# WILD
## guide

## Wales & the Marches
Hidden Places, Great Adventures
and the Good Life

Daniel Start & Tania Pascoe

WILD
THINGS
PUBLISHING

Above G'day Level, Dinorwig p75

# WILD
## guide

Afon Glaslyn above Llyn Gwynant, p71

# Contents

# Regional
# Overview

Trevallen Cove, p226

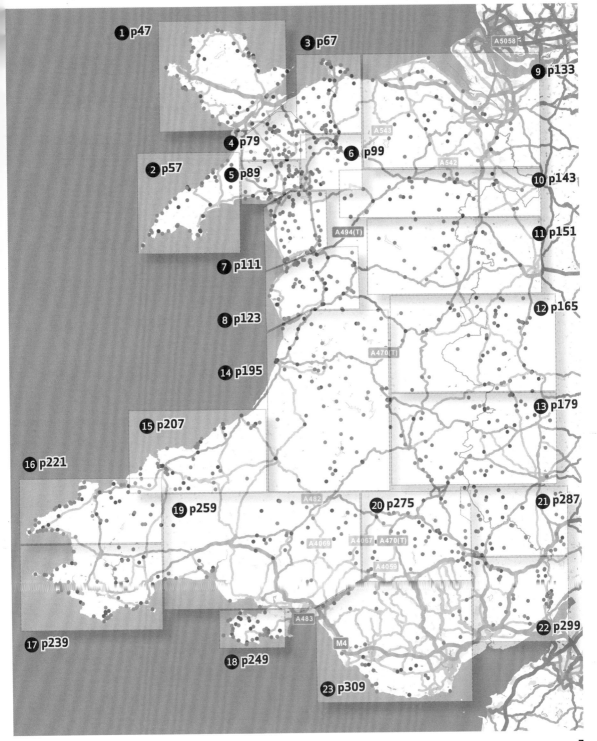

1 p47
3 p67
9 p133
4 p79
6 p99
2 p57
5 p89
10 p143
11 p151
7 p111
8 p123
12 p165
14 p195
13 p179
15 p207
16 p221
19 p259
20 p275
21 p287
17 p239
22 p299
18 p249
23 p309

A5058
A543
A542
A494(T)
A470(T)
A482
A4069
A4067
A470(T)
A4059
A483
M4

Conwy Gorge, p93

# Introduction

Wales is an awe-inspiring land with wild and dramatic landscapes that abound with natural wonders and an epic history that's matched by its many myths and legends. It may be a small country, but the opportunities for adventure are immense.

## Volcanoes to rainforests

The story of Wales begins with some of the oldest rocks in the British Isles, formed over 700 million years ago on Anglesey and the Llŷn Peninsula, and the nearby volcanic landscapes of Snowdonia, now weathered to pinnacled mountain peaks and ridges. Running through to mid Wales are rich sedimentary seams of slate, later mined into tunnels, pits and caverns as Wales 'roofed the world'. To the south, the country is abundant in limestone, formed below a vast tropical sea and now carved into sea caves and spectacular waterfalls. Glacial scarring across the whole Welsh landscape has created dramatic U-shaped valleys, serene mountain tarns, and lowland lakes dammed by terminal moraines. No wonder the first pioneering geologists came to Wales to understand how the world was formed and took Welsh words to describe entire periods of geological time ('Cambrian' from Cymru, the Welsh word for Wales, and 'Silurian' after an ancient tribe from south-east Wales).

Such varied geology brings with it diverse ecosystems too. On the high mountains alpine plants survive in the harshest conditions. In deep, damp gorges 'temperate rainforests' flourish, internationally renowned for their rare species of ferns, lichens and mosses and just as precious as their tropical counterparts. Along the coast towering piles of shifting sand form bizarre dunescapes dotted with

Ynys Gifftan and Portmeirion from Caerwych, p103

pioneering plants, fungi and over 500 insect species. Know where to look, and what to look at, and these sandy slopes become just as interesting as the stunning beaches which they border. There are rich finds in estuarine marshes and in extensive bogs such as at Cors Caron National Nature Reserve. These primeval peaty mosaics of reedbed, pond and wet grassland are not only important refuges for insects, and birds but also vast carbon sinks of international importance.

## Cromlechs to quarries

People first settled in Wales hundreds of thousands of years ago, and we can still touch and feel many of the mysterious monuments they left behind. Seek out the sea cave of The Red Lady of Paviland in the Gower, one of the earliest examples of a ritual burial in Europe dated to over 30,000 years ago, at a time when Britain was connected to Europe by a vast savannah. On Anglesey, the Neolithic burial chamber of Barclodiad y Gawres is decorated with the earliest examples of Welsh art and in the Preseli mountains we can find the quarry from where bluestones were transported all the way to Stonehenge 5,000 years ago. The Iron Age is marked by the presence of over 600 hill forts, later a defence against the Roman invaders, greedy for the mineral riches of the land. When the Romans finally left at the end of the 4th century, after 300 years of occupation, Emperor Magnus Maximus, then ruler of Britain, and reputedly married to a Welsh noblewoman, transferred sovereignty back to the Welsh princes. Thus began a golden era of Christian saints and mystics: now-ancient yews groves were planted, and rock hermitages, holy wells and stone chapels were built in some of the most sacred places in the landscape. The earliest versions of Arthurian legend, and the tales later recorded in the Mabinogion, were first told at this time and, in 780AD, Offa, the Anglo-Saxon King of Mercia, built a defensive dyke defining the Welsh nation for the first time, a line you can still walk from sea to sea today.

When the Normans conquered England in 1066 much of Shropshire and Herefordshire were under Welsh rule; throughout the Marches (which means 'frontier') a string of superb ruined castles stand, testimony to the bloody border conflicts of these brutal times. In the 13th century, Edward I

Entering California, p74

finally conquered Wales, though for centuries the Anglo-Welsh barons faced a series of revolts, the most famous being the uprising led by Owain Glyndŵr, a Welsh prince still seen by some as the last true Welsh king. But it was not until 1707 that Wales legally became a part of Britain, through the Act of Union.

Centuries later the discovery of iron and coal in the green valleys of South Wales fuelled the Industrial revolution and saw landscapes transformed by mines and towering iron furnaces that belched fire like the Welsh dragons of legend. In the north, new slate tunnels, pits and tramways marched across the mountains, and exports further fuelled the economy. This set Wales on a course for the greater autonomy and growing self-confidence that it enjoys today.

## Land of adventure

The Welsh language is a living embodiment of the long history of the Welsh nation and although not all Welsh are fluent, it's taught in all Welsh schools and appears on road signs, trains and public buildings. There are many places in north, west and mid-Wales where Welsh is still the mother tongue and a *diolch* (thank you) or *bore da* (good morning) will always help you on your travels.

This Wild Guide is a celebration of all these wild and historic places that lie hidden, sometimes just off the beaten path. It's also a guide to some of Wales' best local food, historic inns and cosiest places to sleep out under the stars. As you explore this incredible country, play on its shell sand beaches, camp in its verdant valleys, swim in its sparkling mountain lakes and follow its ancient roads all the wonder, magic and mystery of Wales is there to discover.

We wish you many happy adventures. Siwrne dda!

**Daniel and Tania**

adventure@wildthingspublishing.com

# Finding your way

Most places listed are on a public right of way, permissive path, open-access land or benefit from long-use rights. However some places, usually marked ❓, may not have such clear rights. **You will need to make your own judgment about whether to proceed or seek permission from the landowner.**

An overview map and directions are provided, but the latitude, longitude for each location, provided in WGS84 decimal degrees, is the definitive reference and can be entered into any online map site, such as Google, Bing or Streetmap. The latter two provide Ordnance Survey mapping overlays, which show footpaths. OpenStreetMap increasingly shows paths, too. Print out the map before you go, or save a 'screen grab'. Map apps such as ViewRanger or Memory-Map are useful, and you can also enter the co-ordinates into your smartphone GPS or car sat nav (enable 'decimal degrees'). Postcodes are provided for convenience, but only provide a rough location. If you have paper maps, look up the equivalent National Grid reference in the conversion table at the back of the book. If a parking place is mentioned, always make your own judgment and be considerate. Where two places are named in the title, the focus of the text is always the first. Walk-in times given are one way only, allowing 15 mins per km, which is quite brisk. Abbreviations in the directions refer to left and right (L, R); north, east, south and west (N, E, S, W) and direction (dir). There are also: National Trust (NT), English Heritage (EH), Royal Society for the Protection of Birds (RSPB), National Nature Reserve (NNR) & Youth Hostel Association (YHA).

# Wild & responsible

1. Fasten all gates and only climb them at the hinges.
2. Keep your dogs under close control, especially around livestock and in nature reserves.
3. Take your litter home, and gain good karma by collecting other people's.
4. If you wash in streams or rivers, use only biodegradable soap, or none at all.
5. Take special care on country roads and park considerately, to allow room for a tractor or truck.
6. Take map, compass, whistle and waterproof clothing when venturing into remote or high areas.
7. Always tell someone where you are going, and do not rely on your mobile phone.

## Glossary of Welsh place names

| | | | |
|---|---|---|---|
| afon | river | llech | stone, slate |
| bryn | hill, mound | llyn | lake |
| bwa | arch | melin/felin | mill |
| bwlch | pass | moel/foel | rounded hill |
| caer/gaer | fort | mynydd | mountain |
| coed | woods | nant | stream |
| capel | chapel | ogof | cave |
| carreg | rock | pant | hollow, dell |
| chwarel | quarry | pen | head, top |
| craig/graig | rock | pistyll | spout |
| cwm | valley | plas | big house |
| dolydd | meadow | pont/bont | bridge |
| ddu/du | black, dark | porth/borth | cove, bay |
| eglwys | church | pwll/twll | pool, pit, hole |
| fyynnon | spring | rhaeadr | waterfall |
| gors | marsh | scwd/sgwd | waterfall |
| gelli | small wood | traeth | beach |
| glas | blue, grey | tre | town, settlement |
| gwyn | white | trwyn | headland / nose |
| hafod | summer house | ty | house |
| hendre | winter house | uchaf | upper(most) |
| llan | parish | ynys | island |

# Best for
# Wild swimming & canoeing

With so many lakes, tarns, waterfalls and rivers, Wales is a paradise for wild swimming ⬛ and boating ⬛. Water quality is generally excellent, and a hot spell will quickly warm up shallower waters. Jumping and rope swings can be fun, and we've marked where this is often possible with a ⬛ but always check the depth before you jump, even if you were there just the day before.

Take your swimming costume and a small cotton sarong on every trip, and you'll always be ready for a dip; bring a plastic bag with you so you can pack away your wet things. If you don't fancy swimming, there are many new and affordable types of boat. Plastic 'sit-on-tops' are unsinkable, while inflatable canoes are much easier to transport, and stand-up paddleboards (SUPs) provide a higher vantage point and are great fun on placid waters.

Bear in mind that just because a river or lake is on a footpath or open-access land, that doesn't mean there is a legal right to swim or canoe. ⬛ means access is not encouraged and discretion is urged. Please never swim when there are fishermen; they have usually paid to be there. Always be polite and leave if asked.

# Be safe

**1** Never swim alone, and keep a constant watch on weak swimmers.

**2** Cold water can dramatically decrease swimming ability, create cold shock and cause drowning through panic. Know your limits, enter slowly and stay close to the shoreline.

**3** Never jump into water unless you have thoroughly checked for depth and obstructions.

**4** Avoid strong currents, such as those directly under large waterfalls or weirs, or those found in river rapids during floods: they can drag you under.

**5** Always make sure you know how you will get out before you get in.

**6** Wear footwear if you can.

**7** Avoid direct contact with blue-green algae, and be wary of water quality in lowland areas during droughts and heavy rain. Cover cuts with plasters if worried, and if you develop flu-like symptoms tell your doctor you have been in a river.

Llyn Gwynant, p71

# Best for
# Secret beaches

Gower, Pembrokeshire, Ceredigion, the Llŷn Peninsula and Anglesey have some of the best beaches in the world, yet many are little known  and rarely visited. Access isn't always straightforward, and some are difficult to find, but that's half the fun. There's almost always a path down, sometimes with the help of a rope or some rough steps. Your reward is often utter seclusion and unmarked sand where you can skinny dip and maybe even have a driftwood fire.

On these wild beaches you won't find lifeguards, so take care where there are a lot of breaking waves and rip currents tend to form. A rip only goes out to the back of the surf, but to escape one you need to swim out of it parallel to the shore, and come back in on the waves. Many secret beaches are tidal, so check the tide times carefully before setting off to make the most of the sand and avoid being cut off. Remember that when spring tides occur (every fortnight, at full and new moons), low tides are lower and high tides higher, so more water moves and tidal currents are stronger too. Spring lows are great for beach hunters, and these tend to be about 2pm in Pembrokeshire and 4–5pm in North Wales.

Porth Ysgo p52

# Best for
# Coasteering & caves

Between the beaches and bays of Wales lie some of her wildest places, in an intertidal zone of incredible sea stacks, inlets, pools and arches. Limestone coasts like South Pembrokeshire and Gower are particularly rich in caves ⚑ and arches, but also seek out the indented coast of North Pembrokeshire, Ceredigion, Llŷn and Anglesey. Sea caves are magical, and can open up a world of watery adventure if explored carefully, but watch out for swell and for seal pups that sometimes shelter inside.

Invented in Pembrokeshire, coasteering ⚑ is a mixture of swimming and scrambling along the edge of the water, exploring features, playing in the swell and jumping off ledges. Choose a very calm day and survey the route from the coast path first. Wear a wetsuit and old trainers or water shoes, and in swell assume a squat or 'armchair' position with your feet out in front to push off the rocks as the main form of defence.

Inland, natural caves are formed by water running through limestone fissures over thousands of years. See safety notes on p25 and watch out for flash flooding.

## Be safe

**1** Never swim alone and ideally join an organised trip.

**2** Wear a helmet, wetsuit, trainers and buoyancy aid.

**3** Caves amplify swell as they narrow, sometimes bumping you on their ceiling, so enter only when the sea is calm.

**4** Never jump or dive into water unless you have checked it for depth and obstructions. When looking down, water always appears deeper than it is.

**5** Swim within the shelter of coves and bays unless you understand the tidal streams at headlands and in the open sea.

**6** Walk your route first and identify escape routes from the sea.

**7** Do not approach seals or pups.

Confucius Hole, Box Bay, p226

# Best for
# Waterfalls & gorges

An abundance of water and helpful geology have made Wales a picturesque wonderland blessed with misty, fern-filled gorges and sublime waterfalls 🅛. Some of the best can be found in Snowdonia and the limestone landscape of the southern Brecon Beacons. The rivers of the Cambrians, Ceredigion and Carmarthenshire are also excellent, often with easy access but very few visitors.

Most waterfalls and gorges have a good pool or two for a bracing plunge or jump, and some people like to explore up or downstream, half swimming, half scrambling. This is also known as canyoning, gorge walking or gill scrambling 🅺 and you can join guided sessions.

On more gentle rivers, with no waterfalls, drops or major rapids, an inflatable ring or float can help you swim downstream with the current. This is called 'river bugging' in Scotland, 'hydrospeed' in France, 'river boarding' in the US and 'white-water sledging' in New Zealand. Take great care!

## Be safe ▼

**1** Never jump into the centre of a waterfall, as the undercurrents can be very powerful there.

**2** Never jump into pools that haven't been checked for depth.

**3** Never descend something you can't climb back up. If in doubt, scramble up the gorge, not down.

**4** Wear a wetsuit, to avoid hypothermia and protect from cuts. In narrow gorges wear a helmet, due to the danger of rock falls.

**5** Beware of flash flooding after heavy rainfall upstream.

Horseshoe Falls, p263

# Best for
# Quarries & caverns

Love them or hate them, it's difficult not to be awed by abandoned quarries now returning to nature. There is often much to see above ground, but the pits, caverns and mining tunnels ⛏ are also intriguing and the product of awe-inspiring industry and immense physical labour.

Wales' mining history is a grand one, of world-wide importance. On Anglesey you can climb the moonscape remains of Parys 'copper mountain', once the largest copper mine in the world. North Wales was home to hundreds of great slate quarries which roofed the world, such as those at Dinorwig, Dorothea, Blaenau Ffestiniog and Corris. In these you will find the ruins ▣ of inclines with old wheelhouses, reservoirs and waterwheels, dressing sheds and sleeping quarters, and of course deep pits, some now filled with sparkling turquoise water, coloured by fine dust from the surrounding rock. Many were also excavated underground, and adit tunnels lead into a vast underworld of chambers and tramways. Those new to caving and keen to go under should join a guided tour: Go Below and Corris Mine Explorers in Snowdonia offer some of the most exciting trips.

## Be safe

**1** Always carry back-up torches.

**2** Always tell someone where you are going.

**3** Always wear a helmet — a single small rockfall can kill.

**4** It is dangerous to enter any mine tunnel without an experienced guide. Peer in from the outside.

**5** Mine tunnels that are propped with wood are more risky than tunnels hewn through sheer rock.

**6** Rotten false floors may be concealing deep voids, which could give way at any moment. Partially flooded tunnels, with water underfoot, are somewhat safer as the void is already filled.

# Best for
# Ancient ruins

The long human history of Wales has left us an incredible number of sacred remains and lost ruins. They are often sited on choice spots, high on hills or looking out to sea, so visiting draws us into their wild and beautiful landscapes.

The earliest of these remains date from prehistoric times and the Bronze Age ☸, when Druids were at the height of their power. You can find ceremonial burial chambers, walk around remote stone circles or climb inside megalithic cromlech tombs – some even pre-dating the Egyptian pyramids. Hill forts date back to before Roman occupation and offer wonderful places to watch a sunset 📷. Lost chapels, holy wells and hermitages ✝ were founded by saints, sometimes more than 1,500 years ago. A vast array of castles across Wales and the Marches tells the story of the Norman conquests during the 11th and 12th centuries, and ruined abbeys are testament to the destruction of the 16th-century dissolution.

Lamphey Bishop's Palace, p231

# Best for
# Easy peaks & scrambles

Snowdonia, home to England and Wales' highest mountains, is a paradise for hill climbers, and the Brecon Beacons, Berwyns and Cambrian Mountains also provide some fine and famous summits. But there are many lower fells that yield immense satisfaction and panoramic views in exchange for much less effort, and far fewer visitors. They make exceptional places to wild camp and watch the sunset ◨. They are also great for children or for shorter trips.

The rocky landscapes, particularly of Snowdonia, make for great scrambling ◨. This tends to mean anything that requires you to use your hands but doesn't need ropes. Routes are classed from Grade 1 (easy), which don't need ropes, to Grade 3 (difficult), which do require knowledge of ropes in order to protect yourself on some steeper sections, and involve more exposure and more 'committing' sections where it's harder or impossible to avoid difficulties. Most of the routes mentioned in this book are Grade 1.

Llyn Eiddew & Moel Ysgyfarnogod, p105

## Be safe ▼

**1** On high ground be prepared for the weather to deteriorate, faster than you can retreat.

**2** On high ground be prepared with waterproofs, warm clothes, whistle, compass, map, torch, snacks and water. A 'group shelter' and GPS are also useful.

**3** Always be prepared to turn back if you don't feel confident on a scramble or climb.

**4** Many scrambles are in high and remote locations; be especially cautious on wet and windy days, when some scrambles will feel even more exposed.

**5** Research the scramble route thoroughly before you leave – there is much information online.

# Best for
# Forests, meadows & wildlife

The diverse wildernesses of Wales are home to an equally wide range of wildlife ◪. Along the coast are cliffs and islands harbouring globally important colonies of Manx shearwaters and puffins, while porpoises, dolphins and seals dance amongst kelp forests in the sea. In rock pools you will find mind-blowingly colourful crustaceans, starfish and anemones, and in the some of the largest dune systems in Europe, rare orchids and fungi. Enchanting Atlantic rainforests ◘ can be found from Pembrokeshire right up to Northern Snowdonia, literally dripping with rare bryophytes and lichens, and full of birdsong. The vast bogs and marshes and estuarine salt marshes are havens for birds ◪ and you cannot mention Wales without celebrating the comeback of the red kite, whose V-shaped tail can now been seen soaring high all over the country. Whatever the season there is a wondrous spectacle to enjoy. Springtime flowers ✿ carpet the grassy coast paths and wooded valleys, while midsummer meadows return us to an innocent time past. We can watch salmon leap in the autumn and starling murmurations in winter dusks, and – if we are really lucky – see something as wild as a polecat.

Ty Canol woods, p217

# Best for
# Slow food & drink

To travel well is to eat and drink well, and gilding any adventure is the feast that awaits at the end – the ultimate reward for climbing that high mountain and swimming in that freezing tarn. We like to travel cheap, explore for free, sleep wild and dine like kings. Luckily for all of us, Wales has transformed into a seriously good food and real-ale destination, and the revolution shows no signs of abating.

From remote hill farms to coastal smallholdings, seashore foragers to bakers, brewers and artisan cheese-makers, wondrous fare is flowing from field to fork 🍴, and from the taps. Michelin-starred chefs, micro-breweries, beachside cafés and cosy pubs 🍺 across the land work as taste alchemists, enthusiastically celebrating their region's delights and allowing us to savour the very *terroir* we are exploring. So whether you're collapsing with a pint by the roaring fire of a characterful lost-in-time parlour pub, or feasting on a fresh-fish tasting menu, you won't be disappointed.

Bessie's Pub, p219

# Best for Camping

Wales boasts a multitude of fantastically run, wild havens to fit every taste and budget. You can rent a gypsy caravan with woodburner hidden in a flower-filled meadow or camp on a high hill farm and enjoy fantastic sunsets with the cool comfort of a compost loo and cold-water tap .

Those seeking out real solitude can wild camp ⊞ on a high mountain, shelter in a prehistoric cave, or stay in one of the remote bothies **B** managed by the Mountain Bothies Association. Whatever the level of luxury, we demand a characterful, charming place where we can really feel the landscape. We know that good design doesn't have to cost the earth and now, thanks to the Greener Camping Club, more and more campsites ⬜ are signing up to responsible land and waste management. No matter what the weather or season, these idyllic hideaways, organic sheepskin-strewn yurts and wild, windswept campsites will make you want to return again and again.

## Wild camping

**1** Camp above the highest fell wall, well away from towns and villages.

**2** Leave no litter, remove other people's, and don't bury litter.

**3** Do not light any fi res, even if there's evidence that fi res may have been lit by others.

**4** Stay for only one night.

**5** Keep groups very small – only one or two tents.

**6** Camp as unobtrusively as possible, with inconspicuous tents that blend into the landscape.

**7** Do not trespass and seek permission.

**8** Perform toilet duties at least 30m (100ft) from water, and bury the results with a trowel. Take toilet paper and sanitary products home in a plastic nappy / dog poo bag.

Llyn Gwynant campsite, p78

# ANGLESEY & MENAI

## Our perfect weekend

- → **Walk** along the coast to the ruined porcelain and brick works at Porth Llanlleiana and Porth Wen
- → **Creep** inside the chambered tombs of Barclodiad, Lligwy or Bryn Celli Ddu – built at the same time as the pyramids and Stonehenge
- → **Explore** the flower-studded dunes and sandy beaches of Newborough Warren and Llanddwyn Island, then retreat to The Marram Grass Café for a delicious seafood feast
- → **Discover** the incredible moonscape of Copper Mountain – one of Britain's oldest mining sites
- → **Marvel** at the extensive stone remains of the Iron Age village at Din Lligwy and imagine Anglesey life 3,000 years ago
- → **Swim** around beautiful islets at Borthwen and buy some freshly caught crab for your supper
- → **Kayak** down the sandy estuary from Abberfraw to discover six secret coves along the southern shore, perfect for a wild camp
- → **Run** barefoot on the secret sands of Traeth yr Ora then refuel in Moelfre on cake and ice cream

Ynys Môn is an ancient island steeped in antiquity, with lush farmlands ringed by a golden coastline of beaches, islands and coves. A land of Neolithic burial cairns and Iron Age villages, it boasts dramatic natural features, from caves and arches to volcanic lava flows. Separated from the mainland by the Menai Strait, with the mountains of Eyri as a backdrop, it's not difficult to see how this land so inspired the druids and saints.

The early Welsh certainly knew how to give their leaders a good send-off, and here you will find many of Wales' finest chambered cairns and cromlechs. Bryn Celli Ddu (the mound in the dark grove), has an eight metre passage aligned with the midsummer sunrise. Barclodiad – the largest Neolithic tomb in Wales – faces west on a clifftop and enjoys glorious views.

Holy wells and tiny chapels are hidden in stunning locations: St Cwyfan is set on an island reached by a cowrie-scattered causeway, St Seiriol's Well pours forth from rocks within a peaceful well house. Holy Island – so called due to its high concentration of sacred sites – is the land of early Christian saints and now also renowned for its high cliffs and birdlife.

More recent remains include medieval castle mottes in the woods, ruined factories set on remote beaches, cliff quarries and even the extraordinary overgrown remains of a mansion dating back to before the Civil War.

Perhaps the most beautiful beach is at Newborough Warren, with its tidal island and abundant wildlife. From here there are secret coves up to Aberffraw with no public access, as the farmer has refused all requests for a coast path. To reach these untouched gems you will need to walk for several miles along the shoreline, or bring a boat. Borthwen (White Bay) is a favourite, lost-in-time swimming cove, with little islets and a good pub for afterwards. To the north, the white, sandy beaches of Porth Trwyn and Church Bay are perfect for families, with seafood cafés and home-made ice cream.

The fertile fields and rich seas that have long made the island the larder of North Wales still provide rich pickings, and after your explorations you'll be fed well on world-famous Menai mussels, oysters and crab, and discover some excellent new eateries celebrating the local produce.

And finally, don't miss the opportunity to explore the bizarre mineral stained landscape and tunnel systems of the copper mines of Parys Mountain – once the largest in the world – and historic Amlwch port which fuelled the industrial revolution changing our planet for ever.

1

## TINY ISLANDS

### 1 LLANDDWYN ISLAND, NEWBOROUGH

About 570 million years ago during the
Cambrian era much of Wales lay beneath
the ancient Iapetus Ocean. Volcanic islands
were common, with lava spilling out of vents
on the sea floor. Some of this pillow lava is
still visible around the neck of Llanddwyn
Island, a narrow isthmus studded with sandy
inlets that is set against the vast tracts of
Newborough Warren and forest (see entry).
There are several beautiful coves and an
awe-inspiring backdrop of mountains and
sea. It was home to St Dwynwen, patron
saint of lovers. Seek out the remains of
her chapel, and visit her holy well. There
is an old lighthouse and pilot cottages for
the seamen who used to guide the slate
ships through the Menai Strait. Beyond lie
miles of wildness along Traeth Penrhos and
Malltraeth Sands.

→ In Newborough, turn opp post office
(Church St, signed Llys Rhosyr) past LL61 6SG
then toll road £2 to shore and car park (fee
charged). Follow beach/forest track NW 1 mile
and cross to the 'island'. Best coves on SE side.
30 mins, 53.1382, -4.4096 🏊🏖️🅿️🚶

### 2 CRIBINAU ISLAND & CHURCH

The ancient whitewashed chapel of St
Cwyfan stands on a tiny island connected
by a rockpool isthmus, walkable at low tide.
Sandy beach.

→ Follow Church St from Aberffraw 1 mile,
past LL63 5PJ, to park at the road end.
10 mins, 53.1854, -4.4919 🏊✝️

### 3 BORTHWEN & BWA GWYN ARCH

Idyllic sandy crescent bay, scattered with
little islets, perfect to swim or canoe around.
From here walk along the coast path to find
the white and black sea arches through which
the adventurous could try swimming.

→ At the end of a long narrow lane with a small
car park. The road can become congested
in summer so easier to walk from the White
Eagle pub, LL65 2NJ. Beautiful Silver Bay is
1 mile to the E on the coast path. Or bear W
on the coast path 1 mile to reach Bwa Gwyn/
white arch (30 mins, 53.2539, -4.6108). The
steep bank on opposite slope offers a difficult
scramble down to water. Bwa Du (black arch) is
300m beyond. Return on walled track, which
arrives behind Rhoscolyn church and the pub.
2 mins, 53.2440, -4.5913 🏊🏖️🔽🚶

### 4 YNYS Y FYDLYN, CARMEL HEAD

Remote west facing island tombolo,
sheltering a rocky cove, with sea arch to
swim to/through at high tide.

→ On lane N of Llanfairynghornwy (½
mile beyond LL65 4LR). Parking is signed
Mynachdy NT. Follow the main path W.
20 mins, 53.3947, -4.5705 🐚🏖️🏊

## SECRET BEACHES

### 5 PORTH TWYN-MAWR & ABERFFRAW

Almost inaccessible without a boat, this is the
largest of six perfect secret sand coves (also
known as 'Sixpenny' to yachties). There is no
right of way to them, but they can be reached
via the foreshore, or canoe. Or just explore
Aberffraw beach and dunes – you can even
swim down the sandy creek at high tide.

→ From Aberffraw (car park E off A4080)
head to beach via the dunes footpath (20 mins)
then follow the foreshore 1 mile SE. Or canoe in
from Malltraeth. Try Llys Llewelyn tea rooms in
Aberffraw (LL63 5AQ, 01407 840847).
45 mins, 53.1618, -4.4454 🐚🏖️🏊

### 6 TRAETH CYMYRAN, RHOSNEIGR

Meaning 'beach at the confluences', the
sand strand and dunes are great for anyone

who doesn't mind being adjacent to the MOD airfield. At low tide you could even try wading across the estuary west to the perfect crescent sands of Silver Bay.

→ Head for the tiny parking area at LL65 3LF, 2 miles S of Caergeiliog (A55) then continue down the estuary 1 mile. You can also walk up from Rhosneigr, across Traeth Crigyll.
20 mins, 53.2453, -4.5490 🌊🏖

### 7 PORTH-Y-POST COVE, TREARDDUR

The largest in a string of tiny south-facing coves situated right by the road. Perfect for an easy dip.

→ This penultimate cove is a mile along the coast road from Trearddur Bay Hotel (LL65 2UN). Also a low-tide sea cave with amazing coloured rocks at 53.2848, -4.6606, ½ mile W from parking at Porth Dafarch.
2 mins, 53.2843, -4.6372 🏖🏊

### 8 PORTH TRWYN & CHURCH BAY

Trwyn beach is tucked away a short walk off the lane, best at low tide. Nearby Church Bay (Porth Swtan) is busier, with café, restaurant and campsite (see listings), perfect as a family holiday base.

→ Signed 'Church Bay' off A5025 at Llanfaethlu. After 1¼ mile find track and parking area on L, with footpath sign and info board. For Church Bay continue on road another mile.
1 min, 53.3591, -4.5631 🌊🍴⛺↩

### 9 PORTH WEN & BRICKWORKS

Superb hidden bay with old ruined harbour, brickworks buildings and beehive kilns. Also a rock arch and white pebble beach.

→ First R off A5025, 2 miles W of Bull Bay (before LL67 0NA) with a layby. 800m, by L bend, find 2 footpath signs on R. Take second footpath up track then descend to bay (500m).
10 mins, 53.4245, -4.4061 🌊🏖🏚

### 10 TRAETH YR ORA, DULAS

Long, secret sand beach adjacent to the wonderful wild sandflats of the Dulas river estuary.

→ Footpath leads from behind the Pilot Boat pub (LL70 9EX, 01248 410205) up to heathland then down to beach, bearing L at Penrhyn. Alternatively walk from road end past LL70 9DJ at low tide, or follow coast path N from popular Traeth Lligwy with parking (signed from A5025 ½ mile E of the pub), or connect with either for a circular walk.
30 mins, 53.3727, -4.2712 🌊🚶✨

11

## WILDLIFE & TREES

### 11 HOLYHEAD MOUNTAIN & SOUTH STACK

The ruined coastguard lookout provides a stunning and accessible ocean sunset viewpoint. Wildlife here is renowned, with auks, choughs, puffins, grey seals, and if you are lucky, dolphins and porpoises. If you have more time, explore the heathland, rich in butterflies, and the mountain summit, popular with climbers. There are impressive Iron Age hut circles, named Cytiau'r Gwyddelod (Irishmen's huts) here too.

→ From Holyhead follow South Stack Rd past LL65 1YH. The hut circles are signed opp first RSPB car park. Continue to visitor centre parking for Ellin's Tower (good lookout for cliff birds). Beyond, steps lead down to the island (entry fee) or a path up to the old lookout and heathland. Also seek out double standing stones at 53.2957, -4.6616 on Plas Rd near LL65 2LT.

5 mins, 53.3080, -4.6939 🅿️➡️🏔️

### 12 CEMLYN BAY TERNS

Visit between May and July to see thousands of terns breeding in the shallow lagoon. Head out onto the headland, Trwyn Cemlyn, for the chance of spying bottle-nosed dolphins and a view of the now closed nuclear power station.

→ Signed from A5025 3 miles W of Cemaes roundabout, dir LL67 0DY. After 1½ miles take dead-end road R with small NT sign to car park by beach.

5 mins, 53.4086, -4.5049 🅈🏖️

### 13 LLANDDEINIOLEN YEW

Impressive ancient yews in St Deiniolen churchyard, one of which you can climb inside.

→ Church on lane ¼ mile S of B4366 at LLanddeiniolen (car park here), towards LL55 3AR. No parking at church.

10 mins, 53.1703, -4.1772 🅿️⛪

13

### 14 NEWBOROUGH WARREN

The forested NNR is one of Britain's best coastal sand-dune systems and a haven for wildlife. From spring through to autumn, flora and fungi decorate the dune hollows – discover vast colonies of orchids in spring and summer and waxcaps in autumn. Skylarks, oystercatchers and lapwings also thrive here. A network of paths leads through the reserve and down to the tiny, remote tidal island of Llanddwyn.

→ From Newborough village follow road and park as for Llanddwyn Island (see entry). Walk SE for paths through dunes.

45 mins, 53.1442, -4.3656 🅿️🅈🚻🏔️

14

### 15 ST GWENFAEN'S WELL, RHOSCOLYN

In a field just back from the coast path are the remains of a medieval holy well house with steps down to a pool. White pebbles were thrown in by those seeking help for mental disorders.

→ From Borthwen (see listing) head W along coast path. After coastguard lookout bear up over peak to find well in fields below.

15 mins, 53.2476, -4.6049 ✚

### 16 PENMON PRIORY & HOLY WELL

The ruins of a 13th-century priory ruins and 16th-century dovecote share this site with St Seiriol's Well – one of the more enchanting holy wells in Wales, and possibly the oldest. An unmarked track by the dovecot leads down through gate and fields to the shingle beach and substantial remains of Flagstaff limestone quarry which provided the mortar for Liverpool docks. Walk back along the beach to make a loop.

→ Beyond Castell Aberlleiniog (see listing) head towards LL58 8RP. This is a free CADW site, but to park for free, park on the lane layby 100m before the priory, otherwise £2.50.

5 mins, 53.3057, -4.0564 🖼️🚻✚🚶

### 17 BARCLODIAD Y GAWRES TOMB

Set above popular Porth Trecastell beach, this is the largest Neolithic tomb in Wales. It was constructed at the same time as the Egyptian pyramids and Stonehenge, and built as a public grave for the local farming community. A key is needed to explore inside. Look for the carved zigzags, lozenges and spirals.

→ Signed off A4080, just S of LL63 5TE, but drive on to park at Porth Trecastell beach, then walk the coast path up the headland. The key is held at nearby premises (find directions on information board) and may be borrowed on payment of a returnable deposit.

5 mins, 53.2074, -4.5037 ❓✚🖼️🚴🐾

### 18 BRYN CELLI DDU TOMB

One of the best-preserved passage tombs in Wales, set within its own stone circle. Enter through the tall stone slit to find the unusual pillar within the chamber, and the carved pattern stone beyond. Druids greet the sunrise here on the summer solstice.

→ Off the A4080 SW of Menai Bridge (dir Llanddaniel Fab). Small signed car park beyond school at LL61 6EQ. Another tomb (Bodowyr) is 3 miles along lanes at 53.1883, -4.3030.

10 mins, 53.2076, -4.2361 ✚🐾

### 19 DIN LLIGWY, MOELFRE

A trio of atmospheric ancient sites, spanning millennia. The walled village is Romano-British, and its massive stone foundations make for a surreal secret playground surrounded by woods. En route explore the 12th-century ruined chapel, and afterwards, walk back along the lane 300m for the Neolithic burial chamber, which you can climb down inside.

→ From Moelfre head SW on A5108, then signed R by roundabout, past LL72 8NG.
10 mins, 53.3505, -4.2592 ⊠✝☆♦

### 20 ST BAGLAN'S & FORYD BAY

Isolated in a graveyard in the middle of a field, this tiny medieval church escaped Victorian renovation; its door lintel is from a 6th-century predecessor and the lych gate is from the 18th century. It overlooks Y Foryd estuarine nature reserve (many wildfowl).

→ Follow the slow coastal lane from bridge in Caernarfon W towards LL54 5RA. The church can be seen surrounded by trees off to L after about 2 miles, with layby parking.
3 mins, 53.1209, -4.3094 ✝🚗

## LOST RUINS & HILL FORTS

### 21 BARON HILL RUINS, BEAUMARIS

On private land, but with a dense network of paths, this is an extraordinary and completely overgrown ruined country mansion and gardens, slowly returning to nature and rhododendron forest.

→ Locals seem to climb up by the bus stop opp the school and Maes Hyfryd turning (LL58 8HN) in Beaumaris.
5 mins, 53.2668, -4.1040 ⊠?⬛

### 22 LLANLLEIANA PORCELAIN WORKS

China clay was quarried from the cliff here, but the porcelain factory burnt down in 1920, leaving a picturesque ruin above the remote cove. The detached chimney was to direct the noxious fumes away from the working areas. The next cove east, Hell's Mouth, has high cliffs and good jumps.

→ Footpath starts 300m E of LL67 0LN (narrow lane with no parking). Head down, over the farm track and bear L at bottom (or R for Hell's Mouth). Also reached by a coastal walk from St Patrick's church to the W (Llanbadrig, with parking), which has a famous cave in cliffs beneath, or from Porth Wen (see listing).
10 mins, 53.4272, -4.4272 ♦⊠

23

23

24

### 23 BWRDD ARTHUR HILL FORT

Small limestone hill with Iron Age remains, wildflowers (rockrose and orchids) and magnificent sea views. Just below is a tiny medieval church, with a holy well in the woods up behind.

→ Head for LL58 8YB (NE of Llandonna) and park at the dead-end road junction by sign. A wooden kissing gate leads up to the heath. Head to NW edge and you can loop back down, through the farm, via the church and lane on the E side. NB 1 mile E along the lane is Mariandyrys Nature Reserve, limited layby parking at 53.3090, -4.0967.

10 mins, 53.3116, -4.1207 ⬛✿✝🎋

### 24 CASTELL ABERLLEINIOG & WOODS

11th-century motte deep in woods overlooking the Menai Strait, topped with 17th-century Civil War castle fortifications.

→ From B5109 N of Beaumaris head for LL58 8RN (signed Penmon). After ½ mile, 50m E of Tros y Arfon, find tiny parking area on L. Follow footpath, bearing R across bog, then zigzag uphill. More parking and connecting path at Leiniog picnic spot on road further along.

20 mins, 53.2927, -4.0771 📷⬛

### 25 PARYS/COPPER MOUNTAIN

This vast orange crater is awe-inspiring to behold. Copper has been mined here since the early Bronze Age and this wondrous landscape, created by hand tools, was the largest copper mine in the world in the 18th century. You can shelter inside the ruined windmill that tops the site, climb one of the many golden spoil heaps for views to the sea or descend into the heather-filled pit to find caverns and tunnels below.

→ Car park high on the B5111 S of Amlwch ½ mile beyond LL68 9PL. Nearby Copper Kingdom in Amlwch Port (LL68 9DB, 01407 830298) tells the further story of how copper was processed and shipped around the globe.

10 mins, 53.3883, -4.3424 ⬛🎦🎦

### 26 LLANEILIAN CLIFF QUARRIES

A flight of perilous steps, carved into the cliffs, lead down to slate quarries above the sea. A tunnel, blocked by a slate wagon, plummets down to one level and then into a small sea cave with a quay, where the slate was taken out by boat. Sheer drops and many hazards, so view from a distance, or coasteer in from the sea at low tide.

→ Follow lane through Llaneilian to beach past LL68 9LT, then uphill to park (limited space) before lighthouse gate. Footpath on R shortly before parking leads to coast and then S to quarries. At low tide explore from the shore below, with some swimming and coasteering.
15 mins, 53.4067, -4.2843 🅻🆅⬛🔵

## SLOW FOOD

### 27 ANN'S PANTRY, MOELFRE

In a house just steps from the harbour this lovely café/restaurant is open for breakfast and lunch (and dinner on weekends). Eat in the colourful garden or cosy up in the café, which transforms into an intimate bistro at night. Look out for their tapas nights. On the doorstep is the Moelfre Ice Cream Parlour.
→ Moelfre, LL72 8HL, 01248 410386.
53.3522, -4.2365 🍴

### 28 LLIGWY BEACH CAFÉ & CAMPING

A small family-run café overlooking the long sands of Lligwy beach, selling everything from gin cocktails to locally sourced bacon baps and bowls of fish stew. It stands at one side of the beachside car park and campervan campsite (£10 per night, no tents).
→ Moelfre, LL72 8NL, 07935 331145.
53.3592, -4.2612 ⛺🍴

### 29 Y CWT MWG SMOKEHOUSE, DULAS

Stop off at this tiny farm shop and buy delicious kiln-smoked Anglesey fish, meats and cheeses from this family-run smokery.
→ Cors Yr Odyn, Dulas, LL70 9DX, 07584 093619.
53.3652, -4.3208 🍴

### 30 THE CRAB SHOP, BENLLECH

Stock up on fresh, dressed Anglesey crab, whole Anglesey lobsters, cooked or alive, and fresh local fish from this small shop.
→ Benllech LL74 8SW, 07909 773665.
53.3217, -4.2255 🍴

### 31 THE OUTBUILDINGS, LLANGAFFO

Open to non-residents for lunch and afternoon tea, this remote B&B serves fresh and local food from a small, ever-changing menu in their airy restaurant in a converted barn. In the field nearby lies Bodowyr Neolithic burial chamber (53.1883, -4.3030).
→ Bodowyr Farm, Llangaffo, LL60 6NH, 01248 430132.
53.1912, -4.3038 🍴🛏

### 32 LOBSTER POT & WAVECREST CAFÉ

Ignore the uninspiring bungalow setting of The Lobster Pot restaurant and you will be rewarded with locally landed lobsters, fish, crabs, mussels and oysters when in season. It's informal and very friendly. Just down the road is the Wavecrest Café, with home-made ice creams and colourful tea garden.
→ Church Bay, LL65 4EU, 01407 730241.
53.3718, -4.5546 🍴

### 33 BLAS LLYNNON TEA ROOMS

The 18th-century Llynnon Mill is the last of its kind in Wales to still be producing stoneground organic flour. The bakery and small tea shop use the flour to make delicious breads, cakes and pasties. Buy some to go home with and climb the windmill (entry fee).
→ Melin Llynnon, Llanddeusant, LL65 4AB, 01407 730633.
53.3378, -4.4942 🍴

### 34 OYSTER CATCHER, RHOSNEIGR

Behind the dunes of popular Traeth Llydan, this glass-fronted restaurant serves up Menai 'moules', sharing platters and classic fish and chips with views. The large terrace enjoys lovely views of the dunes and water.
→ Maelog Lake, Rhosneigr, LL64 5JP, 01407 812829.
53.2231, -4.5103 🍴

### 35 THE MARRAM GRASS CAFÉ

Just inland from Newborough Warren (see entry) is this wonderful and much-acclaimed eatery. Much more than just a café; Anglesey oysters, lobsters, fresh fish, meats and wonderful Welsh cheeses and vegetables are served simply and imaginatively. If you're celebrating, book the surprise set menu to share. Open for lunch and dinner Thurs–Sun.
→ White Lodge, Newborough, LL61 6RS, 01248 440077.
53.1592, -4.3488 🍴

### 36 MENAI OYSTERS & MUSSELS

Pick up the freshest oysters and mussels along with a bottle of champagne direct from the farm HQ. Oysters come by the dozen, and mussels in bags of 2kg or 5kg. It's always best to phone in your order if possible. Open Wed and Sun only (closed BH weekends).
→ Tal y Bont Bach, Llanfairpwllgwyngyll, LL61 6UU, 01248 430878.
53.1742, -4.3150 🍴

### 37 HOOTON'S HOMEGROWN

Home-grown, home-reared and home-cooked to eat in or takeaway from this family-run farm. Lots of seasonal vegetables and fruit for sale, and in summer their own Welsh Black burgers are barbecued on the terrace.

→ Gwydryn Hir, Brynsiencyn, LL61 6HQ, 01248 430322.
53.1847, -4.2599 🍴

### 38 SOSBAN AND THE OLD BUTCHERS

A gourmet delight housed in the old butcher's shop. Using only the finest local ingredients (truly) there is no menu, and you must book ahead. Open for dinner Thurs–Sat, lunch Sat.

→ Trinity House, 1 High St, Menai Bridge, LL59 5EE, 01248 208131.
53.2261, -4.1630 🍴

### 39 BLUE SKY, BANGOR

Excellent ethical café in the town centre serving innovative breakfasts and lunches using the best local ingredients, often organic and with lots of vegetarian and vegan offerings. Great coffee.

→ Ambassador Hall, Rear of 236 High St, Bangor, LL57 1PA, 01248 355444.
53.2264, -4.1257 🍴

### 40 THE MILL, PONT-RUG

Located at Seiont Riverside Camping, this converted mill is a spacious bistro serving delicious laverbread Welsh breakfasts, inventive salads, goats cheese tarts and warming Welsh lamb stews. Open Wed–Sun 8.30am-5pm, Fri and Sat evenings.

→ Llanberis Rd, Pont-rug, LL55 2BB, 01286 676549.
53.1419, -4.2350 🍴

### 41 HOLY ISLAND SEAFOOD, RHOSCOLYN

Pick up fresh fish and shellfish on your way back from St Gwenfaen's Well (see entry). Telephone first to check what is available.

→ Llainysbylldir, Beach Road, Rhoscolyn, LL65 2NJ, 01407 861699.
53.2485, -4.5927 🍴

### 42 THE WHITE EAGLE, RHOSCOLYN

After an afternoon on pretty Borth Wen beach (see entry), head back to the sun-warmed deck for a feast of fresh dressed crab, fish and chips, delicious burgers, moules and steak frites, all served by friendly and attentive staff.

→ Rhoscolyn, LL65 2NJ, 01407 860267.
53.2495, -4.5944 🍴

### 43 THE BLACK LION INN, LLANFAETHLU

Whitewashed 18th-century inn, renovated and reopened by a local couple in 2012, with views to Snowdonia. Simply does it here, from uncluttered decor to the unfussy menu serving good Anglesey-sourced produce.

→ Llanfaethlu, LL65 4NL, 01407 730718.
53.3480, -4.5256 🍴🛏

### 44 THE SHIP INN, RED WHARF BAY

This charming traditional seaside pub is just the place to enjoy a pint or hearty pub grub meal, overlooking sandy Red Wharf Bay. Just up the road is The Boathouse restaurant, with a more modern feel.

→ Harry's Way, Red Wharf Bay, LL75 8RJ, 01248 852568.
53.3055, -4.2090 🍴

### 45 CHURCH BAY COTTAGES & CAMPING

Within walking distance of Porth Swtan's lovely sandy cove is this little village camping ground. Packed in summer, it's filled with families coming to play on the beach and kayak around the bay. Three self-catering stone cottages have their own outdoor space away from the campers. Up the road is the Church Bay Inn, or just minutes away are the Lobster Pot and Wavecrest Café (see entry).

→ Ty Newydd, Church Bay, Rhydwyn, LL65 4ET, 01407 730060.
53.3712, -4.5535 ⛺🚐

### 46 NANT BYCHAN FARM, MOELFRE

Set up a summer camp overlooking the sea in this basic grassy site behind a farm, between the seaside village of Moelfre and sandy Traeth Bychan. Yes there are caravans, but the tent pitch is flat and dolphins are often spotted from the rocky beach below.

→ Moelfre, LL72 8HF, 01248 410269.
53.3459, -4.2352 🚐⛺

### 47 FEDW UCHAF, MOELFRE

A quiet high spot enjoying views out to sea, with resident donkeys, goats and pigs (so no dogs allowed). Between March and October you can set up your tent, camper or caravan on the hardcore pitches. Facilities are basic but clean.

→ Moelfre, LL70 9HZ, 01248 410414.
53.3520, -4.2885 ⛺

## RUSTIC HAVENS

### 48 AEL-Y-DON, BORTHWEN BAY

With steps down to the secluded sands of Porth Trwyn, this white stone house sleeping 14 has been a family holiday home since 1919. There's no television, no wifi, no central heating – but there is a stove, a piano and a garden.

→ Borthwen Bay, Llanfaethlu, LL65 4HD, 020 7281 1118. cottageguide.co.uk
53.3595, -4.5600 🏖️🐚

### 49 PLAS ESGOB, RHOSCOLYN

Borthwen is a beautiful sheltered arc of sand, with clear waters and little rocky islands to jump from. Steps away from the beach, this bright self-catering house for six is the perfect place to stay and enjoy this charming coast and hamlet.

→ Rhoscolyn, LL65 2NQ. menaiholidays.co.uk
53.2429, -4.5860 🏖️🏄

### 50 POINT LYNAS LIGHTHOUSE

Enjoy fantastic views from the two lighthouse-keepers cottages situated on the rocky headland. Both of the cottages (sleeping 6 and 12) in the castellated complex are decorated simply and stylishly, but it's the location that really wins. Dolphins are regularly seen frolicking from the windows and it's a wild experience in all weathers.

→ Llaneilian, Amlwch, LL68 9LT, 01407 831509.
53.4160, -4.2895 🏖️🏄

### 51 PLAS CADNANT, MENAI BRIDGE

Set on a secluded estate in the lush Cadnant valley, five holiday homes get to enjoy the restored gardens and SSSI woodland, waterfalls and meadows. The valley garden is wonderfully picturesque and the wildlife tangibly present. The gardens and tea shop are open to the public April–Oct on Wed, Thurs, Sun; otherwise the place is yours to discover.

→ Cadnant Road, Menai Bridge, LL59 5NH, 01248 717174.
53.2307, -4.1588 ♿🏖️🔁

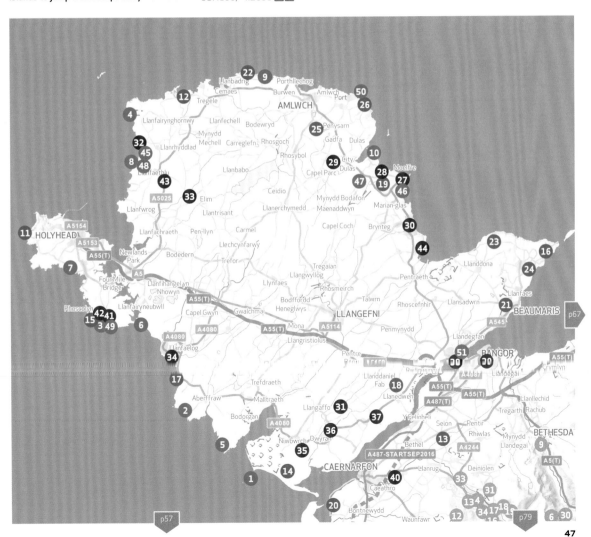

# LLŶN PENINSULA

## Our perfect weekend

→ **Play** on the white sands at perfect Porth Iago, then watch the sunset from the hill fort above

→ **Greet** the dawn and marvel at the magnificent views from Tre'r Ceiri hill fort, then descend via giant Trefor quarry for an early morning swim

→ **Seek** out the remote ancient churches – St Beuno with its reed-strewn aisle, St Tudwen with a giant lych gate and St Cybi with the ruins of a medicine cottage

→ **Make** a wish at St Mary's Well, then watch the sun set over Bardsey Island from Mynydd Mawr

→ **Take** a summer walk out onto the flower-strewn headland of Porth Dinllaen and swim in the crystal waters of Borth Wen before enjoying a pint on the beach at the Ty Coch Inn

→ **Coasteer** out to giant sea caves from Porth Llanllawen and enjoy fish and chips at Aberdaron

→ **Find** tunnels and ruins on the way down to dramatic Porth Ysgo

→ **Surf** at Porth Ceiriad and survey the rolling waves from your base at Nant-y-Big campsite

Tiny lanes lined with wildflowers lead to empty coves and rugged cliffs, and a timeless island feel pervades this magical and too-often-overlooked peninsula – some say the Llŷn is like Cornwall 50 years ago. Welsh is spoken more often than not, and as on Anglesey, sacred places abound. A strong surf culture exists around Porth Neigwl (Hell's Mouth), and in pockets around the Llŷn you can taste the beginning of a good-food revolution.

The coast starts in rugged fashion along the north side with the towering peak of Yr Eifl, home of Tre'r Ceir, an Iron Age settlement with some of the best roundhouse remains in Wales. Below is Nant Gwrtheyrn, a former quarry village reached by dramatic mountain roads that snake down through forest to the quarry remains and a deserted shingle foreshore.

Porth Dinllaen is a narrow rocky headland, looking out across two sweeping bays. Seashore cottages huddle by the beach around the red-roofed inn, only reachable on foot along the sand. Isambard Kingdom Brunel had once hoped to build a port for Ireland here, but Thomas Telford's proposals won the day for Holyhead and the more accessible north Wales coast.

Southwards from here, the coast becomes gentler, revealing a string of pearly coves with tiny seasonal campsites. Porth Towyn has two small coves with good rocks for scrambling; Traeth Penllech is a long stretch of sand with a stream for paddling; Porth Iago is wild-swimming heaven, its perfect west-facing white sand guarded by kestrels and a sunset hill fort, and the farmer will let you wild camp.

Sacred Bardsey Island sits at the distant tip, glimmering across the tidal waters. There's been a church here for 1,500 years, and it was once considered as sacred as Iona in Scotland or Holy Island in Northumberland. Take a boat trip from the slipway at Porth Meudwy to see its Manx shearwater colonies.

Exploring the lanes south-east, beyond charming Aberdaron, a leafy path along a stream glade leads down to the hidden bay of Porth Ysgo, one of the most beautiful parts of this coastline. Here are old mine workings and tunnels overgrown with ragwort and bindweed, and on the grassy cliff-tops there are ruined engine houses and rusted turning wheels. Beyond is Porth Neigwl, the wildest beach on the peninsula, and a serene spot for building driftwood fires and bivvying under the stars.

## HIDDEN BEACHES

### 1 YNYS FAWR & TRAETH YR EIFL, TREFOR
Wonderful views of the peaks of Yr Eifl greet those who travel this coast. A very tricky scramble leads down to an isolated shingle cove with the huge pyramid rock of Ynys Fawr. Continue on to the main beach below Yr Eifl.

→ Park at Trefor quay (beyond LL54 5LB) and follow coast path W ¾ mile, past the old pier – you can swim here, but look out for anglers – and just around the headland. After ½ mile a faint path zigzags down the L side of the narrow, grassy gully on the far SW side of a cove (tricky slab at bottom, be careful). Or continue on ½ mile to reach the main beach below Yr Eifl, by the house, and return in a loop via the ruins of the old hotel to Trefor.
20 mins, 52.9980, -4.4372 🌊💧🏖️📷🐟🚶

### 2 BORTH WEN & PORTH DINLLAEN
The main Porth Dinllaen beach with Tŷ Coch Inn (see entry) is superb, but also try the quiet shingle beach with rock pools on the far side of the peninsula, Borth Wen. The coastal flowers in summer are a delight. Walk to the end of the headland between them for the lifeboat station in a cove with wonderful views and a chance to see seals.

→ From Morfa Nefyn, follow the B4417 coast road signs for beach and golf course, past NT car park R, to club house car park at road end (dir LL53 6DB). Continue on along the path and Borth Wen is below L after ½ mile.
10 mins, 52.9393, -4.5707 🏖️🚣🐟🚶

### 3 PORTH TOWYN, TUDWEILIOG
Small crescent beach of 'squeaky' sand, with even smaller cove to the north. Farm camping (see entry) and a tiny refreshment hut.

→ Signed traeth/beach from B4417 just NE of Tudweiliog; parking on verges or in a field shortly beyond LL53 8PD.
5 mins, 52.9061, -4.6329 🌊🏕️

### 4 TRAETH PENLLECH, LLANGWNNADL
At low tide almost a mile of white sand is revealed; at high tide there are three separate sections, with the most secret to the north. No facilities.

→ Follow lane N of Llangwnnadl ¾ mile past LL53 8PA to car park and picnic tables.
5 mins, 52.8769, -4.6705 🌊🍴

### 5 PORTH WIDLIN COVES
Two super-secret sand coves face each other across a narrow bay.

→ From Llangwnnadl follow lanes 1½ miles SW past LL53 8NU. At 52.8527, -4.6952 (some tight parking on verge) the Llŷn coastal footpath crosses an iron gate, and down to the coast, through a kissing gate. Straight on is the easier beach, or continue R for 200m for the sandier beach. Or park at Porth Iago (see entry) and walk 1¾ miles along coast path.
15 mins, 52.8594, -4.6960 🚶🌊

### 6 PORTH IAGO, RHYDLIOS
One of the best little beaches on the Llŷn: west facing, sheltered, with golden sands, clear waters and an ancient hill fort lookout above. You can even wild camp here, included in the parking fee. The rocks around are a good place for bass fishing – we barbecued one, spear-fished only minutes before, and scented with wild thyme.

→ Signed 1½ mile NE of Rhoshirwaun on B4413. Take second R after 2½ miles, then first L, signed Iago (LL53 8LP), then second track on L through Ty Mawr Farm. Parking £5.
2 mins, 52.8516, -4.7217 🌊🏕️🐟📷♨️

### 7 WHISTLING SANDS & LOOKOUT
Popular white-sand bay (Porth Oer) said to whistle in certain winds. There's a NT shop and large car park. Walk south along the

coast path to sea caves and inland to the ruins of a lookout tower on Mynydd Carreg.

→ 1 mile N of LL53 8LH. As for Porth Iago (see entry), but continue beyond the Iago sign 1½ miles to find R turn with NT Porthoer sign. For lookout tower, head ½ mile SW, then bear L inland to 52.8286, -4.7269. Further along coast, the small island headlands of Dinas Bach and Dinas Fawr have sea caves to explore.
5 mins, 52.8349, -4.7242 🌊📷🏴🐚

### 8 PORTH YSGO, LLANFAELRHYS

Remote sand and shingle beach below a particularly dramatic section of coast, rich in serpentine and gabbro volcanic rock, green-black and crystalline. Reached via a secret valley with intriguing mine ruins (wheelhouse, tunnels). At high tide an offshore rock, once used to moor ships, is fine to dive from.

→ 2½ miles E of Aberdaron on B4413, turn R at dog-leg crossroad, signed Porth Ysgo. Pass LL53 8AN and park in small layby just after L turn. The footpath S is at this junction.
15 mins, 52.8054, -4.661 🌊⛴🏊🚶🏴

### 9 HELL'S MOUTH/PORTH NEIGWL

A long, wild south-west bay, with four miles of sand and dunes. Perfect for bivvying.

→ From Abersoch take Lon Engan through Llanengan, then continue 1 mile to find the beach parking 300m after LL53 7LG.
1 min, 52.8078, -4.5503 🏖🏴

### 10 PORTH CEIRIAD, ABERSOCH

A favourite with surfers, and geologists. Look out for giant glacial boulders trapped in the cliffs above, then golden sandstone layers, folded and contorted over millions of years. Campsite above.

→ From Abersoch head through Sarn Bach. After 1 mile (before LL53 7DB) take second L down narrow dead-end lane. Continue through Nant-y-Big campsite (see entry) to parking.
5 mins, 52.7942, -4.5064 🏖🏕⛺

## SEA CAVES

### 11 PORTH LLANLLAWEN, UWCHMYNYDD

Narrow pebble cove with clear water, great jumps and huge sea caves in the cliffs if you swim/coasteer 100m to the right.

→ From bridge in Aberdaron follow signs for Whistling Sands (see entry), then after ½ mile L for Uwchmynydd. After 1 mile (after LL53 8BY), find metal kissing gate on R after Penbryn Bach restaurant on L. No parking, but limited space to pull off by old chapel shortly

before this, at 52.8029, -4.7378. Follow footpath 1 mile to creek bottom on shore.
20 mins, 52.8054, -4.7518 🍴🅿️🌳🚲

### 12 OGOF DDEUDDRWS ARCH

Several sea caves and a rock arch you can swim through at high tide. Discover more along the coast around the headland.

➜ From Aberdaron (car park between bridges, S of LL53 8BE), walk 1 mile E along Aberdaron beach to headland.
25 mins, 52.7966, -4.6922 🏊🚶

## HILLTOPS

### 13 MYNYDD MAWR & ST MARY'S WELL

Watch the sun set over Bardsey Island (see entry) from this spot on the very tip of the Llŷn. Below, pilgrims would have made their way down to the steep and dangerous cove to board tiny boats for the perilous trip across the sound, stopping to drink at St Mary's well near the water line.

➜ As for Porth Llanllawen (see listing), but continue beyond LL53 8BY to park just beyond Mynydd Mawr campsite. Find footpath on L as road bends up R, and bear downhill to the inlet.
10 mins, 52.7921, -4.7602 📷✝️🧗

### 14 TRE'R CEIRI HILL FORT, YR EIFL

This 'home of the giants' is one of the best-preserved and most dramatic Iron Age hill forts in Europe, with the scattered remains of 150 roundhouses and four-metre high perimeter walls. The sea and mountain views are phenomenal. Yr Eifl means 'the forks' or 'the strides' due to its three distinct summits.

➜ From Llanaelhaearn head SE on B4417 (dir LL54 5BB). After ¾ mile find small layby on R and footpath ¼ mile beyond, following wall up steeply on R then curving up L flank to SW entrance. Or a longer approach from the car park on the Nant Gwrtheyrn road LL53 6NU.
40 mins, 52.9745, -4.4238 📷🚌🧗

## LOST RUINS

### 15 TREFOR QUARRY, YR EIFL

An old granite quarry complex with sea views. The massive concrete stone crusher has been gutted but is still impressive.

➜ From Trefor follow Eifl road through village to the bus depot/industrial area (LL54 5LH) and park. The long, straight quarry road heads up the mountainside. A footpath also leads into the site from the lane at 52.9885, -4.4324 but parking is tricky.
20 mins, 52.9880, -4.4373 🚌📷

### 16 PORTH Y NANT, NANT GWRTHEYRN
Explore the remains of the granite quarry, which produced cobble sets for Liverpool's roads, and take a walk on the long pebble beach below.

→ Signed Nant Gwrtheyrn from Llithfaen, dir LL53 6NU. Spectacular drive down. Park at Caffi Meinir (see entry) and head SE along the coast path. Ascend on the old incline.
7 mins, 52.9723, -4.4656 ⬛🚗

SACRED & ANCIENT

### 17 ST BEUNO'S & PORTH PISTYLL
Tiny 12th-century church, which maintains the medieval tradition of spreading rushes as a covering on the stone floor. A track runs down to a wild pebble beach in a dell below.

→ From Nefyn follow B4417 E for 1¾ miles and take dead-end road on L to church. Follow the track up beyond church into field. In the bottom far L corner a kissing gate leads down to the wild beach.
10 mins, 52.9555, -4.4924 ⬛✝

### 18 ST TUDWEN'S CHURCH & LYCH GATE
Remote 16th-century church with a huge lych gate, in meadows, said to have been built over the saint's grave. Holy well.

→ From Dinas take lane NE, signed Rhyd-y-clafdy and Pwllheli, past unsigned turning to LL53 8UB, church is up next unsigned L. Limited space to pull off. A holy well has been rediscovered at the spring at 52.9008 -4.5666 – look for the new kissing gate on R as approaching the church, then 200m across boggy fields to a wooden cross marker.
1 min, 52.9013, -4.5675 ✝

### 19 ST CYBI'S WELL, LLANGYBI
Intriguing ruins of a 6th-century enclosed holy well and 18th-century cottage for patients, who drank well and sea water, bathed in the well, and stayed at the cottage. The water was also used for divination in romances . Super views from Garn Bentyrch hillock, a short walk above.

→ From the church in Llangybi (LL53 6LZ), follow the path from the far L corner of the graveyard up the hill 100m. Continue up through woodland to reach the hillock summit.
2 mins, 52.9455, -4.3421 ⬛✝

MEADOWS & WILDLIFE

### 20 CAEAU TAN-Y-BWLCH
Owned by the charity Plantlife, Caeau Tan-y-Bwlch means 'the fields below the pass' and

even if you're not really into bucolic summer meadows rich with orchids, wildflowers and butterflies, then come just for the stunning views. Best between May and July before the meadows are cut for hay.

➜ Along lanes 1½ miles SE from Clynnog Fawr, at LL54 5DL. Pull off by reserve entrance gate on L (limited space).
2 mins, 53.0140, -4.3411

### 21 PLAS YN RHIW NT
Hidden in the woods overlooking Cardigan Bay this intimate NT house and garden was left by the Keating sisters, keen conservationists who created a garden for the benefit of the wildlife. Still organically managed and a haven for nature, it's a romantic place with wonderful views. You can rent the Trust's Tan y Bwlch, a charming restored crog loft cottage (01758 780219).

➜ Signed from Abeerdaron; follow the minor road through Rhiw, dir LL53 8AB to find entrance on L after ¾ mile. Check open times.
10 mins, 52.8217, -4.6190

### 22 YNYS ENLLI (BARDSEY ISLAND)
A place of pilgrimage since early Christian times, Barsdey has ancient remains, wonderful wildlife and stunning scenery that continue to entice visitors seeking spiritual or natural inspiration. It's home to over 300 bird species including an important colony of Manx shearwater. Grey seals breed on the island and dolphins and porpoises are often spotted in the surrounding sea. Open to visitors Mar–Oct as a day trip or as guest in one of the Bardsey Island Trust's characterful holiday cottages.

➜ All trips depart from Porth Meudwy, dir LL53 8DA (follow signs). Parking at 52.7989, -4.7319, then 10 min walk to the harbour. bardseyboattrips.com, 07971 769895.
20 mins, 52.7584, -4.7917

## SLOW FOOD

### 23 PLAS GLYN Y WEDDW
Set on the coast path just behind Llanbedrog beach is this gothic mansion, now an art gallery, heritage centre and café. Exhibitions, theatre performances and kids' holiday messy-art sessions ensure there is something for everyone. Don't miss a wander around the lovely woodland.

➜ Llanbedrog, LL53 7TT, 01758 740763. oriel.org.uk
52.8544, -4.4829

### 24 THE CRAB KITCHEN, SARN
No luck fishing? Stop off at this little seafood stall and pick up some local, freshly caught and prepared lobster, crab or fish of the day.

➜ Selective Seafoods, Ffriddwen, Sarn, LL53 8BJ, 01758 770397.
52.8796, -4.6128

### 25 CAFFI PORTHDINLLAEN
Good coffee, home-made pancakes, scones and ice creams from this little beach café on the road for Borth Wen and Porth Dinllaen (see entry). Open 10am–5pm, Apr–Oct. The Ship Inn in neighbouring Edern (01758 720559) serves evening meals.

➜ Golf Road, Morfa Nefyn LL53 6BE, 01758 721210.
52.9351, -4.5588

### 26 Y GEGIN FAWR, ABERDARON
Café housed in a white cottage that once served pilgrims to Bardsey Island, selling delicious locally caught sweet crab and generous slices of homemade bara brith. Don't miss St Hywyn's seaside church which pilgrims visited en route – and still do today.

➜ Aberdaron, LL53 8BE, 01758 760359.
52.8042, -4.7125

### 27 SBLASH CABAN PYSGOD FISH BAR

A short stroll away from the beach, find great fish and chips, crab cakes and locally caught fish to eat at the long table inside, outside, or to take away and enjoy on the beach.

→ Abadaron, LL53 8BE, 01758 760442 .
52.8043, -4.7119 🟦

### 28 CAFFI MEINIR, NANT GWRTHEYRN

'The Nant' is a former Victorian quarrying village and now home of the National Welsh Language and Heritage Centre, with a museum, holiday cottages and café. It's a stunning location (see Porth y Nant entry) and free to visit. The café serves breakfast and lunch using Llŷn produce. Nearby Tafarn Y Fic (01758 750473), a Welsh community pub in Llithfaen, holds Welsh music nights.

→ Nant Gwrtheyrn, Llithfaen, LL53 6NL, 01758 750442.
52.9749, -4.4596 🟦🟦

### 29 PORTH TOCYN, MACHROES

Relaxed, family-run country hotel perfectly located for all the beaches, with a pool and an AA rosette restaurant open to non-residents.

→ Bwlchtocyn, LL53 7BU, 01758 713303.
52.8069, -4.4950 🟦🟦

### 30 PLAS BODEGROES

If you are seeking luxury on the Llŷn, book a table or a weekend at this romantic wisteria-clad manor. Dine on the best Welsh produce, including much from their kitchen garden, served with flair in their art-gallery-cum-restaurant. Open to non-residents for dinner Tues–Sat and for Sunday lunch.

→ Nefyn Road, Pwllheli, LL53 5TH, 01758 612363.
52.8898, -4.4466 🟦🟦

### 31 MICKEY'S BOATYARD & BEACH CAFÉ

Right by the edge of the water, this friendly café with lots of outdoor seating serves up bacon baps, sandwiches, ice cream and good coffee from its metal boatyard home.

→ Machroes Beach, Bwlchtocyn, LL53 7EU, 07584 181185.
52.8097, -4.4969 🟦🟦

### 32 TY COCH INN

Virtually on the beach, this popular nautical pub is perfect for a pint and a bowl of chips while the kids play on the sand. Food served 12–2.30pm only, reduced hours in winter.

→ Porthdinllaen, Morfa Nefyn, LL53 6DB, 01758 720498.
52.9432, -4.5679 🟦🟦

### 33 MYNYDD MAWR CAMPSITE

Right on the very western tip of the Llŷn, enjoying wonderful views out to sea and, if you climb the hilly peak, as far as Bardsey Island. Hot showers (50p) and a little café serving breakfasts and home-made cakes (weekends and summer holidays), take nothing away from the sense of wild isolation that you'll find here. Sunset camping at its best.

→ Llanllawen Fawr, Aberdaron, LL53 8BY, 01758 760223.
52.7991, -4.7460 🟦🟦

### 34 PENISARLON FARM CAMPING

Sunset campsite on a rural smallholding overlooking Porth Nefyn. Open grassy pitches are exposed but offer good sea views. Feed the donkeys and buy the farm eggs for your breakfast.

→ Pistyll, LL53 6LR, 01758 721533.
52.9484, -4.4947 🟦🟦

### 35 TOWYN FARM CAMPING

With easy access to a lovely sandy cove (see Porth Towyn entry) this family-only campsite on a working farm is a place families come back to year after year. There are washing machines, freezers, hot showers, sunset views and of course the wonderful beach.

→ Tudweiliog, LL53 8PD, 01758 770600.
52.9051, -4.6297 🟦🟦🟦

### 36 PENRALLT COASTAL CAMPSITE

This is a quirky, simple sunset campsite that often feels uncrowded even in high season. Sculptures made from beach flotsam decorate the site to encourage everyone to recycle as much as they can, and there are a couple of camping pods. It's a 10-minute walk down to the small rocky cove, which is great for rock pooling, or a half-hour trundle along the coast path to Traeth Penllech (see entry).

→ Penllech, LL53 8PB, 01758 770654.
52.8943, -4.6550 🟦🟦🟦

### 37 NANT-Y-BIG CAMPSITE & TOURING

If you have a tent you can take it down to the quiet (but exposed) field nearest the beach and enjoy fantastic sea views and friendly camping cameraderie. Facilities are basic, clean and there are hot showers to warm up after surfing. Best of all, it's minutes from the sandy shores of Porth Ceiriad (see entry). Caravan facilities near the farmhouse.

→ S of Bwlchtocyn, LL53 7DB, 01758 712686.
52.7969, -4.5113 🟦

## 38 TREHELI FARM

What it lacks in modern facilities it makes up for in views and peace. Sitting above the sea, the very basic Treheli Farm campsite looks out over wind-lapped Porth Neigwl (see entry). Plas yn Rhiw NT (see entry) is nearby.

→ Rhiw, LL53 8AA, 01758 780281.
52.8253, -4.6140

## 39 ABERAFON, GYRN GOCH

Set behind a rocky beach (some sand) and with views of Gyrn Goch mountain, this family-friendly site is perfect for an evening campfire on the beach watching the sunset. Choose from grassy pitches sheltered behind the trees, or, if the wind is low, directly behind the beach. Simple, clean services include pay showers. Open Easter–Oct.

→ Gyrn Goch, LL54 5PN, 01286 660295.
53.0107, -4.3886

## RUSTIC HAVENS

### 40 RED WELLY, CLYNNOG FAWR

Beautifully decorated farmstead complex offering complete seclusion with its own private beach and a grassy field by the sea for house guests wanting to camp under the stars. Perfect for groups, the dairy barn seats up to 20 people for communal dinners, children can run free, safe from any roads, and a footpath leads to the village. Three properties sleep 12.

→ Ty Coch Farm, Clynnog Fawr, LL54 5PD, 07866 467979.
53.0277, -4.3608

### 41 YR HEN FYNYDD

Escape to this idyllic stone cottage nestled under Yr Eifl. Perfectly rustic and warmed by blankets, a woodburner and cooking range. Step outside and the vast vista of the mountain opens up. Sleeps five, no pets.

→ Llanaelhaearn, LL53 6PB, 0844 5005101.
underthethatch.co.uk
52.9633, -4.4167

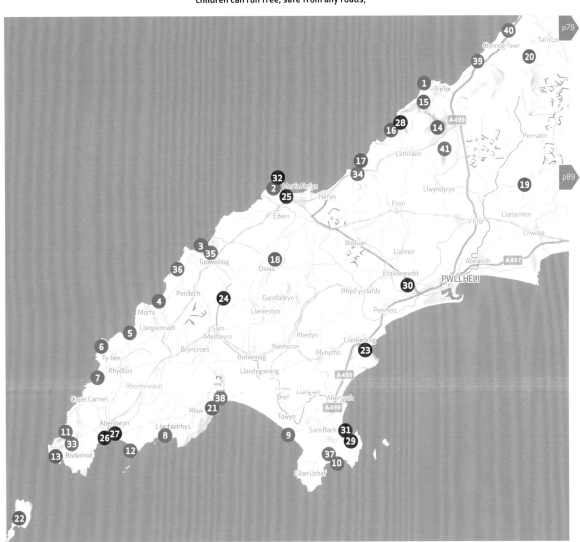

# CONWY & LLANDUDNO

## Our perfect weekend

→ **Look** for Tylwyth Teg (Fairy Folk) in the magical mossy woods between the Klondyke ruins and the Clogwyn slate chambers

→ **Swim,** canoe and picnic at Llyn Geirionydd, perfect for family summer fun

→ **Dip** in the waterfall pool of Afon Dulyn, en route to your overnight camp at Dulyn bothy and lake

→ **Discover** fabulous fungi, mountain goats, and majestic sea views on the Great Orme – home of the fascinating Bronze Age copper mines

→ **Paddle** at Aber Falls, find the ancient round houses then follow the Roman Road up to Foel-ganol for sea views

→ **Dance** around the Druid's Circle high up on the Wales coast path at Cefn Côch

→ **Stock** up on award-winning Welsh artisan produce at Bodnant, then picnic in the gardens

→ **Trek** up to Cwm Caseg and wild camp by the lake, one of the most remote wild spots in Snowdonia

→ **Bivvy** out in a Second World War gun turret on the Great Orme

**The north-eastern corner of Snowdonia is an easily accessible yet quiet land, rich in forest, lakes and lost industrial heritage. As the mountains advance to the coast, sacred and ancient sites abound, many on high trackways commanding dramatic views across the sea.**

Gwydir Forest stretches from Betws-y-Coed to Llanwrst, and its tiny lanes and dense woodland hide many little lakes. Although some are natural, many are naturalised old reservoirs, built to power the lead mines that once operated throughout these sylvan hills. You can explore the mines at Hafna, but the most famous ruins can be found hidden in magical woodland near Llyn Crafnant. Known as the Klondyke mill, it is named after the catastrophic Canadian Klondike gold rush. Swindler Joseph Aspinall bought the failed mine in 1918, though he never actually paid. He stuck lead ore onto its walls, set up a pretend processing unit, and employed an army of mine workers, all of which allowed him to extract vast sums from gullible London investors before he was caught and jailed. The mine is now closed off, and the mill an eerie ruin slowly returning to nature. Even more consumed by the progress of lichen, moss and fern are the earlier mining endeavours at Clogwyn-y-Fuwch, reached on a path through the ancient oaks. Dating from 1790, these were some of the first slate mines in Snowdonia, and adventurers can uncover a vast set of chambers up the hillside.

Heading north, the forest turns first to mountain and then moorland as the coast approaches. At Rowen, a Roman road marches its way from Chester to Caernafon, up the mountains past Maen y Bardd, the 'bard's stone' cromlech, and many Bronze Age remains, to descend near spectacular Aber Falls. Nearer Conwy, along the A55, the mountains meet the sea in a dramatic escarpment and provide stunning coastal views. Gaze over the Lavan Sands and Anglesey, dance around the Druid's Circle, or storm the hill forts of Conwy Mountain.

A short hop across the river Conwy leads to great carboniferous limestone hulk of the Orme – Old Norse for sea serpent. This peninsula teems with rare flora and fauna, and its position affords truly magnificent views of Snowdonia and across the sea to Anglesey. Famous for its 3,500-year-old mine complex – the largest prehistoric copper mine in the world – there is much to discover here, away from the tourists. Explore the network of ruined Second World War gun turrets on the south coast, a good spot for bivvying, and at picturesque Porth Dyniewaid (Angel Bay), seals and their pups can be viewed from the grassy cliffs.

## WILD LAKES

### 1 LLYN GEIRIONYDD

A particularly accessible and popular lake, with car park and little lane along its entire length, but in beautiful scenery. There's a slipway for canoes and dinghies, a meadow for picnics at one end and, for the adventurous, a good gorge scramble at the other down to Klondyke mine ruins.

→ Take signed turning off B5106 in Trefriw, opp Fairy Falls Inn, L after ¼ mile and continue following signs to just beyond LL27 0YX. Gorge scramble is to 53.1397, -3.8465 – watch out for the bit that goes through a tunnel!
2 mins, 53.1268, -3.8501 🏊🏕️🐾🚣🅿️🚻

### 2 LLYN EIGIAU & FAILED DAM

The gap in the dam wall is testament to the disaster that struck here in 1925. Built with poor foundations, it collapsed after five days of heavy rain. 200-tonne boulders were picked up by the deluge, and 16 died when the village of Dolgarrog was flooded. The original, undammed lake remains, and it makes a remote and lonely swim.

→ Heading S on B5106 through Tal-y-bont, turn R after Y Bedol pub, past LL32 8SD and continue, bearing R at split, to park at end of lane at 53.1790, -3.8987. Dam break is another mile on foot; track continues to lake through a second, preventative breach.
30 mins, 53.1698, -3.9103 🏊⛰️🅿️

### 3 CORS BODGYNYDD & LAKE

Two beautiful lakes backed by mountains sit in a strange land of hummocked hillocks and wetland bog – ancient spoil heaps from zinc mining 400 years ago, now re-wilded. On our summer visit there were fungi galore and froglets and toadlets jumping by our feet. The heathland is renowned for its nightjars. The first lake, just a moment from the road, has an old dam wall with deep water for a swim.

→ Drive about a mile S beyond popular LLyn Geirionydd (see entry) to find the gate to the reserve on the R (just beyond turn off L for LL27 0YZ) and limited parking. Walk in 150m, bearing off R through copse around the top edge of the lake to the dam wall. Continue on the main path 400m to arrive at large, more wooded Llyn Bodgynydd.
3 mins, 53.1201, -3.8470 🏊🐾🐾⭐🅿️

## WATERFALLS

### 4 AFON DDU GORGE

Beginners' gorge scramble popular with outdoor groups, with smallish pools and falls. Passes through an SSSI for plant life.

→ Approaching Dolgarrog from S on B5106, find car park R shortly after Conwy Valley Maze and LL32 8JG. Cross road and climb tarmac road, taking footpath on L to stream (see noticeboard and map of scramble). Exit above main waterfall to L, and return down on tarmac road.
5 mins, 53.1785, -3.8359 🏊🅿️

### 5 AFON DULYN WATERFALL

Excellent waterfall with a big pool, just off the lane, in ancient woods.

→ In Tal-y-bont, turn as for Llyn Eigiau (see listing), and continue ½ mile to double hairpin bend and grit bin R just beyond (no parking), where path descends to stream. Ford and continue upstream.
5 mins, 53.1975, -3.8622 🏞️🐾🅿️

### 6 ABER FALLS & ROUNDHOUSE

Also called Rhaeadr-fawr, these very impressive and popular falls are reached through the beautiful Coedydd Aber nature reserve and accessible by wheelchair. There is no dipping pool, but a stream and several Iron Age hut remains. Foel-Ganol, at the end of the access lane, makes a great mini peak too.

→ Signed Abergwyngregyn from A55, then follow road ½ mile (past LL33 0LP) to signed entrance for car park with WC. The best roundhouse is on R by path, after 400m (53.2137, -3.9969). Falls are a further mile. 30 mins, 53.2107, -3.9956 🅻🚻🐑⛰🚲

### 7 CWM CASEG & LAKE

The Caseg valley is a magnificent but remote entrance to the mighty but lesser visited Carneddau range, with quarries and a truly wild spot to camp at Cwm Caseg by the tarn.

→ From Bethesda drive beyond LL57 3UD to park at road end at pump station, then follow path E upriver. After 1 mile find tunnel which leads to a quarry chamber (53.1805, -4.0185). 90 mins, 53.1656, -3.9785 🚲🅺🏕⛰🏔

## BEACHES & COAST

### 8 PORTH DYNIEWAID, LITTLE ORME

A wild shingle cove on the lesser-known Little Orme's Head set under cliffs and popular with climbers, also known as Angel Bay. Seals regularly visit with their young in autumn and winter – please keep off the beach if you see them.

→ Park at far end of Penrhyn Beach East (past LL30 3RN), in Penrhyn Bay. Take steps to footpath and bear R to end of headland. 10 mins, 53.3278, -3.7763 🌊🏊🚶

### 9 PIGEON'S CAVE, GREAT ORME

Huge sea cave with beach. Very tricky access. Popular with climbers and anglers.

→ Follow Happy Valley Rd/Marine Drive ¾ mile N of Llandudno pier (LL30 2LR); limited space to park L. Rough anglers' path descends R onto slabs. If you want to get down to the entrance, there is a tricky descent from far W end of the beach, ½ mile beyond, at low tide. 1 min, 53.3374, -3.8360 🅻▼🅺📷

## CAVERNS

### 10 ELEPHANT CAVE, HAPPY VALLEY

The largest of the Great Orme quarry caverns, and right near the town centre. Cave lovers might also like Sheep Cave on the other side of the headland, high up with sea views and just big enough to bivvy in.

→ From Llandudno Pier ascend road past cable car and café (LL30 2ND), to park at dry ski slope. Return back on foot to find path opp botanical garden, to an obvious rock face on R. Sheep cave is at 53.3247, -3.8444 at top of zigzag footpath from Abbey Rd (LL30 2AT). 10 mins, 53.3296, -3.8332 🅺🚶

## 11 CLOGWYN-Y-FUWCH, LLYN CRAFNANT

Very impressive set of large slate caverns from the 1790s, before safer honeycombed chambers were introduced. The first level can be entered via a short tunnel, or bypassed, and contains splitting and dressing huts (waliau) inside the cavern itself. Persevere up the steep incline, through the waste, to the largest chambers on levels 4 and 5. From here a beautiful walk through ancient woodland leads down to Klondyke mill (see entry). Llyn Crafnant lake is beautiful, but no swimming due to fishing.

→ Signed Llyn Crafnant opp The Fairy Falls inn in Trefriw B5106; follow road past LL27 0JZ to forestry car park and toilets ½ mile further R. Cross road and take forestry track up. At first bend bear off L to find ruins at base of mine and first level entrance.

10 mins, 53.1396, -3.8560 🏴‍☠️🔦📷🧗

## 12 CAE COCH SULPHUR MINE

A 'fools gold' (pyrites) and sulphur mine complex with several ruins plus tunnels leading to a large network of chambers. The water runs red and there are fantastic coloured yellow stalactite formations. Peer in but do not enter: the water is acidic and wooden props have rotted away.

→ A mile N of Trefriw B5106, turn into Coed Gwydyr forestry road on L (by mirror, a little N of LL27 0JS). It is usually gated. Continue up, then first L, and follow track ½ mile to mill ruins at 53.1691, -3.8304. From here a footpath rises NW through woods 300m to Level 3, main mine/quarry area.

20 mins, 53.1707 -3.8336 🔦📷🧗

10

## LOST RUINS

## 13 HAFNA MINE SMELTER

In forest off a minor lane, this was one of the most important lead mines in the area from 1879 to 1915. The vast covered factory was state of the art, designed by the French in 1889. Follow the smelting process down the hillside: each floor has a different function.

→ About ½ mile N of the Outdoor Pursuits Centre (LL27 0JB) in Gwydyr Forest, with parking.

1 min, 53.1241, -3.8234 📷

## 14 KLONDYKE MINE RUINS

Huge ore mill ruins from 1900 in beautiful woods. The mill and associated mine (sealed off) were the site of a great mining scam in 1918. A challenging gorge scramble ascends up to Llyn Geirionydd (see listing).

14

→ Best approach is via Clogwn-y-Fuwch (see entry); continue round on the contour, bearing down L on smaller track as main path begins to rise after 50m. Cross wall into ancient oak woods and follow old trackway ½ mile to the mill tailings. Return on lane in loop. Gorge scramble is at 53.1397, -3.8465.
25 mins, 53.1421, -3.8478 ▨▨▨▨▨▨

### 15 ROYAL ARTILLERY SCHOOL RUINS

The Royal Artillery coastal gunnery school was built in 1940 and abandoned at the end of the war. There are several sets of gun houses near the beach, and a further lookout higher on the cliff, which could make a great bivvy spot. Also underground bunkers.

→ From the car park at Great Orme's Head (LL30 2XD, see entry) continue ½ mile SW on road to find metal gate on R at 53.3376, -3.8758 (no parking here). Paths lead ¼ mile S to main guns, but another trio is directly below the gate, at 53.3366, -3.8784. Another single lookout is just to 200m to the N below the cliff, at 53.3385, -3.8772. You can also cycle (sometimes drive) to the bottom sites from the end of Llys Helig Drive (LL30 2XB).
10 mins, 53.3327, -3.8758 ▨▨

### 16 BRYN EURYN RUINS & HILLTOP

This little urban enclave yields the remains of a 15th-century grand house (the Llys), derelict for centuries, set within a nature reserve of rare butterflies and wildflowers. Make the easy climb to Bryn Euryn's summit to look out across the Great Orme.

→ From A55 head N on B5115 through Rhôs-on-Sea. Cross roundabout then take 2nd L at lights, Rhos Rd (past LL28 4TT) and cross into Bryn Euryn Nature Reserve at end. Find ruins on R, before car park. Continue on track to hilltop.
5 mins, 53.306, -3.7526 ▨▨▨

### 17 GREAT ORME MINES

Incredible network of caves and tunnels dating back 4,000 years. If you don't want to pay there are also some ancient copper mine caves in the cliffs just north of Llandudno pier.

→ Well signed, at LL30 2XG, with parking. Mar–Oct only. Llandudno mines at 53.3297, -3.8282, N of pier, down stone steps. £7 entry fee.
2 mins, 53.3305, -3.8471 ▨▨▨

## SACRED & ANCIENT

### 18 DRUID'S CIRCLE, CEFN CÔCH

Large stone circle with 29 stones and great views. The coast path rises to 400m here,

and there are two more circles to be found on the ridge, including the smallest in the UK, and the Craig Lwyd Neolithic axe factory.

→ Park by pillars at the top of Mountain Lane (beyond LL34 6YP) then 1½ miles on a good track. Craig Lwyd outcrop is to the NW at 53.2562, -3.9240.

30 mins, 53.2535, -3.9157 🖼🚶🚴♿

### 19 MAEN Y BARDD, ROWEN

The 'bard stone' is a perfect little cromlech with a capstone on four uprights. There are stunning views out over the Conwy valley. It is situated on an age-old trackway, once a Roman road, and there are several other standing stones and hut circles. A remote YHA can be found a little further along track. Tal y Fan is an easy peak above and a wonderful lookout point across Anglesey.

→ Take the turning by Y Bedol Inn in Tal-y-Bont past LL32 8YZ (B5106). Ascend for 4 miles. At 53.2251, -3.9019, a mile before the road end and car park, a footpath ascends N to Tal y Fan (1 mile), and the ancient trackway begins to the E. Bear L off track after ½ mile to find the cromlech. YHA Rowen can be booked exclusively (0345 3719038).

20 mins, 53.2281, -3.8880 🖼✝🚴♿🏞

### 20 ST TRILLO'S WELL, RHÔS-ON-SEA

A 6th-century holy well established by St Trillo in a tiny stone chapel, possibly the smallest in Britain, almost on the shore.

→ On promenade, Marine Drive, Rhôs-on-Sea, 100m N of LL28 4HS (near end of Trillo Ave). 2 mins, 53.3144, -3.7405 ✝

### HILL FORTS & PEAKS

### 21 MYNYDD Y DREF & PENSYCHNANT

Spectacular views out over Anglesey and the Orme from this ancient hill fort on Conwy Mountain. Earthworks, burial cairns and stone circles. Pensychnant House, adjacent, is a community nature reserve with ancient woodland, Scots pines and many bird species.

→ Leave Conwy on Upper Gate St / Sychnant Pass Rd. Continue 2 miles, past Pensychnant LL32 8BJ, to parking at top of pass. Take footpath on R for 1 mile bearing N then E. For a shorter walk, Alltwen hill fort is up a fork L from the path.

30 mins, 53.2827, -3.8617 🖼🚴🐕

### 22 FOEL-GANOL PEAK

An easy mini peak with sea views (536m). Many cairns and Iron Age ruins on the way; Carnedd y Saeson sits in a group of 7 cairns.

→ As for Aber Falls (see listing), LL33 0LP, but continue on to parking at lane end. Then a 1 mile steep ascent E, past Carnedd y Saeson at 53.2263, -3.9813; more cairns along gentler but longer ascent path around N side.
40 mins, 53.2251, -3.9666

### 23 LLECH DDU SCRAMBLE
Set in a truly wild and beautiful mountain environment, this pyramid of rock on the side of Carnedd Dafydd makes a brilliant Grade 1 (easy) scramble, which few know about. The white quartzite bands on the shoulder above the crag mark the beginning of the scramble.
→ Park in Bethesda/Gerlan and follow lane ¼ mile to end at LL57 3UB. Walk 2¼ miles, then climb up to the crag L of Cwmglas Bach.
90 mins, 53.1535, -4.0019

## ANCIENT TREES & WILDLIFE

### 24 LLANGERNYW YEW
The oldest living tree in Wales, possibly 4,000 years old – older than the great pyramid of Giza. Now split into several trunks.
→ St Digain's Church is at the crossroads in Llangernyw, just E of LL22 8PQ.
2 mins, 53.1923, -3.6851

### 25 GREAT ORME'S HEAD
Explore spongy, grassy cliffs and enjoy awesome sea views. Wild mountain goats, sea bird colonies, wildflowers and a vast array of fungi in season.
→ Parking by tiny café at far W end of (one way) Marine Drive (LL30 2XD). Explore W on the cliff tops.
10 mins, 53.3413, -3.8700

## SLOW FOOD

### 26 CONWY FARMERS MARKET
Monthly farmers market held at the RSPB Conwy nature reserve. Lots of local, seasonal and artisan food produce. Last Wednesday of every month, 9am–1pm.
→ RSPB Conwy Nature Reserve, LL31 9XZ.
53.2798, -3.8057

### 27 CONWY HONEY FAIR
Conwy's Honey fair has been going for 700 years and is probably one of the oldest food fairs in the country. Buy honey and beeswax products and learn about beekeeping. Annually in mid-September.
→ Lancaster Square, Conwy, LL32 8DA. conwybeekeepers.org.uk
53.2808, -3.83048

### 28 BODNANT WELSH FOOD CENTRE
Come and stock up on a smorgasbord of award-winning Welsh artisan breads, meats, ciders and ales, cheeses and vegetables. This is a large enterprise and deservedly the winner of numerous awards. Eat in the attractive Hayloft restaurant or tea room. Also on site is Wales' National Beekeeping Centre, and nearby is NT Bodnant garden.
→ Furnace Farm, Tal-y-cafn, LL28 5RP, 01492 651100.
53.2339, -3.8046

### 29 BLAS AR FWYD
A Welsh food hub, this little deli is packed with artisan products and a long line of locals coming for their lunch. Next door is a great wine shop with knowledgeable staff, and opposite is their bright and friendly Amser Da Café serving breakfast and lunch (open 8.30am–4pm Wed–Sat).
→ 25 Heol Yr Orsaf/Station Rd, Llanrwst, LL26 0BT, 01492 640215.
53.1392, -3.7995

### 30 FFIN Y PARC
Don't miss a visit to this beautifully restored country-house art gallery, showcasing contemporary Welsh artists. It has a lovely conservatory tea room piled with art books and serving light lunches and cakes. Book a room, or rent The Old Laundry or Caretakers Cottage. Open Wed–Sun 10am–5pm.
→ Betws Rd, Llanrwst, LL26 0PT, 01492 642070.
53.1213, -3.7801

### 31 LLYN CRAFNANT LAKESIDE CAFÉ
Family-run café serving breakfasts, lunches and cakes in a stone cottage by the lake. Buy a trout fishing permit and book a ghillie or maybe hire yourself a row boat. Camp overlooking the lake at nearby Cynllwyd Bach (see listing). Open daily 8am–5pm, Mar–Oct.
→ Tal y Llyn, Llanrychwyn, LL27 0YX, 01492 640818.
53.1305, -3.8693

### 32 MOSTYN GALLERY CAFÉ
Bright café above the art gallery. Come for breakfast, coffee and cakes, or a whole rotisserie chicken with all the trimmings.
→ Mostyn Gallery, 12 Vaughan St, Llandudno, LL30 1AB, 01492 879201.
53.3210, -3.8257

### 33 CAFFI CONTESSA, LLANRWST
Excellent coffee, teas, Welsh rarebits,

breakfasts and more, all made with local ingredients and love.

→ Ancaster Square, Llanrwst LL26 0LG, 01492 640754.
53.1381, -3.7979 🍴

### 34 BRYN WILLIAMS AT PORTH EIRIAS

This celebrity chef industrial-styled bistro overlooks Porth Eirias and the moody sea. Fantastic Welsh produce from the open kitchen focuses on fresh, seasonal seafood.

→ The Promenade, Colwyn Bay, LL29 8HH, 01492 577525.
53.2953, -3.7169 🍴

## COSY PUBS

### 35 THE QUEEN'S HEAD, GLANWYDDEN

Braised local lamb with creamed leeks and hearty Sunday roasts of Welsh rump beef are served in the traditional pub, with bar area, restaurant and outdoor terrace. Cosiest in winter when the woodburner is flickering.

→ Pen-y-Bont Rd, Glanwydden, LL31 9JP, 01492 546570.
53.3071, -3.7762 🍺🍴

### 36 THE OLD SHIP, TREFRIW

A roaring fire, friendly service, a riverside garden, real ales – 'Yr Hen Long' is a proper traditional pub with home-made food.

→ Trefriw LL27 0JH, 01492 640013.
53.1524, -3.8240 🍺🍴

### 37 GROES INN HOTEL

Expect lots of Welsh lamb, Welsh Black beef and fresh seafood in this characterful dining pub with inglenooks and bedrooms.

→ Llanrwst Rd, Conwy LL32 8TN, 01492 650545.
53.2492, -3.8348 🍺🛏🛌

### 38 THE WHITE LION, LLANELIAN

Real ales, real fires and pub grub, including delicious home-made pâté, at this very friendly traditional pub.

→ Llanelian, Colwyn Bay LL29 8YA, 01492 515807.
53.2724, -3.7057 🍺🍴

## WILDER CAMPING

### 39 DULYN LAKE BOTHY

Deep in the Carneddau, miles from anywhere in an imposing cwm by the lake – in which at least one plane wreck lies – this stone cottage maintained by the Mountain Bothies Association has a woodburner, but you

will need to bring your own fuel. There are Bronze Age hut remains on the path 200m before reaching the bothy.

→ From parking for Llyn Eigiau (see listing) take path over steps around ridge, then NW for the Dulyn Reservoir. 400m E of the reservoir, by the path. 60 mins walk in.
53.1789, -3.9388 🏕🏔🎣⛺🅱

### 40 CAE WENNOL YURTS

Painted Mongolian yurts, ponies, eco-loos and showers, outdoor pizza oven and peace on a smallholding in the Conwy Valley. The quirky common room/kitchen has a woodburner stove as well as a gas hob.

→ Ty Hwynt i'r Ffwrd, Hen Efail, LL32 8SP, 01492 650138.
53.2398, -3.8375 🏕

### 41 CYNLLWYD BACH

Described as semi-wild camping, there is room for two tents and two campervans at this tiny no-frills camp spot on Llyn Crafnant, with a potty loo in a shed and cold water tap. Lakeside café is down the road.

→ Llyn Crafnant, LL27 0JZ, 01492 641888.
53.1335, -3.8666 ⛺

## RUSTIC RETREATS

### 42 THE LIGHTHOUSE B&B, LLANDUDNO

What a location! Housed in a castellated lighthouse on the very edge of the cliffs. Three quirky, dated rooms offer unrivalled sea views and come with much-praised breakfasts.

→ Marine Dr, Llandudno LL30 2XD, 01492 876819.
53.3422, -3.8689 🏖📷

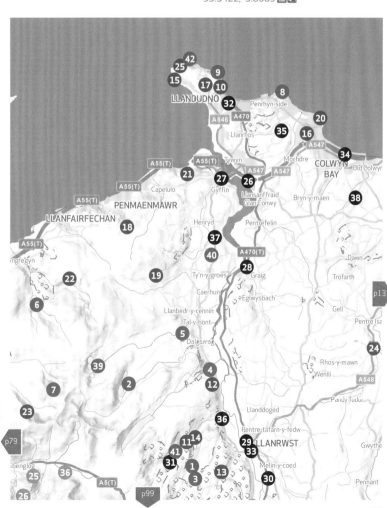

# SNOWDON & LLANBERIS

## Our perfect weekend

→ **Wild** camp by the picturesque Lyn Glas, a perfect mountain infinity pool complete with island

→ **Greet** the dawn with a long swim in Llyn Gwynant, pitch your tent at the lakeside campsite and feast on wood-fired pizza

→ **Scramble** from Tryfan to Bristly Ridge, to the Cantilever and down the Gribin – some the finest Grade 1 scrambles to be had in one day

→ **Swim** in the emerald plunge pools of Cwm Llan or crystal clear tarns of Llynnau Silyn

→ **Climb** to the highest levels of Dinorwig to see Wales' largest quarry frozen in time

→ **Dive** into the blue lagoons of Dorothea, Tryfan and Glanrafon, some over 100m deep

→ **Wonder** at the lives of the mine workers amid the haunting remains of Anglesey Barracks

→ **Treat** yourself to old-style comforts surrounded by climbing antiquities at the Pen-y-Gwyrd mountain hotel, where Hilary and Tenzing trained for Everest

**The towering mountain massif of Eryri is a fairytale land of jagged peaks and glacial valleys. This small area contains Wales' 18 highest peaks, and some of its greatest adventures, from the remains of the largest slate quarries in Welsh history, to exciting scrambles over the pinnacled ridges.**

Although the area attracts many visitors, it's surprisingly easy to escape the crowds and find true solitude. Most tend to aim for the highest peaks, and the routes to these can too often feel like a busy 'walking motorway' in the high summer months. Break with tradition and the best views of these grand mountains can be enjoyed from their adjacent peaks and ridges. These are often easier to access, emptier and even more beautiful – so try exploring Eilio, Nantlle or Clogwyngarreg.

Scrambling is an exhilarating way to reach some of the wilder summits. Thanks to the Ice Age, these are plentiful, so forget Crib Goch and discover some lesser-known Grade scrambles – Senior's Gully leads up to Cwm Cneifio, a valley near Cwm Idwal that is sheltered, even on a rainy day. Or for a really big day out, try the Tryfan to Bochlwyd Horseshoe.

For more grand adventures, scout out the two largest slate mines in Welsh history, which both closed in 1970 and are slowly returning to the wild. Magnificent Dinorwig consumed an entire mountainside above lake Padarn. At its peak it employed 3,000 men on over 30 levels, creating pits over 250m deep. With names such as California, Australia and Tasmania, these are a mecca for climbers. The rite of passage is the 'snakes and ladders', an extraordinary route between the various pits accessed via climbing rockwalls on old iron ladders and descending through tunnels into the Lost World. In places – such as the huge shed with 100 circular saw tables, or a caban where workmen's coats still lie waiting – time stands still. Take care if you enter these sites, as each winter frost sees another collapse. Access issues also flare up here from time to time, so be respectful.

Dorothea in Nantlle is less visible, but covers a similar area. The many pits have now amalgamated into one giant lake, over 100m deep in parts, unofficially used by divers but open to swimmers too. Swimming near to the cliff face wearing goggles is a vertigo-inducing experience. The quarry wall plunges down to a lunar landscape of moraine and boulders that appears far beneath. The village of Talysarn was moved west as the quarrying expanded, and today the remains of the old village and many fascinating ruins, including a Cornish beam engine and the overgrown remains of the chapel at Plas Talysarn, can be found. Only the baboons of Angkor Wat are missing.

## LAKES & TARNS

### 1 LYNNAU CWM SILYN

Two super-clear, blue tarns, looking out to sea. Perfect for catching a midsummer sunset swim.

→ Park at the very end of the mountain lane, beyond LL54 6RT, and follow track for 1 mile. Upper lake is deeper. Nearby Llyn Cwm Dulyn has a similar aspect, but is lower and closer to road, at 53.0238, -4.2531, via LL54 6EA.

20 mins, 53.0350, -4.2214

### 2 LLYN NADROEDD, CWM CLOGWYN

One of a trio of beautiful tarns in west-facing Cwm Clogwyn. Superbly clear and super cold!

→ Take footpath from main car park just S of Rhyd-Ddu A4085 (LL54 6TN). Take Rhyd-Ddu path for Snowdon but veer L around Llechog ridge; in total some 2½ miles of walking and 300m of climbing. Glanrafon quarry (see listing) is nearby.

90 mins, 53.0677, -4.0980

### 3 LLYN GLAS & CWM GLAS

This enchanting wild tarn has an island, on which grow two picturesque Scots pines. It sits in the secret Cwm Glas, one of the least trodden areas of Snowdon, with an infinity-pool view to the pinnacles of Crib Goch rising up before you. From here you can ascend to Llyn Bach and on up the scrambling ridge of Gyrn Lâs/Crib y Ddysgl (the Cwm Glas horseshoe).

→ 1½ mile NW of Pen-y-Pass on the A4086 (LL55 4NY) there is layby parking, by the Cromlech boulders, and a few more spaces ¼ mile further. Walk ¼ mile past these to second bridge and follow Cwm Glas Mawr up, then head L to tarn. A map is needed, as there are few paths.

80 mins, 53.0807, -4.0638

### 4 LLYN PADARN SHORE

A large, glacial lake, perfect for a quick canoe or swim among wooded islands, coves and peninsulas – all created by slate waste.

→ From A4086 at the far N end of Llanberis, almost opposite turn into town (dir LL55 4PX), turn towards lake to find several different separate parking/drive-on beach areas among the trees. Good spot for an easy overnight.

2 mins, 53.1273, -4.1332

### 5 LLYN GWYNANT & ELEPHANT ROCK

Stunning lake surrounded by mountains with beaches and easy access along much of the eastern side. Make your way round to Elephant Rock cliff for epic jumps from all heights. Nantgwynant campsite (see listing), on the lakeside, makes for a perfect base.

→ The cliffs are obvious on the far NW shore of the lake. There is some limited space on the roadside at 53.0475, -4.0174, 50m NE from entrance to YHA Bryn Gwynant (LL55 4NP) where the shoreside footpath and beaches begin, but it is probably best to park at the campsite entrance. Follow the footpath through the campsite to the footbridge upstream, then double back towards the rocks, ¾ miles, keeping below the mountain wall. Scramble down to shore at end. Or reach by boat from the road.

10 mins, 53.0492, -4.0244

### 6 CWM CLYD LAKE

This little glacial lake has a peninsula, towering mountains and epic Ffrancon valley views. At 600m it's an imposing place to wild camp or swim.

→ From the NT Ogwen Cottage visitor centre, parking and café (off the A5 at LL57 3LZ), climb up to Llyn Idwal. Bear R at the lake, then climb up to the W between Pinnacle Crag and Castell y Geifr.

60 mins, 53.1168, -4.0412

**10**

copper mine, with many ruins and tunnels, at Cwm y Bleiddiaid (53.0367, -4.0712)

90 mins, 53.0570, -4.0394 🖼️🚷🏊📷⛰️

### 9 OGWEN BANK, BETHESDA

If you ignore the mobile homes, this is as beautiful as any river scene, with a view up the Ffrancon valley, a stone bridge, ancient oaks, waterfalls and a huge pool for swimming. Scramble up slate on the other side of the bridge to peer down into the flooded part of Penrhyn quarry, once the biggest slate production site in the world.

→ Easy parking in layby off A5 by entrance of the caravan park (LL57 3LQ). Walk down entrance way to bridge.

2 mins, 53.1681, -4.0561 🏊📷

## BLUE POOLS

### 10 MOEL TRYFAN BLUE LAGOON

Set under Dolomite-like pinnacles in a lunar landscape of slate ruins (closed in the 1970s), find four iridescent blue open-access lakes and the mini peak of Moel Tryfan with sunset views out over the Llŷn.

→ Entering Y Fron from W on A487, turn L at telephone box (dir LL54 7BT) and park immediately on R, by track. Follow track ¼ mile up NE to reach first crater lake (53.0740, -4.2245, skirt round on its L to find way down). Continue on NE on quarry tracks another ½ mile to reach the main trio of lakes.

20 mins, 53.0816, -4.2138 🏊🍴📷

### 11 LLYN-Y-GADER QUARRY & CYCLE

The old quarry tramway, now the Lôn Gwyrfai cycle path, runs along the shores of Llyn-y-Gader to quarry ruins with a blue lake crater, and continues all the way to Beddgelert.

→ Park as for Llyn Nadroedd (see entry), but take path on opp side of road. Follow ½ mile around lake; when path turn E, the quarry is 100m above to W.

20 mins, 53.0453, -4.1429 🚴🏊

### 12 BWLCH-Y-GROES QUARRY POOLS

A remote mountain road leads up to huge quarry craters, silent since 1890. Two have part-filled with blue water – descend if you can find a safe way down!

→ Head E from crossroads in Groeslon 1½ miles, past LL55 4EX to parking area. Bear R past parking ½ mile, to find pit above on R. (Second pit, Cefn-du area, is N of parking, at 53.1175, -4.1655, and also has a tunnel).

10 mins, 53.1157, -4.1580 🏊🔽⛰️

**7**

## WATERFALLS

### 7 CWM LLAN FALLS, WATKIN PATH

Cascading down the mountain, deep blue and decked with rowan, these sunny, south-facing pools are popular with Snowdon walkers. Footpaths lead on up to Cwm Llan ruins or Merch falls (see entries).

→ Park at Pont Bethania pay car park off A498 N of Beddgelert, opp LL55 4NQ turning, and follow Watkin Path signs.

30 mins, 53.0441, -4.0551 🚶🏊🖼️🏃

### 8 MERCH FALLS & LLIWEDD MINE

Situated on remote mountainside beneath the Y Lliwedd ridge, this copper mine has huge chambers and many old artefacts. It sits at the head of the Merch river stream with many waterfalls, slides and pools.

→ As for the Cwm Llan falls (see entry) then turn R as falls start, just before gate, and cross the slate bridge. Follow path 1½ miles up mountainside to reach copper mine ruins above. Return following the Merch down, exploring its falls, finally through the woods into Hafod-y-Llan NT farm and campsite and back to road. Or ascend direct from the campsite, or combine as part of a loop via Y Lliwedd ridge. NB there is another abandoned

**11**

15

### 13 GLYN RHONWY & BOMB STORE

This quarry lake has always been popular with locals due to its clear water and rock ledges, though plans are afoot to develop for pumped hydro storage. Nearby is a once top-secret bomb store, now abandoned.

➔ As for Llyn Padarn (see listing) but continue N on A4086 200m and turn L into Glyn Rhonwy. Park on R, by barriers, opp caravan park. Walk through barriers into the nascent business park. After 300m, second R, at far end, you can peer down into the old bomb store area (several bunkers run off from this site, 53.1271, -4.1383). Another 200m along main drive, plot on L leads to gates for the lake. If these are open descend down path to pit bottom. Do not trespass.

15 mins, 53.1260, -4.1434 ? V ☂ ⛵

### 14 GLANRAFON QUARRY, SNOWDON

A vast azure crater, on this remote western flank of Snowdon. Tunnels lead from the quarry galleries westwards to the mill and tipping areas. Ruined barracks, waterwheels and a mill, all from 1875, can be seen.

➔ Park as for Llyn Nadroedd (see entry). Bear NE across boggy ground, crossing the railway, to reach the slag heaps after 1½ miles. The crater is at the top of the waste. Possible to

walk on to Llyn Nadroedd. Also 'Glan-yr-Afon'.

40 mins, 53.0646, -4.1190 ☂☒▲▼

### 15 DOROTHEA QUARRY LAKE & RUINS

A vast, wild site with many fascinating overgrown ruins, like a Welsh Angkor Wat. Circumnavigate the lake to discover old railways and a beam pump house. Over 100m deep in places, the lake is the culmination of many flooded quarry pits. Swimmers are welcome at the diving pontoon, at the end of a rough vehicle track. Currently open to the public, but development plans afoot.

➔ Park near the roundabout at the far E end of Talysarn (LL54 6AF). Follow access track E: after 70m a stile R leads to a swimming lagoon in fields. 100m on is a new security gate. Continue on main track 700m to reach the parking for the main dive/swim location (open to vehicles) at listed lat long. But bear L on footpath for ruined Talysarn Hall and barracks on R at 53.0559, -4.2439. Beyond the lake dive site, detour off E along the deep tramway cuttings, and find many more ruins to the N and E. Circumnavigate lake to find to find the magnificent Cornish beam pumping engine at 53.0542, -4.2435, with a second lake to the SW with tall island.

15 mins, 53.0561, -4.2393 ☂☒▼

9

15

## LOST RUINS

### 16 DOLBADARN CASTLE, LLANBERIS

Climb the romantic tower of this much-visited 13th-century ruined castle to admire the dramatic ruins of Dinorwig slate quarry and marvel at the lake and mountain views.

→ There's a large pay car park (follow signs for the County Park) but nicer approach at secret parking S of the castle instead: coming N on the A4086, there is a bend, turn R opp the 'Croeso Llanberis' down a track (53.1154, -4.1128, just before LL55 4UB).
2 mins, 53.1164, -4.1140 🖼🏔

### 17 ANGLESEY BARRACKS, DINORWIG

Explore the deserted street of roofless terraced cottages, home to workers from Anglesey until it was closed and abandoned in 1948. A poignant place filled with past lives. More ruins can be explored from here.

→ Park at the National Slate Museum LL55 4TY (entry to the museum is free and you can peer into the azure depth of Vivian quarry). Backtrack to the mini roundabout and the power station road to find a steep walled path on L. The clear path zigzags up for ½ mile, crossing an old railway bridge and entering woodland above. From the far end of the street explore E to find another set of ruined houses in 50m, or bear L to follow the railway, to reach the incline and climb up to Dali's Hole (see entry) near the viewpoint.
20 mins, 53.1205, -4.1092 🖼🗝🏔

### 18 DALI'S HOLE LEVEL, DINORWIG

One of the greatest adventures in Snowdonia, in the heart of the massive Dinorwig quarry. Much used by climbers, but mostly private land, so be respectful and discreet. Dali's Hole is a transient blue lake with waterfalls, empty in dry weather. From here explore through the waterfall double tunnel into 'California' with its giant snake chain and Banksy-style grafitti art by 'Panik' (Jack Murray).

→ Climb up from Anglesey barracks (see entry) or park at the bus stop layby car park (300m N of LL55 3ET) and follow track from SW of circle. Pass the huge derelict building after 600m and turn L through gate. Climb over metal field gate where the public path turns R. A tunnel on far side of Dali's Hole (53.1232, -4.1007) leads into California and 50m N of tunnel, in corner, is a tight squeeze down through a jumble of fallen boulders into long tram tunnel leading into bottom of Australia pit. (Enter at your own risk; many climbers use this approach and it has

74    Snowdon & Llanberis

19

been stable for some time). On far side of the massive pit is a ladder network up the far face to reach G'day level (see listing) about 150m above. 10 mins, 53.1233, -4.1007 ▣🌧❓🔦▽🖼

### 19 G'DAY LEVEL, DINORWIG

At the very top of the 'Australia' pit, the largest in Dinorwig, reached by a very long flight of mountain steps. Here, overalls still hang in old cabans (cabins), Blondin cable runways rust and iron ladders descend into the abyss below. Hike up further to find the great dressing shed, still complete with banks for circular saw tables.

→ From Dali's Hole (see listing) climb up to the level above (from here you can begin to look down into Australia) and then take slate steps on R, up, up, up to G'day level (Blondins and cabans, 53.1244, -4.0981), and up 2 more short levels, and SE, to dressing shed. The deep pits below, W are the Lost World and Mordor. Allow 30 mins Dali's Hole to dressing sheds direct. 40 mins, 53.1217, -4.0935 ▣🌧❓🔦▽🖼

### 20 BWLCH CWM LLAN QUARRY, SNOWDON

Up on the top of the world, to the west of the Yr Aran to Snowdon ridgeline, rock tunnels link overgrown pits and ruined mill buildings dot the hillside. Several old reservoirs and big views make this a great wild camp spot.

→ Park at main carpark just S of Rhyd-Ddu A4085 (LL54 6TN). Take Rhyd-Ddu path for Snowdon, but bear R off this after 1½ miles. 100 mins, 53.0482, -4.0900 🌧▣🖼✢

### 21 CWM LLAN QUARRY, SNOWDON

Just off the Watkin Path, look out for the ruins of Plas Cwm Llan, the old mill, workers' barracks and old quarry pits.

→ As for Cwm Llan waterfalls (see listing), follow main path another mile. Or bear up L after ¼ mile (before ruined Plas) then follow old tramway. 25 mins, 53.0509, -4.0700 ▣📙

19

20

18

24

22

23

### 22 MOEL EILIO SUMMIT

Lesser known peak (726m) with sublime sea and mountain views. Or continue as ridge walk to Foel Goch, returning in horseshoe loop.

→ Walk on from Bwlch-y-groes quarry lake (see listing). Or from Llanberis, find road end 300m beyond LL55 4SR (some parking on byway track after final gate).

50 mins, 53.0973, -4.1582 🏞️🚶

### 23 CLOGWYNYGARREG & ISLAND

A very easy quartz knoll peak (336m) overlooking Nantlle and Snowdon. The island on little Llyn Dywarchen beckons below. This is a reservoir, so be discreet if taking a dip.

→ Small parking bay by lake on B4418 a mile W of Rhyd-Ddu, dir LL54 6BT. Follow lake shore around to L and then ascend.

20 mins, 53.0611, -4.1543 🏞️🏊🚶

### 24 NANTLLE RIDGE WALK

A classic on the Snowdonia skyline, but surprisingly quiet. Seven peaks, up to 734m, with easy scrambling, sweeping arêtes, grassy saddles and superb sea views.

→ From car park just S of Rhy-Ddu on A4085 (LL54 6TN) starting with the easy ascent of Y Garn. Descend and return via Talysarn if you have a transport link up. For a longer, wilder walk via the top of Cwm Pennnant (and the Prince of Wales quarries), start from road beyond LL51 9AX (parking at bridge after 1 mile, or at very end).

150 mins, 53.0510, -4.1626 🏞️🚶🏃

### 25 TRYFAN SCRAMBLES

This superb popular peak has many scrambles. The North Ridge is a classic Snowdonia Grade 1, stretching from the valley floor to the summit. Or try one of the routes up from the Heather Terrace – a goat track/ledge along the east face, from which to ascend the Little and North Gully scramble and Nor Nor Groove. Once at the summit find Adam and Eve, two huge stones between which the daring leap, or take a seat on the Cannon cantilever rock.

→ Start from the A5 laybys and kissing gate 1 mile E from LL57 3LZ. Follow the path up, keeping to L of the wall, to reach the highest stile. Path L leads up N Ridge, normal summit path continues. Or contour further around to the E side to find the Heather Terrace path.

For the descent, head down the S Ridge to Bwlch Tryfan, then the rocky path down to Llyn Bochlwyd, Bochlwyd Buttress and back to road. Descending N end of Tryfan is far harder, best avoided.
60 mins, 53.1193, -3.9944 🔆 🔽 ⛰️ 🖼️

### 26 BRISTLY RIDGE, GLYDER FACH
South of Tryfan, another classic Grade 1 scramble along a fantastical pinnacled ridge. Link this up with Y Gribin ridge scrambles (see listing) to complete the Bochlwyd Horseshoe.
→ From the NT Ogwen Cottage visitor centre, parking and café (LL57 3LZ), follow the Cwm Bochlyd path past the lake up L to Bwlch Tryfan and then ascend via Sinister Gully – despite its name, this is the one to the R. If descending Y Gribin, the W side is the easier.
120 mins, 53.1084, -4.0031 🔆 🔽 🖼️

### 27 SENIOR'S GULLY, CWM IDWAL
Sheltered, easy Grade 1 scramble with a waterfall that you can walk behind. For something harder try South Arête, Foel Goch.
→ Park as for Bristly Ridge (see listing) and head around Llyn Idwal, following up to Cwm Cneifio (literally 'the shearing valley' but often called the 'nameless cwm'). For the South

Arête, bear R at Llyn Idwal, pass underneath the Pinnacle Crag and the Mushroom Garden, to find East Gulley on the S edge of Creigiau Gleision (53.12901, -4.0415).
60 mins, 53.1106, -4.0241 🔆 🔽 ❄️ 🖼️

### 28 Y GRIBIN & Y LLIWEDD, SNOWDON
An easy scramble up from Glaslyn that avoids all the crowds. Continue on via Y Lliwedd, keeping to the north face to really appreciate the highest cliff in Wales, 300m of sheer rock wall.
→ From Pen-y-pass car park (LL55 4NY) follow the Miner's Track past Llyn Llydaw. At Glaslyn, cross the stream and head directly up the blunt ridge ahead to the S.
135 mins, 53.0622, -4.0612 🔆 🖼️ 🖼️

### 29 CARNEDD Y CRIBAU
A scrambly and adventurous mini peak (591m) on the remote north Moelwynion range. The graceful double lakes of Diwaunedd are below.
→ From LL55 4NP head N on A498 to park on the corner layby 1 mile after road heads up from Llyn Gwynant. Opp L find bridle path up to the Bwlch y Rhediad saddle, then pick your own path up the ridge NE to the summit.
90 mins, 53.0642, -3.9771 🔆 ⛰️ 🖼️

### 30 CWM IDWAL LAKE

Wales' first National Nature Reserve, and deservedly popular with walkers, this picturesque glacial lake, surrounded by rising cliffs, harbours many rare Arctic Alpine plants including the incredibly rare Snowdon lily which blooms in May. Busy, but worth it.

→ Signed from Ogwen Cottage, LL57 3LZ on A5. 15 mins, 53.1183, -4.0239

## SLOW FOOD

### 31 LODGE DINORWIG

Stunning views, great food and a good selection of books, convenient for Dinorwig explorations. Popular with climbers and adventurers. Also a bunkhouse.

→ Dinorwig, LL55 3EY, 01286 871632. 53.1348, -4.1179

### 32 CAFFI GWYNANT

Get your avocado toast here! This great café in a renovated chapel near Snowdon's Watkin Path, serves delicious local food. Full Welsh breakfasts, homemade granola with Greek yoghurt, kippers on sourdough, cheese and leek sausages with home-made chilli jam, all beautifully presented. Open 9am–5pm, limited days out of season.

→ Bethania, Nant Gwynant, LL55 4NL, 01766 890855.
53.0343, -4.0491

### 33 CABAN CAFÉ

Lovely social-enterprise café at the foot of Snowdon. Delicious locally sourced sweet potato soups, vegetarian Thai curries and sausages with parsnip mash can be eaten outside on the tables amongst the trees or in the wooden cosy café. Open 9am-4pm.

→ Yr Hen Ysgol, Brynrefail, nr Llanberis, LL55 3NR, 01286 685500.
53.1423, -4.1543

### 34 PANTRI CAFÉ

Although 'Pete's Eats' up the road is the iconic climbers' café, with a map library and giant portions, the coffee there is terrible! Instead come to the Pantri for your flat white fix and highly-rated accompaniments.

→ High St, Llanberis, LL55 4SU, 01286 238070.
53.1190, -4.1260

### 35 PEN-Y-GWRYD HOTEL

An absolute institution, this mountain inn with its authentic old fashioned, simple decor is now so right on that it hurts. There are old leather walking boots hanging from the beams, wooden settles and sparse tables, Welsh-blanketed bedrooms and shared bathrooms with roll-top baths – and then of course there's the gong which calls guests in for dinner and breakfast. Don't be late. The restaurant and bar is open to non-residents.

→ Nantgwynant, LL55 4NT, 01286 870211. 53.0825, -4.0019

### 36 GWERN GOF ISAF CAMPING

Four generations of one family have run this old hill farm since 1906 as a base camp for explorers. Open all year, with two bunkhouses sleeping 12 and 6, and plenty of room for campers.

→ Capel Curig, LL24 0EU, 01690 720276. 53.1217, -3.9658

### 37 HAFOD Y LLAN NT CAMPSITE

With a little stream, mountain views and the Watkin Path up to Snowdonia minutes away, this simple farm campsite has clean facilities, pay showers and campfires. Tents only. Open April–Oct, no bookings.

→ Nantgwynant, Beddgelert, LL55 4NQ, 01766 890473.
53.0403, -4.0491

### 38 LLYN GWYNANT CAMPSITE

It's hard to beat the stunning lake and mountain surroundings of this large campsite on the banks of Llyn Gwynant with its own beach, launching area and rope swings. Pitch up near the surreal turquoise river and enjoy wood-fired pizzas, great coffee, kayaking and camping cameraderie. It does get busy here, with bank holidays feeling like a bit of a festival without the music, but the scenery and the access to the serene lake and wooded paths straight from your tent make it all worth it. Mind the midges!

→ Nantgwynant, LL55 4NW, 01766 890853. 53.0519, -4.0167

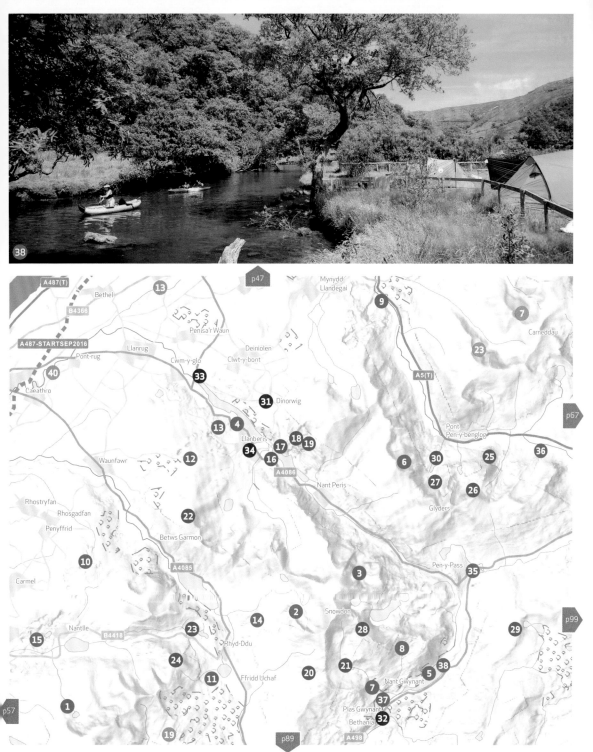

# GLASLYN & CWM PENNANT

## Our perfect weekend

→ **Dip** in deep hidden pools under Pont Aberglaslyn

→ **Picnic** and bathe in the secret waterfalls of the Croesor valley

→ **Follow** the Afon Dwyfor on its short journey from source to sea, starting at the Prince of Wales quarry and finally plunging into tidal pools on a wild beach near Criccieth

→ **Wild** camp at Llynnau Cerrig-y-myllt, explore the old quarry ruins of Croesor then descend along the old slate tramway to the Oriel Caffi for lunch

→ **Make** the wild foreshore walk from Porthmadog via Cei Ballast past Pen y Banc to Black Rock Sands and Criccieth Castle, eat at Dylan's then return by train

→ **Climb** up the waterfalls to find the restored cast-iron waterwheel and pumping machine at Ciprwth copper mine, a beautiful Victorian relic that even locals don't know about

→ **Enjoy** fine views of gnarled oaks, craggy outcrops and parched gorse from the coppery crest above Bwlch-y-Sygyn

As the Glaslyn river flows towards the sea, Snowdonia opens out into a more gentle landscape of blessed estuaries, sandflats and beaches. The secret valleys of Cwm Pennant and Croesor have many charms and few visitors, making this an excellent base for wild exploration.

Crowned by the peaks of the Nantlle ridge, the remote and beautiful Cwm Pennant, along the Afon Dwyfor, was once a far busier place than it is today. The minerals of north Wales made many investors rich but just as many poor, and the Prince of Wales slate quarry at the valley head showcases the wildly optimistic investments made. Here, an entire village was built to house 200 workers in barracks, a tramway routed for many miles up the mountain, an unnecessarily graceful arched dressing shed constructed and a reservoir dammed to provide the constant water supply essential for running the machinery. You can tour many of its remains and swim in the serene lake, secluded in its sheltered little valley and surrounded by the crumbling ruins of a long-gone industrial age.

Close by, Gorseddau quarry under Moel Hebog also rode a wave of optimism, and was started by two northern railwaymen with little knowledge of slate. Another small village, a railway and the eerie ruins of Ynys-y-Pandy mill are the main monuments to their folly, for there was no good slate to be found.

On the other side of Glaslyn, in the sheltered folds of the sublime Croesor valley – now much loved by artists – the quarrymen were more successful, and an elaborate system of inclines and tramways can still be followed, including the remains of a 1904 hydroelectric station which powered the quarries and the village. Higher up is a network of serene lakes that welcome walkers descending from Cnicht. Below are waterfalls, idyllic places for a picnic and a skinny dip, and the eccentric home and gardens of the late Clough Williams-Ellis, visionary architect of Portmeirion.

Down towards the coast, Porthmadog is where legendary prince Madog is said to have set sail to discover America 300 years before Christopher Columbus. The soft sands of the estuary are ever changing, with pools and great sand flats to explore at low tide, all set against a backdrop of the Rhinog range. If you time it well you can cross to Whitesands and Portmeirion – indeed this was the only way to cross before the turnpike roads and bridges were built. Easier is the walk from Borth-y-Gest around to Black Rock Sands, or a short stroll out to Cei Ballast, an island in the sands formed entirely by jettisoned ballast from the great slate ships that docked at Porthmadog over so many decades.

## RIVERS & WATERFALLS

### 1 AFON CROESOR WATERFALLS

Follow the tiny stream up a secret valley below Croesor, amongst rowan and ancient trees, to find a series of magical deep pools and waterfalls. Many are big enough to jump and swim in.

→ On A4085 ½ mile NW of LL48 6SG (beyond Croesor turning) the road crosses a bridge and turns hard L. Park on L (limited space) and take the track on R. After Gelli, the final house, keep to the stream. The first pools are very deep and shady – good for jumps – but the stream soon opens out after 200m.

15 mins, 52.9730, -4.0562 🚶🏊🍴🚗

### 2 CWM PENNANT POOL

This is the most easily accessible pool on the Dwyfor river, just below a road bridge and popular with families, who picnic on the grassy banks enjoying the beautiful secret valley setting.

→ Up a dead-end road from Llanfihangel-Y-Pennant, ¾ mile beyond LL51 9AX. Space to pull off by the bridge.

1 min, 53.0060, -4.1890 🏊🚗

### 3 AFON DWYFOR, LLANYSTUMDWY

A bend in the river with a pretty pool and rope swing, just along the riverside path from David Lloyd George's birthplace and final resting place.

→ Free parking in the village 130m E of the museum (LL52 0SH). Follow signs from bridge to Lloyd George's grave ('bedd') 120m E of LL52 0SW, then continue on the riverside path for ¾ mile.

15 mins, 52.9317, -4.2636 🏊🍴🚶✝️

### 4 PONT ABERGLASLYN, NANTMOR

A secret swim in a wooded gorge with pebble beach and deep river pools. In summer the water can reach 22°C, warmed by its route through Gwynant. Swim up and under the bridge or down into the junction pool.

→ Park at the Aberglaslyn car park on A4085, between the bridge and the turning into Nantmor dir LL55 4YG. Walk along A4085 back to the bridge and hop over wall L, opp kissing gate, down to beach.. Also explore the riverbank path upstream from the bridge for many smaller pool and waterfalls.

5 mins, 52.9943, -4.0945 🏊❓🚶

## LAKES

### 5 LLYN MAIR, TAN-Y-BWLCH

With a backdrop of wooded hills, this clear lake decorated with lily pads is easily accessible from the small picnic area by road. You could even arrive at Tan-y-Bwlch Station on a Ffestiniog Mountain Railway steam train.

→ On A487 E of Porthmadog, turn L at Oakley Arms (01766 590277) dir LL41 3AQ, and continue ¾ mile to car park on R, picnic area opp. The adventurous could also climb up to Llyn y Garnedd reservoir ¾ mile to the NE (52.9584, -4.0010).

2 mins, 52.9519, -4.0072 🏊🚗📷

### 6 LLYNNAU CERRIG-Y-MYLLT

The ridge of Cnicht conceals a land of wild enchanting lakes. This pair, at 410m, are completely hidden by crags and perfect for a summer wild swim and camp after an ascent of Cnicht.

→ From the Nantmor Mountain Centre hostel (see listing) a mile S of LL55 4NL, park and head up the footpath, bearing up to the R along a wall after ¾ mile. After about 450m, over another wall, find first lake.

50 mins, 53.0042, -4.0384 🏊⛺🏔️📷

## BEACHES & ISLANDS

### 7 PEN-Y-BANC, BORTH-Y-GEST

With secret sandy coves and tidal pools, rocky islets, golden estuarine sand and soaring mountains, this stretch of beach boasts one of the best views of any in Britain and is very easy to reach. Rich in bird life: curlews, redshanks and black-necked grebes visit in winter, and large flocks of sandwich terns can be seen in summer. Beware of strong currents out in the estuary.

→ In Borth-y-Gest (signed from Porthmadog) park in seafront car park in (LL49 9TU) and follow road and then path S around headland and down to shore.

5 mins, 52.9110, -4.1414

### 8 CEI BALLAST ISLAND

This island in the sand flats was created entirely from the ballast stone carried by inbound slate ships for stability. They would unload the ballast here before filling up with slate. Look for an old quay and mooring posts.

→ Limited parking at Ffestioniog Station, Porthmadog (LL49 9NF). Follow the footpath beside the lines E, cross the lines at the first signal box and drop down to the sand. Some shallow wading required. If you leave 2 hours before low tide you could also walk out to Whitesands (see entry) on the Portmeirion headland opposite (Trwynypenrhyn). Only about a mile there, but tides come in fast and some deep low tide pools. Be careful.

10 mins, 52.9194, -4.1279 

### 9 WHITESANDS, PORTMEIRION

At the far end of the Penrhydeudraeth headland is a ferryman's cottage with cliffs, forest at Trwynypenrhyn, and Portmeirion's beautiful white sand beach. Tricky navigation.

→ Park in layby off the E end of the Cob, just N of LL48 6HT, by the cycle path arch. Cross A497, up steep road to railway tracks, then follow coastal footpath ½ mile SW up through woods to near Penrhyn-isaf farm. To its R find a wooden gate in stone wall leading onto the headland (no public footpath). Cottage is on far SW side, and a tricky path leads down to the W end of beach. The E end of beach leads into Portmeirion.

20 mins, 52.9092, -4.1053 

### 10 DWYFOR BEACH, LLANYSTUMDWY

As the Dwyfor meets the sea it travels through shingle banks backed by inviting deep pools, finally reaching a wild beach with a mountain backdrop.

→ Travelling W from Criccieth on A497, take first L after Llanystumdwy, about 400m after LL52 0LS. Cross bridge and find footpath on L along river leading to estuary beach (limited space to pull off). Or walk 1½ mile W along beach from Criccieth.

20 mins, 52.9105, -4.2635 🏖️🛶

### 11 BLACK ROCK SANDS CAVES & GRAIG DDU

This huge, drive-on sand beach is pretty charmless, but there are superb sea caves at the far west end. Escape the crowds by scrambling over the granite knoll of Craig Ddu and down to the eastern extremity of Criccieth beach (you can walk around at low tide).

→ From Porthmadog head towards LL49 9YL, but after Morfa Bychan follow road straight onto beach.

2 mins, 52.9138, -4.1977 🏖️🛶

### WILDLIFE

### 12 GWAITH POWDWR & ESTUARY

Once the biggest gunpowder production site in Europe, supplying all slate workings in north Wales, now a wildlife reserve and a complex of ruins. Bushwhack out across the crag top to reach a secluded section of the Dwyryd estuary with salt marshes and a cove.

→ 300m E of Penrhyndeudraeth station (LL48 6LL), before the estuary bridge , turn L at Cookes Workshops estate and gates are ahead. The beach is at 52.9276, -4.0485, with quicker access from the new pedestrian gate and steps nearer the bridge.

5 mins, 52.9292, -4.0599 🚶🖼️🛶

### 13 PLAS BRONDANW GARDENS

The formal and wild gardens of Plas Brondanw – home of the Portmerion architect Clough Williams-Ellis – are set against a stunning mountain backdrop and worth visiting for the views alone. Little café with seating outside serves locally sourced, home-made light lunches and cakes. Entry fee.

→ Signed from A4084 just N of Garreg, dir LL48 6SW. Admission £5.

5 mins, 52.9601, -4.0610 🛶🍴

### LOST RUINS

### 14 CIPRWTH MINE WATERWHEEL

This exquisite cast-iron waterwheel has recently been restored but remains a well-kept secret, high on the mountainside and surrounded by ruined copper mine buildings from the Victorian era. It was supplied from Truro, Cornwall, and worked a drum

17

15

and pumps via rods. Explore upstream for waterfalls and pools.

→ From the bridge ¾ miles N of LL51 9AX, follow the 'Tir Gofal' path markers NW up through the woods (past Gilfach mossy ruins at 53.0073, -4.1907), bearing left at the flooded tunnel. At the top of the slope, the Cwm Ciprwth ruins come into view across open moorland.

20 mins, 53.0068, -4.1983 🖼️🏊

### 15 YNYS-Y-PANDY MILL

This overly grand three-storey slate slab mill sits on an outcrop above the lane, like a ruined abbey, with rows of great arched windows. It processed slate from nearby Gorseddau quarry (see listing), and was built in 1855 but only used for a decade before the business went bankrupt.

→ From A487 NW of Porthmadog take turning for Cwm Ystradllyn and follow 2 miles to just after LL51 9AZ.

2 mins, 52.9680, -4.1607 🖼️

### 16 GORSEDDAU QUARRY, MOEL HEBOG

This huge quarry tells the sad story of over-enthusiastic investment in poor-quality slate, and suffered the same fate as Ynys-y-Pandy mill (see entry). A railway was constructed all the way to the sea, and a three-street village was built for the workers. Look out for the curved tramway wall and many ruined workers' sheds. Wonderful views from above, and a good starting point for ascending Moel Hebog.

→ From Ynys-y-Pandy bear L and continue on up valley 1 mile to park at the end of the lake dam. Continue up on SE side of lake and then climb the incline. Return in a loop via the village ruins at 52.9865, -4.1470, ½ mile to N of lake.

30 mins, 52.9855, -4.12916 🖼️🏊🏔️🚶

### 17 FRON-BOETH QUARRY

A remote valley side in Croesor with impressive estuary views. Atmospheric ruins include a Cornish boiler furnace, ruined mills, and an epic tunnel through the hill that once connected the mine to the Croesor tramway. Above are the remains of Pant Mawr plus the Moelwyn Mawr incline head and tramway.

→ From Croesor village head for Tan-y-bwlch (dir LL48 6DQ) and after ½ mile find a tractor track on L through field up mountain (verge to pull off on R). After a mile, bearing L off the track, tunnel is at bottom of incline. Pant Mawr quarry ruins are E 400m and the incline head is up NE 300m (52.9853, -4.0136).

30 mins, 52.9822, -4.0181 🖼️🏔️🖼️

### 18 CROESOR QUARRY & LAKE

On the top of the world, this high quarry enjoys superb views of Cnicht and the Croesor valley below. The plateau location makes a great wild camping spot with the remains of vast sheds, a wheelhouse and a fan house to explore. Advanced for its time, it was powered by pneumatics and hydroelectricity, and after 1930 it was used for the mass storage of high explosives. NB if the gated tunnel is open, be very careful, as this is an unstable mine.

→ Park in Croesor village (LL48 6SR). Head NE up the valley road and after ½ mile, when the tarmac ends, bear up R. This wide track leads directly to the quarry, a further 1½ miles. From here, head NE to famous Rhosydd quarry (see listing) via Llyn Croesor.
60 mins, 52.9907, -4.0029 🚫🏔️⛰️🔥

### 19 PRINCE OF WALES, CWM PENNANT

At the head of one of Wales' most beautiful lost valleys lie the remote ruins of a quarry that never made money. In the manager's house you'll still find the iron range in the inglenook. Beautiful arched doorways frame the old mill and a tramway leads to a street of barracks high on the mountainside, almost as impressive as the Anglesey Barracks at Dinorwig (see listing). There's also a sheltered blue reservoir to swim in; the double-skinned stone wall is a dam that was once filled with clay.

→ Follow road past LL51 9AX as for Ciprwth mine (see listing) but continue to very end of valley and parking near last house (Beudy'r Ddol). Follow the faint path up the hill E, via ruined Cwm Trwsgl manager's house. Behind is the great mill and the reservoir beyond. Above this the mine tramway runs up to the barracks ruins on the top level, above the

waste. Tunnels and pits of connected Princess Quarry can be found ¼ mile up to the E of the lake (53.0238, -4.1592).
25 mins, 53.0270, -4.1651 🚫🚫

### 20 HENDRE-DDU & MOELFRE QUARRIES

A deep pit with a high terrace leads to a tunnel. Many mossy ruins, and beautiful views of sea and mountains. Above is Craig-y-garn mini peak (363m). Moelfre quarry has a wet tunnel that leads to a tiny secret lake.

→ Follow steep track L (gated, cattle grid) 2 miles before LL51 9AX (no parking). Moelfre is at 52.9830, -4.2056. Take track L across Pont Gyfyng, 1 mile before LL51 9AX.
15 mins, 52.9761, -4.2093 🚫❓🚫

### EASY PEAKS & HILL FORTS

### 21 MOEL-Y-GEST ROCK CANNON

This prominent knoll (263m) with hill fort near Porthmadog has vast views over all of Snowdonia, the estuary and the sea towards the Llŷn Peninsula. Find the 'rock cannon', a series of deep holes drilled in the summit slab. Gunpowder was put in the holes and laid between them, then ignited – flash, bang, a ceremonial or celebratory noise that was heard for miles around.

→ Head W out of Porthmadog on A497 dir Criccieth. Just before LL49 9LzB, opp petrol station, find path rising through woods. After a stile, path splits, bear L and up through woods to summit (stay above quarry).
45 mins, 52.9279, -4.1594 🚫

### 22 BWLCH-Y-SYGYN

For glorious views climb to 318m above the famous Sygun copper mine. From here return via the shore of Llyn Dinas for a swim, or descend into Cwm Bychan and/or return along the beautiful Glaslyn river with its pools and falls. You can also strike out to

Mynydd Sygyn and down to Beddgelert.

➜ Park at the large Sygun Copper Mine, signed off the A498 mile NE of Beddgelert, dir LL55 4NE. The marked footpath is next to entrance gate. Follow it to the exit of the Sygun Mine (people finish their tour here, at level 3). Bear R on the path, then L after ½ mile to climb the mini peak. More old workings are just below the peak to the S. Mine tour is a £9 entry fee, but recommended.

25 mins, 53.0143, -4.0798 ▣▣▣

### 23 DINAS EMRYS CASTLE

These 5th-century hill fort remains stand on a wooded knoll where the original red dragon of Wales and a 'foreign' white dragon (credited to the Saxons) emerged from a pool and battled. Look out for the pool and spring below the fort, as described in the legend, and the square remains of a 12th-century tower. There is a pretty waterfall pool on the way, and the crag-bounded Llyn Dinas nearby is a good place to dip.

➜ Take A498 NE from Beddgelert and 300m after LL55 4NG turn L into Craflwyn Hall NT. A signed permissive path leads up from behind the house, crossing the Afon-y-cwm after ¼ mile (waterfall pool by footbridge) and after another ¼ mile bearing R up to the peak.

30 mins, 53.0221, -4.0786 ▣▣▣▣▣

## SLOW FOOD & PUBS

### 24 CARIAD GELATO

The best ice cream for miles, family made in Dolgellau! Enjoy delicious ice creams, sweet or savoury crêpes and milkshakes from either their Porthmadog store or the van on the beach at Criccieth.

➜ 125 High Street, Porthmadog, LL49 9HA, 07717 290165.
52.9277, -4.1328 ▣

### 25 DYLAN'S, CRICCIETH

Dylan's three North Wales restaurants – one at the Menai Bridge, one in Lladudno, and this one on the beach at Criccieth – all focus heavily on local produce, from Menai mussels, Welsh beef burgers and Caerphilly cheese to Welsh craft ales. You can also find their travelling pop-up vans at the many food festivals around North Wales.

➜ Esplanade, Maes y Mor, Criccieth LL52 0HU, 01766 522773.
52.9198, -4.2239 ▣

### 26 ORIEL CAFFI CROESOR @ CNICHT

Charming community-run café and art gallery in the beautiful Croesor valley. Enjoy Welsh-roasted coffee and home-made food. Closed Nov–Mar.

➜ Hen Bryngelynen, Croesor, LL48 6SS, 01766 771433.
52.9820, -4.0382 ▣

### 27 THE BIG ROCK CAFÉ, PORTHMADOG

Delicious, organic, fairtrade and inventive breakfasts and lunches, artisan breads, patisseries, gluten-free and vegan delights at this wonderful relaxed café in town.

➜ 71 High St, Porthmadog LL49 9EU, 01766 512098.
52.9266, -4.1308 ▣

### 28 HEBOG, BEDDGELERT

Relaxed, cosy café/bistro with rooms, serving well-sourced Welsh produce. Enjoy good coffee, rarebits, creative salads, cheese platters and evening three-course feasts.

➜ Beddgelert, LL55 4UY, 01766 890400.
53.0123, -4.1035 ▣▣

### 29 MOORINGS BISTRO, BORTH-Y-GEST

With big windows and a little terrace (with Welsh blankets to snuggle under) overlooking the bay and the mountains beyond, this cosy bistro gets rave reviews for its seasonal, local food. Closed Wednesdays.

➜ Ivy Terrace, Borth-y-Gest, LL49 9TS, 01766 513500.
52.9155, -4.1365 ▣

### 30 THE GOLDEN FLEECE INN

Cellar bar, B&B and pub bistro serving real ales in Tremadog's market square.

➜ Market Square, Tremadog, LL49 9RB, 01766 512421.
52.9392, -4.1418 ▣▣

## WILDER CAMPING

### 31 CNICHT CAVE

A very simple stone shelter above a shallow, islanded tarn, all in a wonderfully wild location just below Cnicht, the 'Welsh Matterhorn'. Bring a tent just in case!

➜ From Croesor take road 160m past LL48 6SR, continue as it becomes a track, and take path R 250m after (60 mins). Or follow path from Nantmor Mountain Centre (see listing).
52.9987, -4.0371 ▣▣▣

### 32 TY'N LLAN CAMPSITE

Wonderfully wild riverside campsite in the peaceful Cwm Pennant valley. Home is a pretty glade right on the bank of the idyllic river Dwyfor, and happy days can be spent stargazing and messing about in the crystal waters. Open Apr–Sept.

→ Plas Hendre, Cwm Pennant, LL51 9AX, 01766 530242.
52.9767, -4.1999

### 33 CAE AMOS MOUNTAIN BOTHY

Renovation was completed in 2017 at this Cwm Pennant hill-farm bothy. Used as a climbing hut for half a century, it's now open for walkers to shelter in thanks to the Mountain Bothy Association. With a woodburner and stunning wild surroundings, the best things in life are sometimes free. Bring fuel.

→ Best approach is from parking opp Capel Horeb in Garndolbenmaen, nr LL51 9SJ. Walk NE up adj lane, taking second R, then R fork to meet bridleway between track gates at 52.9766, -4.2330, and follow approx 2 miles to bothy. Bring a map.
52.9860, -4.2108

RUSTIC HAVENS

### 34 BRYNKIR TOWER

Cwm Pennant is a magical valley filled with crystal streams, mossy boulders and twisted oaks, rising to mountains. Sitting atop a wooded hillock is the strange Gothic folly of Brynkir Tower, renovated from a ruin to sleep four in two bedrooms reached by a spiral staircase.

→ Dolbenmaen, LL51 9AQ, 01248 430258. menaiholidays.co.uk
52.9678, -4.2009

### 35 NANTMOR MOUNTAIN CENTRE

Basic 22 bed/4-bedroom hostel in an excellent wild location. £10 per person per night. Bookings online only.

→ Gelli-Iago, Nantgwynant, LL55 4NL. nantmormountaincentre.co.uk
53.0146, -4.0386

### 36 CROESOR BACH

A secluded, traditional country-style farmhouse in the stunning Cwm Croesor. With its range cooker, open fires and glorious valley position, this is the perfect adventure base for a couple of families (sleeps nine).

→ Croesor, LL48 6SS, 0345 2680813.
52.9865, -4.0329

### 37 ABER COTTAGE & THE RETREAT

Right on the banks of the Glaslyn, next to the Pont Aberglaslyn river pools (see listing), this stone house and annexe is a perfect location for wild swimmers and children with boats. Together, the two properties sleep up to 11.

→ Beddgelert LL55 4YF, 07970 291971.
52.9936, -4.0955

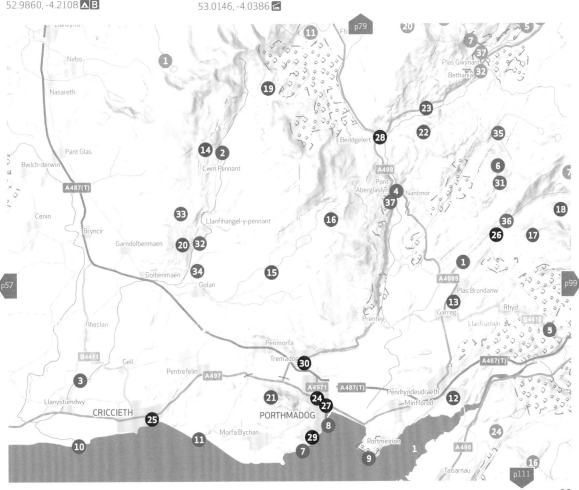

# BLAENAU TO BETWS-Y-COED

## Our perfect weekend

→ **Wonder** at the ruins of Rhosydd, a mountain mining village lost in time, then wild camp by Llyn Clogwyn-brîth, once a reservoir but now perfect for swimming

→ **Find** the Roman Bridge, decked in ivy, then descend to the hidden gorge between Conwy Falls and Fairy Glen

→ **Swim** in the waterfalls of the Llugwy river, at Pont Cynfal and the Miner's Bridge, then picnic on the shingle beaches of the Conwy confluence

→ **Scramble** up Daear Ddu to remote Moel Siabod, passing ruins and blue lakes along the way

→ **Follow** Rhiwbach tramway past lakes to discover the amazing wild ruins and chambers of Cwt-y-Bugail and Rhiw-Bach

→ **Explore** 60 miles of underground tunnels at Cwmorthin – borrow the key or join a tour

→ **Trek** ten miles from Blaenau Ffestiniog, across the Rhoysdd ruins, down through Croesor to the coast at Penrhyndeudraeth, to return on the mountain railway

There is much wild land to explore around Siabod and Penamnen, the lesser-visited, gentle-giant mountains of the Moelwyns. The histories of Blaenau Ffestiniog and Betws-y-Coed at either side could not be more different: one created by the slate boom, on mountainsides forever transformed by industry, the other, the epitome of unspoilt nature, filled with woodland and waterfalls, and a famous destination for 19th-century artists and travellers seeking the sublime and picturesque.

You should not overlook Blaenau however, for its old workings reveal spectacular industrial remains. Quarrying was started here in the 1760s by Methusalem Jones, who claimed he was instructed by God in a dream to come and dig in the area. He made a fortune and his quarry, Diffwys, became the mam-chwarel or 'mother quarry' of Blaenau and inspired the opening of many more slate mines. Its ruins make for excellent exploring and are mixed up with the modern ruins of Maen-offeren. Above is the mountain tramway, leading past wild lakes and over the plateau to Rhiwbach, with other derelict quarries along the way.

Slate extraction began about 50 years later, on the other side of the valley at Cwmorthin above Tanygrisiau, but here the seams were underground and over 60 miles of tunnels were eventually dug. Experienced cavers can borrow the key to the mines and explore by themselves (lamps and helmets obligatory); for others, Go Below will take you on guided tours around the vast underworlds. Climb higher, to Rhosydd, for another Hades, and the haunting, misty remains of a ruined quarryman's town. There is also a network of over 20 mountain lakes here, some natural and some old reservoirs, all within a couple of miles of each other. The two lakes of Llynnau Diffwys stand at the head of Croesor's U-shaped valley, enjoying views down the mountains, across the sandy flats of Traeth Mawr, and out to sea. Relatively shallow, they warm up quickly and beg to be swum in.

Over the pass from Blaenau the road drops into the valley of the Lledr, passing the 13th-century tower of Dolwyddelan Castle, to the river Conwy and Betws-y-Coed. This is waterfall country, brimming with scenic gorges such as Cynfal and the Fairy Glen and secret, sylvan swimming holes. These transcendent places have long been a place for the romantics and the 1840s landscape painter David Cox spent long summers sketching here, joined by a growing colony of artists. The picturesque qualities are still very much in evidence today, and a peaceful swim in a fern-hung gorge or a walk through ancient woodland, along a river cascading over boulders, will still inspire.

## RIVERS

### 1 FAIRY GLEN, RIVER CONWY

A picturesque gorge with access for £1. The big grassy junction pool is good for a longer, sunnier swim and family picnic. Upstream the gorge has some large rocks to sit on and a deep section down the middle to swim through (if not in spate). Also find a huge, easy-access river pool beneath the A470 bridge.

→ S of Betws-y-Coed take A470 (dir Blaenau Ffestiniog). Signed on L just before bridge (dir LL24 0SL). For bridge pool, turn R after bridge.
15 mins, 53.0725, -3.7953 🅿🏞🏊🏖

### 2 ROMAN BRIDGE & CONWY GORGE

Beneath this enchanting ivy-clad packhorse bridge (actually medieval but with Roman origins) is a small pool with rope swing. Further down the lane find a (free) lookout over the mighty Conwy Falls, and a scramble route down for those keen to descend. Downstream the gorge remains spectacular and wild, before joining the Fairy Glen section (see listing).

→ At the A5 Conwy Falls café (LL24 0PN, popular pay paths to falls viewpoint), take B4406 dir Penmachno. After ½ mile turn R, past LL24 0PP, to bridge. Just possible to park on L. The old Roman bridge and pool is below on R. For Conwy Falls lookout continue down lane ½ mile to layby on R and path. (R hand lookout and pump house has a scramble down to water level). Another ½ mile down lane, near end of forest and open fields, the river gorge bends to N and there is another dramatic viewpoint into the top end of Fairy Glen. At very low water levels it might just be possible to canyon the whole route, if properly equipped, from below Conwy Falls to the bottom of Fairy Glen / A470 road bridge.
1 min, 53.0599, -3.7823 🅿🚶🅿🍴📷

### 3 CONWY & LLUGWY CONFLUENCE

Bring a picnic and enjoy an afternoon playing on the gravel beaches at the confluence of the rivers Conwy and Llugwy. With an inner tube you can ride the gentle rapids.

→ Follow path from end of Station Rd car park in Betws-y-Coed (LL24 0AG) to river, under railway and downstream ¼ mile to confluence. Footpath continues around the golf course and back to start by crossing the lines again via the station bridge.
10 mins, 53.0995, -3.7960 🏊🚣🏖🚶

## WATERFALLS

### 4 CYFYNG FALLS, RIVER LLUGWY

Huge pool beneath a towering waterfall and steep rock walls. The site is well used by local lads in summer, and sometimes fenced off, it has become notorious for dangerous daredevil leaps. Upstream are easier pools, across the bridge opp Cobden Hotel.

→ 50m W of Bryn Glo on A5 (LL24 0DT), find a small layby on L and an alcove in the stone wall. The gorge is a steep scramble below, but is sometimes fenced. Cobden pools at 53.1004, -3.8967.
5 mins, 53.0958, -3.8904 🏊🚶🅿🍴❓🏞

### 5 MINER'S BRIDGE, RIVER LLUGWY

Fun gorge with steeply sloping bridge and pools. The best pool and waterfall is 100m upstream with some good jumps; some easy riverside scrambling required.

→ Heading W out of Betws on A5, take L to park in Rhes Dolydd street (LL24 0BU). Cross A5 and continue W 40m to find stone stile and steps down to river. After 100m reach Miner's Bridge stairs. Head upstream. Or walk from Betws bridge on the far river path (L bank), 1 mile.
10 mins, 53.0962, -3.8238 🅿🏞🚶🍴🏞🏖

## 6 CEUNANT CYNFAL

Magical, remote gorge with huge waterfalls and exciting swimming and scrambling. A mile south-east of Llan Ffestiniog at Bont Newydd take lane opp LL41 4PY then turn right to find footpath on right into woods after 70m (52.9494, -3.9181). There is a small paddling pool immediately upstream, but follow river downstream for the best: five mins leads to the viaduct, which allows access upstream 100m into gorge pools (52.9498, -3.9215).

→ Another 5 mins passes the main cascades, with accessible pool and gorge 200m below, leading into canyon pools. (Another 300m downstream is an old iron footbridge. There are more high falls below, but access is difficult. Canyon companies run courses here).
10 mins, 52.9507, -3.9248 🚶🌊🐾▼

## LAKES

### 7 LLYNNAU DIFFWYS & CLOGWYN-BRÎTH

There are many beautiful high lakes amid the Moelwynion peaks . LLynnau Diffwys are a favourite pair and the northerly tarn has an island to swim to and views out to the sea. Perfectly located after a descent from Cnicht. Llyn Clogwyn-brîth, nearer the

Rhosydd quarry ruins (see listing), is an old quarry reservoir and offers good swimming surrounded by sheltering cliffs.

→ As for Rhosydd quarry, but then walk on ½ mile NW. Clogwyn-brîth with cliffs is ⅓ mile due N at 53.0007, -3.9909.
80 mins, 53.0027, -3.9987 🚶⛰️📷✦🏕️

## 8 AFON GAM WATERFALL & BLUE POOL

This is an easy car camping spot by Llyn Dubach, deep in the wild lands of the Migneint moors. A short walk leads to an impressive waterfall and on up to a dramatic blue pool in the old quarry.

→ From B4391 E of Llan Festiniog, take B4407. After ⅓ mile at Llyn Dubach (52.9638, -3.8686). Cross road, walk back 75m and follow vehicle track. Waterfalls are below R after 200m. Continue, bearing L to reach flooded quarry pit. Another good waterfall further up the road at 52.9696, -3.8617, no parking.
15 mins, 52.9641, -3.8580 🚶🌊▼⛰️

## MINES & CAVERNS

### 9 RHOSYDD QUARRY

This slate quarry complex is one of the most extensive and atmospheric ruins around, with abandoned barracks, mills and old

engines scattered across the high mountain plateau, often shrouded in mist. The route up passes the ruined lakeside Rhosydd Chapel and Plas Cwmorthin. The fabled (and wet) Level 9 adit tunnel can be found just behind Rhosydd. Driven in 1870 and known as Piccadilly Junction, it continues for over ½ mile into the mountainside, leading eventually to several huge chambers, internal inclines and a network of railway junctions with tracks and points still in place. Further up the mountainside are higher levels with vast open cast caverns and more ruins. Suitably equipped risk-takers can explore the tunnel. It's well used and in good condition for its age, but rockfalls do occur.

→ From Tanygrisiau follow narrow Ffordd Dolrhedyn steeply up, take dead-end Rhesdai Dolrhedyn R on bend at LL41 3ST, and park in the car park at the road end. Follow path up to lake and ruined houses. Continue along L shore of lake, then follow the old tramway up valley, past chapel ruins on L, through Conglog quarry ruins (Plas Cwmorthin is just off to the R at 53.0009, -3.9816) and climb to finally reach plateau and many ruins. The upper caverns are up ½ mile S at 52.9886, -3.9888.
60 mins, 52.9963, -3.9901 ▣🅢🅴🚶🆅

## 10 CWMORTHIN MINE, GO BELOW

Considered to be the largest and deepest slate mine in the world, Cwmorthin was a quarry only in name and boasts more than 60 miles of underground tunnels, levels and chambers. Casual visitors can admire the ruined terrace of cottages by Llyn Cwmorthin shore, and the brave can take a dip. Those with caving experience and equipment can borrow a key and enter the gated entrance to explore on their own, or there are some excellent guided family and adventure trips organised by Go Below.

→ Park and walk to lake as for Rhosydd quarry (see listing), but follow shore to R for the mine entrance. Keys can be checked out from Go Below office behind Conwy Falls café (LL24 0PN, 01690 710108) by those with caving experience and a £20 cash deposit. Or join one of their guided tours. You must have proper lighting (including backup) and helmets. There are many pitches and traverse possibilities in the mine, but also plenty on level ground requiring no rope work. Wet in parts.
15 mins, 52.9963, -3.9676 🅢🅴🆅

## 11 WRYSGAN QUARRY & TUNNEL

On a spectacular mountain plateau overlooking Llyn Cwmorthin, this old mine

13

14

14

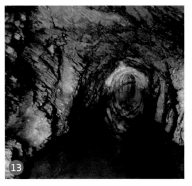
13

13

is most famous for its incline and tunnel through the mountainside; and building it bankrupted the first mining company. Reaching the mine by this incline and tunnel is an exciting and challenging adventure for kids. There are ruins everywhere and several vast interlinked caverns to explore.

→ Start as for Rhosydd Quarry (see listing), as far as the ruined houses. Track back down the stream (footbridge lower down is closed) and find the good path that leads up through the levels and waste, eventually following miners' steps to reach the plateau level. On the way up, find wet tunnel far R below cliff, which leads into lowest chambers. On plateau level the incline head and drum is to the L. Explore above plateau to R to find several upper chambers in the crag. Another, more dramatic approach is up the incline itself. Follow Ffordd Dolrhedyn L past bus stop after LL41 3ST, cross bridge, turn immediately R and park. Follow gated power station road ½ mile to the bottom of incline, with tunnel looming up ahead.
30 mins, 52.9902, -3.9706 🅿️🚶‍♂️⛰️🔽🔅

## 12 DIFFWYS CASSON

Diffwys Casson mill ruins rest high above Blaenau Ffestiniog like a Welsh Machu Picchu. The 'mother quarry' of the slate industry, it opened in 1760 leading to the very existence of the village, and in 1859 became one the world's first integrated slate mills and is still impressive today. Nearby are the colossal processing sheds of modern Maen-offeren, now closed and succumbing to dereliction.

→ Park at the very end of Manod Rd, past LL41 3DQ. Climb steeply E following the yellow footpath posts, bearing L at top. Once at the crag and a wall with tramway, bear L up slag heaps to find Diffwys Casson ruins. Return down and continue on footpath up mountainside past two tiny and lovely tarns (refreshing cool down after the climb). Continue on to Cwt-y-Bugail.
25 mins, 52.9970, -3.9217 🅿️🔅🏊

## 13 CWT-Y-BUGAIL

Approach on a tramway through empty mountain terrain with numerous swimming lakes. Find giant caverns, old underground ghost trains, tunnels and ruins. Above the derelict mill a tunnel leads into the main pit. On the far wall another cavern contains a tramway with rolling stock and the remains of a carbide generator.

→ From Diffwys Casson (see listing) tarns continue on footpath across mountain wall and boggy ground to reach the Rhiw-bach mountain tramway. Follow E around Llyn Bowydd (good swimming, 53.0028, -3.9047) ½ mile to mine. (NB If you head W ½ mile, the tramway arrives at the head of the old incline down to Maen-offeren, a good approach if you wish to view or approach this area. Rights of way are limited and access is best at weekends only).

60 mins, 53.0048, -3.8886 🚶📷▽⛰

### 14 RHIW-BACH

Vast mill complex ruins, incongruous in such a remote place. Underground are flooded blue lakes, which can be explored with Go Below.

→ From Cwt-y-Bugail (see listing) continue on tramway S and E another mile, past Blaen-y-cwm. Or from Cwm Penmachno side of mountain, follow track at bend in dead-end road after LL24 0RT. Subterranean trips with Go Below ( 01690 710108), or BCA members can obtain key via Cave Access Limited (caveaccess.co.uk). Also lake in the woods.

90 mins, 52.9978, -3.8793 🚶📷▽⛰

### 15 RHOS & MOEL SIABOD QUARRIES

Many ruins and a beautiful blue quarry lake decked with ledges and heather on the wild slopes of lesser-visited Moel Siabod. Rhos quarry is en route, with more intact remains of workers' barracks and the slate and slab works.

→ Park in layby on the A5 near turning into Pont Cyfyng. Walk into the village, taking farm road on R to and past LL24 0ED). Follow footpath 300m and take L for Rhos Quarry 300m off path at. Back on main path, continue another mile and keep to the R of the lake and L of the ridge to reach Moel Siabod ruins and flooded pit (53.0821, -3.9150).

20 mins, 53.0885, -3.8980 📷⬆⛰▽

## ANCIENT RUINS

### 16 DOLWYDDELAN CASTLE

This brooding, romantic 13th-century castle tower stood sentinel over the Lledr valley for Llewellyn the Great. For the most beautiful approach, walk in from the high ground to the west, to see the castle ruins beneath you at the head of the valley.

→ Shortest route is from car park on the A470 ⅓ mile W of LL25 0JG (entry fee, pay at farmhouse as you walk up). For a better walk, start from Roman Bridge train station (or park after the river bridge 53.0463, -3.9239, beyond LL25 0JG). Continue along lane ⅓ mile to Pen-y-rhiw farm on corner, to find footpath on R (actually byway). Entry fee is probably

optional via this route! NB Locals swim at quarry lake behind A470 car park, if you are adventurous, but be careful.

20 mins, 53.0530, -3.9084 📷⬆▽🏊🚶

### 17 CAPEL GARMON TOMB

A little-visited Neolithic chambered tomb, situated amongst gently rolling hills with views to the Snowdonia mountains. It has several open passages, impressive walls and one chamber with a huge capstone; the kerbstone circle marks the original extent of the mound.

→ Heading S from Betws-y-Coed on A5, take fork up L shortly after Conwy Falls Café. Take gated fork L, around Rynys campsite (see listing), and find footpath at start of track on L at bend (53.0685, -3.7691) before next farm (LL26 0RU). Path is indistinct but heads NNE for ½ mile, through 3 fields. Bring a map/GPS!

10 mins, 53.0731, -3.7701 🚶📷

## HILLTOPS & SCRAMBLES

### 18 NANT DWR-OER INCLINES

Follow the path of the slate wagons up consecutive levels to arrive at this desolate plateau. From here you can enjoy views out across the slate lands, with ruins and two lakes – great for sunsets. Or continue even higher on the next incline.

→ Park on street near LL41 4DD, where a short track between houses leads to the bottom of the incline, which rises to L.

40 mins, 52.9907, -3.9137 📷⬆📷⛰

### 19 BRYN Y CASTELL

A remote, little-known Iron Age hill fort occupying a small mount, with partially reconstructed stone walls and ramparts. Inhabited and producing iron on an impressive scale until the Romans arrived; Sarn Helen Roman road runs past the site.

→ Head E of Llan Ffestiniog on B4391, and ½ mile after LL41 4PS, at junction, park on track/ drive on L. Walk up drive past house ½ mile (all open access), then bear R for another ¼ mile. 19th-century Drum Quarry is ½ mile E at 52.9694, -3.8864.

20 mins, 52.9691, -3.8955 🚶⛰📷✲

### 20 DAEAR DDU SCRAMBLE

Excellent Grade 1 scramble on the south-eastern ridge of Moel Siabod (872m) with views to the Glyders.

→ Approach from Pont Cyfyng LL24 0ED via Rhos Quarry (see listing) and Llyn y Foel.

100 mins, 53.0725, -3.9290 📷⛰🚶

## WILDLIFE & WOODS

### 21 GOEDOL WATERFALLS & WOODS

Waterfalls aplenty adorn the Afon Geodol as it cascades down through the ancient oak woodland of Coed Cymerau – an NNR and temperate rainforest. This fall is right by the road and leads on down to more below. At the bottom footbridge you'll find a small gorge section where the water is deep and emerald.

→ Heading S from Tanygrisau on A496, find second parking layby on R after about ½ mile, shortly before LL41 4BW. Just beyond, a track R (red and white poles) leads over the waterfall and pool. The footpath continues, bears R, past Dol-wen to a major set of falls (⅓ mile). Return or continue on down to the bottom footbridge, either along the river 1 mile (no path) or on footpath up over hill. Alternatively, park further down A496, just N of LL41 4NT (layby with telephone and post box), cross road and follow path 200m to 52.9625, -3.9531.

3 mins, 52.9771, -3.9476 🏞️👣

### 22 TY MAWR WYBRNANT, NT

Wildlife-rich traditionally managed farmland, woodland and wildflower meadows. At the centre is a 16th-century farmhouse and museum, birthplace of Bishop William Morgan, who first translated the bible into Welsh in 1588. Wonderful walks can be taken around the estate, but there's a fee to enter the house. Or take a pony trek with Gwydyr Stables (01690 760248) next door.

→ Signed from Penmachno, heading W on Glasgwm Road and forking R to follow NT signs to LL25 0HJ. House open afternoons, Thu–Sun, closed winter, 01690 760213. Download walks from the NT website.

5 mins, 53.0547, -3.8365 🚶🔄🚲

## SLOW FOOD

### 23 OLIF, BETWS-Y-COED

Fantastic tapas created using Welsh produce in a bright restaurant in town. Delight in local cod in beer batter, Lon Farm belly pork, Anglesey goats' cheese, artisan breads, real ales and – on Friday and Saturday evenings – gourmet burgers.

→ Plas Derwen, Holyhead Road, Betws-y-Coed, LL24 0AY, 01690 733942. 53.0930, -3.8047 🍴

### 24 PONT YR AFON GAM CAFÉ

This was once the highest petrol station in Wales; now the remote cottage café

serves wholesome home-made breakfasts, cakes, lunches and afternoon teas. Lovely views into the Cynfal waterfall gorge. Open 11am–4pm, Wed–Sun (closed winter).

→ Llan Ffestiniog, LL41 4PS, 01766 762766. 52.9595, -3.8687 🏞️🍴

## COSY PUBS

### 25 TY GWYN HOTEL

Traditional family-run whitewashed coaching inn with log fires, low beams and friendly locals. Good food comes either from their polytunnels down the road or from farms in the surrounding area, including forest reared pork from Gelli Farm.

→ Betws-y-Coed, LL24 0SG, 01690 710383. 53.0847, -3.7943 🍴

### 26 BRYN TYRCH INN, CAPEL CURIG

As popular with walkers as it is for destination restaurant-goers, this rather plain looking inn on the A5 redeems itself with a riverside beer garden, AA Rosette, locally sourced food and a very friendly atmosphere.

→ Capel Curig, LL24 0EL, 01690 720223. 53.1027, -3.9071 🍴

## WILDER CAMPING

### 27 LLECHRWD RIVERSIDE CAMPSITE

Simple riverside campsite in the verdant Vale of Ffestiniog. Camp on the flat grassy fields bordering the River Dwyryd – just beware of the midges! Campfires with a permit.

→ Llechrwd Farm, Maentwrog, LL41 4HF, 01766 590240. 52.9521, -3.9690 🏕️

### 28 CWMLANERCH CARAVAN PARK

Riverside camping on a working farm within walking distance of Betws. Tents and campervans can set up camp on the flat field abutting the River Conwy.

→ Betws-y-Coed, LL24 0BG, 07751 374527. 53.1063, -3.7939 🏕️

### 29 RYNYS FARM CAMPING SITE

Set up camp on grassy fields bordered by stone walls, maybe under a big oak, to enjoy the view down the Machno valley by day and stargaze by night. You can walk to Capel Garmon (see listing) from here. Pay showers and sadly no campfires.

→ Betws-y-Coed, LL26 0RU, 01690 710218. 53.0659, -3.7699 🏕️

## RUSTIC HAVENS

### 30 FOEL GOPYN
Far, far away from the madding crowds, this little NT stone cottage sits high on a remote moor. Enjoy cosy comfort and far-reaching views along with your seclusion. Sleeps four.
→ 1 Bryn Ysgol, Ysbyty Ifan, LL24 0NY, 0344 8002070. nationaltrust.org.uk
53.0235, -3.7424

### 31 HENDRE ISAF BUNKHOUSE
A beautiful 400-year-old cruck barn, sleeping 18. The National Trust has kept the decor simple with lots of comfy seats

and an open-plan main room with kitchen and big table. Outside is a large garden and barbeque area.
→ Pentrefoelas Road, near Betws-y-Coed, LL24 0HP, 0344 3351296.
53.0456, -3.7100 B

### 32 TY UCHAF, TY CAPEL & TY COCH
In these stunning wild uplands, the Landmark Trust has renovated three unique, separate buildings into the ultimate hideaways, a ten-minute walk from the forestry car park. Ty Uchaf is an old crog loft, Ty Capel is the former chapel and schoolhouse, and Ty Coch is an 18th-century cottage.

→ Rhiwddolion, nr Betws-y-Coed, LL24 0DE, 01628 825925. landmarktrust.org.uk
53.0866, -3.8404

### 33 BLAEN Y BUARTH
Stylish and secluded, this beautifully renovated rural cottage in the Machno valley offers complete isolation – without wifi or a phone signal, but with glorious mountain views and underfloor heating! Sleeps six.
→ Penmachno, near LL24 0AJ, 0844 5005101. underthethatch.co.uk
53.0336, -3.7844

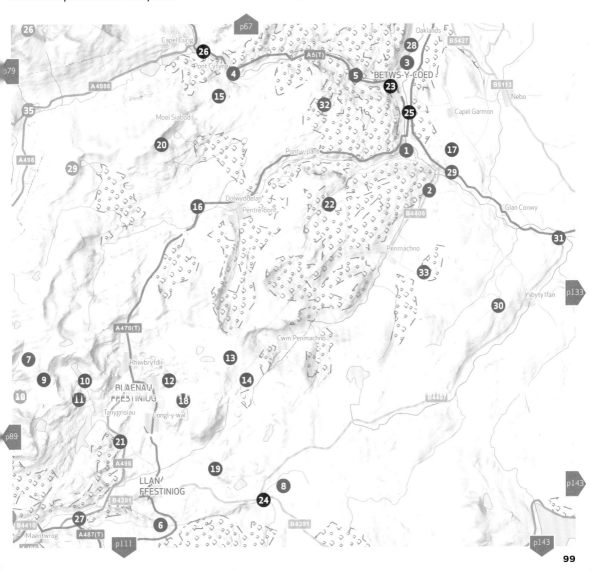

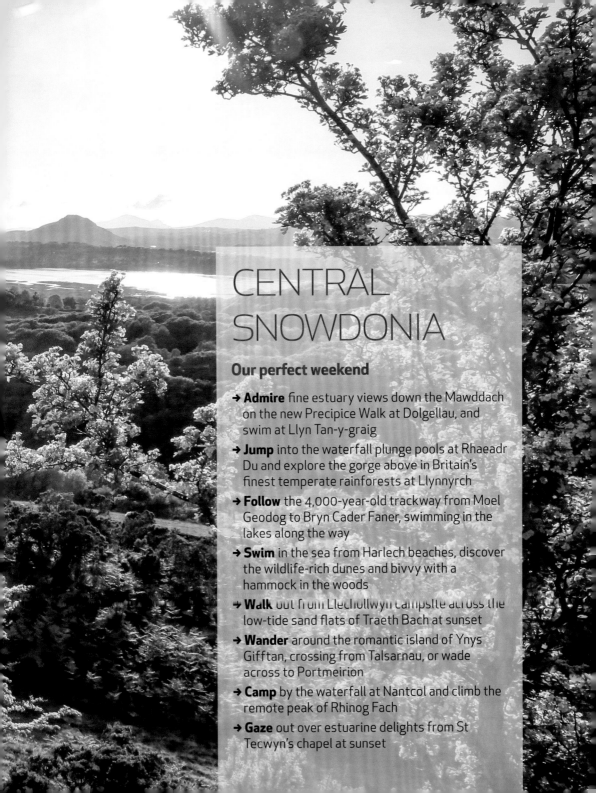

# CENTRAL SNOWDONIA

## Our perfect weekend

→ **Admire** fine estuary views down the Mawddach on the new Precipice Walk at Dolgellau, and swim at Llyn Tan-y-graig

→ **Jump** into the waterfall plunge pools at Rhaeadr Du and explore the gorge above in Britain's finest temperate rainforests at Llynnyrch

→ **Follow** the 4,000-year-old trackway from Moel Geodog to Bryn Cader Faner, swimming in the lakes along the way

→ **Swim** in the sea from Harlech beaches, discover the wildlife-rich dunes and bivvy with a hammock in the woods

→ **Walk** out from Llechollwyn campsite across the low-tide sand flats of Traeth Bach at sunset

→ **Wander** around the romantic island of Ynys Gifftan, crossing from Talsarnau, or wade across to Portmeirion

→ **Camp** by the waterfall at Nantcol and climb the remote peak of Rhinog Fach

→ **Gaze** out over estuarine delights from St Tecwyn's chapel at sunset

The Rhinogs are probably the wildest place in the United Kingdom with the exception of north-west Scotland. The Cambrian geology of the area, known as the Harlech Dome, is truly ancient, similar to parts of Nova Scotia, of which it was once part. There is little slate here to leave industrial scars, and the absence of grandiose peaks means there are fewer tourists. Instead you will find temperate rainforests, stunning estuaries and sacred stone circles.

The more forgiving landscape, closer to the coast, attracted some of the first settlers. Up among the heather and golden grass are an abundance of Bronze Age sites, such as Bryn Cader Faner, and a prehistoric trackway – now christened the Ardudwy Way – once linked Ireland and Britain via the natural harbours of the coast. Up here are natural tarns galore – our favourite is Llyn Eiddew Bach. On the shallow side of the tarn are grassy, sheep-mown banks perfect for picnics and paddling, and on the deep side are cliff ledges for sun lounging and for those who like to jump. The sense of awe and beauty is completed by a backdrop of bronzed September bracken, bony stone peaks and glimpses of the Irish Sea. Ancient forests are plentiful in the lower slopes, and within the deep river gorges they form very special temperate rainforests, where the constant spray and humidity creates a haven for moss-clad trees, vibrant lichens and hanging ferns. At Ceunant Llennyrch, one of the best examples of such rainforest in the UK, the woods date back over 10,000 years to the last Ice Age, 30m cliffs rise up, and gnarled sessile oaks reach out in a woodland fantasy world of mossy tussocks and bilberry. There are fabulous waterfalls here, particularly in the upper regions, and the remains of the old Harlech coaching road and bridge can be followed.Two more waterfalls can be found below the ruins of the last Welsh gold mine in the rather different woodland plantations of Coed-y-Brenin forest, accessible via the extensive network of mountain-bike trails. Gold mining here is not as ancient as in Carmarthenshire, but since 1911 no fewer than six royal wedding rings have been made of gold from these rocks.

The estuaries and coast provide the final magic in this beautiful region. The foreboding ruins of 14th-century Harlech Castle, built when the sea still lapped the base of its massive crag, now overlook the stunning beach and dunes below. This is one of the few dune systems in the country that is accreting, extending ever further into Cardigan Bay. The beaches continue on and off all the way down to Barmouth and Mawddach. If you're lucky you might also catch a glimpse of dolphins offshore.

## WILD BEACHES & ISLANDS

### 1 YNYS GIFFTAN

This romantic island, set on the tidal sands, was a gift from Queen Anne to Lord Harlech. At low tide you can walk out across the salt marsh and sand flats to explore the strange ripple patterns and tidal sand pools around it. If you are brave you can even wade/swim across the Dwyryd channel to Portmeirion. Dangerous on a rising tide.

→ In Talsarnau turn W by The Ship Aground pub heading for the station and parking at the end of the lane (LL47 6UA). Cross the train line and head straight out a mile. The estuary is empty below mid-tide, so leave on a falling tide to provide plenty of exploring time.
20 mins, 52.9127, -4.0005 🌊🐾🏖️▼

### 2 TRAETH BACH, LLECHOLLWYN

Access onto vast sand flats interspersed with deep pools and rivers, bordered by salt marsh.

→ Take the A496 S from Talsarnau, dir Harlech. After 1 mile at Ynys, on bend, turn R (dead-end) just before bus stop. Pass LL47 6TH to park at road end after ½ mile. At low tide you can walk NE 1 mile to Ynys Gifftan island (see entry) or NW towards Portmeirion. Dangerous on a rising tide. Adventure swimmers can swim 2 miles

upstream with the rising tide, R of Ynys Gifftan. Either get out at Ynys Gifftan for Talsarnau station, or continue on to Llandecwyn station by the bridge (52.9227, -4.0554).
2 mins, 52.9016, -4.0873 🐚🏖️🏊

### 3 HARLECH BEACH

Spend the day playing on miles of white sands backed by dunes beneath Harlech castle. A good place to see dolphins and mountain sunsets, and build driftwood fires.

→ Well signed from Lower Harlech. From A496, turn by the station to car park beyond LL46 2UG. Head N up beach for solitude and the Morfa Harlech nature reserve (see entry).
5 mins, 52.8623, -4.1278 🌊🚗

### 4 Y MAES & ST TANWG'S

A beautiful, easily accessed beach backed by mountains. Discover the 13th-century church and lych gate hidden in the dunes; built on a 5th-century site, this is one of the oldest Christian places in Britain. There is a good local café by the car park, and a quiet tidal lagoon with white sands at the mouth of the Artro, with an ancient harbour used by the first Irish saints and pilgrims. It is particularly warm when the tide rises after a sunny morning, and heats up over hot sands.

→ Signed Llandanwg from the A496 S of Harlech. Pass LL46 2SD to car park and Y Maes Café (01341 241387, 07866 599860 ); church is just behind. Continue on behind the beach 300m to reach the lagoon.
5 mins, 52.8327, -4.1257 ✝️🏖️🚗🍴🍺▼

## RIVERS & WATERFALLS

### 5 NANT STEICYN POOLS

Sparkling clear mountain stream with many enticing plunge pools. The most obvious is by the lane on the way up to Llyn Cwm Bychan. Follow it upstream to discover a second set, running in a little gorge above tiny off-grid cottage, Cwm Mawr, which can also be rented (see listing). Great fun for kids, and wonderfully secret.

→ From Llanbedr head E, following signs for Cwm Bychan. About 1½ miles after the turning to LL45 2PH the lake, there is parking for one by the obvious waterfall over wall on L. Follow the stream course up ⅓ mile to find Cwm-mawr cottage (see listing) with pools, and many above. There are also two footpaths, but the stream course is fun. Llyn Cwm Bychan is also a good longer swim, of course.
15 mins, 52.8625, -4.0305 🏖️🏔️🚶▼

## 6 RHAEADR DU, LLENNYRCH

Set in a picturesque gorge, this 'black waterfall' cascades into a large plunge pool. It was much admired by Victorian travellers, but is now little visited. Head ½ mile upstream, beyond a ruined bridge, for another waterfall with rock slab slide into a large pool; more pools continue above in a zigzag gorge.

→ Head 1 mile W from Maentwrog on A496 and turn L just before Magnox hydro and bridge (¼ mile before LL41 4HY). After ⅓ mile (52.9343, -3.9888) park near gate if space. 100m further find a kissing gate on R. Descend across field and after ¼ mile steep steps on R lead down to waterfall. Reclimb and continue on main footpath ½ mile to reach upper falls and ruined bridge below (52.9271, -3.9820). The gorge can be approached from S side (see Llennyrch rainforest listing). Canyoning companies run gorge adventures here e.g. Snowdonia Adventure Activities (01341 241511).
20 mins, 52.9302, -3.9850 🏊🚶🍴♿🚐🅿️🚌🚲

## 7 CWM NANTCOL POOLS

The waterfall at the Nantcol campsite (see listing) is huge but does get busy. These pools upstream are small, secluded and delicious.

→ Heading up Cwm Nantcol Llanbedr, pass the campsite, and then LL45 2PL. Continue ½ mile, to find footpath on L. Park (limited space) and follow this down to the stream and upstream 200m.
5 mins, 52.8150, -4.0368 🏊🚶🚲

## 8 RHAEADR MAWDDACH & GOLD MINE

Impressive waterfalls with a huge plunge pool and several ruins. Climb above the falls to reach the recently derelict ruins of Gwynfynydd goldmine.

→ 6 miles N of Dolgellau on A470 turn R for LL40 2HS at end of Ganllwyd (where speed limit ends), cross bridge and continue 1¼ miles to Tyddyn Gwladys car park at road end. Walk a mile on track upstream, admiring the river pools, to find Pistyll Cain joining from the L. Cross footbridge to larger Rhaeadr Mawddach for a swim. Climb up above waterfall and continue along river on track ½ mile to find more ruins at 52.8351, -3.8761 and the main Gwynfynydd mine workings up incline into forest above L. Also accessible from the Coed-y-Brenin mountain biking trails (LL40 2HZ, 01341 440728).
20 mins, 52.8301, -3.8777 🏊🚶🏛️🚴🅿️

10

## 9 PONT LLANELLTYD, RIVER MAWDDACH

A late-18th-century stone bridge watches over a huge shingle pool and beach edged with grassy banks. Cymer Abbey ruins are also nearby, adjacent to a caravan park.

→ Signed Cymer Abbey from A470 just S of Llanelltyd (NW of Dolgellau). Abbey at LL40 2HE, but turn L to find parking by river /old bridge first.
1 min, 52.7561, -3.9011 🏊🛶

## LAKES

## 10 LLYN EIDDEW-BACH & TARNS

This perfect tarn in the remote northern Rhinogs has cliffs for jumping and fabulous views. From here an impressive old mining track heads up Moel Ysgyfarnogod past several manganese mines to Llyn Du (not the one on Rhinog Fawr). Nearby is beautiful Llyn Caerwych with sea views.

→ Head N from Harlech on B4573, turn R after 3 miles for Eisingrug (unsigned), after 1 mile take dead-end mountain road R 150m after pond. Follow past turning to LL47 6YB, find parking ½ mile later at road end. Bear R (initially S) to climb track 1½ mile to lake, bearing R after ¾ mile. Llyn Caerwych is NW at 52.8958, -4.0227 (15 mins). Llyn Du is E at 52.8867, -3.9974 (30 mins).
30 mins, 52.8905, -4.0141 🏕️🏊🥾📷🔥

## 11 LLYN DU, RHINOG FAWR

At the top of the Roman Steps below Rhinog Fawr, with infinity pool views over Myndd Bach and the sea, this is a perfect high-level spot to swim and wild camp on the roof of the world.

→ Follow road past LL45 2PH and Nant Steicyn pools (see listing) to the end at Cwm Bychan Farm (paid parking and camping, see listing). Follow the Roman Steps (actually a medieval packhorse path) up as if for Rhinog Fawr, well signed.
90 mins, 52.8454, -4.0009 🏕️🏊🔥📷

## 12 LLYN GELLI-GAIN, TRAWSFYNYDD

A perfect wild-camping tarn with an island in rugged territory. If the mile walk in puts you off, there is also a sweet little river pool off the quiet lane nearby.

→ From A470 in Bronaber turn E dir LL41 4UY and follow 1 mile to park at 52.8690, -3.8937 (by cattle grid and 'bus shelter'). Take hillside track from gate SE then NE around peak. River pool is at Pont Dôl-y-mynach, 1 mile S at 52.8629, -3.8826.
30 mins, 52.8777, -3.8825 🏕️🏊🥾📷🔥

11

12

### 13 LLYN TAN-Y-GRAIG

Follow the New Precipice Walk along an old mountain tramway, and enjoy stunning views down the Mawddach. The first part is flat and wheelchair friendly. It then descends to the super clear Llyn Tan-y-graig, a glassy lake, backed by forest and with views out over Cader Idris.

→ Turn off the A496 into Taicynhaeaf (opp Penmaenpool wooden toll bridge). Continue for 2 miles, bearing R at the chapel (before LL40 2TU), up through several gates, to reach the parking area.

20 mins, 52.7628, -3.9105 🅿️🔁👟

CAVERNS & MINES

### 14 LLANFAIR SLATE CAVERNS

There are slate caverns in the area that you can explore unguided, but if you would prefer a more managed and safer experience, this is one of the best – low key, simple and good value.

→ A mile S of Harlech on A496. LL46 2SA,. £6.50. 01766 780247.

10 mins, 52.8383, -4.1101 🔁📷

### 15 CELL-FECHAN MANGANESE MINE

Follow the old manganese mine trackway up the mountain behind Barmouth, and you'll pass by numerous tunnels and workings before arriving at the ruined houses and buildings of Cell Fechan mine and farm.

→ From St John's Church in Barmouth (some parking), walk up Cellfechan Rd towards LL42 1DE, take the grassy track on the R after 100m. Switchback up the mountainside for 1 mile to the ruins. Gellfawr mine is ½ mile beyond.

30 mins, 52.7243, -4.0544 🔁📷

### 16 HENDRE CERRIG, CAERWYCH

An enchanting lost landscape in the northern Rhinogs. This old, wet manganese tunnel by a stream leads to several chambers. More tunnels in the ancient mossy woods downstream. Further up the lane a beautiful ruined byre illustrates how shepherds used to live, with the fireplace and sleeping quarters upstairs and the cows lowing gently below. On your return there are superb estuary views from the footpath and plateau above Caerwych Farm (Ardudwy Way).

→ From Penrhyndeudraeth go over the road/rail bridge, then straight over A496 and up. Turn L just after LL47 6YR (converted chapel with postbox), continue around Llyn Tecwyn Isaf, then first R and first L through gate (signed Caerwych). Up, up and through Caerwych farm and another gate. Continue

on, and at end of woods, at cattle grid (½ mile before LL47 6YU) find mine ruin on L. 200m further along on R is a stream. Follow it up to find overgrown tunnel on R. The byre is ¼ mile further along on R (52.9081, -4.0108). Very limited parking or turning. Be respectful.

5 mins, 52.9092, -4.0150 🔁👟🔁🔁

SACRED & ANCIENT

### 17 BRYN CADER FANER

One of the most spectacular stone circles in Britain, this is actually a burial cairn, well over 4,000 year old. Only 18 stones remain standing, damaged by treasure hunters and by soldiers during WW2 who used them for target practice. They sit proud like a crown of thorns on an ancient trackway that once linked Ireland to England, which is lined with many more standing stones and cairns. The wild setting under Moel Ysgyfarnogod, or 'hare mountain', only adds to the experience.

→ As for Llyn Eiddew-Bach (see listing) but continue from the lake ⅓ mile N on the ancient path (or on approach, bear L instead of R after ¾ mile).

50 mins, 52.8980, -4.0115 🔁🗺️

### 18 CARNEDDAU HENGWYN & CIRCLES

Explore the gentle and empty slopes of Mynydd Egryn, enjoying fine sea views all along the way. Today this is a quiet place but it was once the site of a large Bronze Age settlement. Many homesteads have been excavated and impressive burial structures remain. Carneddau Hengwyn has two chambers, one of which you can still enter. Beyond is a notable cairn circle, Carnedd Gron. Also look out for the finely cast wheels of a Victorian manganese mine aerial runway nearby.

→ Park off the A496 near the entrance to NT Egryn Abbey, ½ mile S of LL43 2BZ. Follow the track and footpath from Egryn up hillside due E about 1 mile to take the 2nd straight field wall N to the two chambers and stones. About ¼ mile beyond, on the footpath, is the circle (52.7627, -4.0520). About ¼ mile NE of here are the mine artefacts (52.7640, -4.0486).

40 mins, 52.7648, -4.0564 🔁🗺️🔁🔁

### 19 CORS-Y-GEDOL , DYFFRYN ARDUDWY

This area is rich in stone-capped burial chambers, remnants of a once-thriving Bronze Age community that lived here over 5,000 years ago. This chamber lies in heathland near the 16th-century Cors-y-Gedol manor. Back in the village itself, two impressive burial chambers can be found just behind the school.

17

→ From A496 at Dyffryn Ardudwy, follow
dead-end Fford Gors past LL44 2RJ to Cors-
y-Gedol Hall and road end. Follow trackway
S ¼ mile to find on R. For the Dyffryn cairns,
park in Bro Arthur (LL44 2EW) and follow signs
from main road, just behind school.
5 mins, 52.7848, -4.0722 [icons]

## 20 PONT SCETHIN & CRAIG Y DINAS

Follow the old London road into the empty
quarters of the Ysgethin valley to find this
elegant Georgian stone packhorse bridge
under Diffwys mountain. Marvel at the courage
of the horses and packmen of earlier centuries
as they crossed it, burdened with heavy and
precious loads – its low parapets allowed the
cargo to skim above the stonework, and the
surface is smartly cobbled.

→ Park as for Cors-y-Gedol cairn (see listing).
Continue on bridleway 2½ mile bearing SE to
river. There is a walled Iron Age hill fort, Craig y
Dinas, on the knoll ½ mile S of path (52.7871,
-4.0411), a great lookout for a truly wild camp.
50 mins, 52.7922, -4.0265 [icons]

## 21 CERRIG ARTHUR STONES

Three grand stones with superb views of the
Mawddach estuary are all that remain of the
12m circle that can be discerned in the turf.

→ Start as for Panorama hilltop (see listing)
but continue up the lane another 1½ miles,
bearing L through Sylfaen farm (public byway).
Immediately after the wall gate a path leads
up to the L for 250m to the stones.
10 mins, 52.7502, -4.0285 [icons]

SUNSET HILLTOPS

## 22 RHINOG FACH, CWM NANTCOL

One of the finest and wildest peaks in the
Rhinogs (712m), with two lakes, sea views
and the option of some fun scrambling.

→ As for Cwm Nantcol pools (see listing) but
continue up valley another 2 miles, across Pont
Cerrig to Maes-y-garnedd farm (£2 parking). The
path goes straight up between the two peaks,
then bear R over a stile in the wall up to Llyn
Hywel. From the far end a good scramble heads
up to the peak alongside the wall, or cross the
wall to follow the much gentler summit path.
120 mins, 52.8241, -3.9829 [icons]

## 23 PANORAMA WALK, BARMOUTH

An easy outing to an awe-inspiring viewpoint
over the Mawddach estuary and mountains.
In the Victorian era this was known as the
Panorama Pleasure Grounds and laid out as a
woodland garden. There was a tearoom beyond

19

21

the gate and views from many points on the path. Now the oak trees have grown up, and you must reach the crag to enjoy the vistas.

→ Leaving Barmouth on A496 inland, take steep dead-end fork up L on bend (Panorama Rd). After 1 mile parking is on R (just before L turn for LL42 1AL). An iron gate R leads up to the woods, then R through another gate.
15 mins, 52.7264, -4.0358 🖼️🚶

### 24 ST TECWYN'S & LAKE, LLANDECWYN
The Welsh often reserved the best spots for God, and this little chapel enjoys one of the finest, with stunning views west out over Ynys Gifftan (see listing) and the Dwyryd sand flats. Stop for a dip on your way up at idyllic roadside Llyn Techwyn Isaf, or follow the old coaching road from the church along the shore of Llyn Techwyn Uchaf.

→ As for Hendre Cerrig (see listing) but at the lake, after LL47 6YR, take fork bearing up L.
2 mins, 52.9188, -4.0357 ⛪🖼️🏊

### 25 MOEL GOEDOG & PEREGRINES
The views out over Portmeirion, the estuary and the Llŷn are sublime, especially at sunset. There are two stone circles and a hill fort summit. Buzzards and sometimes peregrine falcons can be seen hunting. The

track continues on into the wildest stretch of the new Ardudwy Way, to Bryn Cader Faner stone circle (see entry) and lakes.

→ From higher Harlech centre take the steep lane up past the Lion Hotel. After a mile turn L past LL46 2TN and continue 1½ miles to find track on R. Circle is ½ mile along track, on R.
15 mins, 52.8714, -4.0658 🚶🖼️

### 26 PRECIPICE WALK & LLYN CYNWCH
Created by the Nannau estate in 1890, this is an easy and popular walk circumnavigating heather-clad Cwynwch mountain and lake, with fine views of the Mawddach estuary.

→ Take Llanfachreth road N from Dolgellau 2½ miles and find large car park on L just beyond LL40 2NG.
15 mins, 52.7725, -3.8712 🏞️🖼️🏕️🚶

## FORESTS & WILDLIFE

### 27 LLENNYRCH RAINFOREST
Walk among gnarled oaks festooned with mosses and ferns, and steep banks clothed with bilberry, wood anemones and wood sorrel in the summer. Mosses, liverworts, ferns and lichens are abundant.

→ Start as for Hendre Cerrig ruins (see entry), but after lake continue on 2 miles, past LL47

6YT, to road end (52.9205, -3.9974). Walk R over fields to find the head of Ceunant Geifr stream gorge and follow this down and into the most remote part of the woods, and the deepest section of the Llennyrch gorge. Downstream are the upper waterfalls of Rhaeadr Du (see entry) and a ruined coaching bridge (52.9287, -3.9844) that carried the old Harlech road. To return, follow this old road from the bridge as it switchbacks up the hillside and out via Llenyrch Farm.

45 mins, 52.9257, -3.9819 🅿️🏊🧗⛺🏔️🥾

### 28 MORFA HARLECH DUNES & WOODS

One of the few expanding sand dune systems in Britain – nearby Harlech castle once stood by the sea. Orchids, fungi and stoats are just a few of the wildlife highlights that thrive in the sheltered inland hollows of Morfa Harlech NNR. Explore the far northern end of the beach (3 miles) or there are paths inland where you can spend hours discovering this rich sandy world. The plantation forest behind the dunes is a wild, lost world of sandy hillocks, pine needles and giant blackberries, just waiting for you to string up your hammock.

➜ Pay car park signed opp train station in Lower Harlech (past LL46 2UG). Head R up the beach 15 mins before exploring inland over the dunes.

20 mins, 52.8749, -4.1284 🏖️🐚🏊🌲🦌

### 29 COED CRAFNANT

Ancient woodland has covered this site for over 6,000 years and it's rich with mosses, ferns and lichens and a beautiful place for a walk. If you can, rise early and come for the utterly heart lifting spring dawn chorus.

➜ From Llanbedr head E following signs for Cwm Bychan (dir LL45 2PH). After just under 3 miles (and ½ mile past turn off for Dinas caravan and camping) find signposted footpath on R with wooden gate leading down to stone bridge (small car park can be found ½ mile further along lane on R). Cross river, enter wood and follow red waymarked path, or sheep paths to view point.

10 mins, 52.8398, -4.0531 🅿️🐦🥾

### 30 COED GANLLWYD & RHAEADR DDU

Enjoy a beautiful waymarked circular walk along the tumbling River Gamlan with its famous Rhaeadr Ddu (not to be confused with the Rhaeadr Du or Llennyrch listing). The steep gorge is a NNR, rich in ancient oak forest, mosses, lichens, ferns and bats. The waterfall has a great plunge pool for a swim.

→ From the NT car park in Ganllwyd on A470 (LL40 2TF) cross road and take lane by 'tin tabernacle', becoming a woodland footpath and arriving at footbridge and waterfalls. Cross S to explore woodland and return on circular trail.

15 mins, 52.8022, -3.8956 🏊🔦💧🚶

→ Head S from Ganllwyd on A470. After 1 mile turn L for Llanfachreth, and find Glasdir forestry car park signed R after a mile just, 300m after LL40 2NW. Continue on lane to find gate opp into picnic field and follow red waymarked path upstream (on opp bank).

15 mins, 52.7857, -3.8717 🏊

## LOST RUINS

### 31 TOMEN-Y-MUR & LAKE

A Roman fort was constructed here in AD78 under the infamous Roman governor Agricola and occupied for about 60 years. Some remains of the (reconstructed) walls and a small amphitheatre can still be seen. A millennium later the Normans occupied the site and built this motte mound, which you can climb. Expansive views out over the Prysor valley, and a lovely lake to dip in.

→ Climbing the A487 from Maentwrog, 300m beyond the A470 junction at LL41 4RD, turn L down lane to parking on R with signboard after 1 mile. From the bend beyond the cattle grid a byway track leads ¼ mile on up to Llyn yr Oerfel.

2 mins, 52.9298, -3.9272 Q61

### 32 MOEL Y CROESAU, TRAWSFYNYDD

The 'hill of crosses' is the site of a 1943 Wellington bomber crash and remarkable survival story. The crash happened in thick fog, and four men died, but two survived and one walked through darkness, mist and bogs, following the stream to Doldinnas and a track to Bwlch-gwyn farm. You will also find the remains of the Prince Edward mine (winches, buildings and holes), which produced gold used in royal rings, and the mock forts made by Roman army for practice at Doldinnas.

→ On the A4212 turn R to Bwlch Gwyn ½ mile W of LL41 4TP (park opp turn). Then walk 2½ miles NE, to retrace the route but in daylight. Or walk in from lake at Tomen-y-mur fort (see listing) continuing on byway, then paths E for 3 miles, joining the track at Dolddinas.

60 mins, 52.9292, -3.8719 🏔🏊💧⛺

### 33 GLASDIR COPPER MINE

These ruins hidden by a stream in the woods near Coed-y-Brenin are the remains of a revolutionary copper mine: in 1896 it pioneered flotation extraction of ore, which made copper wire cheap and ushered in 20th-century telecommunications. Walk up the stream and explore the industrial-sized flotation tanks, now overgrown on the hillside.

## SLOW FOOD

### 34 BISTRO BERMO

Maybe the decor could be cosier, the lighting better, but the Conwy lamb, 30-day dry-aged Welsh Black rib-eye and fish of the day are fresh and delicious in this unassuming little bistro. Open Tues–Sun evenings.

→ 6 Church St, Barmouth LL42 1EW, 01341 281284.
52.7205, -4.0528 🍴

### 35 LLEW GLAS CAFÉ, HARLECH

Lovely local-produce café serving Welsh cheese plates, their famous scones and home-made cakes.

→ 3 Plas y Goits, Blue Lion Square, Harlech LL46 2YA, 01766 781095.
52.8585, -4.1084 🍴

### 36 CASTLE COTTAGE, HARLECH

Four-star local produce served up with flair. The decor is somewhat stuffy, but for a delicious meal and friendly service you won't be disappointed.

→ Y Llech, Harlech, LL46 2YL, 01766 780479.
52.8596, -4.1078 🍴

### 37 BWYTY MAWDDACH RESTAURANT

Winning all the awards, this bright restaurant with fantastic estuary and mountain views serves super-fresh, super-local food. Enjoy rare-breed cured meats, herbs fresh from the garden, Mediterranean-inspired dishes and Sunday roast joints.

→ Llanelltyd, LL40 2TA, 01341 421752.
52.7567, -3.9134 🍴

## WILDER CAMPING

### 38 SHELL ISLAND

Gigantic sprawling campsite on the beach, with room for everyone. Choose your spot hidden in the sandy dunes or on the busier grassy pitches. Bars, restaurants, shops and even a laundrette.

→ Llanbedr, LL45 2PJ, 01341 241453.
52.8191, -4.1427 🏊⛺

### 39 CAE GWYN FARM

Majestic mountain and valley views at this rustic campsite, bunk barn and simple B&B on a working farm.

→ Bronaber, Trawsfynydd, LL41 4YE, 01766 540245.
52.8502, -3.9110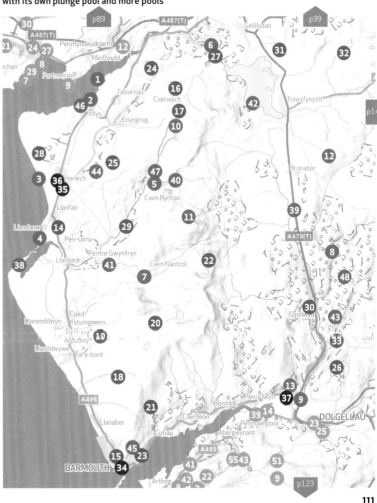

### 40 CWM BYCHAN CAMPING

A simple site in wild Rhinog mountain scenery. At the foot of the Roman Steps by the lake.

→ Cwm Bychan Farm, LL45 2PH, Llanbedr, 01630 657001.
52.8635, -4.0130

### 41 NANTCOL WATERFALLS CAMPSITE

Build dams, play on the rope swing and relax on your lilo. If you're brave enter the waterfall chasm for a deeper swim or jump. This is a basic campsite, but there is a good little shop and campfires are allowed.

→ Cefn Uchaf, Llanbedr, LL45 2PL (misleading, follow Rhaeadr Nantcol signs), 01341 241209.
52.8205, -4.0663

### 42 CAE ADDA

Beautiful lakeside positioned campsite with open, flat grass pitches and a small camp kitchen. Simple lake cabin and cottage also available.

→ Trawsfynydd, LL41 4TS, 07783 873532.
52.9029, -3.9488

### 43 PENRHOS ISAF

This stone cottage deep in the woods of southern Snowdonia is large by bothy standards and has the luxury of an outdoor earth loo. Many cycle here, but you can't drive to it. Please beware of fire risk to the forest – no outdoor fires.

→ Park as for Glasdir copper mine (see entry). Walk N on road over river and past fork to find signed footpath into woodland R. Continue N on footpath uphill for ¼ mile to junction with forestry track. Turn R on track for 118m then take track on L approx. ½ mile. At footpath junction continue straight to bothy.
52.7976, -3.8737

### 44 MERTHYR FARM CAMPSITE

Awesome estuary and mountain vistas and sunsets (if the weather's kind) at this family-focused hill-farm campsite high above Harlech.

→ Harlech, LL46 2TP, 01766 780897.
52.8667, -4.0796

### 45 BUNKORAMA CAMPING

Amazing estuary views from this campsite and bunkhouse.

→ Gwastad Agnes, Barmouth, LL42 1DX, 07738 467196.
52.7286, -4.0412

### 46 LLECHOLLWYN CAMPING

Simple camping right on the shores of the Dwyryd estuary, opposite Portmeirion. Perfect for sand, sunsets and samphire foraging. You can even bring your own boat.

→ Ynys, Talsarnau, LL47 6TH, 01766 781130.
52.90126, -4.08881

## RUSTIC HAVENS

### 47 CWM-MAWR COTTAGE

A small stone cottage up a remote trackway, with its own plunge pool and more pools

above. For many years it was all candles and paraffin lamps, but there are now solar panels and even some solar-heated water.

→ Llanbedr, LL45 2PH. A family-owned cottage, contact Paul Cooper, 020 8947 6046.
52.8676, -4.0303

### 48 TYN Y SIMDDE

This little cottage hidden from the world is just the place from which to enjoy the wild Hermon Valley. Lovingly restored by the family who spent their holidays there in the 1950s, its two bedrooms, valley and mountain views, woodburner and simple rustic furnishing are simply heaven.

→ Dolgellau, LL40 2LH, 01341 247200.
secludedsnowdoniacottage.co.uk
52.8177, -3.8663

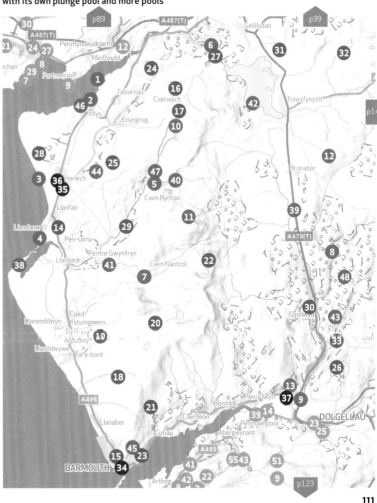

# SOUTHERN SNOWDONIA

## Our perfect weekend

→ **Investigate** the Abercwmeiddaw binoculars, giant boreholes through the cliffs

→ **Swim** in the Blue Lake at Golwern quarry, found through a tunnel in the rocks

→ **Leap** in from Aberdovey Pier near the top of the tide and swim upstream with it to Picnic Island

→ **Dip** in the secret waterfalls of Penrhyn-gwyn, deep in a wooded ravine with a tunnel

→ **Scramble** up the rocky knoll of Cefn Hir, above the islanded lake of Cregennen for superb estuary, lake and sea views

→ **Enjoy** a proper pint at the lost-in-time parlour pub of the Dovey Valley Hotel, or an organic lunch at Andy and Adam's café in Corris

→ **Paddle** down the Dysynni to the Broad Water lagoon and on to Tonfanau beach

→ **Watch** the sunset from Birds' Rock or Castell y Bere and camp by the river at Llanllwyda farm

→ **Sleep** in a handmade bowtop gypsy caravan and wake up to bird song and mountain views

**Cader Idris, the grand mountain fortress of a mythical poet warrior, matches the drama of any mountain in Snowdonia. It rises up from the Mawddach estuary at the north, with fantastic views south down the Dyfi estuary to the sea.**

Many make the iconic climb to the summit from Minfford, passing by Llyn Cau, but for the best views explore the northern approaches, and dip in the lesser-known tarns of Gafr and Y Gadair, scooped out of mountain walls by glaciers over 10,000 years ago. Bathing in their pure waters provides total immersion in the landscape and a sense of the wild, bolstered by a supernatural feeling of elation and achievement. The route up this side also passes the exquisite, islanded Cregennen lakes and provides a chance to discover two magical waterfalls with a tunnel in the totally secret, wooded gorges by the Penrhyn-gwyn ruins.

Those who love dramatic lakes will also be amazed by the Blue Lake in Golwern Quarry. You can walk up from Fairbourne, or drive in via the spectacular mountain road past the Cregennen lakes, although you will have to open and close at least ten gates. The pool is reached through a short railway tunnel, which quickly opens out into an almost perfectly rectangular amphitheatre, with smooth, vertical rock walls that make it as close to a natural swimming pool as you can imagine.

To the west of Cader Idris is the Dysynni, a secluded valley with Bird's Rock, a rocky knoll giving magnificent views, and Castell y Bere, a ruined castle encircled by twisted oaks. The river spreads into the remote tidal lagoon of Broad Water and then flows out on a wild beach beyond, north of Tywyn. To the south, the coast turns in to the Dyfi estuary, past the seaside village of Aberdovey.

Another band of the Ordovician slate that made Blaenau Ffestiniog appears at Abergynolwyn and Corris, and quarries here have created vast chasms in the mountain at Aberllefenni, and left fascinating 'binocular' tunnels at Abercwmeiddaw.

The area's alternative and eco-minded communities mean there are plenty of quirky and beautiful places to stay – such as the amazing treehouses at Living Room – and some brilliant wholesome places to eat in Dolegellau, Corris, Machynlleth and Dinas Mawddwy. Close to nature and celebrating the wonderful bounty of the land and sea, we think a good adventure should always begin and end with a good night's sleep in beautiful surroundings and a feast of ethical local produce.

## RIVERS & LAKES

### 1 LLYN GAFR & LLYN Y GADAIR

Two lovely tarns – Gafr at 410m and Y Gadair at 560m – below the great mountain wall of Cader Idris, with expansive views and few visitors. Good for wild camping.

→ The main path ascends from Gwernan lake LL40 1TL, or bushwhack from Penrhyn-gwyn waterfalls (see listing).

60 mins, 52.7055, -3.9139

### 2 BLUE LAKE, GOLWERN QUARRY

This slate quarry has stunning views out over the estuary and Cardigan Bay. There are several relics, including tramways and an old iron winding wheel, but the main attraction is a very deep, green-blue rectangular pool. It is entered by a short railway tunnel that opens out into a great quarry amphitheatre. ACCESS TUNNEL REPORTED BLOCKED / CLOSED 2019.

→ Heading S on A493, 300m after turning for Fairbourne, turn L at Fford Panteinion (opp LL38 2NJ and telephone box) and continue ⅓ mile on narrow dead-end lane to ind gate, stream and steep track up on R (very limited parking, so consider leaving car in layby on main road). After track turns L, 250m, enter quarry through

archway on R and then climb inclines and paths to reach top plateau (iron wheel) with tunnel into the lagoon. Or park at Llynnau Cregennen (see entry) and walk up to the single-track Fford Ddu and SW, a total of 4 miles (past LL39 1LX) to drop down on track from 52.6841, -4.0412 – a much more scenic walk in.

20 mins, 52.6891, -4.0413

### 3 LLYNNAU CREGENNEN

Set in a secret valley below Cader Idris, this NT-managed lake is sublime, with a boathouse, stunning sea views and mystical peaks rising around. The whole shore is open access and the sunsets from here are worth the climb.

→ On A493 ¼ mile E of Arthog, turn signed Cregennen Lakes just N of LL39 1YT. Continue up the lane 1½ miles to find first lake L and car park on R.

2 mins, 52.7103, -3.9875

### 4 PONT RHYDYGWIAL, RIVER DOVEY

Good riverside banks for paddling, picnic and a dip, if nobody is fishing.

→ At Cemmaes, 8 miles E of Machynlleth on A470, turn into Maes-y-Llan, past SY20 9PS, and continue to river bridge.

2 mins, 52.6405, -3.7243

### 5 TAL-Y-LLYN & LLYN MWYNGIL

Stretching out along the lush valley floor under the southern flanks of Cader Idris, this is a tempting lake on a summer day, and not too cold either. Stop at the no-frills Pen-y-Bont Inn for a post-swim pint.

→ Take the B4405 dir Tywyn from the A487, follow towards LL36 9AQ, and reach the lake after 1⅓ miles; limited parking in a couple of laybys. The Pen-y-Bont (01654 782285) is on the R at the far W end of the lake, after the Ty'n-y-cornel Hotel (see listing), and you could follow the lane from here along the N shore of the lake, beyond the Old Rectory – it's a public byway.

1 min, 52.6673, -3.9082

## WATERFALLS

### 6 AFON DULAS POOLS

Oak-wooded stream gorge just by the road, leading to a little waterfall and pool with rope swing.

→ As for Aberllefenni slate caverns (see listing) but don't turn L at SY20 9RX. Continue almost ½ mile to a large layby on R on bend. Descend, open access.

2 mins, 52.67403, -3.8108

### 7 NANT GWERNOL & BRYN-EGLWYS

Sparkly little woodland waterfall pool, perfect for nymphs. A Cascade Trail (marked yellow) leads up the wooded valley from the station and reaches the small pool almost immediately. Follow the Quarryman's Trail (marked blue) through the reforested remains of the once-busy Bryn-Eglwys slate quarry: an incline, winding-house and some vast, tree-filled pits, one of which has a waterfall cascading into it.

→ In Abergynolwyn (LL36 9YA) walk up from behind the post office to Nant Gwernol station (or take the train from Tywyn). There are also the busy Dolgoch Falls in the next valley SW, LL36 9UW, with a viewing platform, 52.6191, -3.9884.

10 mins, 52.6413, -3.9501 🚻🏊👣👁

### 8 ARTHOG WATERFALLS

Enjoy a steep walk up the picturesque, waterfall-filled wooded gorge. It starts with some little plunge pools and ends with a pool under a clapper bridge and the site of Llys Bradwen, the manor of an early medieval Welsh chief (there's not much left of this, but it's a lovely spot). Continue on to Hafotty-fâch, the intriguing ruins of a more recent farmstead, or Maen Du standing stone.

→ Start as for Llynnau Cregennan (see listing) but park after ¼ mile at the gate for Pant Phylip (LL39 1LQ). Continue 200m through gate for the stream bridge (permissive path). The waterfall path heads steeply up about ½ mile. Hafotty-fâch (52.7022, -3.9845) or Maen Du (, 52.7001, -3.9966) are further S by road. 3 mins, 52.7105, -4.0036 🚻👁📷📖🚶

### 9 PENRHYN-GWYN WATERFALLS

Beyond the usual attractions of an old slate quarry – a ruined mill and waterwheel, old inclines, a vast overgrown quarry pit and amazing views – Penrhyn-gwyn also offers other treasures. Follow the secret track and you'll enter a steep sylvan glen boasting two beautiful waterfalls and plunge pools, and a dark, mysterious tunnel leading into the bottom of the pit. From the top of the pit a cross-country bushwhack leads up to Llyn Gafr (see listing).

→ Heading W on Cader Rd in Dolgellau, turn L signed Cader Idris. After LL40 1TL (Llyn Gwernan and hotel) continue ½ mile to the Ty Nant car park R. Pony Path path starts 200m further, over bridge and past possible further field parking. Follow to just after the farm (was a hostel) then follow L branch of stream through a copse 200m, then L through gate,

soon leading to the mill ruins, waterwheel pit below. Climb incline to second main level (52.7161, -3.9220) and contour around 100m NE to stream. Take care.

20 mins, 52.7165, -3.9195 🚶📷🔧🌀Ⓥ

## BEACHES & ESTUARY

### 10 TONFANAU BEACH, TYWYN

Pass the abandoned Second World War army barracks to reach a long, wild beach foreshore where the rapids of the Aber Dysynni meet the sea.

→ Park opp Tonfanau train station, ¾ mile S of LL36 9LS. Cross the track on footpath and follow past the farm to the beach. Or approach from Tywyn, following Idris Villas then R before level crossing, to a mile beyond LL36 9AU at road end. This is also an approach to the Broad Water lagoon on R (see listing).

5 mins, 52.6128, -4.1285 🐚🚶🏕

### 11 BROAD WATER, AFON DYSYNNI

Explore the birdlife, reed islands and tidal sand flats of this large, shallow, coastal lagoon, fed by the Dysynni river.

→ To swim or canoe it's best on an incoming or high tide. Down- stream access from Dysynni Bridge (railway bridge at Tofanau beach, see

listing), with footpath on S side. Upstream access from the old bridge, below the new one: turn L off A493 ½ mile W of LL36 9LF. Or walk down the lane to find a little pontoon: first L, 300m beyond LL36 9LH, no parking).

2 mins, 52.6037, -4.0805 🏕🚶🌀Ⓨ❓

### 12 ABERDOVEY PIER & ESTUARY

Join the kids leaping and diving from the pier next to the sandy beach at high tide – check the depth! For a bigger adventure swim with the incoming tide up the estuary to Picnic Island beach (see listing) or as far as Smuggler's Cove Boatyard and camping at Fron-gôch (see listing). Or do in reverse on an outgoing tide, but don't get swept out to sea.

→ Seafront carpark just W of LL35 0ED. Picnic Island swim is 1 mile. Fron-gôch is about 4 miles by high tide direct route or 6 miles by more curving low tide channel. Tidal currents can be dangerous.

2 mins, 52.5430, -4.0451 🏕Ⓨ❓Ⓥ🌀

### 13 PICNIC ISLAND, ABERDOVEY

A small headland leads down to a beach, providing access to the sand flats and low-tide pools of the Dyfi estuary.

→ A mile E of Aberdovey on A493, 180m past

Philip Ave turning up to LL35 0PY, find layby on R with path over bridge. At low tide you can usually walk to Aberdovey on the remains of the ancient old Roman foreshore road, cut from the rock.

2 mins, 52.5464, -4.0273 🏖️⭕

### 14 MAWDDACH TRAIL

This converted railway line is a perfect way to explore (cycling, walking or running) the best parts of the sandy tidal estuary foreshore, most of which are unreachable by car. Follow the whole circuit, or the adventurous (with boat support) could even try swimming up with the tide from Barmouth, and running back afterwards.

→ E of Dolgellau, A493, find a car park by the toll bridge, near George III pub (see listing) just upstream of LL40 1YJ. Nice pool halfway to Fairbourne at Abergwynant (52.7395, -3.9702).

2 mins, 52.7484, -3.9328 🚴🚶

### 15 LLANGELYNIN BEACH & CHURCH

This wild beach is overlooked by the atmospheric 13th-century church of St Celynin, virtually unaltered since the early 1500s. The horse-bier hanging on its wall was once used to allow two horses to carry coffins long distances.

→ Park at layby and postbox on seaward side of A493, ⅓ mile S of LL37 2QL. Walk down into hamlet just to N. There is usually a path across the railway and down the cliffs to the boulder beach, but it depends on storm erosion.

5 mins, 52.6436, -4.1132 ⛪🏖️

LOST RUINS & CAVERNS

### 16 CASTELL Y BERE, ABERGYNOLWYN

Built for Llewellyn the Great in the 1220s, the castle fell to Edward I in 1283 and has remained a ruin ever since. Its position high up on a rocky promontory offers handsome views down the valley to Birds' Rock, and the extensive ruins are fun for children.

→ In Abergynolwyn, turn off B4405 at Railway Inn. After 1⅓ miles, signed R up dead end at staggered crossroads (dir LL36 9TS). Castle parking after ½ mile on L.

10 mins, 52.658, -3.9713 🏰🐾

### 17 DARREN SLATE QUARRY

Below the scarp of Tarren-y-Gesail, this slate quarry sits in the forested plantations of Esgair and is an adventure best suited for seasoned mine explorers, and best discovered by mountain bike due to the long walk in. Stocks of cut slate and ruined cutting sheds abound, and many impressive (wet) tunnels lead into deep pits. Bring the right kit and stay safe.

→ Unsigned turn off A487 just S of SY20 9AS leads to parking area at 52.6246, -3.8523. Then forest road (no vehicles) for 3 miles up valley. 60 mins, 52.6326, -3.8890 ⬛🥾🆅🚴

### 18 MINLLYN QUARRY & BRIDGE

A very ruinous slate quarry high in the hills. Look out for the mill, compressor house, workshops, weigh-houses and the drum house, with several tunnels and chambers for the properly equipped. Take a swim under the 17th-century packhorse bridge at Merion Mill afterwards.

→ Heading N to Dinas Mawddwy on A470, 30m after SY20 9LP, find layby and then 100m further footpath on L ¾ mile steep track up through woods. Bridge is at 52.7105, -3.6892. 30 mins, 52.7113, -3.6995 ⬛🥾♨️🆅

### 19 ABERCWMEIDDAW BINOCULARS

These double bore test tunnels, high on the quarry side, were cut by a machine patented by George Hunter in 1864. Beyond the pit, continue further up the main path to discover the manager's house ruins. Corris Mine Explorers is nearby and runs fantastic guided tours of nearby mines. There are also many remains and tunnels at the (reforested) site of Abercorris. The footpath up passes a quirky miniature recreation of the famous buildings of Italy!

→ About a mile N of King Arthur's Labyrinth A487 (SY20 9RF, home to Corris Mine Explorers 01650 511720/07721 043136), turn R 100m before SY20 9BW and Corris Uchaf. At T-junction, find wide double-gated track and park. Follow this up on a zigzag track to reach ruined dressing sheds. 200m further along is the main pit on R: descend then climb up to binoculars opp, or bear R and descend to bottom of pit for main tunnel. Abercorris at 52.6638, -3.8428 with Little Italy on footpath, 5 mins above SY20 9TT at 52.6581, -3.8484. 10 mins, 52.6666, -3.8555 🥾🆅⬛

### 20 ABERLLEFENNI & RATGOED QUARRIES

Only recently closed, this was one of the largest slate producers in the area. The great square hole in the mountainside is the top of Foel Crochan quarry, which descends vertically the entire height of the mountain. Peer down into it from the top of the vast, curved retaining wall that rises up the centre of the mountainside. Keen quarry explorers might walk up to Ratgoed (ruined chapel in the woods) or cycle to the more remote

Hendre-ddu. Or, for a safer experience, try King Arthur's Labyrinth, set in slate caverns, or join a trip with Corris Mine Explorers.

→ About 5 miles N from Machynlleth on A487, turn R signed Corris/Aberllefenni just before King Arthur's Labyrinth (SY20 9RF) on L. Continue just over 2 miles, taking L at millpond just after SY20 9RX. Find parking area on L after 400m with various buildings, at bottom of main incline with hut on R. Ascend from here. The area to NW of slag is all open access, and a footpath leads across the main level, but be discreet. Ratgoed ruins (52.6896, -3.8075) are a long walk in, and Hendre-ddu is lost in woods near Aberangell (52.6967, -3.7797); both best approached by mountain bike. 10 mins, 52.6769, -3.8212 🥾⬛🆅🚴

## HILL FORTS & CAIRNS

### 21 BIRDS' ROCK & RIVER DYSYNNI

This famous outcrop provides a fantastic vantage point down the valley, and in the Iron Age was fortified. It is famous for the cormorants that nest here – unusual as they are so far from the sea. The Dysynni river below is lovely for a swim.

→ As for Castell-y-Bere ruins (see listing) but at staggered crossroads turn L, to Llanllwyda

Farm (LL36 9TN, see listing) after a mile. Just beyond, park at layby and follow footpath L, bearing R uphill ½ mile. For the river, follow the footpath into the farm and L before the caravan field to the river. A deeper section is upstream (actually accessed from further up the caravan field). Or continue through caravan section and bear L to the beach.
30 mins, 52.6424, -4.0050 🖼️

### 22 CEFN HIR HILL FORT SCRAMBLE

Easy scramble to hill fort with views out south over Cregennen lakes and west to the estuary and sea.
→ Park as for Llynnau Cregennan (see listing) and walk back along lane from lake 300m to find footpath sign on R, leading to wall stile and then up ridge line.
20 mins, 52.7165, -3.9798 🖼️

## SLOW FOOD

### 23 T.H. ROBERTS

There are lots of good places to refuel in Dolgellau, but this lovely café has character, great food and excellent coffee. Housed in a tall, old pharmacy, with much left just as it was, home-made cakes of every kind spill off their plates, soups are hearty and there are maps, magazines and newspapers to browse.
→ Parliament House, Bridge St, Dolgellau, LL40 1BD, 01341 423573.
52.7432, -3.8854 🍴

### 24 TŶ TE CADER TEA ROOM

Fill up on home-made soups and cakes at this little cafè, ready for your ascent up the Minffordd Path to Cader Idris. Attached to the Cader Idris Vistor Centre, it was built with timber hauled from the surrounding woodland by heavy horses. Open Wed–Sun, daily in school holidays.
→ Minffordd, LL36 9AJ, 01654 761505.
52.6873, -3.8818 🍴

### 25 GWIN DYLANWAD WINE

A lovely wine merchant, wine bar and friendly café serving small plates. Open Tue–Wed 10am–6pm, Thur–Sat 10am–11pm.
→ Porth Marchnad, Dolgellau, LL40 1ET, 01341 422870.
52.7424, -3.8849 🍴

### 26 PROPER GANDER

Local seafood, meats, Welsh charcuterie and cheeses in a relaxed high-street bistro.
→ 4 High St, Tywyn, LL36 9AA, 01654 712169.
52.5869, -4.0877 🍴

### 27 HENNIGHAN'S TOP SHOP FISH & CHIPS

Queues down the street to any eatery are always a good sign, and this family run, MSC certified, award-winning fish and chip shop is the best for miles. Gluten-free batter also available.
→ 123 Heol Maengwyn, Machynlleth, SY20 8EF, 01654 702761.
52.5911, -3.8460 🍴

### 28 NUMBER TWENTY ONE, MACHYNLLETH

Delicious, beautifully served and sourced food makes this little bistro a favourite place for a light lunch or special dinner. The changing menus sing of the seasonal delicacies of land and sea, and the relaxed ambience adds to the gastronomical joy.
→ 21 Heol Maengwyn, Machynlleth SY20 8EB, 01654 703382.
52.5906, -3.8521 🍴

### 29 CAFFI'R CEUNANT

The changing menu of this much-loved no-frills café says it all; Clywedog trout, 'caught by Tommy', salad leaves from 'my garden' and fresh herbs from 'Marion's house next door'. Good home cooking using plenty of local produce.
→ Y Ganolfan Gymunedol, Abergynolwyn, LL36 9UU, 01654 782372.
52.6437, -3.95657 🍴

### 30 THE SALT MARSH KITCHEN

With a strong ethos of local, seasonal and sustainable, this bright, friendly bistro in Tywyn town serves excellent seafood and much, much more. Large range of real ales, good wines and wonderful service.
→ 9 College Green, Tywyn, LL36 9BS, 01654 711949.
52.5873, -4.0862 🍴

### 31 ANDY & ADAM'S, IDRIS STORES

A fantastic café/deli serving warming bowls of vegetable chilli, home-reared pulled pork, soups and salads and excellent coffee. Sadly for sale at the time of writing, but we hope its excellence will continue.
→ Bridge St, Corris, SY20 9SP, 01654 761391.
52.6545, -3.8420 🍴

### 32 SEABREEZE RESTAURANT, ABERDYFI

Right on Aberdovey's main front, this simple restaurant with rooms is a wonderful celebration of fresh and local fish. Dyfi crab is served with house sourdough, fish and chips are light and fresh, the home-made chips just perfect. Try dry-aged Welsh black rib-eye or see the catch of the day for a selection of freshly caught treats from the harbour. Pick up fresh caught fish and shellfish to take home from Dai's Shed on the harbour.

→ 6 Bodfor Terrace, Aberdovey, LL35 0EA, 01654 767449.
52.5440, -4.0478 🍴

### 33 CAFFI CAMLAN

Lovely café in this garden centre and craft shop, serving locally sourced and home-made products.

→ Dinas Mawddwy, SY20 9LN, 01650 531685.
52.7124, -3.6912 🍴

## PUBS & ALES

### 34 CROSS FOXES

This award-winning, bright and modern dining pub sits on the busy road at the foot of Cadair Idris. Potted laver cockles, Welsh sirloin steaks, local venison and super-food salads packed with kale and blueberries revive tired walkers and drivers alike. Sit on the sun terrace, in the conservatory or in the garden overlooking the stream.

→ Brithdir, Dolgellau, LL40 2SG, 01341 421001.
52.7337, -3.8282 🍴

### 35 TAFARN DWYNANT

A quirky, friendly pub with art gallery and jukebox, serving home-made locally sourced burgers and chickpea and spinach stews. Closed Mon & Tues. Food served Thur–Sun evenings.

→ Ceinws, Machynlleth, SY20 9HA, 01654 761660.
52.6371, -3.8347 🍴

### 36 WYNNSTAY ARMS HOTEL

Welsh real ales, superb pizzas and delicious locally sourced pub food at this large (but still cosy), eclectic hotel and restaurant on Mach's main street.

→ Heol Maengwyn, Machynlleth, SY20 8AE, 01654 702941.
52.5904, -3.8528 🍴🛏

### 37 THE BLACK LION INN

Cosy traditional Welsh pub with log fires, cask ales and hearty plates of pub grub.

→ Derwenlas, SY20 8TN, 01654 703913.
theblacklion-machynlleth.co.uk
52.5743, -3.8892 🛏🛍

### 38 DOVEY VALLEY HOTEL

A rare and historic parlour-style inn. A little like having a drink in someone's front room.

Loads of character, very good beer and music, opens about 5pm; has rooms.

→ Cemmaes Road, SY20 8JZ, 01650 511335.
52.6241, -3.7448 🛏🛍

### 39 GEORGE III HOTEL

Enjoy wild boar sausages, dressed crab and bubble-and-squeak in this characterful pub with rooms overlooking the Mawdach estuary and the wooden bridge.

→ Penmaenpool, LL40 1YD, 01341 422525.
52.7479, -3.9360 🍴🛏🛍

### 40 THE RED LION, DINAS MAWDDWY

Traditional Welsh pub with rooms owned and run by mother and son, with open fires, real ales and home-cooked food. The name on the front is in Welsh – Gwesty'r Llew Coch.

→ Dinas Mawddwy, SY20 9JA, 01650 531247.
52.7188, -3.6904 🛏🛍

## WILDER CAMPING

### 41 GRAIG WEN

Incredible estuary and mountain views from this well managed campsite with yurts, cabins and B&B. Bring your tent and you can camp in the estuary fields nearest the magnificent Mawddach. Campervans and tourers must camp nearer the road.

→ Arthog, LL39 1YP, 01341 250482.
52.7223, -3.9939 📷🚻🛍

### 42 PANT Y CAE CAMPING

Relaxed streamside camping on an organic family farm just below Llynnau Cregennen (see listing ). Cottage also available.

→ Arthog, LL39 1LJ, 01341 250892.
52.7146, -3.9971 🏕🛍

### 43 HAFOD DYWYLL CAMPSITE

Wake up to the sounds of the dawn chorus at this simple campfire campsite by a small river in a sheltered, wooded glade rich with wildlife. YHA Kings is very close by.

→ Islaw'r-dref, LL40 1TR, 01341 423444.
52.7253, -3.9488 🔥🏕🚻

### 44 ECO RETREATS GLAMPING

In meadow glades hidden amid the wooded wilds north of Mach is a selection of furnished tipis and yurts offering complete off-grid seclusion, starry skies and magical woodland living.

→ Way beyond postcodes, 7 miles NE of Machynlleth , 07962 186563
52.6600, -3.7776 🔥🚻🏕

### 45 CAE DU CAMPSITE

Camp metres from the beach and revel in sea views, sunsets and campfires. This is traditional family camping – and indeed the site has been open since the 1930s. Beware of windy days, but if it's sunny and calm expect dolphins, cricket on the beach and some very good rockpooling.

→ Rhoslefain, LL36 9ND, 01654 711234.
52.6316, -4.1194 🛇 ◪ ⛵

### 46 SMUGGLERS COVE BOATYARD

Right on the bank of Dyfi estuary and looking south over the sparkling waters to the mountains beyond is this quirky campsite on a working boatyard, with space for three lucky tents.

→ Fron-gôch, Aberdovey LL35 0RG, 01654 767842.
52.5566, -3.9735 🛇 ◪ ⛺

### 47 Y FELIN GREEN HOLIDAYS

Idyllic riverside camping for up to four tents, plus a kitted-out caravan on a wildlife-rich permaculture farm. Buy organic vegetables and honey from their beehives, take a dip in their pond and sit around your campfire.

→ Melinbyrhedyn, SY20 8SJ, 01654 702718.
52.5733, -3.7475 🛇 ◪ ❀

### 48 BWLCHGWYN FARM CAMPSITE

Stunning sunsets and estuary and mountain views, flat grass pitches and hot showers. Particularly good for caravans and tourers – just ignore the static caravans! The working farm also runs pony trekking and gallops along the beach.

→ Fairbourne, LL39 1BX, 01341 250107.
52.7002, -4.0375 ◪

### 49 LLANLLWYDA FARM CAMPSITE

Peaceful, small riverside campsite on a working farm, with views of Cadair Idris and great wild swimming.

→ LLanfihangel-y-pennant, Abergynolwyn, LL36 9TN, 01654 782276.
52.6517, -3.9973 ⛺

### 50 GWALIA FARM CABIN & CAMPING

Rent this cabin in the woods overlooking the lake, and take a jump from the jetty after soaking and stargazing in the wood-fired hot-tub. Wilder secluded camping pitches for tents also available. Sadly no kids.

→ Cemmaes, SY20 9PZ, 01650 511377.
52.6289, -3.6934 ⛺ 🏕

### 51 GWERNAN HOTEL

If you're coming down the Fox's Path from Cadair Idris, this cosy little hotel on Llyn Gwernan is a truly welcoming sight. Restaurant open to guests only.

→ Islaw'r-dref, Dolgellau, LL40 1TL, 01341 422488.
52.7252, -3.9201 🍴 🏕

### 52 NANTCAW FAWR FARM

Secluded stone farmhouse at the foot of Cader Idris in the stunning Dysynni valley. Sleeps seven.

→ LLanfihangel-y-pennant, Abergynolwyn, LL36 9TR, 01654 782286.
52.6653, -3.9920 🏕

### 53 LIVING-ROOM TREEHOUSES

There is something so magical about a treehouse, and these six unique, high-up hideaways make life in the branches cosy, with woodburners, spring-water showers and compost loos. Constantly booked up, so you'll need to plan ahead.

→ Brynmeurig, Machynlleth SY20 9PY, 01650 511900.
52.6339, -3.7048 🏕

### 54 GWYLIAU BEUDY BANC

Stylish hideaways in the stunning Dyfi valley. Choose from the big eco-barn sleeping eight, mini-cabins for two, or bell tents, or pitch your own tent in the meadow. Every detail is done with humour and with respect for the environment.

→ Cwmllywi Uchaf, Abercegir, SY20 8NP, 01650 511495.
52.6090, -3.7611 🏕 ⛺ 🛇

### 55 CAE EINION, GALLESTRA

A cosy and utterly charming stone farmhouse sleeping four in two double rooms. Remote and with stunning views of Cader Idris.

→ Islaw'r-dref, LL40 1TR, 0844 5005101.
undertherthatch.co.uk
52.7253, -3.9577 🏕

### 56 AFON GELLI FARMHOUSE

If I were to draw the perfect Snowdonia farmstead, this would be it: a stone farmhouse (Afon Gelli) and barn (Little Gelli), open fires, four-poster beds, and no TV or phone to distract from the sweeping valley views, misty mountains, mossy woods, streams and starlight beyond the porch.

→ Cwm Cywarch, Dinas Mawddwy, SY20 9JG, 0844 500 5101. underthethatch.co.uk
52.7505, -3.7032 🏠🏕️🛶

## 57 MOUNTAIN TOP GYPSY CARAVAN

On a small holding high in the hills, is the home of friends Jony and Pippa, artists who have hand-built this beautiful traditional bowtop gypsy caravan. It sits overlooking a stunning rolling mountainscape, quiet but for the birdsong. Enjoy a woodfired sauna and take a dip in the plunge pool.

→ Penrallt, Melinbyrhedyn, Machynlleth, SY20 8UP. airbnb.co.uk
52.5774, -3.7520 🛶🏔️

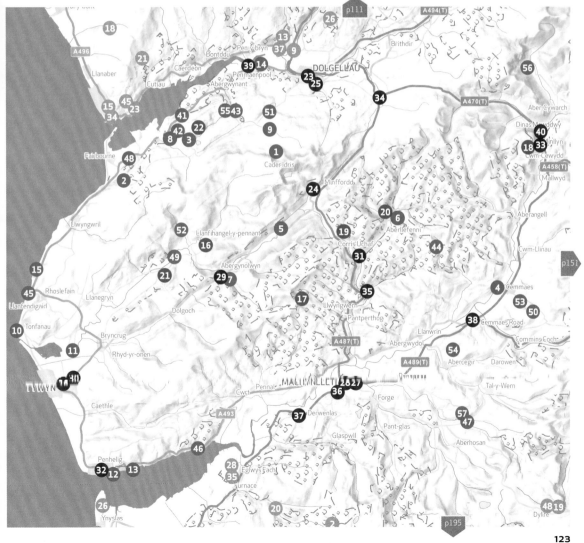

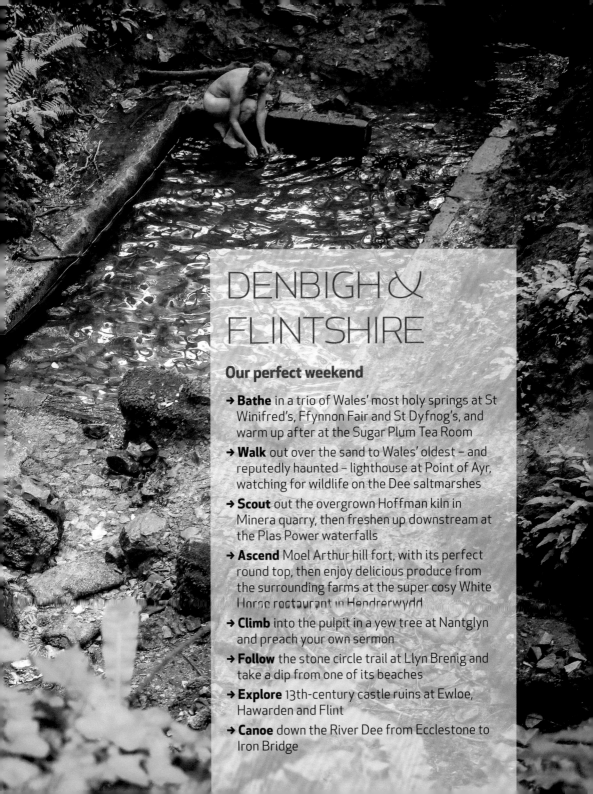

# DENBIGH & FLINTSHIRE

## Our perfect weekend

→ **Bathe** in a trio of Wales' most holy springs at St Winifred's, Ffynnon Fair and St Dyfnog's, and warm up after at the Sugar Plum Tea Room

→ **Walk** out over the sand to Wales' oldest – and reputedly haunted – lighthouse at Point of Ayr, watching for wildlife on the Dee saltmarshes

→ **Scout** out the overgrown Hoffman kiln in Minera quarry, then freshen up downstream at the Plas Power waterfalls

→ **Ascend** Moel Arthur hill fort, with its perfect round top, then enjoy delicious produce from the surrounding farms at the super cosy White Horse restaurant in Hendrerwydd

→ **Climb** into the pulpit in a yew tree at Nantglyn and preach your own sermon

→ **Follow** the stone circle trail at Llyn Brenig and take a dip from one of its beaches

→ **Explore** 13th-century castle ruins at Ewloe, Hawarden and Flint

→ **Canoe** down the River Dee from Ecclestone to Iron Bridge

**Many tourists zoom through north-east Wales without stopping, heading for the high peaks of Snowdonia. But this area has its own mountains and many intriguing sites that are part of the rich tapestry of Welsh history.**

The Clwydian Range has views galore and a string of impressive hill forts such as Moel Arthur, plus some excellent pubs. Further south you'll find some of the best limestone pavement in Wales at Bryn Alyn, and the relics of some of the industries built on that stone, including the remains of a great underground multi-chamber Hoffman Kiln at the old Minera limestone quarry. Further down the Clywedog valley at Plas Power are lead mines, a wooded glen and old ironworks, important remnants of the industrial revolution.

Along the coast there are several castles from much earlier periods, including Flint which was the first castle built in 1277 by Edward I as part of his 'Iron Ring' of fortresses. Other lesser-known castles nearby include Hawarden and Ewloe, both hidden in woodland. There is even a great Victorian pastiche castle, Gwrych Castle, whose derelict 'battlements' stretch along the hill looking out to sea.

Even greater antiquity is found at Bontnewydd caves, where the oldest Neanderthal remains in Britain, from over 220,000 years ago, were found. There are other ancient cave shelters at Gop, and above Llyn Brenig a series of well-preserved cairns and stone circles remind us of the spiritual life of the Bronze Age.

Indeed the area is well endowed with holy sites, particularly wells. St Winifred's Well, the 'Lourdes of Wales', has been attracting pilgrims for some 1,300 years and the 16th century chapel is exquisite. Ffynnon Fair used to attract almost as many visitors, and its beautiful octagonal star-shaped bath may be an homage to St Winifred's, but is now off the beaten track and sadly overgrown and neglected. There is also a wilder well to bathe in at St Dyfnog.

You can rent the medieval manor of Dolbelydr and spend evenings staring into an inglenook fire or feasting on local meats and cheeses on the long table. Or better still, head to one of the area's lovely pubs, such as The White Horse Restaurant in the far-from-anywhere-hamlet of Hendrerwydd, and dine on first-class seasonal food cooked with love.

## RIVERS

### 1 TWT HILL & CLWYD, RHUDDLAN CASTLE

There are fine views of 13th-century
Rhuddlan Castle from Twt Hill motte, the
upstream site of the original castle, built in
1087. Below is the river Clwyd – ships once
sailed all the way here to supply the castle
from the sea.

→ From Rhuddlan Castle car park (opp LL18
5AD) follow Hylas Lane and take footpath
forking R at bend, which leads towards the
river bank and up to Twt Hill.

5 mins, 53.2869, -3.4618

### 2 RIVER DEE, ECCLESTONE

Convenient riverside car park from which to
reach the water for swimming or canoeing.
Footpath heads both up and downstream,
but upstream leads to the beautiful Crook of
Dee meander.

→ From Ecclestone take Paddock Rd dir CH4
9JE, following L past gates to ferry parking at
end of road.

10 mins, 53.1534, -2.8760

### 3 IRON BRIDGE, RIVER DEE

This is undoubtedly one of the finest
remaining examples of a Thomas Telford
cast-iron bridge. Spanning a wide, bucolic
stretch of the river Dee, with footpaths up
and downstream.

→ In Aldford (CH3 6HX), park at church side
entrance and take footpath through white
gates and across fields down to woods and
river bridge, ½ mile.

10 mins, 53.1349, -2.8711

## LAKES

### 4 STRYT-ISAF LAKE

An old sand-and-gravel pit lake, good for a
discreet dip on a hot day.

→ From Hope, take Stryt Isa by the Red Lion
pub. Continue on 1 mile N (½ mile beyond
LL12 9PU) to reach a footpath and gate on
L, across railway, leading to lake shore. Park
responsibly.

5 mins, 53.1311, -3.0498

### 5 BOD PETRYAL POOL

Large woodland lake with trails, perfect for a
dip and very easy to get to.

→ Follow B5105 from Clawdd-newydd W.
After 3 miles take L signed Melin-y-wig before
LL21 9PR. Forestry car park is on R.

3 mins, 53.0477, -3.4373

## 6 LLYN BRENIG & BONCYN ARIAN

Remote, expansive reservoir with beaches,
fishing, bicycle hire, and an archaeology
trail leading past several stone circles. The
most impressive is Brenig 51, a 22m Bronze
Age platform cairn on a plateau overlooking
the lake. An adult and child were buried
around 1700 BC beneath the stone platform
that surrounds the perfect inner circle of
26 small stones. Near the dam there is an
exhibition/visitor centre with café, showing
some of the finds from the excavation. A
good place to see otters, osprey and red
squirrels too.

→ Signed off the remote B4501, about 1 mile
SW from LL16 5RN. Pay parking. Head for the
archaeology trail, NE corner. Brenig 51 is on
the 440m contour, head ½ mile S on shore
footpath, then climb E to 53.0966, -3.5102.

10 mins, 53.1042, -3.5199

## WATERFALLS

### 7 DYSERTH WATERFALL

An impressive waterfall, ravine and plunge
pool in the middle of a little village. The path
passes between massive walls, probably
for a mill wheel, and leads up to a woodland
walk. Put 50p in the box.

→ In Dyserth village centre (with small shop, pub and gardens), signed opp LL18 6ET.
2 mins, 53.3021, -3.4165

### 8 PLAS POWER FALLS, CLYWEDOG

The weirs along the Clywedog supplied power for the many important surrounding ironworks and corn mills. The sylvan valley trail through damp woods is a botanists' dream, and you'll also find one of the best-preserved sections of Offa's Dyke.

→ From Bersham old ironworks, LL14 4LL, head W 250m past St Mary's church to find horseshoe weir on R (53.0371, -3.0393). Park here. Take a dip and follow river upstream on far bank to the more impressive waterfall weir, ½ mile further along the Clywedog Trail. Offa's Dyke crosses river here. Another mile upstream leads to Nant Mill country park and visitor centre (53.0434, -3.0620). Further upstream are the Minera Lead Mines and country park. Downstream you can explore more of the Clywedog at the Erddig country park, S of Wrexham.
10 mins, 53.0381, -3.0487

### RUINS & FOLLIES

### 9 GWRYCH CASTLE, ABERGELE

With a 300m façade, this elaborate castle was mostly built in the 1820s by wealthy industrialist Lloyd Hesketh Bamford-Hesketh, and was his family home for a century, with a few extensions along the way. It was left to George V in 1924, but he refused it, and after changing hands several times it fell derelict in the late 20th century. It is now being restored, starting with the garden and the Gardener's Tower, by the Gwrych Trust, who organise self-guided tours (gardens), and events and guided tours (the only way to enter the buildings).

→ Gwrych Castle Woods, which adjoins the castle, is open access. A rough path leads in up over the low wall opp the end of Clipterfyn (LL22 8EH). Or pay £5 for self-guided access to grounds, book a guided tour for £15, or attend an event (gwrychtrust.co.uk).
25 mins, 53.2832, -3.6089

### 10 FLINT CASTLE

The first castle, started in 1277, of what would later become known as Edward I's 'Iron Ring' encircling conquered Wales. In a commanding position over the sand flats (and now the industrial parks) of the Dee

13

estuary, it is a fine place for sunsets and coastal wandering. The estuary once ran right up to the slopes of the castle's bailey to form the moat. The corner-tower keep, or donjon, is a French design unique in Britain; look out for the scratches of mason's marks on stone blocks throughout.

→ From Chester St/A548 in Flint, follow Castle Dyke St to shore dir CH6 5PE and park on street or in car park. Free entry, open access.
2 mins, 53.2515, -3.1302 ▣

## 11 HAWARDEN MILL, ESTATE & OLD CASTLE

The remains of a corn mill, with giant iron gears and wheels littered around. On open days in summer you can also visit the ruins of the old castle, a 13th-century stone keep on a motte, where the final Welsh conflict with Edward I began in 1282. They are in the private estate of 'new' Hawarden Castle, home of William Gladstone. The parkland has many ancient trees.

→ From Gladstone memorial fountain in Hawarden, at crossroads S of CH5 3NN, take A550 (dir Wrexham) and find car park on L after 100m. Bear SE on footpath – mill is to R after 100m. The old castle ruins are at 53.1809, -3.0197 (hawardenestate.co.uk).
5 mins, 53.1823, -3.0256 ▣ ⬤ ⛰

## 12 EWLOE CASTLE & WOODS

Climb to the top level of these native Welsh 13th-century ruins, romantically situated in Wepre Park woodland.

→ On B5125 heading NW from Ewloe, find field gate and parking layby R just after CH5 3BZ (opp the kennels). Follow signed footpath 300m across field and into woods.
5 mins, 53.1999, -3.0668 ▣ ⬤ ↪

## 13 MINERA HOFFMAN KILN

This vast limestone quarry, distinct from the lead mine of the same name, was once the largest in Wales. It has towering cliffs, woodland ruins and the spooky remains of an underground Hoffman kiln, built in 1868. There are 24 chambers around a central chimney, each capable of holding 120 tons of limestone, which was burned sequentially with the fuel fed from above.

→ From B5426 in Minera take Church Rd dir Gwynfryn, then L after ½ mile onto Maes-y-Ffynnon road, and continue past LL11 3DE to park at road end barrier. Continue along track, with stream to L, and after 200m bear into woods L to find ruins. These lead through to the Hoffman kiln, a raised area beyond.
10 mins, 53.0595, -3.1108 ▣ ↪

11

12

### 14 DENBIGH MENTAL ASYLUM

On every ghost hunter's bucket list, it's extraordinary that this massive Victorian building still lies empty and derelict. Private, but can be viewed from gates and boundary.

→ Main gates at LL16 5SR, ½ mile S of Denbigh castle (LL16 3NB, an easier ruin to visit). Or a footpath runs around edge of site from beside the entrance gate of the quirky Cae Dai 1950s Museum (01745 817004) on bend near LL16 4ST (53.1754, -3.4255), emerging 400m S of hospital entrance gates.
1 mins, 53.1754, -3.4189 🚫❓

## SACRED & ANCIENT

### 15 BONTNEWYDD CAVE

Some of the oldest Neanderthal remains in Britain, dating back to 230,000 BC, were found here. In limestone cliffs above the lane, the cave has now been walled-up but the door is sometimes open and you can look through the window. Nice pool beneath river bridge further down lane.

→ Start as for Fynnon Fair well (see listing), but continue just over a mile past footpath turn. Turn L at cottage with central chimney and continue another mile. Downhill, 300m before LL17 0HD, cave is visible through trees above road on R; path in is a little further back. Find another cave at 53.2288, -3.4913 a mile beyond. No parking at caves, park responsibly.
2 mins, 53.2272, -3.4762 🚶‍♂️🏊‍♂️🚲

### 16 GOP CAVE & MOUND

Enjoy panoramic views from the second highest Neolithic man-made mound in Britain after Silbury Hill, built about 4000–3000 BC atop Gop Hill. Its purpose remains unknown, but possibly it was built as a lookout or hill fort. Below is a cave used as a burial place throughout much of the Neolithic.

→ From A5151 E of Dyserth, in Trelawnyd, turn up High St next to church, signed Llanasa (LL18 6DT) and park. After 150m find footpath / driveway on L just after Bron Haul. Follow path across open land about 450m; cave is 120m up on R. Path circles hill and comes back to road above village, with path in to summit at 53.3107, -3.3659.
10 mins, 53.3099, -3.3732 🚶‍♂️📷🚲

### 17 ST WINIFRED'S CHAPEL & WELL

The 'Lourdes of Wales', where in the 7th century St Winifred is said to have been beheaded by a spurned nobleman and restored to life by her uncle St Bueno – the well sprang up where her head rolled to a stop. The well is mentioned in Sir Gawain

and the Green Knight, and the exquisite chapel was built over it in the early 16th century. Bathe in the waters – many healing miracles are claimed here – and gaze up at the beautifully carved ceiling, cleaned and conserved in recent years.

→ On B5121/Greenfield Street, in Holywell, just S of CH8 7PN, with layby parking on the road. Entrance £1, bathing at 10–11am and 2.30–3.30pm, not Sundays (01352 713054).
2 mins, 53.2773, -3.2238 ⛪🏊‍♂️

### 18 ST DYFNOG'S WELL

Steps lead down into this sacred pool, a short woodland walk behind the church (which has a Jesse window, saved from Cromwellian destruction by being buried during his rule). Beware, the water is freezing – legend has it the saint's penance was to stand in it!

→ Off A525, the church is opp the King's Head, Llanrhaeadr, LL16 4NL. At the back L of the graveyard a path leads up the stream 300m.
5 mins, 53.1592, -3.3778 ⛪🏊‍♂️🚶‍♂️

### 19 FFYNNON FAIR WELL & CHAPEL

A ruined chapel, probably dating back to the 15th century, and an ornate hexagonal well-basin of similar design to St Winifred's (see listing). Hidden in the woods and now sadly overgrown, this was once a much-visited shrine, but the ancient riverside footpath, used for centuries, is now contested.

→ Leave Nant-y-Patrick on B5381, then 2nd L after a mile, after river, dir LL17 0ET. After ½ mile turn L down track (signed footpath) and park immediately. Continue down past houses, over gate and along river to the site in woods at end of field. Or, to be more discreet, walk up hill along road then bear L into woods on any track, staying in woods about ¼ mile, dropping to chapel.
15 mins, 53.2278, -3.4557 ⛪❓

## HILLTOPS & EASY PEAKS

### 20 MOEL ARTHUR HILL FORT

The Clwydian Range has many Iron Age hill forts, linked together by Offa's Dyke. Built around 500 BC, Moel Arthur is perfectly domed, and a very easy little climb from the car park below. Although it is a small hill fort, it boasts some of the largest banks, ditches and ramparts in the area. Penycloddiau hill fort to the north is one of the largest, enclosing a 50 acre settlement. Foel Fenlli, to the south, is easily accessible.

→ From B5429 in Llandyrnog take Gladstone Terrace and follow lanes 3 miles E, a mile

(23)

beyond LL16 4NB, to car park. Penycloddiau is at 53.1989, -3.3074, car park 1 mile E of LL16 4NA. Foel Fenlli is at 53.1312, -3.2524, Moel Famau car park is 1¼ miles W of CH7 5SH.
15 mins, 53.1851, -3.2809 🔲🐾

### 21 BRYN ALYN LIMESTONE PAVEMENTS
Super little peak, with some of the most extensive limestone pavement in Wales. Much less busy than Moel Famau, but with great views. There's also a cave nearby to explore.
→ From A494 ¾ mile S of Llanferres take L signed B5430 Llanarmon-yn-Ial, then L at cross roads by postbox (sign Bryn Difyr cattery). Continue 200m past cattery (CH7 5TG) to find footpath on R and parking for one car, opp farm. Cave is in Dig Covert woods at 53.1361, -3.2002 about a mile N of the lane.
20 mins, 53.1209, -3.2011 🔲🐾🕳️

### 22 GARREG HILL TOWER & CROSS
A mysterious 17th-century tower – maybe a beacon watchtower, possibly a windmill – restored as a folly in 1897, with good views in a clearing on a hill. Also visit the very fine 10th-century Maen Achwyfan cross, with Viking-influenced carvings.
→ In small lanes a mile W of Whitford, park near CH8 9DD for the cross, which stands in a field (53.2986, -3.3086) with a sign and gate. Then take lane slightly S signed Whitford, with windowless stone building on corner, and find footpath on R. Climb ½ mile to woods, then turn L to summit.
15 mins, 53.2943, -3.3013 🔲🐾

(20)

## ANCIENT FORESTS & TREES

### 23 NANTGLYN PULPIT YEW
A stone pulpit and steps have been built into this yew's hollow trunk. John Wesley, the founder of Methodism, is said to have preached from here.
→ Nantglyn is 3 miles SW of Denbigh, and St. James Church is just N of LL16 5PL.
1 min, 53.1469, -3.4903 🔲✝️

### 24 COED CILYGROESLWYD
Small 'wood of the grey cross' is particularly glorious in spring and summer, when wild daffodils, bluebells, orchids and rare wildflowers unfurl. It's also an important place for the ancient yews that grow on the limestone pavement.
→ A494, 2 miles S of Ruthin, turn dir Llanfair/ LL15 2EG, limited parking over bridge. Footpath entrance is back over bridge, opp turning.
5 mins, 53.0875 -3.3065 🔲🐾

(22)

### 25 CYFYLLIOG YEWS & WATERFALL

Four ancient yews, at least one of which is older than the 12th-century village church of St Mary's. Upstream is a small waterfall pool with rope swing.

→ Village is 5 miles W of Ruthin, church opp LL15 2DW. 100m on footpath on R leads upstream to falls (also viewable from the lane).
5 mins, 53.1093, -3.4071 🍴🅿️♿🚌🍴🐾

## WILDLIFE

### 26 POINT OF AYR RESERVE

See thousands of birds on the saltmarshes of the Dee Estuary. Oystercatchers, curlews, skylarks, avocets, greenshanks, hobbies and peregrines all come to feed, flock or breed in this rich habitat. Look out for Wales' oldest lighthouse – said to be haunted. Beach café near the car park.

→ Car park at the end of Station Rd, Talacre (beyond CH8 9RP turning). Walk SE to the saltmarshes or N to the beach and lighthouse.
10 mins, 53.3532, -3.3166 🚌🍴

### 27 RHYDYMWYN VALLEY

This 35-hectare site in the Alyn Valley has been used by a variety of industries since the 1700s, but during the Second World War it was known as the 'Ministry of Supply Factory Valley', and used by the government for assembly of mustard gas shells and atomic weapons research. Many of the buildings and tunnels still survive and the whole area is now a richly diverse wildlife reserve (birds, fungi, butterflies, mammals) with restricted access.

→ Visitor centre entrance is on Nant Alwyn Rd, Rhydymwyn, CH7 5HQ. Check newwildlife.org.uk for more information on public events.
10 mins, 53.1924, -3.1919 🚗🅿️

## SLOW FOOD

### 28 THE SUGAR PLUM TEA ROOM

Tucked away in Homewood Bound vintage homewares store, this vintage-styled tearoom with tin lights and painted furniture serves excellent coffee, rarebits, cream teas and salads. Mon–Sat 9.30–4.30pm, Sun 10–4.

→ The Old Station, Rhewl, LL15 1TN, 01824 702852.
53.1340, -3.3285 🍴

### 29 THE MACHINE HOUSE

Tasting menus, set menus or à la carte – good food, sourced locally, cooked respectfully and presented beautifully, and always with a spot-on wine suggestion.

→ Chester Rd, Rossett, LL12 0HW, 01244 571678.
53.1085, -2.9465 🍴

### 30 HAWARDEN ESTATE FARM SHOP

The funky décor is a refreshing break from the usual aisles of chutneys and fake 'country-kitchen style' cafés. Much of the meat, vegetables and fruit comes from the estate. Pick your own fruit when in season, buy artisan cheeses, breads and eggs or sit in the buzzing café.

→ Chester Rd, Hawarden, CH5 3FB, 01244 533442.
53.1801, -3.0119 🍴

### 31 SWAN'S FARM SHOP

An award-winning farm shop selling free-range beef, pork and chicken raised on their Flintshire farm, alongside local honey, ice cream, pies and cakes.

→ Treuddyn, Mold, CH7 4LE, 01352 770088.
53.1129, -3.1135 🍴

## COSY PUBS

### 32 THE WHITE HORSE, HENDRERWYDD

Enjoy excellent food using seasonal Welsh produce, much of it from the surrounding farms, in this cosy 16th-century pub with leather armchairs, wooden pews and passionate foodie owners.

→ Hendrerwydd, , LL16 4LL, 01824 790218.
53.1609, -3.3155 🍴🍺

### 33 THE WHITE HORSE HOTEL / INN

Gastropub food in a friendly village free house. Open 5–11pm on Wed–Sat, and Sundays for lunch.

→ Llandyrnog, Denbigh, LL16 4HG, 01824 790582.
53.1759, -3.3364 🍴

### 34 KINMEL ARMS

Food using great local produce is presented like art here at this excellent country pub with rooms.

→ St George, Abergele, LL22 9BP, 01745 832207.
53.2688, -3.5394 🍴🛏️

### 35 THE BLUE BELL, HALKYN

CAMRA cider pub of the year in 2017. An independent pub with post office, live music, and real fires.

→ Rhosesmor Rd, Halkyn, CH8 8DL, 01352 780309.
53.2241, -3.1857 🍺

## 36 THE PANT-YR-OCHRAIN

A huge rural pub with lots of room, fires and a large garden, matched by a large and consistently good pub-food menu.

→ Old Wrexham Rd, Gresford, LL12 8TY, 01978 853525.
53.0731, -2.9786 🍴

## 37 THE FOX, YSCEIFIOG

Traditional friendly village pub serving real ales and home-cooked food beside real fires.

→ Ysceifiog, Holywell, CH8 8NJ, 01352 720241.
53.2342, -3.2725 🍴

## 38 SPORTSMANS ARMS & RUIN

Up in the Denbigh Hills is the highest pub in Wales. Very remote and not much to look at outside, but inside out of the wind you'll find a friendly atmosphere with live music, parties, pub grub and log fires. Above is Gwylfa Hiraethog, once the highest inhabited house in Wales, now a forboding ruin.

→ Bylchau, Denbigh LL16 5SW. 07825 630214. Head up footpath and turn L to the ruin, about ½ mile. 53.1184, -3.5745
53.1184, -3.5666 🏕🔺

## 39 RAVEN INN, CASTLE & CAVE

Friendly community-run village pub with outdoor seating overlooking the church. Much here is locally produced, including the real ales. The village also has a 12th-century castle mound by the bridge on the river Alyn, and an intriguing cave on the hillside through gate opposite, and over a field. Fish & chip night Fridays. Closed Mondays.

→ Ffordd Rhiw Ial, Llanarmon-yn-Ial, CH7 4QE, 01824 780833.
53.0970, -3.2104 🍴🥾

## 40 THE ROYAL OAK

Just reopened at the time of writing, we can only hope this friendly village pub with real fires and real ales continues to thrive. Early reports are promising.

→ Kinnerton Ln, Higher Kinnerton, CH4 9BE, 01244 660871.
53.1475, -3.0006 🍴

RUSTIC HAVENS

## 41 DOLBELYDR

This 16th-century stone manor house with inglenooks, exposed beams and slate floors sleeps six. It is surrounded by quiet farmland near the River Elwy, and the name translates as 'meadow of the sunbeams'. Managed by the Landmark Trust.

→ Trefnant, LL16 5AG, 01628 825925.
53.2267, -3.4529 🛏

## 42 MORGANS BED & BREAKFAST

A lovely B&B with views and delicious breakfasts, made by Kate using local eggs and meat, and their own garden-grown veg.

→ 2 Penllan Cottages, Axton, CH8 9DH, 01745 570981.
53.3125, -3.3489 🛏

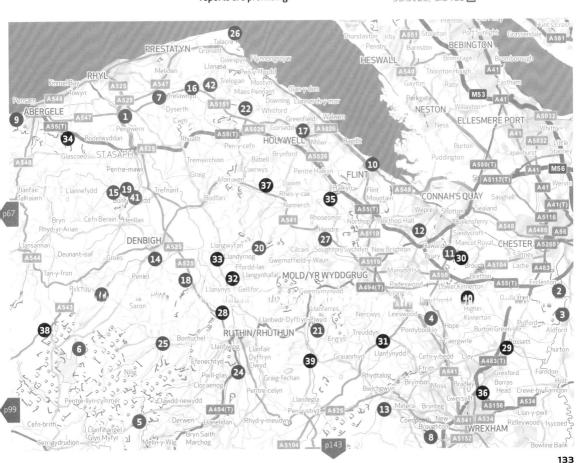

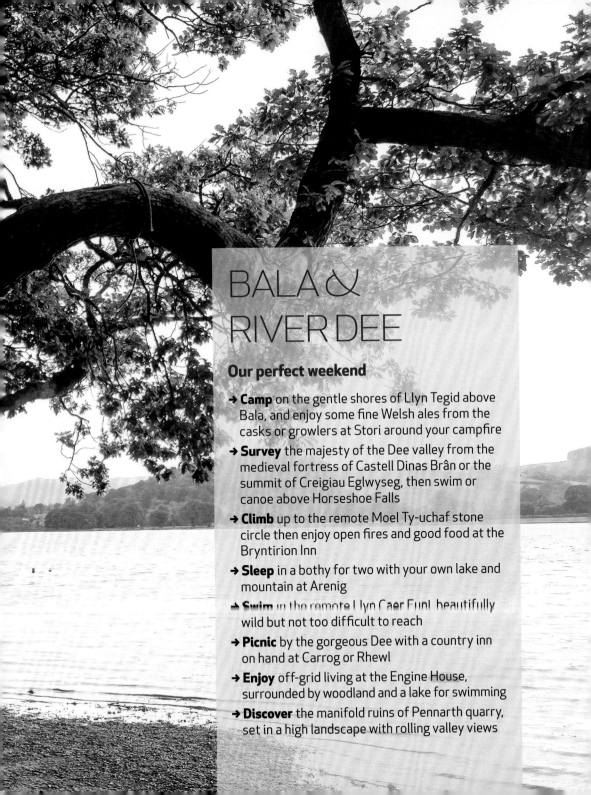

# BALA &
# RIVER DEE

## Our perfect weekend

→ **Camp** on the gentle shores of Llyn Tegid above
Bala, and enjoy some fine Welsh ales from the
casks or growlers at Stori around your campfire

→ **Survey** the majesty of the Dee valley from the
medieval fortress of Castell Dinas Brân or the
summit of Creigiau Eglwyseg, then swim or
canoe above Horseshoe Falls

→ **Climb** up to the remote Moel Ty-uchaf stone
circle then enjoy open fires and good food at the
Bryntirion Inn

→ **Sleep** in a bothy for two with your own lake and
mountain at Arenig

→ **Swim** in the remote Llyn Caer Euni, beautifully
wild but not too difficult to reach

→ **Picnic** by the gorgeous Dee with a country inn
on hand at Carrog or Rhewl

→ **Enjoy** off-grid living at the Engine House,
surrounded by woodland and a lake for swimming

→ **Discover** the manifold ruins of Pennarth quarry,
set in a high landscape with rolling valley views

**The Dee is not the longest river in Wales, but is perhaps its most iconic, shaping the historic boundary of the mountain kingdom of Gwynedd. At its headwater is the well-named 'fair lake', Llyn Tegid (Bala to the English).**

Famously deep and clear, this was the largest natural lake in Wales even before Thomas Telford raised its level. It makes a tranquil oasis for swimming and boating, blessed by a backdrop of mountains and a shoreline of shingle beaches dotted with ancient trees. Tegid is also rich in legends, including the lost palace of the enchantress Ceridwen, said to light up beneath the waters on a moonlit night.

Llyn Celyn, to the north, also laps over a sunken village, but this one is all too real. The controversial reservoir, started in the 1950s, obliterated the village of Capel Celyn, a stronghold of Welsh language and culture. Liverpool City Council needed the water supply but knew they wouldn't get permission from the Welsh authorities, so brought a private member's bill to Westminster to bypass Welsh involvement. Years of angry protests and political dissent followed, fuelling the growth of Plaid Cymru and ultimately Welsh devolution. Today, scheduled water releases make the Tryweryn below one of the most reliable rivers for white-water rafting and kayaking in the UK.

From Bala, the Dee flows though a fine fertile valley that grows top-notch produce much-celebrated locally. Try The Hand or The West Arms, both in Llanarmon, the Boat at Erbistock, the Michelin-starred dining at Tyddyn Llan, and a bonanza of farm shops, including organic Rhug Estate.

The most beautiful and accessible stretch lies between Carrog and Llangollen. Wide meanders are overlooked by the dramatic ruins of Castell Dinas Brân, and wooded slopes lead down to shingle beaches. Try a dip in Carrog by the Grouse Inn, or along the more wooded, secluded stretch at Rhewl, near the Sun Inn. If you are riding the heritage Llangollen Railway you can get out at Deeside Halt and follow a bridle path down to a pool above a small weir. Above Berwyn is the elegant crescent of Thomas Telford's Horseshoe Falls, which feeds the important Llangollen Canal, carried by the grand arches of the aqueduct at Cysylltau. The Dee is a renowned and expensive fishing river so be respectful when you dip, and give fishermen a wide berth. Canoeing and swimming are generally allowed before 3pm, however.

## RIVER DEE

### 1 CARROG BRIDGE, RIVER DEE

River meadows, beach and pools by an old stone bridge, perfect for an easy swim and picnic. Then enjoy lovely river views and real ale on the terrace of the friendly Grouse Inn.

→ Turn off A5 at Llydiart y Parc, dir LL21 9BD signed Carrog, and after ½ mile park R before river bridge. Cross to kissing gate at bridge and follow riverside footpath upstream for ½ mile. Grouse Inn is over bridge (LL21 9AT, 01490 430272). Also nearby is Station campsite (01490 430237).

2 mins, 52.9799, -3.3218

### 2 OVERTON, RIVER DEE

Remote meander of the Dee in open fields with a sunny shingle beach. Explore the riverbank both ways on the Wat's Dyke Way.

→ On A528 (A539) ⅓ mile NW through Overton, look out for two ornate wooden gates into woods, just before LL13 0HF. Parking for one here. Descend on footpath through woods, bear R on reaching the open fields, downstream to the river 200m.

10 mins, 52.9715, -2.9464

### 3 HORSESHOE FALLS, RIVER DEE

Set in parkland in a beautiful valley, the graceful curve of this weir may be beautiful but it creates dangerous currents – never swim below the weir. Above, however, the water is deep and calm and can be accessed from the footpath. Built by Thomas Telford in 1804–06, to supply the Llangollen canal.

→ A5 heading W from Llangollen, take R signed Ruthin over river by the train station in Berwyn. Turn L at end, uphill to the pay car park on L, ½ mile before LL20 8BT. Follow riverside path to falls.

5 mins, 52.9816, -3.1996

### 4 RHEWL, RIVER DEE

Easy roadside paddle and swim spot, not far from The Sun Inn (see listing). If you are travelling on the Llangollen steam railway you can also find your own private spot near Deeside Halt.

→ Start as for Horseshoe Falls (see listing) but continue past car park to Rhewl. There take L for LL20 7YT and follow L past the Sun Inn to find pulling off space ⅓ mile further along, where road runs along river. Deeside Halt pools are above the little weir 300m downstream of the halt, at 52.9736, -3.2276.

1 min, 52.9905, -3.2285

### 5 CYSYLLTAU BRIDGE, RIVER DEE

Follow the wooded footpath along the river, enjoy fine views of Pont-Cysyllte Aqueduct, and discover plenty of places to stop for a paddle or bathe.

→ From Froncysyllte A5 take B5434 1 mile, dir LL20 7YS, and park before bridge on R. Cross bridge and find riverside path down on R.

3 mins, 52.9707, -3.0913

### 6 PONT CILAN, RIVER DEE

The deep, peaty Dee runs under a remote stone bridge on the Crogen Estate. Do not swim if fishermen have beaten you there!

→ Head W from Llandrillo B4401, dir LL21 0SY, turning R after ½ mile to reach stone bridge; limited parking just beyond. Deep swimming upstream or downstream from footpaths.

2 mins, 52.9255, -3.4573

## LAKES & WHITE WATER

### 7 AFON TRYWERYN WHITE WATER

Scheduled dam releases ensure plenty of lively river flow, even in summer, making it perfect for a six-mile kayak or canoe all the way down to Bala. Only for the suitably experienced and equipped: Grade 3-4 in the upper reaches, Grade 2 lower down.

→ Well signed off A4212 NW of Bala, before the dam, just E of LL23 7NU. Check release times at nationalwhitewatercentre.co.uk. There is a £14 fee if you start at the National White Water Centre (courses and river rafting trips and a café and car park). You can also launch from the excellent Tyn Cornel campsite (see entry) if staying there. Or from path at the end of residential cul-de-sac Glan Tryweryn another mile downstream (LL23 7NT). You can swim in Treweryn lake from the picnic spot at its W end, on A4212 a mile SW of LL23 7NY.
2 mins, 52.9470, -3.6514

### 8 LLYN CAER EUNI

A secluded and sheltered lake hidden in rolling moorland, perfect for a summer picnic and swim.

→ On the A494 3½ miles NE of Bala, turn into Sarnau (LL23 7LG) and continue 1 mile to gate at road end. Walk another ½ mile on track and L down across open access land to SE shore.
15 mins, 52.9534, -3.5163

### 9 HANMER MERE

A warm, serene mere, formed in the last Ice Age, with sandy bays looking out over parkland. It's a quiet place with no boats or fishermen.

→ Turn off A539 into Hanmer 3 miles E of Overton and head to Glendower Place, (SY13 3DF). Follow lakeside footpath ½ mile through woods to reach open fields and little bays.
10 mins, 52.9474, -2.8146

### 10 LLANGOWER, LLYN TEGID, BALA

The largest natural lake in Wales, also called Bala Lake, with gravel shores and swimming freely allowed. There's a very easy cove by Llangower station car park, and more shore to explore, lined with ancient oaks, leading on to campsite at Pant Yr Onnen (see listing).

→ Take B4403 just S of Bala, follow 2½ miles along lake Bala, ½ mile before (E of) LL23 7DA. Cross tracks to shore.
2 mins, 52.8757, -3.6331

### 11 COLEMERE COUNTRY PARK

In an area of glacial lakes, Cole Mere is one of the more easily accessible, with a quiet shore path where a dip might go unnoticed, but be discreet. Blue-green algae possible. Orchids decorate the hay meadows in spring.

→ Signed from the A528, 2 miles S of Ellesmere. Follow road taking L fork after crossroads, past turning for SY12 0QL, then L at T-junction to lakeside car park. Follow path around to wooded N shore for quieter spots.

12

Some also swim from NW shore of Ellesmere (52.9122, -2.8815).
5 mins, 52.8910, -2.8402 🏊❓📺✿

## LOST RUINS & CAVERNS

### 12 CAMBRIAN SLATE QUARRY
In a gaping chamber at the bottom of a wooded crater are long tunnels, abandoned equipment, and traces of forgotten structures disappearing into the greenery.
➔ ¼ mile E of (the turn off for) LL20 7DE, find dirt pull-in for one, and a footpath sign leading down into woods. After 100m where the path levels out, bear L to reach edge of crater with cave at bottom. A steep track leads down. (Or approach from Glyn Ceiriog via Quarry road, past LL20 7DA. Longer walk, less driving).
5 mins, 52.9334, -3.2117 🚶📺📷

### 13 PENARTH QUARRY, CORWEN
Superb views out over the rolling river valley and Carrog can be had from this old quarry vantage point, sprinkled with the ruins of mills, finishing houses, tramways, and tracks disappearing into tunnels. There is a higher and wilder slate quarry at Moel Fferna, which only closed in the 1960s and links to a Deeside slab quarry by tramway; it

is notorious for its vast chambers, vertical shafts and suspended 'Bridge of Death' – one for properly equipped and experienced cavers only.
➔ Turn off A5 Llydiart y Parc, opp Carrog, up dead end to LL21 9EL. Park near here then walk on up road to find footpath on R at end. Follow this SE straight for a mile up to quarry. (Moel Fferna is at 52.9487, -3.3032, park at end of road beyond LL21 9HP then 30 mins walk).
30 mins, 52.9721, -3.3290 📷🚶📺

### 14 CASTELL DINAS BRÂN
High above the Dee valley the divinely picturesque remains of 13th-century castle crown a craggy hill. Glorious when viewed from inside or from the Panorama Walk lane along the valley. Tan y Castell farm, on Panorama Walk, takes campers and sells home-reared lamb. Nearby, Valle Crucis abbey ruins (entry fee) were founded by the same family 50 years earlier; now incongruously encircled by a campsite.
➔ Leave A539 in Llangollen up Wharf Hill (by Bridge End) then R at T junction along Wern Lane, keeping L past fork for LL20 8DU to leave the town, with steep climb and narrow lane for 1 mile. Pass gate to castle footpath on L, then turn L after cattle grid to pull off on L. Tan y

12

13

139

Castell farm is just beyond. Or walk 1 mile from Llangollen on footpath at the top of Wharf Hill. Valle Crucis ruins are at 52.9887, -3.1864.

10 mins, 52.9792, -3.1595 🖼️🔲🏞️

### 15 CASTELL CARNDOCHAN

You'll need to use your imagination to rebuild this rubble, set high on a steep defensive crag, into the lost medieval castle, but recent conservation work helps, and the awesome views of the Aran Benllyn ridge round to Bala and beyond make it worth the climb. Built in the 13th century, this may have looked much like Castell y Bere, but an intriguing square foundation resembles Dinas Emrys near Beddgelert.

→ From the A494 at SW end of Llyn Tegid, take turn dir Trawsfynydd. Follow 1⅓ miles to park by pretty bridge with river pool at Dolhendre Isaf. Cross bridge and turn R at crossroads. 50m beyond LL23 7TA find track L at 52.8630, -3.7129, up S onto open access land.

20 mins, 52.8610, -3.7139 🔲🖼️🏞️

### HILLTOPS

### 16 CREIGIAU EGLWYSEG

Dramatic white limestone cliffs that translate as 'church rocks' stretch across three miles of the Dee valley. Rich in rare flora and history, this is a place of spring flowers, amazing views and Bronze Age cairns.

→ Start as for Castell Dinas Brân (see listing) but turn R after cattle grid and continue ½ mile on the Panorama Walk road past Trevor Quarry to pull off on hairpin bend, where the footpath is signed up to the old quarry above and onto the plateau.

20 mins, 52.9962, -3.1605 🖼️➕🔲

### 17 ARENIG FAWR

This is a wonderfully serene Snowdonia peak, with fine views to historic sights. The summit cairn commemorates the 1943 crash of an American bomber; eight men died, and some of the wreckage (pieces of fuselage) can still be found in a line about 300m north-west from the peak. To the north-east there are views to the bitterly contested Llyn Celin reservoir.

→ Signed Arenig off the A4212. Within ½ mile there is a dead-end track on R (about a mile before LL23 7PB). Park and follow this, then climb up via Craig y Hyrddod. A loop descends from the summit via Llyn Arenig Fawr, where there is a bothy (see listing).

120 mins, 52.9171, -3.7461 🖼️🔲

## TREES & WILDLIFE

### 18 LLANARMON YEWS

Two yews (a male and female) stand either side of St Garmon church path. At over 1,000 years of age, they are older than the present church, and maybe its medieval predecessor. The church here is said to have been founded in the 5th century by St Garmon, and the circular Tomen Garmon mound in the churchyard is claimed as his resting place, or his preaching mound.

→ Llanarmon Dyffryn Ceiriog, LL20 7LD.
3 mins, 52.8862, -3.2530 ✝

### 19 CROGEN OAKS, RIVER CEIRIOG

Two giant oaks on the Offa's Dyke path. The Oak at the Gate of the Dead and the Duelling Oak, together called the Crogen Oaks. This place became known as Adwy'r Beddau or 'pass of the graves' after a ferocious battle was fought here in 1165, when the outnumbered soldiers of prince Owain Gwynedd saw off the invading force of Henry II. There is a pleasant pool under the river bridge nearby.

→ 2 miles W of Chirk on B4500, at LL14 5BL, a footpath leads into the NT Chirk estate opp turning to bridge; turn and park near river bridge. The trees are 100m along path on R with a tree swing too. The pool and little beach below are just over bridge.
2 mins, 52.9314, -3.0953 🚻🏊

### 20 WOOD LANE NATURE RESERVE

A great example of re-wilding, Wood Lane's large lakes were carved out of the countryside by excavation for sand and gravel but are now a haven for birds, with over 180 species recorded since it opened nearly 20 years ago. Bird hides and good access. Managed by Shropshire Wildlife Trust.

→ On the A528, leaving Ellesmere to S, at crossroads just after SY12 0HS turn L dir Colemere. Reserve and car park ¾ mile further on R.
5 mins, 52.8896, -2.8575 🦅

## SACRED & ANCIENT

### 21 LLANGAR, RIVER DEE & CAPEL RHUG

All Saints church, Langar, has some extraordinary 15th-century wall paintings, including one of the grim reaper. Below are white shingle beaches on a meander of the River Dee. The church key can be obtained from Capel Rhug nearby, known for its exquisite painted ceiling and angels.

→ Signed off B4401, opp turning into Bryn Saint dir LL21 0HW; pull off in turning layby. Follow signed track to Llangar Church. For river pass church gate, over stile and railway track into field. Beach is 50m on R. Church open 2–3pm Wed–Sun. Capel Rhug is well signed just NE from LL21 0ER crossroads (£4 entrance).
10 mins, 52.9712, -3.3997

### 22 MOEL TY-UCHAF CIRCLE

A superb ring of 41 stones on the isolated grassy summit of Moel Ty-uchaf (440m) with spectacular views.

→ Follow B4401 1 mile N from Llandrillo, turn R up dead end just before bridge, dir LL21 0SN, and continue past postcode another ⅓ mile up steep hill and through final gate to park at crossroads of tracks (this is a public byway for all vehicles). Circle is ½ mile SE – continue up bridleway and bear L to summit.
15 mins, 52.9236, -3.4055

### 23 QUINTA STONE CIRCLE

This impressive, if scaled-down, homage to Stonehenge was built in the mid-19th century as a folly.

→ Head W from Chirk on B4500, and turn L ½ mile beyond roundabout , over river bridge 'unsuitable for HGVs' dir SY10 7RW. Footpath is R in trees 130m before postcode; park and walk back. Footpath leads up to woods 200m and then R around woods 200m.
10 mins, 52.9198, -3.0715

## SLOW FOOD

### 24 RHUG ESTATE ORGANIC FARM SHOP

A field of bison is your first welcome to this commercially slick organic farm shop, selling home-farm meats, local cheeses and deli goods for your camp larder. Afterwards you could paddle/swim at the ford at 52.9746, -3.4039 (back to lights and turn R).

→ Rhug Estate, Corwen, LL21 0EH, 01490 411100.
52.9814, -3.4117

### 25 TYDDYN LLAN, LLANDRILLO

Michelin-star dining in a chintzy but relaxed country house, with rooms. Bryan Webb's famed cooking is an ode to the best Welsh ingredients including Cardigan lobster and wild-caught fish with laverbread sauces. Try the set price for three courses, or indulge in a six- or nine-course tasting menu.

→ Llandrillo, LL21 0ST, 01490 440264.
52.9236, -3.4423

### 26 STORI BEERS & WINES

If you like craft beers, gins, liqueurs and wines, with a strong emphasis on the local, then this new bottle shop and tap room is a must-visit. Taste, drink in or take home.

→ 101 High St, Bala, LL23 7AE, 01678 520501.
52.9096, -3.5999

### 27 LEWIS'S FARM SHOP

Welsh cheese, Cheshire farm ice cream and locally sourced meats including lamb from the farm. Closed Mondays.

→ Brook Cottage, Eyton, Wrexham, LL13 0SW, 01978 780852.
52.9972, -2.9707

### 28 HOME FARM, OVERTON

Farm shop selling free-range local produce, much from the rare-breed pigs that you'll see snorting around. Open 10am–4pm, Thur–Sun.

→ Bryn-y-pys, Overton, LL13 0HG, 01978 710141.
52.9762, -2.9508

### 29 WHITTINGTON CASTLE

A community-run café and craft shop in a community-run castle! The moat, bailey and grounds are free to explore. 10am–4pm, Thurs–Sun.

→ Castle Street, Whittington, SY11 4DF, 01691 662500.
52.8735, -3.0027

## COSY PUBS

### 30 THE CORN MILL & WATERFALLS

Amazing views of the tumbling River Dee as it passes through Llangollen. Good pub food and a lovely deck from which to watch the crazy canoeists negotiating the white waters below. A popular paddling and swimming

spot with slabs and pools is just upstream – be careful in high flow.

→ Dee Ln, Llangollen, LL20 8PN, 01978 869555. 52.9707, -3.1706 🅟🅐🅱

### 31 THE SUN INN, RHEWL

A pint-sized 14th-century drovers' inn with Dee valley views and friendly locals. Serves good local beer from Llangollen Brewery alongside pub grub.

→ Rhewl, LL20 7YT, 01978 860860. 52.9935, -3.2257 🅟

### 32 BOAT INN, ERBISTOCK

A characterful old pub serving local free-range meats and seasonal vegetables, inside by the fire or outside on the grassy banks of the River Dee. Popular for fly fishing, so if you want to dip in the river, you'll need to head a long way upstream on the footpath, or try the weir at the mill (52.9729, -2.9634).

→ Erbistock, LL13 0DL, 01978 780666. 52.9650, -2.9612 🅟🅗

### 33 THE BRYNTIRION INN

Open fires, real ales, organic wines and good home cooking. Try the Welsh Black beef casserole, which comes in a home-made loaf. It's also near Pont Fawr, under which there's a beautiful deep pool in the River Dee.

→ Llandderfel, Bala, LL23 7RA, 01678 530205. 52.9163, -3.5104 🅟🅗🅱

### 34 THE HAND AT LLANARMON

A cosy pub that draws both locals and visitors to sit by its fires and enjoy local lamb steaks and real ales. Cross over the road to visit the church and ancient yew trees (see listing). The West Arms Inn over the road is also very good.

→ Llanarmon Dyffryn Ceiriog, LL20 7LD, 01691 600666. 52.886199, -3.254386 🅟

### 35 THE MULBERRY INN, LLWYNMAWR

With a lovely garden looking out over verdant hills and a fire to warm you, this colourfully furnished restaurant and bar is home to the fantastic Dafydd Burger: Welsh Black beef with laverbread, rarebit, cockle fritters and crispy leeks. Rooms available.

→ Llwynmawr, Glyn Ceiriog, Llangollen LL20 7BB, 01691 718281. 52.9248, -3.1542 🅗🅱

WILDER CAMPING

### 36 ARENIG FAWR BOTHY

A truly tiny stone MBA-maintained bothy with a small open fireplace, beside Llyn Arenig Fawr. Sleeps two on sleeping platforms, can fit one on the floor. Stunning location.

→ Start as for Arenig Fawr peak (see entry) but continue to ⅓ mile beyond LL23 7PB to find small layby on L and track with stile on R. Walk up track for approx 1¼ miles to E side of Llyn Arenig Fawr. Bothy is below the dam wall. 52.9262, -3.7116 🅐🅱🅱🅱🅑

### 37 FELIN UCHAF CAMPING

Streamside camping (albeit with a few caravans) and a waterfall swimming hole.

→ Waterfall Road, Cynwyd, Corwen, LL21 0LN, 01490 413371. 52.9540, -3.3952 🅐🅱🅱

### 38 TYN CORNEL CAMPING

Large, flat grassy site surrounded by trees on the banks of the River Tryweryn, perfect for those wanting to access white water rafting straight from your camp.

→ Off the A4212, Frongoch LL23 7NU, 01678 520759. 52.9455, -3.6447 🅐🅱

### 39 PANT YR ONNEN, LLANGOWER

Camp right on the gravel shore of Llyn Tegid/Bala Lake and enjoy a beach campfire surrounded by mysterious twisted oak roots. Glorious sunsets and an altogether very friendly – and popular – family site.

→ Llangower, Bala, LL23 7BT, 01743 718283. 52.8786, -3.6314 🅱🅱🅱🅱🅱

RUSTIC HAVENS

### 40 PLAS UCHAF, NR CORWEN

The Landmark Trust renovated this medieval hall-house between the River Alwen and Dee from dereliction. With its incredible timbers and large inglenook it makes a lovely holiday house, sleeping four.

→ Corwen, LL21 0EW, 01628 825925. 52.9735, -3.4116 🅱

### 41 ENGINE HOUSE - OFF GRID LIVING

Idyllic off-grid red-brick cottage, surrounded by woodland with a lake for swimming. Enjoy dinner by candlelight, baths heated by the woodburner and the joy of peace.

→ Redbrook Maelor, Whitchurch, SY13 3AL, 07969 626827. airbnb.co.uk 52.9691, -2.7377 🅱🅱

41

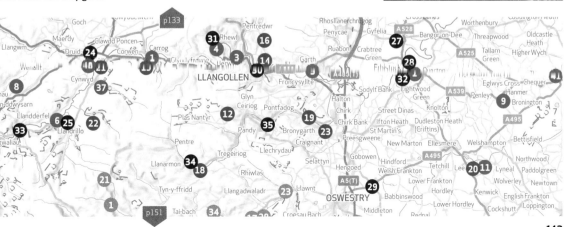

# BERWYN &
# VYRNWY

## Our perfect weekend

→ **Find** the secret cave hideout of 'Wild' Humphrey
  Kynaston in the red cliffs of Nesscliffe

→ **Canoe** or swim down the Afon Vrynwy from
  Dolanog to Meifod, or down the River Severn
  from Royal Hill to Shrawardine

→ **Descend** on the second-highest road in Wales
  from Bwlch y Groes to find the tallest tree in
  Wales at Lake Vyrnwy

→ **Commune** with sacred yews at Llansilin,
  Pennant Melangell or Llanerfyl

→ **Delve** into the shadowy underworld of the
  Hoffman kiln chambers at Llanymynech and
  ascend to the cave house at Kynaston's cliffs

→ **Dip** with the fairies in Pistyll Rhaeadr, visit the
  sacred stone row on the moor above, then climb
  to Berwyn's highest peak at Moel Sych

→ **Treat** yourself to seasonal, organic food, game
  and wine at Pen-y-Dyffryn Hotel

→ **Glamp** in beautiful yurts at a secret location on
  the Bodynfoel Hall estate and take a moonlit
  row around the lake

The vast, isolated range of the Berwyn mountains is a moody, lonely place of moorlands, crags, waterfalls and sacred stones. Even on the loveliest summer's day you are unlikely to see another soul up here, and a good place to start your peregrinations is Pistyll Rhaeadr, the most perfect waterfall in Wales. Its passage down the mountain has two stages, first falling to a natural stone 'fairy' arch, and then passing through a variety of plunge pools, one named the Druid's Bowl.

The area was settled first by the Celts, who brought their mythology and language, and then by the Romans, who brought their own cultural influences: the beautiful shrine in the church at Pennant Melangell is a mix of Celtic and Roman motifs.

The principle river of the area is the Vyrnwy, as large and as lovely as the Dee or Severn to the north and south, but far more secret and with more places to canoe or wild swim with ease. It also boasts wooded gorges at Pont Llogel, thundering waterfalls at Dolanog and great meanders through open pasture and ancient oaks at Meifod.

This area is rich in spiritual sites, with many of the churches dating back to the 6th or 7th centuries, but the yews found in their graveyards point to an even earlier sacred history. Llansilin has the largest gathering of ancient yews in one place in Wales, while Pennant Melangell, one of the holiest churches in Wales, has equally impressive yews in its curious circular churchyard, and the Llanerfyl yew is a vast and sprawling ancient life form, intriguingly with male and female parts.

More recent relics include the quarries at Llanymynech, and the impressive wooded limestone hills they were carved from. You can explore inside a Hoffman kiln, a massive oval structure with many chambers that were filled, fired and emptied in turn to create lime continuously in a circuit, over a six-week cycle.

More underworld curiosities can be found within the red sandstone cliffs of Nesscliffe – a man-made cave house with a staircase, reputedly the home of outlawed 'Wild' Humphrey Kynaston, a real life Robin Hood who lived here 600 years ago.

Nearby, beyond the pub at Royal Hill you too can find solitude on the river; taking a picnic from Churncote farm shop, launch your canoe and float away downstream along the lazy meanders and hardly see a building or person for miles.

## WATERFALLS

### 1 PISTYLL RHAEADR

One of the highest waterfalls in Wales thunders down a vertical cliff and then escapes through a circular hole. Small pools for plunging are below the footbridge. Adjacent are tea rooms, loos and campsite, so it can get quite busy, but from here you can also walk on up to Moel Sych (see listing).

→ Signed Pistyll off the B4580 in Llanrhaeadr-ym Mochnant. Follow single-track road 4 miles to end, past SY10 0BZ. Parking £4. You can also park ½ mile before, and walk in on footpath (52.8513, -3.3677).
5 mins, 52.8546, -3.3780 🏊🏕️⛺🚻🔥🅿️🚶

### 2 DOLANOG FALLS, RIVER VYRNWY

Very impressive wooded waterfalls and weir below white cliffs. Enjoy a deep section above the rope swings and all the way up to the old road bridge. Some deep pools downstream too. Allt Dolanog nearby is crowned by the Llys-y-cawr hill fort, or explore more river pools downstream along Glyndŵr's Way.

→ Below B4382, ¼ mile E of Dolanog (beyond SY21 0LQ). Some parking on L adjacent to river or car park at postcode.
1 min, 52.7036, -3.3812 🏊🚶🌳🧗

### 3 EUNANT FALLS & BWLCH Y GROES

This tiny mountain lane ascends from Lake Vyrnwy up to the heady height of Bwlch y Groes at 545m. On the way you'll discover many waterfalls – perfect for a refreshing dip if you are cycling – and at the top you'll be rewarded with superb views.

→ Leave the B4393 at Pont Eunant, at the NE end of lakeshore, taking mountain lane dir Dinas and past SY10 0NF. The biggest waterfall is after 1¼ miles, ½ mile beyond postcode, with space to pause (passing place!) beyond the salt bin. Drive on up and turn R for the bwlch. The Pistyll Rhyd-y-meinciau (Rhiwargor Waterfalls) are at 52.8087, -3.5538, 1 mile from the picnic site at NW end of the lake.
2 mins, 52.7952, -3.5668 🚴🏊🅿️

## RIVERS

### 4 ROYAL HILL, RIVER SEVERN

Grassy banks, shingle beaches and a pub on one of the few access points to the Severn on this stretch. Put your canoe in here for a paddle down to Shrawardine (4 miles, see listing) or A5 Montford Bridge (6 miles). There is no road or footpath access to the river along these stretches, so it's a haven of wildlife and tranquility.

→ As for Melverley (see listing) but continue past church turning to take next R to SY10 8ES. Large layby opp the Royal Hill Inn and campsite (01743 741242).
2 mins, 52.7498, -2.9627 🚣🏊🍺⛺🛶

### 5 SHRAWARDINE, RIVER SEVERN

From a grassy meadow by a ruined railway bridge, a steep bank leads down to a bend in the river and a deep pool. It's one of the few places where you can get to the young Severn, and also makes a good take-out point if you are canoeing down from Royal Hill (see listing).

→ In Shrawardine follow lane dir SY4 1AJ, park by houses and go through the wooden gate/stile by last house 200m before postcode. Follow the path NW down through 2 small paddocks, ¼ mile.
5 mins, 52.7330, -2.8996 🚣🏊

### 6 PONT LLOGEL, RIVER VYRNWY

An old stone bridge and wooded gorge with an easy-access riverbank walk for over 3 miles along Ann Griffiths Walk (and Glyndŵr's Way). Deep enough for a swim under the bridge.

→ B4395 over river a mile N of SY21 0QD. Forestry car park at N side of bridge.
1 min, 52.7277, -3.4348 🏊🅿️🚶

## 9 MELVERLEY, RIVER VYRNWY

Upstream of Melverley the footpath follows the meandering river Vyrnwy through empty lowland pasture for over four miles with a couple of good drop-off points for a long linear swim, canoe or walk. St Peter's black-and-white church on the bank is one of the oldest of its kind, rebuilt in the 15th century after Owain Glynd^wr burnt it to the ground. There is a Jacobean pulpit and a chained Bible.

→ Leave B4393 at Crewgreen, opp SY5 9BS, for Melverley. After 1 mile the church is signed L (SY10 8PJ, dead end). Follow footpath N past caravan park to explore the river meanders. Upstream there is vehicular byway access to a remote section of the river from SY10 8PQ (about ½ mile on a dirt track), and the road meets the river again ½ mile SE of SY10 8QJ.
2 mins, 52.7425, -2.9903 🏊📷✝

## CAVES & RUINS

## 10 LLANYMYNECH QUARRY & KILN

This vast Victorian limestone quarry has consumed much of the hillside, and can be seen from miles around. Explore along the old tramways in the Heritage Area and climb inside one of the last intact Hoffman lime kilns, a vast catacomb structure which once burnt lime continuously. Continue through a tunnel into the quarry itself to find bee and pyramidal orchids, bright yellow rockrose and many aromatic herbs. There are also old caves on the hillside beyond, including a Bronze Age copper mine.

→ Leaving Llanymynech N on A483, the heritage area is signed on R, after SY22 6EZ, but easily missed. Park here and follow path to the ruins and Hoffman kiln. The tramway then passes under main road and up inclines to the quarry. The cave, Ogof Llanymynech, is at 52.7924, -3.0899, best accessed through the golf course SY10 8LB.
20 mins, 52.7838, -3.0861 📷🧗🐾

## 11 SYCHARTH CASTLE

A perfect circular grass mound and moat, ideal for a picnic and play under the oak trees, is all that remains of the home of Owain Glyndŵr, the last native Prince of Wales. It was burnt to the ground in 1403 during the Glyndŵr Rising.

→ Head S from Llansilin on B4580. After 2 miles turn L signed Llynclys at SY10 9JZ. There is a new parking area and signboard on the L after ½ mile and a footpath leads up behind the house to the mound.
5 mins, 52.8245, -3.1808 📷

## 7 NEWBRIDGE, RIVER BANWY

On the Banwy where it meets the Vyrnwy, you'll find a glorious section of deep river pools either side of the New Bridge, studded with beaches and ancient trees. Uncertain access, and no parking space so best on bikes, but this is a well-known swimming spot.

→ On A495, 2 miles S of Meifod, turn at traffic lights, to and past SY22 6HR and over New Bridge across Banwy. Just after, find stile on L down to river beach. Beach and pool upstream (turn R up lane after bridge and drop down, or go over gate before bridge), but possibly private. From Meifod side of traffic lights, a footpath leads ½ mile upstream to a weir. Or swim all the way down to Meifod (see listing).
3 mins, 52.6928, -3.2692 🏊❓

## 8 MEIFOD, RIVER VYRNWY

Open, sunny and deep with fine views, this is perhaps the easiest place to swim on the beautiful Vyrnwy. Gallt yr Ancr behind Meifod makes a lovely little hill to climb.

→ Turn off A495 in Meifod, dir Recreation Facilities and SY22 6DA past rugby club/ tennis courts to find bridge and limited verge space on far side. Riverside footpaths head downstream for a mile (L bank to a beach).
2 mins, 52.7073, -3.2499 🏊🐾🚶

## 12 KYNASTON'S CAVE, NESSCLIFFE

In red sandstone cliffs, hidden in the woods, is a man-made cave house with staircase, reputedly the home of 'Wild' Humphrey Kynaston, a highwayman who died in 1534. The cave was lived in until at least the 18th century, when a family of 11 made their home here. Woodland walks lead up to Oliver's Point and a hill fort.

→ Park at the Old Three Pigeons (SY4 1DB, 01743 741279, good food and a seat cut from the cave) in Nesscliffe off A5. Gate into Nesscliffe woods 100m up road to Hopton opp. Follow footpath, turning R at top and then up bank to L after 200m to find caves in cliff.
10 mins, 52.7678, -2.9141 🅿️🔵ⓘ🏠🚶

## 13 CRAIG RHIWARTH QUARRY

Discover slate quarry remains, with large caverns, ruins and machinery remnants, and far-reaching sunset views out over the beautiful Tanat valley.

→ Heading N in Llangynog on B4391, cross the river bridge after SY10 0EX and turn immediately R and R again to find track straight up mountain on L (next to Mol Quarry cottage) with limited parking. Caverns visible about ⅓ mile above.
15 mins, 52.8288, -3.4030 🅿️📷🖼️

## ANCIENT TREES & WOODS

## 14 LAKE VYRNWY TREES, LLANWDDYN

Deep and brooding Vyrnwy reservoir is surrounded by woodland, moorland and bogs, which combine to create a haven for flora and fauna. Fungi, skylarks and hen harriers abound in the RSPB nature reserve. There is a Giants of Vyrnwy path to monumental conifers: one of more than 60m stands above a waterfall and plunge pool, and the trunk of what was Wales' tallest tree sculpted into a giant hand. Below on the lakeshore, there is a little beach for a dip. The Artisans café near the dam sells good coffee and rents bicycles.

→ From Llanwddyn take the N shore road in a turning for SY10 0ND, and ⅓ mile beyond find car park on R. Just beyond a path heads into woods on R and tree is 50m above waterfall. Path also leads down to lakeshore picnic area. Café is at the SW end of the dam (SY10 0NA, 01691 870317).
2 mins, 52.7820, -3.4842 🔵🍴🖼️

## 15 LLANERFYL YEW & RIVER BANWY

The long, twisted boughs and multiple trunks of this ancient tree sprawl out over the gravestones. Said to have grown from St Erfyl's staff, it seems to be one tree but three parts are female and one part male, a curious feature also seen in other old yews. Nearby is a swimming spot on the Banwy.

→ On A458 in Llanerfyl parking down turn almost opp SY21 0EQ (signed Workshops). Walk across the road and L for church. For the river, go W over river bridge and turn immediately R. After ½ mile a footpath track on R leads to the river at 52.6811, -3.4277.
3 mins, 52.6770, -3.4301 🔵✝️🖼️

## 16 PENNANT MELANGELL YEWS

Deep in the folds of the Berwyns stand four magnificent yew trees, thought to be at least 2,000 years old. Melangell was the 7th-century patron saint of hares, and the beautiful church and shrine attracts many pilgrims.

→ Turn off B4391 W at Llangynog for SY10 0HQ. Church and car park are signed on bend just before postcode. The adventurous might like to seek out the spectacular cataracts of Pistyll Blaen-y-cwm, a mile further on at the head of the valley.
2 mins, 52.8275, -3.4498 🔵♿🖼️

## 17 LLANSILIN YEWS

Apparently the largest gathering of ancient yews in one place in Wales, some 10 trees,

several very large. St Silin's church is 13th century, but built on a 6th-century site.

→ On B4580 in the centre of Llansilin, 10 miles W of Oswestry, opp SY10 7QB.
2 mins, 52.8454, -3.1748

### 18 GAER-FAWR WOODS & HILL FORT

These beautiful oak woods not only have a sweeping carpets of bluebells in spring, they surround the 'great fort', an Iron Age hill fort with impressively steep ramparts – views are best when the bluebells are out, before the trees leaf up.

→ From B4392 at NE of Guilsfield, turn signed Geufford (dir SY21 9DT). After ½ mile find small car park on R. Follow path uphill NE to circle summit.
15 mins, 52.7085, -3.1515

## HILLTOPS

### 19 BREIDDEN HILLS

The mini volcanic peaks of the Breidden range boast supreme views. Breidden Hill itself sports the massive Rodney's Pillar, built to commemorate a local admiral. Just to the south Middletown Hill is home to a fine hill fort, and Meol y Golfa is the tallest at 403m.

→ Leave A458 at Trewern, taking Garreg Bank lane to a small dirt car park R after 1¾ miles, just before SY21 8ES. This provides access to all peaks.
45 mins, 52.7230, -3.0452

### 20 LLWYN BRYN-DINAS HILL FORT

A fine Iron Age hill fort, rarely visited, with impressive earthwork ridges and views of the Berywn mountainscape.

→ W of Llangedwyn on the B4396, ½ mile W of turning to SY10 9LD, a tiny unsigned lane bears off to the R at 52.8111, -3.2330. After 2 houses, the first field gate on R leads onto hillside. Parking for one.
15 mins, 52.8137, -3.2297

### 21 MOEL SYCH & CERRIG DUON STONES

Moel Sych is one of the highest points in the Berwyns (827m), and looks down over the glacial Llyn Lluncaws. Take a hike up the lake and loop back via the little-known circle and 'stone row' (actually an avenue).

→ From entrance to car park at Pistyll Rhaeadr (see entry) footpath heads N up valley to Llyn Lluncaws, then L up ridge to S of lake. Cerrig Duon stones are 2 miles SW of peak (52.8611, -3.4008); loop back along Afon Disgynfa.
60 mins, 52.8761, -3.3881

## SLOW FOOD

### 22 LYNCLYS HALL FARM SHOP

Drive into the red-bricked old farmyard and you'll be met by baskets of beans, piles of pumpkins and crates of carrots depending on the season. Inside the little wooden farm shop you'll find everything from organic quinoa to pet food.

→ Llynclys Hall Farm, Llynclys, SY10 8AD, 01691 652434.
52.8152, -3.0605

### 23 PEN-Y-DYFFRYN HOTEL

Relaxed country hotel with views and an award-winning restaurant focused on food that's local, seasonal, organic (including the wine), and abundant in local game. Restaurant open to non-residents.

→ Rhydycroesau, SY10 7JD, 01691 653700.
52.8686, -3.1274

### 24 SEEDS RESTAURANT, LLANFYLLIN

A cosy, relaxed restaurant that's old-fashioned in all the right ways, and the perfect place for hungry travellers in need of a good home-cooked meal. Food is cooked and often served by the owners, using local ingredients.

→ High St, Llanfyllin, SY22 5AP, 01691 648604.
52.7657, -3.2724

### 25 CHURNCOTE FARM SHOP & KITCHEN

Farm shop and lovely café selling and serving their home-reared meats, eggs and locally sourced organic flour and vegetables.

→ Welshpool Road, Bicton Heath, SY3 5EB, 01743 850273.
52.7164, -2.8236

### 26 DERWEN FARM SHOP & RESTAURANT

Farm shop and café in garden centre, selling good local produce from beef to beer, organic where possible.

→ Derwen Garden Centre, Guilsfield, SY21 9JH, 01938 551586.
52.6874, -3.1558

## FRIENDLY PUBS

### 27 PLAS YN DINAS

Large, bright village pub serving good gastropub food. The outside still has a touch of the solid country courthouse it was, but it feels much more friendly once you step inside. Local ales, local produce and lots of happy families.

→ Maes Mechain, Llanfechain SY22 6UJ, 01691 829055.
52.7749, -3.2031 🏠🍴

### 28 THE NAVIGATION INN
Quirky and friendly owner-run pub on the canal serving real ales and home-made, locally sourced pies, steak and salads.
→ Maesbury Marsh, SY10 8JB, 01691 672958.
52.8183, -3.0198 🍴

## WILDER CAMPING

### 29 BARNUTOPIA, LLANSILIN
Painted yurts, stables and a bunkhouse sleeping 10, all set around a traditional red-brick farmyard right on the Welsh border.
→ Tanycoed Farm, Cadogan/Cadwygan Lane, Llansilin, SY10 9BS, 01691 791624.
52.8467, -3.1583 🏠B

### 30 UNDERHILL FARM, PANT
Rent your own camping field, the camping barn or a converted dairy sleeping two. The ecologically-minded farm runs bushcraft, natural clay pottery and river ecology trips. The beautiful Llanymynech quarried cliffs (see listing) are within walking distance.
→ Underhill Lane, Pant, SY10 9RB, 07773 046111.
52.7895, -3.0835 🏠▲B

### 31 THE SYCHPWLL CENTRE
Camp in the wildflower meadow or hide away in a unique, hand-built straw-bale barn on this wildlife-loving smallholding.
→ Llandrinio, Llanymynech, SY22 6SH, 07738 702507.
52.7527, -3.0230 🎤🏠

### 32 THE SECRET YURTS, DOLANOG
Lost in the buttercups and surrounded by trees are three well-appointed yurts, each with their own private deck and one with its own wood-fired hot tub. In the shared kitchen is a range cooker and each yurt has its own designated bathroom. This is a place for peace and wildlife watching (sorry no kids).
→ Dolanog, SY21 0JU, 07733 282639.
52.6703, -3.3178 🏠

## RUSTIC HAVENS

### 33 BODYNFOEL HALL GLAMPING
Two beautiful yurts (Old Larch and Jericho) and a quirky vintage caravan (Van Goff) are hidden away behind rhododendrons in the beautiful Bodynfoel Hall estate. Take the boat out onto the lake, stargaze on your private deck with a campfire or walk to the village pub.
→ Bodynfoel Hall, Llanfechain, SY22 6XD, 01172 047830. canopyandstars.co.uk
52.7744, -3.2235 🏠🎤♣

### 34 WYLDWOODS ECO RETREAT
Enjoy views, starlight and wildlife from these two simple but charming cabins with woodburners and Welsh blankets, hidden in large organic gardens under the Berwyn mountains.
→ Cilrhiw, Moelfre, SY10 7QS, 01691 791373.
52.8501, -3.2291 🏠

### 35 ST WINIFRED'S WELL
Utterly charming, tiny black-and-white 15th-century well chapel, later used as a courthouse and a cottage. The well still flows, so you can bathe in the sacred waters by moonlight if you wish – a more comfortable modern bathroom has been added close to the original building by the Landmark Trust. Sleeps two.
→ Nr Woolston Bank Cottages, Woolston, SY10 8HZ, 01628 825925. landmarktrust.org.uk
52.8134, -3.0071 🏠

35

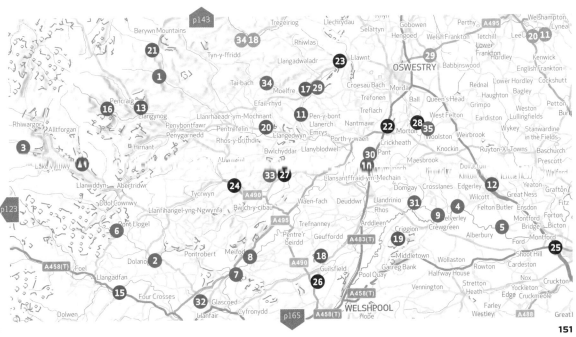

# SHROPSHIRE HILLS

## Our perfect weekend

→ **Forage** for wild bilberries as you explore the heather-clad hills of the Long Myndd, discovering Bronze age remains along the way

→ **Descend** into the tunnels of Snailbeach lead mine, eat cake at The Bog Visitor Centre then climb the Devil's Chair to watch the sunset

→ **Explore** down tiny lanes to find the horseshoe weir on the Teme and the ruined ironworks it fed at Bringewood Forge

→ **Walk** the ancient avenue of beeches along Linley Hill and refuel with a feast of fine Shropshire fare at The Coach House

→ **Tour** the picturesque Marcher castle ruins of Clun, Hopton and Montgomery

→ **Plunge** into the secret Severn at the Roman ford at Rhydwhyman, climb Dolforwyn Castle and watch the sand martins at Dolydd Hafren

→ **Taste** the good life along the River Teme, lunching at Milebrook House, camping at Lower Buckton, and relaxing at Leintwardine with wild swimming and the back-in-time Sun Inn

**The hills of west Shropshire have long been frontier lands, scarred with Celtic hill forts, Roman mines and Norman castles. Bordered by the upper Severn to the west, and the peaceful waters of the Teme, the land still retains a deep sense of remoteness and discovery.**

By the Bronze Age important trade routes crossed the low hills and wooded valleys of the Clun, and ceremonial sites such as Mitchell's Fold stone circle and the barrows on the Long Mynd were built. The sheer number of ancient forts, on almost every hilltop from Caradoc to Bury Ditches, is testament to the power of the Celtic Cornovii tribes who defended this area during the Iron Age – but they could not hold back the Romans, who came for the minerals and metals hidden under the Stiperstones and at Snailbeach. When the Roman empire finally fell, these hills reverted to the Welsh princes of Powys and became a buffer between Celts and Saxons, with Offa's Dyke marking the boundary from the late 8th century.

Peace didn't last, and the Norman invasion saw much of this borderland taken once again. Although princes in north and south Wales were able to regain much of it in the revolt of 1094, the Powys hills remained in Norman hands. The Norman 'Marcher lords' built a network of small castles, such as Montgomery, Clun and Hopton, and new towns, such as Ludlow and Newtown, encouraging English peasants to settle and anglicise the frontier areas. These ruined Norman castles are fun to explore, as are those built by the Welsh princes, such as Dolforwyn and Tinboeth.

Today the hills are a peaceful place. Purple heather, red-tinted whinberry and yellow grasses colour the Stiperstones ridge in late summer. Quartzite tors and tops provide good scrambles and lookouts, and one can only wonder at the isolated life of those 'squatter' families who inhabited the cottages at Brook Vessons. They were allowed to stay if they could build a house and have smoke out of the chimney by nightfall.

The river Teme – 'the dark one' in ancient Celtic – has shingle beaches with deep pools backed by open glades. The stretch near Bringewood Forge is one of the wildest and least visited; although difficult to access, it has two great bridges, weirs and ruins of old iron forges. Extensive fertile pasture has given this Shropshire borderland an enviable reputation for home-sourced gastronomy. Feast on garden grown produce at The Milebrook House Hotel or delight in a seasonally inspired lunch at The Green Café as you relax by this lovely waterway.

## RIVER & LAKES

### 1 CARDING MILL & LIGHTSPOUT FALLS

Sitting in a sheltered glen at the top of New Pool Hollow, this disused reservoir was built in 1902 to power the textile mill in the valley below. Owned by the NT, swimming is permitted. Continue up north west to Lightspout Hollow to find a remote waterfall – no pool but fun for a soaking.

→ Signed Carding Mill Valley from B5477/High Street in Church Stretton. Continue about a mile, beyond SY6 6JG, to road end parking (NT). Cross stream on first footbridge and climb SE for Hope Pool Hollow. For waterfall, continue up valley on second footbridge, then bear L up next side valley W to 52.5504, -2.8405

15 mins, 52.5464, -2.8521

### 2 BERRIEW, RIVER RHIW

A pretty village stream that feeds the Severn. You'll find grassy banks and small waterfalls and pools above the stone bridge. Afterwards take tea at the Lychgate Cottage Tea Room.

→ Park in Berriew and walk upstream beyond bridge dir SY21 8PJ. Pools at 50m, but fence ends after 100m. Tea room 01686 640750.

1 min, 52.5992, -3.2028

### 3 LLYN Y TARW, MYNYDD CLOGAU

A trio of wild lakes hiding in the high, rolling emptiness of Mynydd Clogau (420m). Llyn Mawr is a nature reserve, Llyn Du is for fishing, while Llyn y Tarw is the quietest of the three, best for a swim or wild camp.

→ From A470 a mile SE of Clatter, turn (signed Bwlchygarreg) and follow the lane. After 2 miles, 200m after turn to SY17 5NE, find bridle path on R and some parking. Walk ¾ mile NE, or take bridle path L for Llyn Mawr.

15 mins, 52.5657, -3.4481

## SECRET SEVERN

### 4 LLANDINAM GRAVELS, RIVER SEVERN

The meanders of the young Severn are blessed with shingle beaches and deep pools. Tread lightly, as this is a nature reserve with many insects, wading birds and even otters living and breeding in it. In summer the bordering water meadows are decorated with wildflowers.

→ Signed Broneirion/Nature Reserve from A470 just N of Llandinam. Cross the river on narrow bridge, then turn L along a disused railway track dir SY17 5AU. About a mile down find reserve parking L.

10 mins, 52.4814, -3.4387

### 5 RHYDWHYMAN, RIVER SEVERN

The ancient Roman road crossed the river at Rhydwhyman and was defended by Forden Gaer fort, just to the north-east. A perfect place for an easy dip, and another good spot with wide-open beaches is just upstream.

→ Take B4385 NW from Montgomery. After 2 miles turn R just after railway bridge, dir Caerhowel. After ¾ mile, opp the turn to SY15 6HD, find a wooded area by the river on L. For upstream spot, stay on B4385 another ½ mile after railway bridge, to just after L turn to SY15 6RT, then turn R down lane. Park at fork (limited space) and track R leads towards river (footpath, ½ mile) at 52.5762, -3.1783.

1 min, 52.5775, -3.1700

## TRANQUIL TEME

### 6 WESTON, RIVER TEME

This secret swimming spot, best reached by bike, is surprisingly deep and enjoys a large shingle beach. There's a bridge for Pooh Sticks and an overgrown castle motte on the south bank to discover too.

→ 2 miles E of Knighton on A4113, turn L signed Stowe, then after crossing river R dir Buckton/Weston. After 1½ mile, at SY7 0BB, find postbox, stile and gate. Very limited

parking by house. Follow path down to railway cottage, cross lines and continue S 100m to the footbridge. Deep pool and beach below.
5 mins, 52.3520, -2.9841 🏊🚲🚶🏃

### 7 PARSON'S POLE BRIDGE, RIVER TEME

There is some paddling just upstream of this pretty single-track bridge, but the best spot is at the weir downstream, with a rope swing and long deep stretch above, and little shingle beaches and pools below. Private but well used – be respectful.

→ At Brampton Bryan (SY7 0DH), 3 miles W of Leintwardine on A4113, turn N signed Buckton. The bridge is ½ mile on; no parking. Stile on L after bridge for paddling below, but for weir take rough path before bridge on R before, along field edge ⅓ mile.
10 mins, 52.3518, -2.9200 🏊🍴❓🚶🏃

### 8 BRINGEWOOD FORGE, RIVER TEME

Deep in a remote, wooded gorge a grand parapet bridge crosses the river by this elegant horseshoe weir. Built in 1772 by Richard Payne Knight as part of his development of Downton Castle, it fed a forge that used timber from the surrounding woods to smelt iron. The buildings are now lost ruins in the woods, and the river is a quiet place to walk and swim.

→ W of Ludlow on A4113 turn S at crossroads, signed Downton. Opp at next crossroads is Forge Ln down to weir and Bringewood Bridge, beyond SY8 2HY, but it is not a public road, so turn R and take the footpath 120m along the lane on L. No parking. The Herefordshire Trail footpath heads upstream for Castle Bridge, with caves, ruined mill and gorge. Or head downstream for another disused weir and mill.
10 mins, 52.3702, -2.8035 🏊❓🅿️🚶

### 9 BROMFIELD CHURCH, RIVER TEME

A stunning church with ceiling murals. Beyond is a bridge and weir, with riverside path and deep swimming upstream. Or continue into Ludlow to swim below the castle, or onto Ashford Carbonell beach.

→ Turn off A49 for A4113 Knighton, then immediately L dir SY8 2JP, to find church and parking L. Bridge is 200m further. Ludlow Teme is at SY8 1EG by the Green Café. Ashford Carbonell is down bridleway, SY8 4BY.
5 mins, 52.3858, -2.7638 ⛪🏊

### 10 LEINTWARDINE, RIVER TEME

On a stretch of common land and meadow in this delightful village is a deep section above the bridge with rope swing. Upstream find gravel beaches, pools and fun rapids in the

13

meanders. Stop in at The Lion for a pint or a meal after (see listing).

→ Find stile on S side of bridge (A4113, SY7 0JZ); some parking opp. Walk upstream for up to ¼ mile. This is private land but has permissive access, so be respectful.

2 mins, 52.3595, -2.8777 ▣▣▣

## LOST RUINS

### 11 HOPTON CASTLE

A handsome castle tower that fell into ruin after a notorious and bloody siege in 1644 during the Civil War. Restored and cared for by a community trust, it is now a happy place, home to many swallows.

→ SY7 0QF, signed from B4 367 at Hoptonheath, just N of railway bridge. Limited space, please park respectfully.

1 min, 52.3959, -2.9321 ▣

### 12 MONTGOMERY CASTLE & HILL FORT

Classic castle ruins sit on a high bluff looking down over the elegant town and the vale beyond. This is a deservedly popular place, so you won't be alone. Head higher and you will find the original Ffridd Faldwyn hill fort above, with even bigger views, earthworks and ancient woodland.

→ In Montgomery, follow the steep lane up and around from the junction by the Dragon Hotel to find a car park at the top, by SY15 6HN. Continue another ¼ mile (dir SY15 6HL) to find a footpath stile on R leading ⅓ mile to Ffridd Faldwyn (52.5645, -3.1564).

3 mins, 52.5634, -3.1499 ▣

### 13 DOLFORWYN CASTLE

The steep walk up the butterfly-filled lane is rewarded by yet more impressive views from the ruin of this castle, built in 1273 by the last sovereign Welsh prince, Llewelyn ap Gruffudd. Wildflowers abound in the ant-turreted grass surrounding the fort.

→ Turn L off A483, past SY15 6JG, just beyond Abermule. Small parking area ½ mile after postcode, up track on hillside.

15 mins, 52.5465, -3.2524 ▣▣

### 14 CASTELLTINBOETH & ST ANNO

Climb up though woods to these little-known castle remains set in an Iron Age hill fort high above the Ithon valley. Here you'll find part of the old gatehouse, the rest being steep earthworks. St Anno's church nearby is well worth a visit, located by the river – look out for its beautiful carved rood screen.

→ Heading N from Llanbister on A483, find

11

12

layby parking L ½ mile beyond LD1 6TS, with forest track heading diagonally up hillside opp to R. Follow the track ½ mile to the top of the forest line, then turn R to the hilltop and castle. St Anno's is next to layby parking at postcode (52.3596, -3.3295); another car park with WC is opp 150m N.
20 mins, 52.3696, -3.3378 🖵🚳✝

### 15 CLUN CASTLE & RIVER
Impressive towering 13th-century ruins on the side of a large motte, with a gangway into them. Roll down the steep grassy earthworks, wander through the meadow or swim in the river. There are several pubs and tea shops in the village to explore too.
→ In Clun, head S over river from SY7 8JP and turn immediately R for car park with wooden bridge to reach castle. There are some shallow pools by the wooden bridge, but deeper pools in the meadow. Keep going 200m to an old tree, and upstream to the back of the castle.
5 mins, 52.4222, -3.0330 🚳🏊

### 16 SNAILBEACH LEAD MINE
One of the most complete collections of mine building remains in England, and once one of the biggest and richest lead mines in the country. Above ground the ruins are unfenced and open for exploration, with signboards; there are regular volunteer-run open days if you wish to go underground.
→ Signed from the A488 at Ploxgreen, SW of Shrewsbury. After 1 mile, car park in Snailbeach is on R before SY5 0NS; walk up lane opp signed Lordshill. Underground tours can be booked for most Sundays, 11am–4pm (07716 116732). There are also ruins at Tankerville; layby parking on bend 2 miles S, walk into village for tricky-to-find permissive path off R opp the pottery, at 52.5888, -2.9531.
3 mins, 52.6141, -2.9254 🚳📷

## SUNSET HILL FORTS

### 17 CAER CARADOC
A stunning hill fort with fine views to the Long Mynd. Below is a man-made cave, where some claim Caratacus hid after his final stand against the Romans. Below is Comley Quarry, a place of pilgrimage for geologists, where Britain's first trilobite fossils were found in the 1880s. The Lawley is also a popular ridge walk.
→ Park in Church Stretton and walk dir SY6 7AY, along Watling St then Cwms Ln, then continue about 2 miles. Alternatively, leave A49 N of Church Stretton, to and past SY6 7JN

to parking for one at bend, 52.5636, -2.7619. Comley Quarry is through kissing gate then 100m across field (52.5639 -2.7627). 200m W is footpath up Caradoc, and just to the NE is The Lawley.

45 mins, 52.5541, -2.7731 🏞️🚲🚶

### 18 BURROW HILL CAMP

There is plenty to discover around this large Iron Age defended settlement. Multiple entrances lead through several massive banks and ditches, ancient trees and fine views – and if you can find them, ancient springs and hut platforms. Afterwards head to Hopesay Glebe Farm tea room (see listing).

→ On B4368 leaving Aston on Clun, dir SY7 8EP, find bridleway on R by hut (parking for one hut on verge) and walk. After 300m bear L uphill and continue for mile to reach forestry with route map, and another ½ mile up through woods to the hill fort.

40 mins, 52.4424, -2.9091 🏞️⛺🍴🔆🚲

### 19 BURY DITCHES, SUNNYHILL

One of the best hill forts in Shropshire, dating from the 6th century BC. A woodland walk leads up through its original entrance and past new wooden sculptures. Extensive views out from the ramparts.

→ In Clunton on B4368 take signed road N, past SY7 0HX and about 2 miles to car park on L with information boards.

10 mins, 52.4471, -2.9916 🏞️🐾🚲🚶

**SCRAMBLES & MINI PEAKS**

### 20 DEVIL'S CHAIR, STIPERSTONES

Superb views extend out from the dramatic, multi-pinnacled summit tors, great scrambling.

→ Follow road E from The Bog Visitor Centre, ¼ mile S of SY5 0NG (see listing), signed Stiperstones, to reach parking after a mile on L. Then bear NW and N uphill for a mile, via Cranberry and Manstone Rock peaks.

40 mins, 52.5866, -2.9337 🏞️🔆

### 21 FLOUNDERS' FOLLY, DINCHOPE

This grand tower atop Callow Hill was built in 1838. It has been renovated by the Flounders' Folly Trust and is now open to the public one day a month (listed on their website and staffed by volunteers). You can tell it's an open day by the St George's flag that flutters from the tower.

→ A mile NE of Lower Dinchope, signed Westwood at SY7 9JH, a gated forestry track ascends on R, with some verge parking.

20 mins, 52.4606, -2.7953 🏞️🔆

## 22 DEVIL'S MOUTH & LONG MYND

The Long Mynd means the 'long mountain', and the iconic views of the steep, heather-clad hills are stunning whatever the weather. Bronze Age remains abound in this natural place for retreat and fortification, but this earth dyke and knolly lookout are the easiest to visit. Continue up to Shooting Box tumulus car park and Pole Bank viewpoint, where you can see fragments of the Port Way, an ancient trackway that became a Roman road. There's excellent whinberry (bilberry) foraging in summer.

→ Signed The Burway/Longmynd from Church Stretton, opp SY6 6DN. Follow 1¼ miles, over cattle grid and on to parking on L. The dyke is 300m below E, and the knoll rises beyond. Continue on road 1 mile bearing R for Shooting Box (52.5532, -2.8554), or 1½ miles bearing L for parking and Pole Bank R (52.5445, -2.8639).
3 mins, 52.5429, -2.8263 🖼🚶🚲

## 23 NIPSTONE ROCK

One of the most distinctive of the white quartzite tors along the Stiperstones ridge, and a nice easy climb or scramble above regenerating heather slopes.

→ From The Bog Visitor Centre (see listing) head S ½ mile, dir Linley. Find forestry, parking

signboard and track on L, before SY5 0NJ.
10 mins, 52.5652, -2.9500 🖼🚲

### ANCIENT TREES & WILDLIFE

## 24 THE HOLLIES & BROOK VESSONS

Starting at an old chapel, twisted hollies and birdsong pervade this peaceful and magical woodland and open grassland reserve. On a mile to Brook Vessons for more ancient trees, including unusually large birch, crab apples and rowan. A little further are the cottage ruins of Blackmoregate, a remote miner-squatters' settlement. One cottage has now been restored to its original state (open second Sunday each month).

→ Park and walk up lane as for Snailbeach Lead Mine (see entry), keep going past SY5 0NS to the top, ½ mile in all, then turn L down to the reserve sign and chapel. If you are brave you can drive to this point, as there is parking for one car and limited turning (52.6132, -2.9164). Head up track bearing S for Hollies; from here contour via L fork a mile for Brook Vessons 52.6024, -2.9140, or climb via R fork a mile for Blackmoregate at 52.6046, -2.9194. There is also an option to walk in from the lane end at Upper Vessons Farm at SY5 0SG.
30 mins, 52.6087, -2.9126 🅿🚗🖼🚲

## 25 RECTORY WOOD, CHURCH STRETTON

These woodland gardens between the town and the wild hills were influenced by Capability Brown. At their centre is a lake surrounded by ancient yews, an icehouse and folly; other ruins, including a grotto and a pathway, lie hidden in the trees. Bluebells carpet the woods in May.

→ Limited parking outside the church (Churchway, turn by SY6 6DA). A gate in the brick wall at end leads up into the gardens. Bear to the R of the hill for the lake.

15 mins, 52.5402, -2.8126 🅿️✖🏘️

## 26 HELMETH WOOD & GAER STONE

Like a sylvan island in a sea of bare hills, this ancient woodland is carpeted in blue bells in May. The views alone are worth the climb: opposite is the craggy outcrop of Gaer Stone, a great little climb and scramble, leading up to Hope Bowdler Hill.

→ On the B4371 from Church Stretton dir Much Wenlock there is layby parking on L after a mile, just before SY6 7ET. Follow signed track past Gaerstones Farm, then bear L for Helmeth Hill woods; a path leads around the hill. Bear up R before farm for Gaer Stone.

20 mins, 52.5385, -2.7881 🅿️📷🌼

## 27 LINLEY HILL BEECH AVENUE

If you like majestic old trees and awesome views, take a walk up this drovers' road, now part of the Shropshire Way. Vast beeches planted 200 years ago to commemorate the British victory in the Napoleonic Wars, some with battered boughs and ravaged trunks, line the grassy route up to the top. Views spread from your vantage point for miles over the countryside.

→ A mile W of Norbury, turn R just before SY9 5HL, signed Cold Hill/The Bog. After ½ mile find Shropshire Way waymarker on R and room for one to park. Follow path to beeches.

5 mins, 52.5371, -2.9579 🅿️🚶

## 28 BRAMPTON BRYAN SWEET CHESTNUTS

Follow the Herefordshire Trail from this pretty half-timbered village up the tree-lined avenue into the Harley estate (of London Harley Street fame). There are many ancient trees on the parkland, including these enormous sweet chestnuts.

→ In Brampton Bryan, A4113 W of Leintwardine, park near the little triangular green at SY7 0DH and walk up estate driveway for a mile. Another giant sweet chestnut is at 52.3361, -2.9437.

20 mins, 52.3368, -2.9423 🅿️

### 29 DOLYDD HAFREN/SEVERN MEADOWS

If you can manage the bumpy, potholed road to the car park and like bird watching, then you are in for a treat. A short walk through woods and open glades takes you to two hides, both overlooking the ever-changing landscape of the young Severn floodplain. Rich in wildlife, springtime heralds boxing hares, and in late May we saw sand martins in abundance in the steep sandbanks, a grass snake, curlews and plovers.

→ As for Rhydwhyman (see entry), but continue 1 mile beyond the turn to SY15 6HD and take unsigned L at bend, before SY21 8NR. Continue to car park at end of track. A longish path leads round to the hide. You can gain access to the river too: as you walk in, 300m from the car park, the field gate on L is a footpath.

10 mins, 52.5925, -3.1810 🦅🏞

### 30 KERRY RIDGEWAY & OFFA'S DYKE

Two of Wales' greatest ancient roads cross at this point. Offa's Dyke, with earthworks, banks and ancient trees, meets the Kerry Ridgeway from Newtown to Bishop's Castle. Now mostly lane and byway, this was once an important drovers' route for bringing cattle to England. It follows a high, empty ridge along the top of the Shropshire Hills, with burrows, Bronze Age mounds and immense views, and never drops below 300m. Best explored by bike.

→ The Kerry Ridgeway starts W of Bishop's Castle; take Welsh St, signed Pantglas to ½ mile W of SY9 5JR. Bishop's Moat motte is in field R at start, Caer Din hill fort on R after 1 mile. Offa's Dyke crosses at SY15 6TP. The more W sections are more off-road (mainly track byways, good for campervans) so also try Lower Shortditch Turbary, a nature reserve and earthworks at 52.4884, -3.1454. A stone circle is at 52.4661, -3.2415 near SY7 8PS.

5 mins, 52.4992, -3.0940 🚲📷✦🚴

### 31 MITCHELL'S FOLD STONE CIRCLE

This impressive early Bronze Age stone circle has a fine position up on Stapeley Common, in an area that seems to have been a centre of ancient activity, with other circles and an axe factory nearby. There may once have been twice as many stones, and the tallest was once one of a pair, making an impressive entrance.

→ Signed from A488, dir Priest Weston. Follow lane W 1¼ miles to find track R, on bend (½ mile after SY5 0JJ). Follow to parking area at end.

5 mins, 52.5788, -3.0283 🚲📷

### 32 ABBEY CWMHIR

This would be the largest church nave in Wales, if it still stood. Only a few sections of wall remain from a once-extensive Cistercian abbey. Literally the 'abbey of the long valley', it commands a beautiful remote setting with a lake and is thought to be the final resting place of Llewellyn ap Gruffudd, last sovereign Prince of Wales.

→ Abbey-cwm-hir signed off A483 N of Llandrindod Wells, ¾ mile N of LD1 6RS. Follow lane 4¼ miles to LD1 6PH and park at church. Signed opp.

2 mins, 52.3298, -3.3873 🚲✝

### 33 VAN DOESBURGS, CHURCH STRETTON

If you're exploring the Long Mynd, pack your picnic with super sandwiches, quiches, Scotch eggs, sourdough loaves and cakes from this gourmet deli.

→ 3 High St, Church Stretton, SY6 6BU, 01694 722867.
52.5388, -2.8077 🍴

### 34 CULTIVATE, NEWTOWN

Stock up on local fruit and vegetables, bread, honey and milk and at this social-enterprise food shop in Glanhafren Market Hall. Open 9am–5pm Tues–Sat.

→ 26 Market Street, Newtown, SY16 2PD, 07498 756148.
52.5145, -3.3149 🍴

### 35 TEA ON THE WAY, CLUN

Enjoy home-made cakes and light lunches from the garden or in the garden of this lovely little family-run farmhouse café. Open March–October.

→ 3 Guilden Down, Clun, SY7 8NZ, 07795 275557.
52.4379, -3.0169 🍴

### 36 MID WALES ART CENTRE, MAES-MAWR

Quirky art gallery, sculpture garden and B&B with exhibitions, workshops and a little café serving Aga toasties, avocado toast, scones with homemade jam and Welsh-roasted coffee.

→ Caersws, SY17 5SB, 01686 688369.
52.5111, -3.4243 🍴

### 37 THE NAGS HEAD INN, GARTHMYL

Gastropub with rooms serving good locally sourced food and beers in a modernised coaching inn.

→ Garthmyl, SY15 6RS, 01686 640600.
52.5828, -3.1913 🍴🛏

### 38 THE BOG VISITOR CENTRE

A lovely visitor centre and simple community café serving delicious cream teas, cakes and quiche lunches, though less-good coffee. Excellent displays explain the intriguing local geology, mining history and wildlife. Bring cash (cards not accepted) and stock up on home-made jams, pottery and crafts. Free wifi and excellent selection of walking and reference books for sale and to read.

➜ Stiperstones, SY5 0NG, 01743 792484.
52.5756, -2.9516 🍴

### 39 HOPESAY GLEBE FARM TEA ROOM

Little tea room on an organic smallholding just off the Shropshire Way, serving home-made cakes and cream teas, and if you book in advance, soups and ploughman's. Weekends only; closed in winter.

➜ Hopesay, SY7 8HA, 01588 660737.
52.4444, -2.8997 🍴

### 40 MILEBROOK HOUSE HOTEL

This country hotel by the River Teme was once the home of explorer Sir Wilfred Thesiger, and now serves seasonal meals, sourced locally or from their own garden. If it's warm, eat out on the terrace and then take a walk down to the river.

➜ Milebrook, LD7 1LT, 01547 528632.
52.3483, -3.0063 🍴🚲

### 41 LUDLOW FOOD CENTRE & KITCHEN

Buy game and estate-reared meats, seasonal vegetables and deli foods from this slick farm shop, where 80 percent of the produce comes from Shropshire and the surrounding counties. Delicious breakfasts, lunches, coffee and cake are served in the onsite Ludlow Kitchen café.

➜ Bromfield, SY8 2JR, 01584 856000.
52.3892, -2.7608 🍴

### 42 CASTLE KITCHEN, MONTGOMERY

Deli and café with a pretty garden at the back. Stock up on Spanish charcuterie, Welsh cheeses and a host of more unusual delicacies. Open daily 9am–4.30pm (Sun from 11am).

➜ 8 Broad St, Montgomery, SY15 6PH, 01686 668795.
52.5603, -3.1480 🍴

### 43 THE GREEN CAFÉ, LUDLOW

In a pretty setting under the Dinham Bridge, this charming Bib Gourmand café offers simple, seasonal and local lunches and coffees. Open 10am–4pm Tues–Sun, lunch 12pm–2.30pm. Book ahead!

➜ Mill on the Green, Ludlow, SY8 1EG, 01584 879872.
52.3663, -2.7250 🍴

## FRIENDLY PUBS

### 44 THE BRIDGES, RATLINGHOPE

An idyllic location in summer, when children can play in the stream. A rural pub catering to both locals and travellers with classic pub grub and Three Tuns Shropshire ales. Rooms available.

➜ Ratlinghope, SY5 0ST, 01588 650260.
52.5624, -2.8963 🍺🍴🚲

### 45 THE SUN INN, LEINTWARDINE

A real ale, drinks-only pub that remains gloriously unchanged from its days as a traditional parlour pub. Fiddler's Elbow fish and chips is next door, and you're allowed to bring them in and eat them with your pint.

➜ Rosemary Ln, Leintwardine, SY7 0LP, 01547 540705.
52.3597, -2.8745 🍺

### 46 THE LION, LEINTWARDINE

Named the best pub in Shropshire, this large dining pub with rooms serves ribs of roast beef, locally grown pesticide-free salads and local ales, on large wooden tables in the bar or in a garden under the willow trees by the river.

➜ High St, Leintwardine, SY7 0JZ, 01547 540203.
52.3596, -2.8767 🍺🍴🚲

### 47 APPLE TREE, ONIBURY

A lovely community-run pub with garden, serving locally sourced Sunday roasts and home grown veg, pies, soups and sandwiches alongside real ale.

➜ Onibury, SY7 9AW, 01584 856633.
52.4081, -2.8029 🍺🍴

### 48 SUN INN, MARTON

Enjoy delicious, fresh and creative home cooking in this relaxed village pub.

➜ Marton, SY21 8JP, 01938 561211.
52.6149, -3.0550 🍴

### 49 THE CHECKERS, MONTGOMERY

Excellent Michelin-starred six-course dinners in a relaxed but refined, family-run former coaching inn with rooms.

➜ Broad St, Montgomery, SY15 6PN, 01686 669822.
52.5605, -3.1479 🍺🍴🚲

### 50 THREE TUNS INN, BISHOP'S CASTLE

Opened in 1642, this might be the oldest brewery and pub in Britain. Today it's filled with a happy chaos of locals and visitors coming for the real ales and pub grub.

→ Salop St, Bishop's Castle, SY9 5BW, 01588 638797.
52.4945, -2.9968

### 51 THE SIX BELLS, BISHOP'S CASTLE

A quirky pub and brewery serving home-brewed beers alongside curry and fish-and-chip dinners in colourful surroundings.

→ Church St, Bishop's Castle SY9 5AA, 01588 630144.
52.4900, -2.9985

### 52 THE WHITE HORSE INN, CLUN

Real ales, live Welsh bands, home-made local food and B&B in this 16th-century inn near Clun castle.

→ The Square, Clun, SY7 8JA, 01588 418127.
52.4215, -3.0302

### 53 THE COACH HOUSE, NORBURY

Excellent Shropshire-sourced meals, ales, tasting evenings and pie nights. This dining inn with rooms has won many awards for its dinners, breakfasts and use of seasonal local produce. Open Wed–Sat evenings. Also take a moment to visit the massive ancient yew in All Saint's churchyard opposite.

→ Norbury, SY9 5DX, 01588 650846.
52.5297, -2.9385

## WILDER CAMPING

### 54 SMALL BATCH CAMPSITE

Streamside family camping in a pretty valley setting at the foot of the Long Mynd. It's just a five-minute walk from the wisteria-clad Ragleth Inn.

→ Little Stretton, Church Stretton, SY6 6PW, 01694 723358.
52.5229, -2.8261

### 55 FOXHOLES CASTLE CAMPING

Just outside Bishop's Castle is the eco-minded Foxholes, with a bunkhouse, wooden cabins and hedge-lined camping fields amid wildflower meadows, each with their own character and views. Head to the yurt field for a little more peace.

→ Montgomery Rd, Bishop's Castle, SY9 5HA, 01588 638924.
52.5011, -2.9972

### 56 MILLSTREAM CAMP, BUCKTON

Adults-only shepherd's hut with outdoor bath heated by a wood fire and summer swimming in the millstream. Attached to Lower Buckton Country House B&B with excellent meals and breakfasts.

→ Buckton, SY7 0JU, 01547 540532.
canopyandstars.co.uk
52.3548, -2.9054

## RUSTIC HAVENS

### 57 UPPER SHADYMOOR FARM

Feather Down Farm safari tents sit in a woodland glade with a little swimming lake, pontoon and outdoor wood-fired hot tub. There's a deer park and game cooking workshops, as well as all the farm animals. Farmhouse B&B with home-sourced evening meals also available.

→ Stapleton, Dorrington, SY5 7AL, 01743 718670.
52.6140, -2.8076

### 58 THE SHIPPEN, LINLEY

Escape the world, sleep with the stars and wake up to views in this chic and gloriously remote stone-and-wood hideaway in the hills. One double room with an additional sofabed for children.

→ Little Wood House, Linley, SY9 5HP, 07747 115935.
52.5574, -2.9548

### 59 BUCKSHEAD ECO-COTTAGE

An eco-renovated stone cottage on an organic farm near Rhos Fiddle nature reserve. Glorious views out of the rolling hills, where hares, curlews and rare plants are abundant.

→ Brynmawr, Newcastle, SY7 8QU, 01905 339544.
52.4569, -3.1510

### 60 ACTON SCOTT FARM

Four charming holiday houses set on a beautiful historic farm estate, our favourite is the restored Shooting Lodge. On the estate is the Acton Scott working farm museum, preserved to showcase 19th-century farming and rural crafts.

→ Acton Scott, SY6 6QQ, 0345 2680785.
52.5042, -2.8008

### 61 WALCOT HALL

We love this wonderful collection of quirky holiday cottages, camping and glamping, including a fairytale tin church, yurts and a gypsy caravan, all dotted around a stunning Georgian estate with an old arboretum, lake and river.

→ Lydbury North, SY7 8AZ, 01588 680570. 52.4588, -2.9600

## 62 HOUSE-BOX & CLOUD-HOUSE

Stargaze in style and comfort in the cosy converted horse-box or the colourful yurt. Beautiful views abound, and there is extra space for camping if friends want to join.

→ Kinton, SY15 6BU, 0117 2047830. canopyandstars.co.uk
52.5879, -3.0509

## 63 UNDER THE OAK & UNDER THE ASH

A cosy converted wooden railway wagon with a veranda and a showman's wagon, with woodburners, barbecues, a shared hot outdoor shower and utter peace.

→ Green Cottage, Llanbister, LD1 6UN, 0117 2047830. canopyandstars.co.uk
52.3697, -3.3004

55

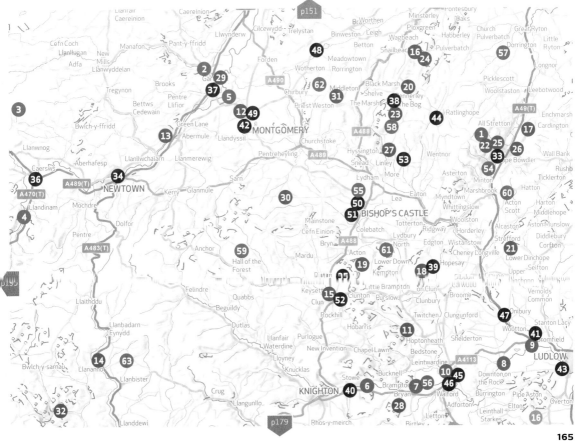

# RADNOR &
# UPPER WYE

## Our perfect weekend

→ **Safari** the Wye by canoe and camp in the orchard at Racquety Farm

→ **Tour** the three white churches in the secret valley of Edw, and picnic by the stream

→ **Sleep** out in Llywelyn's cave and imagine the last night of the last Prince of Wales

→ **Climb** up the ruins of the earliest surviving stone castle in Britain at Richard's Castle

→ **Scale** the ramparts of Croft Ambrey hill fort, with bluebells in spring and ancient oaks to climb

→ **Feast** at The Stagg at Titley, the first ever British pub to win a Michelin star, and take a dip in the cooling River Arrow after

→ **Explore** the fairytale overgrown ruins of Wigmore Castle

→ **Visit** the oldest tree in Britain at Discoed, then walk a section of Offa's Dyke and finish with a waterside picnic at Dolley Old Bridge

→ **Relax** by the fire of the cosy Harp Inn after a fine dinner, then walk back across moonlit fields to the perfectly rustic Stockwell Farm

This rugged pastoral landscape bestows a feeling of timelessness, with millennia-old meadows and medieval trees, meandering rivers and ancient hill forts. It feels so peaceful that it is easy to forget the many centuries of bloodshed that these borderlands have endured.

Offa's Dyke, the 8th-century defensive earthworks built to contain Powys, marches through the parish of Discoed, guarded by a fine display of massive oaks. Powys is renowned for monumental trees, and the yew at St Michael's in Discoed is thought to be one the most ancient in Britain – with a girth of 11 metres, it could be 4,000 years old.

Picturesque ruined castles still mark the landscape, if you know where to look. The stone motte and bailey of Richard's Castle, built before 1066, is now a hushed, verdant place patrolled by goats. The wonderfully wild remains of Wigmore Castle, with its stairways and turrets, beg to be explored. Sometimes you will need to search out any masonry remains amongst the trees and roots, such as those at Cefnllys. Here and at Aberedw and Croft Castle the original hill forts lie nearby, layering history upon history.

In the upper reaches of the Lugg valley, the church of Pilleth, with a deep holy well, still revered for its healing powers, stands below Bryn Glas. In 1402 this was the site of one of the bloodiest battles in the Welsh independence wars, and a great victory for Owain Glyndŵr. The English were decimated, and they say the river Lugg ran red with blood.

Today the Lugg runs clear, and in summer this is a wild-swimming wonderland. At the idyllic Lugg Meadows near Hereford you can sit in meadows dense with wildflowers and butterflies. Parallel to the Lugg is the gentle Arrow, with a long, deep weir pool below emerald alders at Staunton on Arrow, and pools below the bridge at pretty Pembridge. They meet below Leominster, where you can swim behind the church in Bodenham.

But the Wye wears the river crown here. The pools and rapids at Pen-ddôl Rocks at Builth Wells are particularly impressive, and the stretch at Erwood is a delight, rich with kingfishers, peregrines and otters. At the north escarpment of the Brecon Beacons you'll find excellent canoeing and the charming literary town of Hay-on-Wye. The Warren, a community-owned meadow, is a 10-minute walk upstream from the town centre. Used for rabbits in medieval times, today it's an idyllic place to paddle, skim stones or watch canoeists negotiate the rapids.

Best of all this whole area is bursting with excellent places to eat, from fine dining, to cosy old inns to cheerful riverside cafés.

## WILD WYE

### 1 PEN-DDÔL ROCKS, RIVER WYE

An exciting stretch of the Wye, narrowing through rocky cliffs near Builth Wells. Upstream the water is deeper, passing through a small gorge with rock formations. Downstream find safe, white-sand bays.

→ A mile N of Builth Wells on A470 find small layby on L directly opp entrance to Penmaenau Caravan Park, just before LD2 3RD. Stile in fence in layby leads down steep bank to rapids.

2 mins, 52.1613, -3.4195

### 2 ERWOOD BRIDGE SLIPWAY, RIVER WYE

The new slipway track below the road bridge makes this an easy spot to access the grassy shore and beach, where you can play in the rapids and rocky pools so typical of this section of the Wye. You can launch your canoe here and paddle downstream to Glasbury or Boughrood (see listing). Want to canoe? (see listing) can arrange drop-offs and pick-ups.

→ Turn off A470 S of Builth Wells signed Aberedw (dir LD2 3SJ) to find new path on far side of bridge.

2 mins, 52.0848, -3.3293

### 3 BOUGHROOD, RIVER WYE

A large, very secluded pool lies in a kink of the Wye above the rapids.

→ Pull off A470 by suspension bridge 350m N of turning to LD2 3TQ (park on grass). Walk S on verge over bridge to find footpath L just after, and follow S for a mile. Do not swim if people are fishing. Or, from Boughrood take Station Rd N, past LD3 0YF for ¾ mile, to find a small wooden fisherman's gate in hedge on L, at 52.0543, -3.2784 (no parking). The old railway path leads upstream 100m to the pool.

3 mins, 52.0541, -3.2803

### 4 BREDWARDINE & WINFORTON

Bredwardine Bridge is a popular and easy spot for a swim on the River Wye. At low flow there are beaches and shallows, making it good for children. Or head upstream a little and play in the deeper pools, where you can dive back in from the base of the bridge. Upstream further, from Winforton, is a remote curve of the Wye with the remains of an old land quay, excellent for swimming too.

→ Turn off B4352 at Bredwardine, signed Hereford, past HR3 6BT. Footpath is on R before bridge, but parking is by L turn on far side of bridge, beyond Brobury Hs gardens. For Winforton, turn off A438 down Baker's Lane

by red barn (HR3 6EF). Keep going down rough byway (no parking at end, so park and walk) and bear R along field at end to 52.1101, -3.0353.

2 mins, 52.0962, -2.9706

### 5 THE WARREN, HAY-ON-WYE

A deservedly popular stretch of meadow owned by the community. There's a long, white shingle beach, shaded by trees, a pool and shallows below the rapids and deeper section above. A beautiful setting.

→ In Hay turn opp the Swan Hotel (HR3 5DQ), past St Mary's Church. After 500m, drive/walk down bumpy track R to car park at bottom. Or walk upstream from Hay 10 mins; footpath at end of Wyeford Rd (HR3 5BJ).

3 mins, 52.0761, -3.1369

### 6 WANT TO CANOE? HAY-ON-WYE

Our friends Aubrey and Clare run the best place to rent a canoe on the Wye, at Racquety Farm (see listing). They'll make drop-offs and pick-ups for half- or full-day or overnight trips, and guided trips can be arranged.

→ On L immediately after crossing bridge from Hay-on-Wye, on Bridge St/B4351, HR3 5RS, 01497 820604.

2 min, 52.0761, -3.1294

### 7 DOLLEY OLD BRIDGE, RIVER LUGG

Offa's Dyke crosses the River Lugg here, with a coppice grove, gravel beaches with paddling and some deep pools for a dip. Great fun for kids.

→ W of Presteigne on B4356 take turn on bend 350m W of LD8 2NQ, signed Cascob. After a mile, by postbox and barn, park opp by gate. Take footpath by gate, continue 350m across 2 fields to river bridge. Pools are downstream.

10 mins, 52.2811, -3.0597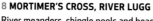

### 8 MORTIMER'S CROSS, RIVER LUGG

River meanders, shingle pools and beaches set within a water-meadow nature reserve and guarded by many ancient, hollow willows. Reported No Swimming signs 2020.

→ Turn off A4110 S of Aymestry at Mortimer's Cross, signed Tenbury (B4362). After 100m park on R before bridge at HR6 9PE, and cross bridge to find footpath downstream. Cross two fields for the meanders across the water meadows. Please check with landowner.

10 mins, 52.2668, -2.8374

### 9 EYTON, RIVER LUGG

Discover over a mile of secluded deep pools and beaches, weirs and footbridges, with shallows meandering through open pasture and little wooded glades. Very pretty and rarely visited.

→ B4361 N from Leominster, turn L signed Eyton/Lucton after a mile. Then L dir HR6 0AQ, signed Aston/Lucton, after another mile (park on verge here). Find double steel gates on L after ⅓ mile, before first house (no footpath sign, but it is) and follow track 400m, bearing R at end, towards to river, bridge and weir 400m. Cross bridge and head downstream for deeper sections and second weir.

15 mins, 52.2474, -2.7849

### 10 FISHPOOL VALLEY, CROFT CASTLE

Deep in the valley, these five spring-fed lakes are rich in trout and dragonflies. Look out for the ruined pumphouse by the upper lake, and icehouse further down. The only swimming lake is at the very bottom, quite near the bottom of the drive. It has a small gravel beach.

→ Turn off the B4362 at HR6 0BL for Croft Castle (NT) and follow the long, tree-lined drive up to the car park on R. From the bottom of the car park follow the track down into the

wooded valley to find the lowest pond. There is also a circular route (yellow markers) to view the top three lakes, and a path to Croft Ambrey hill fort (see listing).

15 mins, 52.2863, -2.7953

### 11 BODENHAM, RIVER LUGG & LAKE

Long, sandy river beach and pools in meadows behind the church. Walk a bit further and you'll find a beautiful, clear, gravel lake (it's a nature reserve, particularly important in winter, so be respectful. Swimming no longer permitted).

→ Village is signed off A49 and A417 S of Leominster. Head into village and turn past HR1 3JU to church. Follow path behind church to river, cross bridge, then downstream 200m for beaches, or stay on near side of river and follow meadow upstream to find corner of lake on R after 400m. Alternatively park at the nature reserve car park just W of village and head S for quieter SE corner of lake.

5 mins, 52.1535, -2.6892

## RIVER ARROW

### 12 PEMBRIDGE, RIVER ARROW

Pretty spot with good paddling by the bridge and deeper swimming holes downstream in the meadows.

→ 7 miles W of Leominster on A44, turn R by Red Lion past HR6 9EY and cross bridge to find car park on L. Paddle by the picnic tables or walk back across bridge and L down track 200m to Long Meadow, following river bank to meanders and deeper pools downstream.

10 mins, 52.2212, -2.8935

### 13 STAUNTON ON ARROW, RIVER ARROW

Grassy riverside and lovely deep water upstream of the weir, good for jumping and diving. Also another deep stretch downstream of village, below Gig Bridge.

→ Staunton on Arrow is signed from B4355, 3 miles N of Kington. After 1½ miles find gate and footpath on R with space for one car, HR6 9HS. Follow hedge down to river. There is also a footbridge and sunny river bank path just downstream of the village at Gig Bridge (52.2331, -2.9240); it's deep here too, above the weir at Court of Noke manor.

2 mins, 52.2373, -2.9392

## OTHER RIVERS

### 14 ALPINE BRIDGE, RIVER ITHON

Beauty spot popular with Victorian sightseers, little visited now. Surprisingly sunken gorge in the river with deep pools below a bridge.

16

15

19

→ Take A483 N from Llandrindod Wells for 2 miles. Just before LD1 5ST and church, after bridge, take unsigned road R. Continue 1½ mile beyond to pull off on R after bungalow. Take path SW through old stile gate across field to river bridge.

5 mins, 52.2585, -3.3338 ⛱

### 15 RIVER EDW WEIR

The Edw stream transforms into deep water at the weir, with a rope swing and pool. The valley is quiet and open, with picnic tables by the water and old quarries over the lane. Perfect for family picnics.

→ Leave Aberedw E past pub then find small weir and picnic spot after 1½ miles, ½ mile beyond LD2 3UR.

1 mins, 52.1244, -3.3138 ⛱🐾🍽

### LOST RUINS & CAVES

### 16 RICHARD'S CASTLE & CHURCH

Overgrown ruins of pre-Conquest 11th-century stone castle in a walled complex – look out for the goats who climb the steep walls. Adjacent St. Bartholomew church is beautiful inside and has a rare detached bell tower.

→ Turn off B4361 at Richards Castle signed Historic Church. After ¾ mile, park outside

church before SY8 4ET. A path from the rear L of church leads up to castle site.

2 mins, 52.3281, -2.7597 🚗✝

### 17 LLYWELYN'S CAVE

Llywelyn ap Gruffydd, last sovereign Prince of Wales, is said to have passed his last night alive in this shelter, before Wales' defeat by Edward I of England on 11th December 1282. You'll find a small cave, with peephole lookout.

→ Head E out of Aberedw, past pub (LD2 3UW) and turn R up hill after bridge. Take hard R up rough track by grit bin, bear L at top of wooded slope. Continue through a gate with the hedge on R. The next gate on R leads to field and path on L to cave, 100m. If driving, you might try and drive all this way, or leave car in Aberedw.

15 mins, 52.1126, -3.3397 🥾🚴❓

### 18 WIGMORE CASTLE

Children will love playing 'capture the castle' among the steps, gateways, turrets and walls of this picturesque ruined fortress. High on a hill and lost in the woodland, the Norman castle was once the stronghold of the powerful Mortimer family; 'slighted' to ensure it couldn't be used in the Civil War, it has been a ruin since. All open access, wonderful views.

→ In Wigmore, turn off A4110 at The Oak inn (see listing) to parking on R at HR6 9UN. Walk back to main road and cross to find signed path to church on R, becoming a lane and then path again at Green Hill Farm HR6 9UB.
15 mins, 52.3184, -2.8696 🖼️🚷🖼️

## SACRED & ANCIENT

### 19 PILLETH CHURCH & WELL

St Mary's is a little white church on a hillside above the young River Lugg. The hill is the site of one of the most famous Welsh victories, the Battle of Bryn Glas in 1402. You can descend the steps into the holy well, still revered for its healing properties. The giant redwoods on the hill mark the site of the battle, where casualties were buried. Down below by the Lugg are the remains of Castell Foel-Allt, an earlier Mortimer castle.

→ Five miles W of Presteigne on B4356, ½ mile before LD7 1NR track N signed Battle of Pilleth leads up to parking by church and holy well. ½ mile E of this a bridleway leads S down to the river and the earthwork remains of a Norman motte at 52.3024, -3.0888
2 mins, 52.3073, -3.0921 ✝️🖼️🖼️

### 20 ARTHUR'S STONE, DORSTONE

This great stone cromlech has nine upright stones, a right-angled passage and a massive capstone. Its name belies its age; it dates from at least 2,700 BC, well before any Arthurian legend. The perfect place to enjoy the sunset.

→ Enter Dorstone on B4348 from E, then signed R at bend. Over the top of the hill take first L (unsigned), to find it on roadside L (some parking, just after HR3 6AX). Continue along lane to sharp R bend for footpath up Merbach Hill, fine valley views (52.0965, -3.0181).
1 min, 52.0823, -2.9954 🖼️🚲🖼️

### 21 WHITE CHURCHES OF THE EDW

Best by bicycle, the little lost valley of the Edw is adorned with May blossom and wild daffodils in spring. Its tiny lanes are home to three ancient white churches, each with its own charm and character.

→ Start upstream with the oldest, 13th-century St David's in Cregrina, 200m S of LD1 5SF (52.1601, -3.2826). Then S to the most secluded, St David's in Rhulen, up a track just S of LD2 3UY (52.1400, -3.2613). Finally St Padarn's in Llanbadarn-y-garreg sits alone in a field by the river just E of LD2 3UT, with paddling too (52.1298, -3.2985).
2 mins, 52.1601, -3.2826 🌀✝️🖼️

18

## HILLTOPS

### 22 THE ROUNDABOUT, BEGWNS

On the high point of the Begwns is the Roundabout, a circular Victorian enclosure around a grove of trees, replanted and rebuilt by the NT to mark the millennium. At the centre is a curious little amphitheatre with seats – perhaps a place to put on a play or sit around a small campfire?

→ A438 a mile N of Glasbury, turn L signed Maesyronnen Chapel (on R 170m after HR3 5NJ). Do look in as you pass – this was the first Nonconformist chapel in Wales, 1690. Continue to Ffynnon Gynydd, turn R and R again then continue 2 miles to brow of hill (½ mile before LD2 3JN). Pull off L and follow path up to trees on hilltop L. Another good hilltop is Twyn y Garth, with a First World War field gun memorial (52.0847, -3.3038).
10 mins, 52.0915, -3.2346 🖼️⛰️

### 23 ABEREDW MOTTE & CASTLE

This pretty old motte stands in a fine position overlooking the Wye and Edw. Further on are the scant remains of a stone castle, overgrown by roots and trees.

→ In Aberedw follow path from rear of lovely St Cewydd church graveyard (LD2 3UN) ,

20

21

26

23

24

next to Seven Stars pub, to climb the mound. Continue along river and turn R along old railway ¼ mile to find remains of stone castle (52.1166, -3.3500).
5 mins, 52.1153, -3.3474 🚗📷

### 24 CASTLE BANK, GILWERN HILL
This fine hill fort enjoys striking views of the wild Radnor hills, and its plateau retains an almost mystical feel. The remains of a stone curtain wall encircle a large rocky knoll.
➔ From A483 Howey, S of Llandindod Wells, turn L signed Hundred House. Continue 2½ mile and look out for field gate on R (½ mile before LD1 5RL) with footpath and some verge parking, leading up to summit – or choose own route across the open-access land.
30 mins, 52.1954, -3.3373 🚗

### 25 CROFT AMBREY HILL FORT & OAKS
Built in the mid-Iron Age, with a Romano-Celtic temple and then a medieval warren added later, this remained a strategic military site until the 16th century. The 32 acres of rampart-defended hilltop boast incredible views, and knobbly ancient oaks and springtime bluebells reward those who make the walk up from Croft Castle.

➔ Park at NT Croft Castle as for Fishpool Valley (see entry). From car park bear R through gate, following the track around to L, and follow blue markers up the hill past a cottage.
30 mins, 52.2967, -2.8179 🚗📷🌼♿🚶

### 26 CEFNLLYS CASTLE, RIVER & CHURCH
Cross the stream on 'Shaky Bridge' to this peaceful pasture headland, protected by a large meander of the Ithon. The scant but complex rubble remains of two Norman castles, an Iron Age enclosure and a medieval settlement lie atop the hill ahead, and hidden in the meadow north is the church of St Michael's, accessible only on foot.
➔ From Llandrindod town centre follow Spa Rd East then Cefnllys Lane past LD1 5PD, continuing ¾ mile after that to reach parking R after bend with track to river.
10 mins, 52.2418, -3.3417 🏊†🚗🛶

### 27 BACH CAMP HILL FORT
Climb the ramparts and roll down the slopes of this peaceful hill fort – its history remains obscure. There is a great tree at the bottom of the field, perfect for climbing. Secluded and little known.
➔ 3 miles E of Leominster, A44, turn L dir Hatfield. First L after a mile, dir Brockmanton.

After 2 miles at rough R fork, just before HR6
0ES, find footpath on L with some parking,
which leads ¼ mile back through fields to the
earthworks.

10 mins, 52.2381, -2.6663 🖼️🌳💦

## TREES & MEADOWS

### 28 LUGG MEADOWS & RIVER

The meandering Lugg creates deep pools and
little beaches as it makes its way across the
county's most important surviving Lammas
meadow – opened for common grazing on the
1st of August, Lammas Day. Look out for the
rare and beautiful snake's head fritillary in
April. Great for wild swimming.

→ Follow A438 Ledbury road E out of
Hereford to 120m past HR1 1QW. At the green
turn L, signed Hereford Nature Trail and park
at HR1 1UT, where signboard and gates lead
into meadow. Head N for ½ mile to reach river.
Hampton Meadow nature reserve downstream
is also beautiful and good for a dip (52.0472,
-2.6447, bridleway ½ mile NW of HR1 4EW,
Hampton Bishop).

15 mins, 52.0657, -2.6829 🏊💦

### 29 DISCOED & CASCOB YEWS

Britain's oldest trees are all yews, and all
found in churchyards – some are remnants of
more ancient, pagan sacred sites. This one, in
the churchyard of St Michael's, is one of the
oldest: a male, 2,500–4,000 years old and
boasting a girth of over 11m. Also seek out
the nearby Cascob yew, at St Michael and All
Angels Church, and Offa's Dyke oak on the
way (see listing).

→ 2 miles W of Presteigne on B4356, turn L on
bend signed Cascob. After a mile, opp postbox
and barn, park by gate. Walk L up smaller
steeper lane to church at LD8 2NW. Continue
W along lane 2¾ miles for Cascob ancient yew
(52.2903, -3.1174, 300m past turn to LD8 2NT)

5 mins, 52.2760, -3.0616 🚲🌳🏛️

### 30 OFFA'S DYKE OAK, DISCOED

Powys is known for its grand, ancient oaks,
and this majestic sessile oak on Offa's Dyke
Path has an undulating girth of at least 7.6m,
making it one of the largest in the county
outside of parkland. Also nearby are the
Discoed and Cascob Yews, and Dolley Old
Bridge over the River Lugg (see entries).

→ Continue ½ mile W from Discoed yew (see
listing) to find signed entrance to Offa's Dyke
Path on L, opp Yew Tree Farm. Park carefully
on verge. Find tree on path after 150m. Offa's
Dyke path in other direction leads down to
river ½ mile.

5 mins, 52.2778, -3.0692 🌳🚲

### 31 BRYAN'S GROUND

Garden lovers will adore this artistic private
garden that's open to the public, with teas
in the loggia. Discover ivy-clad follies,
twisting paths through the wildflower-
strewn arboretum, pond, kitchen garden and
more. Entry fee, open 2–5pm Sun & Mon,
April–July.

→ N of Presteigne on road to Stapleton, 300m
before LD8 2LR, turn signed Kinsham to LD8
2LP (01544 260001).

10 mins, 52.2751, -2.9889 ✳️

### 32 THE CIDER BARN, DUNKERTONS

A relaxed café/restaurant in an old barn, serving excellent Herefordshire-sourced seasonal meals. A favourite in the area. Opening times vary.

→ Pembridge, HR6 9ED, 01544 388161. 52.2033, -2.8866

### 33 THE DUCK'S NEST, PRESTEIGNE

Presteigne is a small, romantic village filled with bohemian, colourful, period houses, and the main street boasts a number of great food shops. The Duck's Nest serves up delicious oxtail croquettes with sumac sauce, steak is local, and foraged delicacies fill the rustic wooden tables. Excellent wine list. Down the road the Salty Dog Deli sells fresh fish and gourmet produce.

→ 10 High St, Presteigne, LD8 2BA, 01544 598090.
52.2739, -3.0071

### 34 THE WORKHOUSE GALLERY & CAFÉ.

An industrial estate is not the place one would expect to find a lovely café and craft gallery, but here it is. Enjoy great coffee, locally sourced light lunches and home-made cakes inside, or in the courtyard garden.

→ Industrial Estate, Presteigne LD8 2UF, 01544 267864. Open 10am–4pm, Tues–Sat.
52.2702, -3.0067

### 35 VAN'S GOOD FOOD SHOP

Open for over 30 years, this is the place to stock up on everything organic, including vegetables, cheeses, dry groceries and wine. Nearby on Temple Street is Arvon Ale House, mid-Wales' first micropub, with ales, ciders and folk Sundays.

→ Elmswood, Middleton St, Llandrindod Wells, LD1 5ET, 01597 823074.
52.2409, -3.3791

### 36 EARDISLAND COMMUNITY SHOP

Village community shops are always a joy, and this one is extra special. Housed beneath a little museum in a 17th-century brick dovecote and staffed by volunteers, the small shop sells artisan bread, cakes, sausages and newspapers. Climb the rickety stairs to see the history of this pretty black-and-white village.

→ The Dovecote, Eardisland, HR6 9BN, 01544 388984. Open 8am–5pm (10am–2pm Sundays), closing 4pm in winter.
52.2233, -2.8511

### 37 QUARRY FARM SHOP, LUSTON

Buy grass-fed, free-range and traditionally raised meats from this and neighbouring farms. Organic ice cream and seasonal veg.

→ Luston, HR6 0AW, 01568 613156.
52.2546, -2.7472

### 38 LLANGOED HALL HOTEL

A very grand restaurant with superb food in an Edwardian country-house hotel by the river Wye. Much of the produce is sourced from the organic kitchen gardens.

→ Llyswen, LD3 0YP, 01874 754525.
52.0518, -3.2848

### 39 THE OLD ELECTRIC SHOP

There are so many wonderful shops and places to eat in Hay-on-Wye, but this is one of our favourites. Selling an eclectic mix of clothes, vintage finds, homewares and books, it also has an offbeat café with excellent locally roasted coffee.

→ 10 Broad St, Hay-on-Wye, HR3 5DB, 01497 821194.
52.0753, -3.1262

### 40 JULES RESTAURANT

Seasonal, organic and local foods are cooked by the chef owners in this bright, homely café/restaurant. Afterwards cross the High St and walk up the track south to Weobley castle earthworks.

→ Portland St, Weobley, HR4 8SB, 01544 318206.
52.1590, -2.8746

### 41 RIVER CAFÉ, WYE VALLEY CANOES

Bright, friendly licensed bistro overlooking the river Wye, serving delicious breakfasts and lunches. Next door you'll find canoe hire and a well-designed bunkhouse in the converted chapel with its own indoor slide!

→ The Boat House, Glasbury, HR3 5NP, 01497 847007.
52.0455, -3.1966

### 42 THE NEW INN, PEMBRIDGE

Old black-and-white 14th-century village inn with real fires, real ales and resident ghosts.

→ Market Square, Pembridge, HR6 9DZ, 01544 388427.
52.2179, -2.8939

### 43 THE STAGG INN, TITLEY

This was the first British pub to win a Michelin star, and the Good Pub Guide named it Dining Pub of the Year for 2018. Excellent local produce, cooked to celebrate its freshness, in a relaxed country pub with rooms. Open Wed–Sun for lunch and dinner.

→ Titley, Kington, HR5 3RL, 01544 230221. 52.2322, -2.9829

### 44 THE OAK WIGMORE

Smart, recently renovated village pub with rooms, serving beautifully presented plates of fresh, locally sourced and foraged food that tastes as good as it looks. Perfect after exploring nearby Wigmore Castle (see listing).

→ Ford St, Wigmore HR6 9UJ, 01568 770424. 52.3164, -2.8610

### 45 THE RIVERSIDE AT AYMESTREY

Sit on wooden settles below hanging hop vines in this cosy black-and-white dining pub to enjoy delicious, fresh, local and sustainably sourced fish and seasonal vegetables, often from their kitchen garden. Braised beef with smoked mash and mussels with local cider and angelica leaf were both excellent. Outside, tables line the river and overlook the pretty bridge.

→ Aymestrey, HR6 9ST, 01568 708440. 52.2839, -2.8443

### 46 THE TRAM INN, EARDISLEY

Traditional black-and-white dining pub, much loved for its home-cooked food using as much locally sourced produce as possible – including seasonal veg from the gardens of Eardisley village. Closed Mondays.

→ Church Rd, Eardisley, HR3 6PG, 01544 327251. 52.1406, -3.0088

### 47 THE HARP INN, OLD RADNOR

One of our favourite cosy pubs, an independently run, old longhouse inn with gorgeous views, open fires and deservedly acclaimed food. Bedrooms and stabling available, or rent the beautifully styled 17th-century Harp Cottage (0777 9737829) or Stockwell Farm (see listing) nearby.

→ Old Radnor, LD8 2RH, 01544 350655. 52.2252, -3.0989

## WILDER CAMPING

### 48 BYECROSS FARM CAMPSITE

Idyllic orchard campsite on the banks of the river Wye with furnished yurt available. The camp shop sells breakfast baps and evening burgers with cider. There's canoe hire on site or you can bring your own.

→ Moccas, Preston on Wye, HR2 9LJ, 01981 500284. 52.0779, -2.9110

### 49 REDWOOD VALLEY, PRESTEIGNE

Two simply styled hand-built yurts and a cabin in the trees, in ancient woodland and only a mile from Presteigne. Lazing in hammocks, running in the woods and stargazing are essential activities at this eco-minded glamping site.

→ Boultibrooke House, Norton Road, Presteigne, LD8 2EU, 01544 598050. 52.2846, -3.0118

### 50 KITE HILL YURTS

Enjoy incredible views of the Black Mountains from one of two cosy furnished traditional Mongolian yurts, each with a woodburner and a camp kitchen.

→ Old Bedw Farmhouse, near Erwood, Builth Wells, LD2 3LQ, 01982 560715. 52.1046, -3.3704

### 51 COSY UNDER CANVAS

Hammocks hang from the trees, and there's a wood-fired hot tub, pizza oven and two kitchens, one with a Rayburn, at your disposal when you stay in one of these cosy geodesic domes hidden amongst the bluebell woods.

→ Dolbedwyn, Newchurch, HR5 3QQ, 01497 851603 52.1349, -3.1570

### 52 DROVER'S REST

Luxurious safari tents on a beautiful working farm at the foot of the Black Mountains, with real beds and woodburners. Enjoy hot showers and pizza from the wood-fired oven, and gather in the fun communal barn. Two holiday cottages also available.

→ Off Watery Lane, Hay-on-Wye, HR3 6AG, 01497 831215. 52.0768, -3.0588

### 53 RACQUETY FARM

A delightful collection of camping, glamping, self-catering, and B&B within walking distance of the river Wye and Hay-on-Wye. Camp wild in the orchard, hire a home-made dome tent, or rent the eco-lodge.

→ Wyecliff, Hay-on-Wye, HR3 5LA, 01497 821520. 52.0780, -3.1361

### 54 DIGEDDI WILDLIFE CAMPING

Set up your riverside camp on the grassy fields bordering the River Wye, or rent the

bow-top or roulotte caravan. Bring your horse, or borrow Digeddi's – they can arrange canoe hire too. Hay-on-Wye is a short drive, trot or paddle away.

→ Little Ffordd-fawr, Hay-on-Wye, HR3 5PR, 07772 554861.
52.0615, -3.1703

### 55 FFOREST FIELDS, BUILTH WELLS

A fantastic campsite with a festival feel in high summer. There's swimming in the lake, paths mown through meadows, a cocktail shack, pizzas and over 500 acres of farm to discover – plenty of space to find your peace. Winner of many awards for its conservation and attention to detail, it has something for everyone. Glamping and cottages available.

→ Hundred House, LD1 5RT, 01982 570406.
52.1715, -3.3165

## RUSTIC HAVENS

### 56 THE PEREN, CLIFFORD

A stylish and cosy open-plan barn by the Wye, flooded with light from large windows, with under-floor heating, woodburner and beautiful wildflower garden. Sleeps five.

→ Lower Wyeside, Clifford, HR3 5EU, 07932 755515
52.1075, -3.1023

### 57 CRUCKBARN, WIGMORE

A beautiful converted oak cruck barn, hidden high on the edge of woods overlooking rolling hills. Underfloor heating (using a

ground-source heat pump) and woodburners keep the bright, open space cosy. Come for birdsong and starlit nights by the firepit. Sleeps five.

→ Wigmore, HR6 9UG, 01568 770036.
52.3151, -2.8765

### 58 WILD MEADOW, DISCOED

An idyllic shepherd's hut (sleeps two, with space for a tent) in a wildflower meadow, and a wooden eco-cottage (sleeps seven) with its own kitchen garden overlooking the verdant rolling Radnorshire hills. Scything courses available.

→ Discoed, Presteigne, LD8 2NQ, 01544 267039.
52.2818, -3.0331

### 59 HAYWOOD CABIN AT HERGEST CROFT

A cosy but spacious wooden cabin for two with glorious views out over the Black Mountains. On the Hergest Croft Estate, with arboretum, decorative gardens and tea room – all of which you can explore for free with your stay.

→ Ridgebourne Rd, Kington, HR5 3EG, 01544 230160.
52.2036, -3.0482

### 60 STOCKWELL FARM, RADNOR

Pretty as a picture inside and out, this rural farmhouse has stunning views, open fires and hillside to play on. Beautifully renovated by the Landmark Trust. Old Radnor with the lovely Harp Inn (see listing) and 15th-century church is only a short walk away across the fields. Sleeps six.

→ Radnor, LD8 2RG, 01628 825925.
52.2266, -3.0967

### 61 HAFOD Y GARREG B&B

Feast on candlelit dinners (AA four-star) and sleep in antique wooden beds in this cosy, unique medieval house, with structural timbers dated to 1402, making it possibly the oldest house in Wales. Stunning views overlooking the Wye valley.

→ Erwood, LD2 3TQ, 01982 560400.
52.0647, -3.3032

### 62 THE NETHOUSE, HAY-ON-WYE

A charming brick cottage right on the bank of the River Wye, with 15 acres of garden to explore. It's near the much-loved summer swimming spot of the Warren (see entry) and a 15-minute walk into Hay-on-Wye. Four old-fashioned rooms sleep eight.

→ Directions on booking, 07919 103933.
52.0727, -3.1329

### 63 NEW INN, BRILLEY

Not a pub – it used to be, but now this organic smallholding has evolved beyond its wildest dreams, offering charming bohemian hideaways to nature-loving guests. Each is made with love by Daphne, your host. Stay in a tin tabernacle, a gypsy wagon, vintage caravans or cosy rooms in the house. Utterly heartwarming.

➜ Brilley, HR3 6HE, 01497 831284.
52.1256, -3.0883

### 64 ECOPAVILION, MONTPELIER COTTAGE

Calling all garden lovers! Overlooking acres of incredible gardens designed by Noel Kingsbury, meadows and pond – which you are free to roam – is this lovely retreat for two, built from timber, straw and clay. The perfect place to relax on the veranda with a glass of wine.

➜ Brilley, HR3 6HF, 01497 831189
52.1286, -3.0823

### 65 BAGE POOL B&B

Traditional B&B in a charming, picture-postcard 16th-century farmhouse in the Golden Valley. Two rooms, a panelled twin

54

and cosy single, and outdoors a lake and eight acres of garden. Delicious full English breakfasts are made with eggs from the farm's own chickens.

➜ Dorstone, HR3 5SU, 01497 831704.
52.0835, -3.0254

### 66 WICKTON COURT B&B

Charming, rambling 15th-century country house with large, comfortable beds (one's a four poster) and locally sourced suppers served by the fire in the panelled room.

➜ Stoke Prior, HR6 0LN, 07812 602122.
52.1864, -2.6988

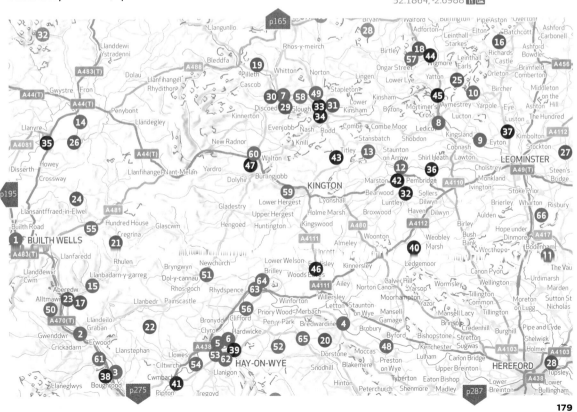

# ABERYSTWYTH & CAMBRIANS

## Our perfect weekend

→ **Lose** yourself in the epic uplands of Plynlimon, Wales' most remote mountain peaks

→ **Follow** the picturesque trails, tunnels and bridges through the woods and waterfalls of the Hafod estate

→ **Descend** into the huge plunge pot of Gyfarllwyd Falls, and discover the ancient woodlands and secret pools of the Rheidol valley

→ **Explore** miles of remote forest, with lakes and wild camping spots, all the way to Llyn Conach

→ **Canyon** into the sculpted shapes and cauldron pools of the incredible Ystwyth gorge

→ **Wild** swim in the waterfalls below Dinas Rock, hunting out the cave of the Welsh Robin Hood

→ **Spend** a day discovering the sea and sand at Ynyslas Dunes, glorious whatever the season

→ **Picnic** at Wolf's Leap canyon, explore its curving innards, then swim at the Washpool before feasting on local produce at the Drover's Rest

**Emptiness, wilderness and water: a land of peaks, forest and lakes, with the source of both the Severn and Wye rivers high on remote Plynlimon. This 'Green Desert of Wales' is still one of the least-frequented places in Britain.**

The Cambrian landscape began to be properly appreciated at the beginning of the 19th century, with the rise of the 'picturesque' movement. At Hafod, where one of the finest county houses in Wales once stood, the enchanting landscape was incorporated into the estate's trails through viewpoints, rustic bridges, tunnels and grottoes, all constructed to frame some natural scene perfectly. The Elan Valley became a romantic inspiration for the revolutionary poet Shelley's early years; he first visited his uncle's estate in the Elan when he was 18, walking there from Sussex over the course of a week. Bathing in the mountain streams and sailing toy boats down the currents with a cat on board, he fell in love with the valley, and tried to settle here.

During this period mining continued its insatiable pillage of the land, leaving fascinating relics above and below ground. At Ystrad Einion and Frongoch, towering ruins beg to be explored, while at Dylife, a remote mountain inn is nearly all that remains of a once-thriving town. Feats of Victorian engineering answered the demand of thirsty English cities, flooding valleys and displacing whole communities; so today, peaceful reservoirs shimmering beneath velvet woods provide tempting places to swim and camp, if you are discreet.

For the water lover there are mesmerising sculpted gorges, swirling cauldron pools and misty waterfalls. One of the best known is Wolf's Leap, where the last wolf in Wales was allegedly seen bounding to freedom in the 16th century. Rugged and beautiful, the valley winds its way down from the sky-scraping wilds above Llyn Brianne, with a tight, rocky canyon on the River Irfon, where the churning water has cut deep down into the rock, eroding potholes, chambers and series of deep river pools.

Wolves were hunted to extinction, and the same fate almost befell the red kite. By the 1930s only a handful of breeding pairs remained in the whole of Wales, these mountains their lonely refuge. With concerted conservation efforts, their populations have literally soared. Maybe one day we will see wolves roaming here again, as evidence mounts on the benefits of rewilding 'sheepwrecked' hills, as George Monbiot so aptly calls them. For now, we can seek solace in the many substantial nature reserves that enrich this region, including Cors Caron, Dinas Rock, Ynyslas Dunes and Ynys-hir.

5

## WILD LAKES

### 1 LLYN CLYWEDOG, LLANIDLOES

The Clywedog reservoir zigzags through verdant valleys, offering deep water and, at the far northern end, shingle beaches. Head around the narrow peninsula to find a little sailing club where you can launch your canoe, and camp above Britain's highest concrete buttressed dam. Below are the impressive ruins of Bryntail lead mine.

→ Well signed off the B4518, 3 miles NW of Llanidloes. The lead mine is signed R before dam. From here continue on up 3 miles to the shoreside section. There is also a parking and picnic spot before this at SY18 6NX; a signed nature trail leads down to a more secluded section of shore. Technically no swimming, but people do. Sailing club 01686 640305.
5 mins, 52.4864, -3.6342 🏊🚲❓⛺

### 2 LLYN CONACH & BEYOND

This is perhaps as remote as you can get by road in Wales. The forestry tracks head higher and higher, passing endless wild swimming lakes and wild camping spots.

→ Turn off A487 Tal-y-bont by the White Lion and Black Lion, and follow signs for Nantymoch, past turning to SY24 5HL. At top, about 5 miles

from pub, turn L onto wide forest gravel track (R is to Nant-y-Moch, see listing), then L after ¾ mile at crossroads and continue 1¼ miles, past lovely little (unnamed) tarn below R (52.5068, -3.8642), to find L turn to Llyn Conach. Back to main track continue E past New Pool lake and the historic Anglers Retreat cabin (R) on the way to Llyn Penrhaeadr (52.5228, -3.8408).
5 mins, 52.5207, -3.8594 🏊⛺✚

### 3 NANT-Y-MOCH & PLYNLIMON

High in the barren uplands of the Cambrians lies this twisting reservoir with long shale shores, many inlets and an empty road hugging its southern shores. Rising above is the hulk of Plynlimon, the highest point in the Cambrians (752m) and source of both the Severn and the Wye. The road here feels like an epic journey in itself, even in a car, and passes several ruined mines and smaller lakes.

→ As for Llyn Conach (see listing), but continue on tarmac road R (SE) at the 5 miles junction. Pass lovely Llyn Nantycagl on L after ½ mile, to reservoir after 2 miles (there are quirky fireplaces in the woods, just off the road at 52.4780, -3.8606). The main beach shore is after another 2 miles; continue up to 3 miles beyond this, turning L after the dam, to explore the little island/peninsula (52.4777,

-3.8120) and the flanks of Plynlimon. At the road end (gates at Maesnant), take the R track (public byway) another mile up to the Afon Hengwm. Also reached following lane from Ponterwyd (SY23 3JX) 4 miles past Hirnant cairn circle (see listing) to dam end.
5 mins, 52.4706, -3.8508 🏊⛺✚🔥

### 4 LLYN RHOSGOCH & MYNYDD MARCH

A trio of pretty tarns adorn the ancient roadway that traverses Mynydd March. Further along are the easily accessible Cow and Calf standing stones, just a few of the many Bronze Age remnants that pepper the area.

→ From centre of Penrhyn-coch, E of Aberystwyth, follow Pendam Mountain Road E about 5 miles, past SY23 3EX, to reach Llyn Pendam. Turn R opp car park signed Ponterwyd for easy Llyn Blaenmelindwr. From here a footpath on R heads down to Rhosgoch, secluded and wilder. Standing stones ½ mile further E on lane (52.4332, -3.8799).
5 mins, 52.4308, -3.8942 🏊♿✚

### 5 LLYN EGNANT, TEIFI POOLS

With easy access and stunning southerly views, this remote family of high lakes makes for a sublime adventure on a sunny day. Together they form the headwaters of

the River Teifi at the start of its journey to Cardigan Bay. Tracks lead off to most of the lakes, and if nobody is fishing, a swim and wild camp shouldn't be an issue. Egnant is the last lake and has a track right along its shore. Llyn Bach is hidden beyond, only a little way on foot.

→ Leave B4343 about 7 miles N of Tregaron at Ffair-Rhos, turning by Teifi Inn for SY25 6BW. Continue 3¾ miles, passing R turns for Llyn Teifi and Llyn Hir. Where road turn to track ('unfit for motor vehicles' sign in Welsh) turn R for Egnant. Llyn Bach is at end of lake, about 200m to R on foot (52.2861, -3.7770).
2 mins, 52.2912, -3.7738 🏊🏕️🏊

## 6 PENYGARREG, ELAN LAKES

This series of spectacular reservoir lakes set within the Elan's rugged valley are the fruits of grand Victorian engineering. Penygarreg hides a secluded picnic area, beaches and an island. Above it, Craig Goch enjoys open access all along its northwestern shore below Pont ar Elan.

→ From Rhayader clocktower follow B4518 past LD6 5AB and Elan Valley for 10 miles, along Caban Coch, Garreg-Ddu and then Penygarreg. Turn R over dam wall of Craig Goch to park by toilets and follow track down

to picnic area. No swimming, but people do. Or continue on towards Pont ar Elan at the very top end of Craig Goch. Cycle Route 81.
10 mins, 52.3020, -3.6190 🏊❓♿🏊

## 7 FANNOG, LLYN BRIANNE

Graceful and sizeable wooded reservoir at the head of the Towy (or Tywi). Several picnic and parking areas dot its shore; Fannog is our favourite, with grassy banks and a beach. There are also good river pools above the little bridge at its top end, 2 miles further up.

→ Either continue on road from Wolf's Leap gorge (see listing) 2½ miles, over the pass and then L (signed Llyn Brianne) down to lake, 3¾ miles from junction to Fannog forest parking R. Or from Rhandirmwyn, N of Llandovery, take lanes past SA20 0PG, continuing 6 miles. Bear R at triangle after 1 mile, and next fork, to follow S and E edge of lake N to Fannog.
2 mins, 52.1482, -3.7416 🏊❓

## RIVERS & GORGES

### 8 WASHPOOL, RIVER IRFON

Large roadside pool overhung with gnarled oaks, traditionally used for washing horses. Swim up into the deep gorge section with its scenic crag and waterfalls.

From Llanwrtyd Wells take Abergwesyn/ Coed Trallwm road. Continue 3 miles to find forestry sign and parking on R and obvious pool, 300m before LD5 4TN.
2 mins, 52.1362, -3.6678 🏊🚻🧺

## 9 PONT RHYDGALED, RIVER WYE

The meeting point of the young Wye and Tarrenig, with a pool and beach below the forestry track bridge and several waterfalls downstream.

7 miles W of Llangurig A44, 270m W of SY18 6SY, find Tarrenig forestry car park. Follow track from car park to bridge pool, or continue and turn L down track for waterfalls, about 200m.
5 mins, 52.4280, -3.7011 🏊🚻

## 10 PONT MARTEG, RIVER WYE

Mossy, ancient woods cloak this hidden gorge, with a footbridge and small pools for paddling. Or follow narrow lanes (cycle route 8) to find a secret spot a mile downstream with a white beach, deeper pools and rope swing.

On A470 3 miles N of Rhayader, park in layby opp turn to St Harmon. Go through gate and across bridge. For downstream spot (52.3237, -3.5454) follow lanes to ½ mile N of LD6 5HA to find old grass avenue to footbridge; 100m upstream is beach, waterfall

and deep cleft where railway used to cross. Be discreet as there is no public footpath.
5 mins, 52.332, -3.5403 🏊🏕🚻❓🅿️♿

## 11 WOLF'S LEAP, RIVER IRFON

A valley of wild beauty, open and sunny with flat rocks. Above the small deep pool is a narrow, sculpted slot gorge. You can also explore the upper parts of the gorge and climb down inside.

From Washpool (see listing) continue on to Abergwesynand turn L signed Lyn Brianne/ Tregaron at postbox. Continue 1¾ miles to uneven road sign and find pool below L, ½ mile before LD5 4TR. Also approach from Fannog, Llyn Brianne (see listing) in the other direction.
5 mins, 52.1788, -3.6949 🏊

## 12 ELAN JUNCTION POOL, RIVER WYE

A wide junction pool not far from Rhayader with shallower paddles upstream by the bridge. No Swimming signs reported 2019.

On A470, 3 miles S from Rhayader, turn R signed Llanwrthwl. Continue through village ¾ mile then R at T junction, signed Elan Village/ Rhayader. ¾ mile beyond LD1 6NP to pull off at bend and take footpath/track to R, to junction pool, 50m. Do not swim if people fishing.
2 mins, 52.2788, -3.5160 🏊❓

### 13 RHAYADER BEACH & FALLS

Swim in the waterfall that gives the town its name. There's also a pretty gravel beach, south facing and secluded, at the bottom of the rugby club.

→ A path leads to the river from behind the Triangle Inn LD6 5AR (see listing). Or head down Water Lane past LD6 5AN to rugby club car park. Follow path at R of car park entrance along the river to very end of playing fields.
5 mins, 52.2962, -3.5116 🏊📖🚶

## WATERFALLS & CANYONS

### 14 DINAS ROCK & TOWY WATERFALLS

Follow the Towy river up into the foothills of the Cambrians to find the wooded slope and conical peak of Dinas. The crag shelters a secret cave, a legendary hiding place of the Welsh Robin Hood. It lies within an RSPB reserve, and there's a double waterfall at the confluence with the Doethie – beware high water levels.

→ Descend from Llyn Brianne (see Fannog listing). Or take Cilycwm Rd from Llandovery and continue about 9 miles dir Rhandirmwyn. Continue past Ystfin riverside camping fields, signed Llyn Brianne, and after ¾ mile (½ mile before SA20 0PG) find layby R

followed by footpath L. Follow this ½ miles to the river junction, and then another ¼ mile to find a path steeply up to the R for the cave (it's about ⅓ the way up the NW side of the hill at 52.1063, -3.7820). NB If coming from Llandovery there is also a good gorge swim right by the tiny lane to SA20 0UH, near Cilycwm (-3.8016, -3.8016).
5 mins, 52.1050, -3.7802 🏊🚴📖🚶

### 15 CWM RHEIDOL WATERFALLS

A tiny lane winds its way up this gentle rocky valley, passing a butterfly centre, ancient woods and many lovely pools and falls. It eventually reaches a super waterfall pool with beach at road end. More adventures on foot beyond.

→ Turn off A44 at Capel Bangor 3 miles E from Aberystwyth, signed Cwmrheidol. After 1¼ miles at a R bend, with a small dirt layby to R, steps lead down to a deep river pool with big gravel banks (52.3915, -3.9600). Continue another 4½ miles, past the Butterfly House, Rheidol Power Station, Rheidol Falls bridge, and SY23 3NB, to layby and gate on R signed Statkraft. There is a deep wooded gorge with good jumps (52.3866, -3.8710) that can be accessed from just downstream above bridge. Finally, 180m on, at 'end of route' sign, find

parking for 3 cars L, signboards and a gate on R down to the main beach and falls. The adventurous can follow the road to the remote waterfall and epic pools of Gyfarllwyd at 52.3817, -3.8492 (steep bushwhack and river scramble required).

2 mins, 52.3858, -3.8686 🅿️🧗🍴👫🎒

### 16 CWM YSTWYTH, HAFOD ESTATE

A fine house was built here in the late 18th century, complete with a network of picturesque paths and bridges that showed off the many waterfalls and wooded ravines. The house is now a pile of rubble, but the walks are being restored, and include a range of canyons and gentle river pools.

→ From the bridge at Pont-rhyd-y-groes (N of SY25 6DN) follow B4343 just over ½ mile to the disabled/cycle entrance (from here it's possible to cycle to the ruin at SY25 6DX). Bear R on B4574, signed Hafod, for another 1⅛ mile to main car park at church on R. Head down by Mrs Johnes Flower Garden on the main estate road. Downstream 200m on the bend are picnic tables and a deep river pool on the Afon Ystwyth. Upstream ½ mile is Pont Dologau (52.3445, -3.8054), where you can scramble into the Ystwyth gorge. There are also lovely pools beneath the wobbly chain bridge another ½ mile upstream (52.3465, -3.7997). The Gentleman's Walk leads to Melyn waterfall (52.3424, -3.8015) and the Cavern Cascade (52.3389, -3.7998) on the Nant Gau.

20 mins, 52.3410, -3.8105 🅿️🧗🍴👫🎒🚶

### 17 YSTWYTH LOWER GORGE

A sculpted slot canyon widens into a wooded gorge with a waterfall and deep pools. It's a tricky scramble down, but explore up the canyon for a real adventure.

→ On B4343 in Pont-rhyd-y-groes, take fork dir SY25 6DQ by bus stop, signed B4340 Cycle Route 81 Llanafan. Follow ½ mile, past café and waterwheel, to layby on R on bend. Follow woodland track down to a tricky, steep rock scramble down to river, then upstream 50 m to the waterfall and canyon.

5 mins, 52.3312, -3.8647 🅿️🧗🍴🚶

### 18 CLAERWEN WATERFALLS

Up the Elan valley from Rhayader is a mini-gorge and plunge pools by the road, and a secret mountain-valley walk with pools all along its happy way.

→ Start as for Penygarreg on Elan lakes (see listing), but 2 miles after Elan village turn L over bridge signed Dyffryn Claerwen Valley. Continue 3½ miles, past Rhiwnant turn off

on L (by telephone box and parking) to 300m before LD6 5HF. A rocky section of the river comes close to the road on L with deep pools and waterfall; park by salt bin. Also explore the Rhiwnant Valley for a waterfall and lovely confluence pool at 52.2314, -3.6453 with mine ruins above and more falls. Return to parking by the telephone box and walk, taking 2nd bridleway on L, after first farm (45 mins).
2 mins, 52.2514, -3.6359

### 19 DYLIFE POOL, FFRWD FAWR & MINE

You can view the spectacular Ffrwd Fawr falls from the road as they crash over 35m down the cliffside. But only locals know about the hidden waterfall pool, concealed in a deep cleft upstream. For details of the Dylife mine ruins see the Star Inn listing.

→ From Llyn Clywedog (see listing) continue on B4518 N and turn dir SY19 7BP and Dylife. Large layby and signboard on R with dramatic views of waterfall and Twymyn valley after ½ mile. Continue to 175m past cattle grid for small pull-off on R, with plateau below and tricky scramble down to the hidden waterfall.
5 mins, 52.5320, -3.6682

LOST RUINS

### 20 YSTRAD EINION MINE

Lost amongst the trees, the above ground ruins of this 19th-century copper mine are intriguing. Risk-takers go deeper and seek out the underground waterwheel, one of only two surviving in the UK. Over 5m high, it was used to pump water out from the lower workings.

→ Turn off A487 at Furnace, signed Artists Valley/Cwm Einion. Continue 2 miles, past SY20 8TD, and at dead-end sign turn R over bridge into parking area. A gate and signboard lead up to mine ruins. Follow path N from below the crusher house to find tunnel at the end of a shallow cutting. The waterwheel is a short distance inside, at the T junction. Another mine with impressive over- and underground ruins is Bwlch Glas, beyond SY24 5DN (52.4724, -3.9002). Take care!
5 mins, 52.5278, -3.9071

### 21 PONT CEUNANT POWER STATION

The giant stone ruins of Pont Ceunant Generating Station stand alone at the roadside in a remote valley. Designed by an Italian for the new Belgian mine owners at the end of the 19th century, it was one of the first of its kind in Wales, using water from the

23

lake above to feed a turbine that powered the nearby Frongoch mine ore processing.

→ Leave B4343 at Abermagwr, signed Pont-rhyd-y-groes. Continue 2¾ miles, past the Frongoch mine ruins above R (52.3502, -3.8857), to find ruin on L with signboard, ¼ mile before SY23 4RR. Space for one car.
1 min, 52.3517, -3.9009 ▣

## SACRED & ANCIENT

### 22 STRATA FLORIDA

In the upper reaches of the Teifi, a Cistercian abbey was built in 1182; its name, Strata Florida, is a corrupted translation of Ystrad Fflur, 'valley of the flowers'. The ornately carved doorway gives a sense of the building's original magnificence. Medieval Welsh poet Dafydd ap Gwilym is said to be buried beneath the yew here, although Talley Abbey claims him too. Entry fee, but you can enjoy the adjacent church and grounds for free.

→ Signed from Pontrhydfendigad (B4343) ¾ mile beyond SY25 6ER.
2 mins, 52.2756, -3.8386 ▣ ✝

### 23 HIRNANT CIRCLE & UPPER RHEIDOL

A perfect stone circle with 16 small uprights, once part of a burial cairn, where beautiful views abound. Down below is a particularly fine and deep gorge section of the upper Rheidol river to explore.

→ From Ponterwyd A44, take tiny lane N next to the old schoolhouse past the chapel. After 2 miles, shortly after SY23 3AG and 3rd cattle grid, find gate and track down to Aber-Peithnant farm. This is open-access land, and circle is by the fence line 100m below. Head down to the river and upstream around the bend ¼ mile to the swimming gorge (52.4440, -3.8375).
2 mins, 52.4392, -3.8355 ▣ ▣

### 24 PARSON'S BRIDGE STONE CIRCLES

This fascinating walk takes in manifold ruins spanning millennia. Start at Ysbyty Cynfyn graveyard, where five ancient stones, some incorporated into the curving wall, indicate the Christian church adopting a pagan site. Cross Parson's Bridge, over the cascades of the Rheidol gorge, to find Dolgamfa round cairn, a Bronze Age stone circle in a stunning setting. Visible from the bridge, 100m upstream, are the 19th-century ruins of the dressing floors of Temple Mine – ore bins, circular buddles, wheelpit and crusher base. This biodiverse wooded gorge is an National Nature Reserve and a beautiful place for a walk in any season.

21

22

26

25

28

→ On A4120 1½ miles N from Devils Bridge, just before SY23 3JR, park in layby L with signboard. Take path to the church, and then onwards down to the gorge and bridge. Beyond, the R footpath (due W) leads 300m up the hillside to Dolgamfa circle (52.3961, -3.8448).
5 mins, 52.3951, -3.8400 🏊📺💷🚶

### WILDLIFE & MEADOWS

### 25 CORS Y LLYN ORCHIDS
Gaze upon fields of orchids and hunt out carnivorous round-leaved sundews. Within a few steps of the car park thousands of heath and common spotted orchids bloom in late June. Good disabled access, and a boardwalk allows visitors to penetrate the bogland areas.
→ Leave A470 at S end of Newbridge on Wye, taking fork R past LD2 3SB. Continue 1 mile and take R onto narrow road, through Craig-gôch farm, to reserve car park opp lane end.
2 mins, 52.1885, -3.4404 🏧🏞

### 26 YNYSLAS DUNES NNR
On a sandy peninsula at the mouth of the Dovey estuary, the vast beach is backed by dunes rich with orchids in May and June, skylarks in summer, fungi in autumn and successfully reintroduced sand lizards.

→ Follow B4353 N from Borth or W from Tre'r-ddôl and take turn on bend, past SY24 5JZ to reach parking at top of beach (keep an eye on the tide) and visitor centre.
5 mins, 52.5269, -4.0521 🏧🏞💷🚻

### 27 MANX SHEARWATERS, BORTH
Between late July and mid-August, tens of thousands of Manx shearwaters – a tenth of the world's population – congregate on the waters of Borth Bay at high tides, fattening up before they migrate south for the winter. At very low tides when the sand has been shifted, you might see the stumps of a buried Bronze Age forest.
→ Take the turning for Ynslas Dunes NNR (see listing) but immediately turn L under barrier, over golf course, and park by sea.
5 mins, 52.5130, -4.0560 💷🏞

### 28 YNS-HIR RSPB NATURE RESERVE
Covering swathes of coastal oak woodland, hill, field, salt marsh and mudflat, and bordering the Dyfi estuary, this is a birds' (and twitchers') paradise. Muddy walks lead through the reserve, with various hides along the way. Car park, kids activities and café.
→ Reserve is clearly signed from the A487 between Eglwys Fach and Furnace, turning dir

SY20 8TA. Entry fee for non-members, open dawn–dusk (01654 700222).
10 mins, 52.5468, -3.9451 🐕🧒♿

### 29 GILFACH FARM NATURE RESERVE
This stunning valley setting, once a traditional hill farm, is now a reserve alive with insects, red kites, otters and hares, and autumn brings the salmon leaping up the Marteg waterfalls. Walks lead from the little visitor centre with summer tea shop.
→ On A470 3 miles N of Rhayader, take turn over cattle grid, dir St Harmon. After ¾ mile, before LD6 5LF, turn hard R just before cattle grid to parking and the old farmhouse, now a visitor centre.
5 mins, 52.3338, -3.5206 🚶

### 30 GIGRIN FARM RED KITES
The story of Welsh red kites, persecuted almost to extinction by gamekeepers and egg collectors, is one of survival against the odds. Gigrin Farm started feeding the kites and became an official feeding station in 1993 at the request of the RSPB. From only a few breeding pairs in the whole of Wales in the 1930s, hundreds now come here every afternoon for a feeding frenzy that is out of this world – watch close up from one of the hides. Entry fee.
→ Signed just S of Rhayader on A470, past LD6 5BL, 01597 810243.
2 mins, 52.2985, -3.4975 🚗

### 31 CORS CARON NNR
Cors Caron bog was formed by a shallow lake during the last ice age. It covers more than 800 acres and is filled with insects, butterflies, rare plants and wild ponies. There are good boardwalks to lakes and the Bog Hide, although the best way to explore is on the cycle path along the old railway line.
→ 2 miles N of Tregaron on B4343, ½ mile beyond SY25 6JF, find parking for Cors Caron.
15 mins, 52.2465, -3.9270 🚶🚴

## ANCIENT FORESTS

### 32 COED SIMDDE-LWYD
Steep, south-facing, ancient sessile oak woodland, with views out over the Rheidol valley. Particularly lovely in late spring, when bluebells carpet the slopes and the call of the cuckoo heralds the summer. Climb up the stream gorge to view the impressively tall Nant Bwa-drain waterfall. The Butterfly House (entry fee) on the way is worth visiting.
→ As for Rheidol waterfalls (see listing), past the Butterfly House and ½ mile after power

station the main reserve gate by Glynrheidol Farm has space for one car, but 450m on find wooden footpath sign and steps L, parking for a car R on bend shortly beyond.
15 mins, 52.3893, -3.8873 🚶🚶

### 33 COED PENGLANOWEN BLUEBELLS
A small woodland reserve, resplendent with bluebells in May. Invasive but beautiful rhododendrons add bursts of vivid pink, and there is the tallest tree in Ceredigion, a giant sequoia. Adjacent on the road is Old Warren Hill, also now a nature reserve, with hill fort.
→ On the B4340 3 miles SE from Aberystwyth, 280m after SY23 4LT, take L signed dead end/ Plas Nanteos Mansion. After ½ mile, park in layby on L near C entrance for hill fort. Walk back up road a little way to find reserve entrance gate on L. Sequoia is at 52.3876, -4.0436.
5 mins, 52.3877, -4.0433 🚶🚶♿

## SLOW FOOD

### 34 GREAT OAK FOODS, LLANIDLOES
Lovely community interest shop selling organic fruit and vegetables, Andy's bread, raw honey and an excellent selection of organic and sulphite-free wine, lots of local produce and even biodegradable nappies.

Stock up your campervan here!

→ 14 Great Oak St, Llanidloes, SY18 6BU, 01686 413222.
52.4482, -3.5385 🍴

### 35 YNYSHIR RESTAURANT & ROOMS
A walk away from the Ynys-hir reserve (see listing) this smart Michelin-starred restaurant with rooms consistently secures best-restaurant awards for its obsessive 'terroir'-focused food, served from set menus. Definitely a special treat.

→ Eglwys Fach, SY20 8TA, 01654 781209.
52.5447, -3.9446 🍴🛏

### 36 CAFFI CLETWR, TRE'R DDÔL

The best community shop and café for miles around, and our favourite stop for an organic ice cream or hearty wholesome lunch. With a kid's corner filled with toys and Welsh books, this is a real community hub offering a warm welcome to visitors.

→ Tre'r Ddôl, SY20 8PN, 01970 832113.
52.5126, -3.9756 🍴🚲

### 37 PYSGOTY, ABERYSTWYTH
Good, fresh Cardigan Bay seafood and sea views from this white weatherboard harbourside café.

→ S Marine Terrace/S Promenade Aberystwyth, SY23 1JY, 01970 624611.
52.4096, -4.0887 🍴

### 38 TREEHOUSE, ABERYSTWYTH

Stock up on all your organic, local produce here and enjoy vegetarian and vegan breakfasts, lunches and cakes in the café upstairs.

→ 14 Baker St, Aberystwyth, SY23 2BJ, 01970 615791.
52.4156, -4.0845 🍴

### 39 ABERYSTWYTH FARMERS' MARKET
Excellent farmers' market every first and third Saturday of the month.

→ North Parade, Aberystwyth, SY23 2NF, 01559 362230.
52.4159, -4.0815 🍴

### 40 THE DROVERS REST RESTAURANT

Views of the river and friendly staff combine with a creative, sustainable approach to sourcing local food, supporting local producers and line-caught fish, plus lots of great vegetarian choices.

→ The Square, Llanwrtyd Wells LD5 4RA, 01591 610264.
52.1073, -3.6388 🍴

### 41 WELSH QUILT CENTRE & CAFÉ-DELI
Come and see the incredible historical and modern quilting culture of Wales and enjoy excellent coffee, lunches and cakes.

→ The Town Hall, High Street, Lampeter, SA48 7BB, 01570 422088.
52.1131, -4.0806 🍴

### 42 CWTCH
Friendly café and village shop serving good home-made hearty breakfasts, lunches and cakes. Buy crafts, bicycle repair kits and groceries. Open 10am–6pm daily.

→ 7 Y Wern, Pon-rhyd-y-groes, Ystrad Meurig, SY25 6DF, 07532 333520.
52.3340, -3.8531

## COSY INNS

### 43 TYNLLIDIART ARMS
Good value locally sourced, seasonal gastro pub menu and home to Bragdy Gwynant, the world's smallest commercial brewery.

→ Capel Bangor, Nr Aberystwyth, SY23 3LR, 01970 880248
52.4036, -3.9771 🛏🍴

### 44 YBLAC/BLACK LION HOTEL
Locally sourced meals, including fresh fish specials, served in a modernised village dining inn. Open Wed–Sat for supper and Fri–Sun for lunch.

→ New St, Talybont, SY24 5ER, 01970 832555.
52.4841, -3.9821 🍴

### 45 Y FFARMERS
This bright dining pub in a pretty village has tasty seasonal, Welsh pub food with a good vegetarian selection, and hosts good live music nights.

→ Llanfihangel-y-Creuddyn, SY23 4LA, 01974 261275.
52.3668, -3.9621 🍴🛏

### 46 Y TALBOT, TREGARON
In the square of this once-important market town is the best food to be had in a pub for miles. Don't be intimidated by the farmers enjoying a pint, they're friendly really. Food is local produce and excellent. Order the shepherd's pie made with braised local lamb neck, or Tregaron beef for two, with bone-marrow beignet and black truffle jus. Cors Caron reserve (see listing) is nearby.

→ The Square, Tregaron, SY25 6JL, 01974 298208.
52.2194, -3.9327 🛏🍴

## 47 DOLAUCOTHI ARMS, PUMSAINT

This bright, simply furnished old drovers' inn with garden and rooms serves aged Welsh steaks, Welsh rarebits and delicious vegetarian fare alongside real ales. It's part of the NT's Dolaucothi estate, where the gold mines date to Roman times and the underground tours (charge for non-members) are fascinating.

→ Pumsaint, SA19 8UW, 01558 650237.
52.0471, -3.9612 🍴🚭🅿️♿

## 48 Y STAR INN, DYLIFE

This rural inn with its local ales and wood fires offers welcome relief from the often wet weather of this mining hinterland. Pick up one of the many books on the area's history and enjoy a local lamb pie with chips and gravy. Rooms available. Below are the remains of the old church graveyard, and ½ mile up the dirt track across the main road is a lead mine cavern and the remains of an old shaft and pump (52.5305, -3.6908).

→ Dylife, SY19 7BW, 01650 521345.
52.5324, -3.6777 🚭🖼️🅿️

## 49 THE ROYAL OAK INN, RHANDIRMWYN

Welsh beef, cockles and bacon, a garden with views, real ales and open fires at this cosy traditional pub. A CAMRA favourite.

→ Rhandirmwyn, SA20 0NY, 01550 760201.
52.0786, -3.7747 🅿️🍴🚭

## 50 THE TRIANGLE INN, CWMDAUDDWR

A 16th-century drovers' inn that feels like a time warp, serving real ales and locally sourced pub grub to eat in or takeaway. Near Rhayader beach on the river Wye and Gigrin Farm red kite feeding centre (see entries).

→ Cwmdauddwr, LD6 5AR, 01597 810537.
52.2984, -3.5153 🅿️🍴

## 51 NEUADD ARMS, CILYCWM

Enjoy real ales and delicious food, including their own farm-raised Welsh Lamb and Welsh Black beef, perfectly served in this old village pub with restaurant and garden. Still sometimes listed as the Neuadd Fawr Arms.

→ Cilycwm, SA20 0ST, 01550 721644.
52.0445, -3.8196 🅿️

## 52 DRUID INN, GOGINAN

Consistently loved by locals and visitors alike this CAMRA 2017 Welsh pub of the year winner, serves up cosiness, real ales and good locally-sourced meals.

→ On the A44 in Goginan, SY23 3NT, 01970 880650.
52.4122, -3.9286 🅿️🍴

## 53 TYDDYN RETREAT, CARNO

In the wilds of the mountains, this enclave of lovely self-catering cottages, summerhouse cabin and tipis offers peace and stunning views to holiday visitors and retreat guests. Can accommodate larger groups.

→ Carno, Caersws, SY17 5JU, 07767 370739.
52.5741, -3.5672 🖼️🚭

## 54 THE GORFANC HIDEAWAY, CARNO

This charming, balconied wooden cottage on an organic smallholding offers all home comforts, hand-crafted with a simple eco-friendly ethos. Buy honey, eggs and home-grown vegetables from the garden. Simple campfire camping also available.

→ Carno, Caersws, SY17 5JP, 01686 420423.
52.5482, -3.5515 🚿🚭🖼️🍴

## 55 GRIBYN COTTAGE, LAWR-Y-GLYN

Wake up to stunning valley views from your converted barn hideaway in the hills. Owner Vicky is a potter and can arrange sessions in her studio for all ages. Sleeps up to five.

→ Llawr-y-glyn, SY17 5RH, 07967 581452.
52.5124, -3.5823 🚭

## 56 NANNERTH HOLIDAY CAMP

A beautiful wildlife-rich farm in the Upper Wye valley. Camp in the hay meadows or by the river, rent Ava the red showman's wagon in a bluebell wood, or stay in one of the farmhouse holiday cottages.

→ Nannerth Fawr, Rhayader, LD6 5HA, 01597 811121.
52.3320, -3.5465 🚭🖼️

## 57 NANT YR ONNEN, RHANDIRMWYN

This eco-conscious hideaway has an octagonal cabin with a composting loo, and a larger stone barn, a wood-fired hot tub, electric car charging, bike storage, woodland walks, waterfalls and views. A five-minute walk away are local ales at the Towy Bridge Inn.

→ Rhandirmwyn, SA20 0PL, 01550 760100, canopyandstars.co.uk for cabin, airbnb.co.uk for barn.
52.0849, -3.8010 🚭

## 58 PENRHYN BARN, RHANDIRMWYN

A large, luxurious converted barn right on the River Towy – good for kayaking or fishing – and near Cwm Rhaeadr mountain-biking trail. Sleeps 10.

→ Rhandirmwyn, SA20 0NT, 01550 760387.
52.0677, -3.7885 🚭🖼️🚿

### 59 TY'N CORNEL, TREGARON

Private hostel (formerly YHA) with open fires and magnificent views. The remote location is great for discovering the wilderness of the Elenydd and Tregaron. Two rooms, each with eight bunks. Camping available.

→ Llandewi Brefi, SY25 6PH, 01980 629259. 52.1655, -3.8281 ⬜⬜

### 60 DOLGOCH HOSTEL, TREGARON

Remote, unmodernized 17th-century hostel, formerly YHA. The three dorms are unlit, so torches are essential, solar panels provide hot water in summer, but in winter there is only a cold supply to the kitchen, and a woodburner heats the common room. There's no fridge and water comes from the stream – boil it for drinking. Sheets are provided. Sleeps 20.

→ Tregaron, SY25 6NR, 01974 298680. 52.1910, -3.7476 ⬜⬜

### 61 RED KITE TREE TENT & BARN

The ultimate in wild luxury, in 80 acres of private countryside. Choose the stunning Forest Retreat barn conversion or one of two fantastical off-grid, globe tents hung in the trees. All with woodburners to keep you cosy.

→ Nr Llandrindod Wells, LD1 6ND. sheepskinlife.com
52.2150, -3.4977 ⬜⬜

### 62 THE YURT FARM, TREGARON

Sleep between organic sheets, atop organic mattresses, on an organic farm. Four hand-crafted yurts and a beautiful converted train carriage, with woodburners to keep you cosy after a meal of organic farm produce.

→ Crynfryn Farm, Penuwch, Tregaron, SY25 6RE, 01974 821594.
52.2327, -4.0754 🍴⬜⬛⬜

### 63 DENMARK FARM

A nature conservation centre with a stylish bunkhouse, eco lodge, glamping or campsite for ten tents, and a tempting calender of sustainable living and rural craft courses.

→ Betws Bledrws, SA48 8PB, 01570493358
52.1631, -4.0684 ⬜⬜B

### 64 TYLLWYD CAMP SITE

Quiet riverside camping in the beautiful rolling hills of the Ystwyth valley. Hot showers (though facilities are limited and across the lane from pitches) and excellent stargazing.

→ Cwmystwyth, SY23 4AG, 01974 282216.
52.3631, -3.7291 ⬜⬜

### 65 DOL-LLYS CARAVAN & CAMPING

A working farm by the banks of the river Wye. Waterside pitches for starlit campfires and hours of messing about in the water.

→ Trefeglwys Rd, Llanidloes, SY18 6JA, 01686 412694.
52.4587, -3.5259 ⬜⬜⬜⬜

### 66 TY-GWYN CAMPING, YNYSLAS

Family-run campsite 300m from beach, dunes and nature reserve. Horse livery too.

→ Ynyslas, Borth, SY24 5LA.01970 871894
52.5126, -4.0477 ⬜

## BOTHIES

### 67 NANT SYDDION BOTHY

A shepherd's house surrounded by forestry and much loved by mountain bikers. Stove, earth privy, bike shed and sleeping platforms.

→ Park by Ysbyty Cynfyn church at SY23 3JR and follow tracks from opp side 300m to N (10 miles, 3½ hrs). Better to mountain bike in on one of the many forestry tracks from near Devil's Bridge (start at SY23 3JN, 8–10 miles).
52.3958, -3.8044 ⬜⬜B

### 68 LLUEST CWMBACH BOTHY

Sitting above Craig Goch reservoir in the peaceful Elan valley, this restored shepherd's cottage has a stove and sleeping platforms.

→ Park in the small parking area near the dam at 52.3051, -3.6227. Walk N, following the reservoir bank, to find bothy up a little cwm after 1½–2 miles. 45–60 mins.
52.3213, -3.6143 ⬜B

### 69 NANT RHYS BOTHY

A former shepherd's house with sleeping platforms and a stove, surrounded by miles of forest plantation. Loved by mountain bikers.

→ Easiest route in is from the bridge near 52.3813, -3.7011. Walk or cycle N up the track/footpath with river Dillw on R all the way to the bothy, approx 2 miles / 45 mins.
52.3990, -3.7111 ⬜⬜B

### 70 MOEL PRYSGAU BOTHY

Hidden in a maze of forestry, this MBA-maintained bothy has a stove, sleeping platforms and stream. Good stopover for mountain bikers cycling the forestry tracks.

→ Cycle or walk the cycle route along the Nant Rhyd-meirth, starting at 52.2655, -3.8252, 1 mile SE of Strata Florida Abbey, Ystrad Fflur (52.2751, -3.8397) where you can park. Approx 6 miles, with ford crossings. 2½ hours.
52.2353, -3.7499 ⬜⬜B

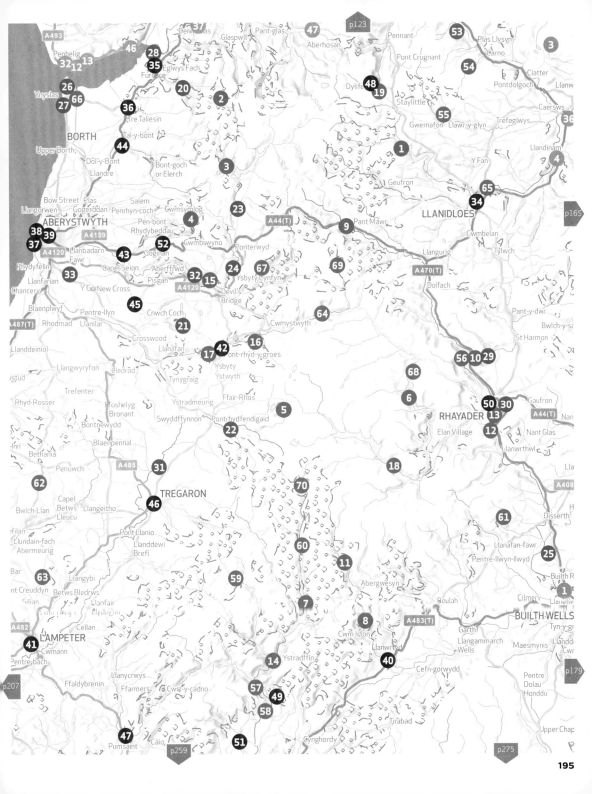

# CARDIGAN &
# TEIFI

## Our perfect weekend

→ **Watch** the sun go down over the perfect golden sands of Mwnt, set beneath an ancient chapel

→ **Drift** through bluebells among the oaks of Pengelli, one of the largest expanses of ancient woodland in west Wales

→ **Explore** Nevern's ruined castle, stroke its bleeding yew and enjoy a picture-postcard cream tea in the village hall

→ **Look** for seals at the remote coves of Traeth Soden, from the ramparts of Castell Bach or around the island at Carreg-y-Tŷ

→ **Camp** in style at Fforest, either at Manorafan near the beach or bordering the secret Teifi

→ **Canoe** or swim down the peaceful Teifi gorge from Cilgerran Castle to the Teifi Marshes

→ **Sup** on vegan ale and wood-fired pizzas at Penlon, a beautiful farmhouse brewery with sea views

→ **Swim** through sea caves into the Witch's Cauldron near Ceibwr Bay, or coasteer around the arches and stacks of Ynys-Lochtyn

**Waterfalls cascade down through a lost valley to a blue sea. Along the coast, sea caves and white sandy coves tempt the swimmer, walker and kayaker, and ancient woodlands and river gorges are abundant with wildlife.**

With a rich local food renaissance in Ceredigion (Cardiganshire), it's perhaps no surprise that discerning adventurers are increasingly heading for these shores, seeking great food to fuel their great adventures. Follow narrow lanes through woodland and along twisting streamside glades and you'll emerge at Cwmtydu, where the cliffs are pocked with caves. Take a short walk on the flower-filled coast path north and find the broken arc of Castell Bach hill fort, with an island and a remote beach beloved of seals – perfect for watching the sunset and enjoying a gourmet picnic of local cheese, ale and artisan bread.

For an easy family holiday, try Llangrannog, a small coastal hamlet at the heart some of the best coastal scenery in Wales. With two sea-facing pubs and two beautiful coves it's a perfect package holiday. A short walk north leads to Ynys Lochtyn headland, with an island, rock ledges, an arch, and a hidden beach, while a short walk south is Carreg-y-tŷ, a bit tricky to reach but easily the most beautiful beach on the Ceredigion coast. National Trust's Penbryn is little way beyond, with a café and long sands.

Continue west along the coast to discover Mwnt, another perfect sandy cove, sheltered by sandstone cliffs, great for snorkelling and watched over by a tiny whitewashed stone church. There's a clifftop campsite here too, if you want to make a base, and funky Cardigan (Aberteifi) is not far away for good food and music. From here you can also explore upstream along the River Teifi, either in the deep, wooded gorge below Cilgerran castle, or at picturesque Cenarth, where the rich culture of coracles still lives on; one of the oldest boat designs in the British Isles, they were used by Bronze Age Britons and invading Romans alike.

If you're yearning for a real wild adventure, hop the county to Ceibwr Bay, where great folds of contorted rock shelve into perfect pellucid seas, ideal for sea-caving and snorkelling. Deep caves and sea tunnel's punctuate the headlands around here – at the Witch's Cauldron, a chasm behind the cliffs harbours an iridescent green pool and beach, and boasts three separate tunnel entrances that meet in a sea cavern. Bring a wetsuit, and plenty of courage!

## SECRET BEACHES

### 1 TRAETH SODEN & CASTELL BACH

Secluded cove at the end of a beautiful valley, also called Cwm Silio. You can swim around to an adjacent cove on the right, or walk around at low tide. Just to the south is scenic Castell Bach, part of an Iron Age hill fort with visible ramparts, guarding its tidal island and cove.

→ Signed Cwmtydu from A487. Follow all the way past SA44 6LQ to park on seafront. Follow the coast path N. Or after 3 miles take R on bend to SA44 6LH, park in layby on R, walk on 200m to St Tysilio's church and take path through graveyard down valley.

15 mins, 52.1985, -4.3977

### 2 YNYS LOCHTYN, LLANGRANOG

This stunning headland flaunts an island, arch, stacks and a long strand of secret sand at Traeth-yr-ynys (morning sun only). It's great territory for kayaking and coasteering, and the coastal walk to it is stunning, from either charming Llangranog (many little coves on the way) or the Urdd Centre.

→ From Llangrannog (pay car park, SA44 6SL) climb steps to follow coast path N. Pass steps to tiny Cilborth cove L (300m) and continue

to headland. Drop down on R of headland to find steps to Traeth-yr-yynys beach. In high season, with limited parking in Llangranog, it might be easier to approach from E: park at the Urdd (youth centre) Centre a mile to the E off B4321, signed up lane from SA44 6AE.

20 mins, 52.1687, -4.4647

### 3 CARREG-Y-TŶ/TRAETH BACH

Secluded and sandy Robinson Crusoe cove, backed by steep, forested cliffs and a little waterfall. It's fun to swim to the little island, which is pierced by a long sea cave, though it is also connected by a low-tide isthmus. Watch out for seal pups after August, and if you see them stay away. The cove is also called Traeth Bach, 'little beach'.

→ On the coast path, a lovely walk 1 mile S of Llangranog (pay car park an extra ½ mile out of village at SA44 6SL) or 1½ miles N of Penbryn (parking by Plwmp Tart café, SA44 6QL see listing). Follow rough path down on R of stream - it ends in a slightly tricky rock scramble. Or there is a very steep descent, but with no scramble, from corner of field near gate on coast path up to W. Also accessible from Morfa, dead end lane at SA44 6RS, but very tricky parking.

15 mins, 52.1533, -4.4855

### 4 TRAETH PENBRYN, ABERPORTH

A mile-long wild beach bookended by cliffs with caves. A path leads down to the beach along the steep, wooded Cwm Lladron (robbers' valley), rich in smuggling history. A good place for a driftwood fire. No dogs May–Sept.

→ From NT car park with Plwmp Tart café (see listing) in Penbryn, SA44 6QL, walk down the lane or take the valley path behind car park.

10 mins, 52.1438, -4.4966

### 5 MWNT, PENPARC

One of our favourite coves in Wales. Perfect west-facing sandy beach with little NT café, a tiny white chapel in the fields above and a good seaview campsite behind. There's a little hill to climb, Foel y Mwnt, and you can coasteer and jump off the rocks below.

→ From Cardigan A487, turn second L at Penparc by petrol station (signed 'Mwnt 3'). Continue across dog-leg junction after 1¾ miles, then second L. Parking is R, before Ty-Gwyn campsite SA43 1QH (see listing). Follow path to R of church NE and along coast path 500m to find large slab rocks below with stacks and caves for coasteering.

5 mins, 52.136, -4.6405

## 6 WITCH'S CAULDRON & CEIBWR BAY

This mysterious and seemingly inaccessible lagoon can be reached by climbing down through the waterfall cave, or by swimming in via one of the sea caves. Caves continue all along this coast, and it's a superb area for coasteering and kayaking adventures. Do not attempt in high swell!

→ In Newport turn off by Llys Meddyg inn (signed 'Moylegrove 5'). After 5 miles at chapel turn L signed Ceibwr past SA43 3BU to park on the roadside just after the cove. Follow coast path W to find lagoon on L. Below mid-tide a cave appears on rocky shore R to swim in; a larger cave is always open in the inlet (more adventurous). Non-swimmers can climb down into a ravine stream passage below the waterfall – tricky, check you can climb back out! From Ceibwr Bay itself a 200m swim SW leads to the giant Careg Wylan (gull rock) headland with sea cave through it; very long tunnel pierces next headland too.

15 mins, 52.0715, -4.7715 🅿️🄿🖼️🅅🄻

### RIVERS & WATERFALLS

## 7 MAESYCRUGIAU, RIVER TEIFI

In the quiet upper reaches of the Teifi, this little river walk leads to a deep pool near an old church and ruin. Below the bridge are luscious pools and lawns; they are private, but you could swim down past them.

→ Signed Maesycrugiau from A485 in Llanllwni. Continue 1¾ miles park L and walk on 150m to find path on R before the Pont Llwni stone bridge, SA39 9LT. Follow the river footpath up from the bridge through woods. There are rapids and pools before arriving at a ruin and a large, deep pool.

5 mins, 52.0496, -4.2257 🅿️🖼️✝️

## 8 CENARTH, RIVER TEIFI

Cenarth is a tourist honeypot, famous for its coracles and the picturesque falls where salmon leap in autumn. There are waterfalls above the ancient bridge and a huge pool beneath. The Coracle Centre (entry fee) tells the story of the Teifi fishermen and their coracles – once common across Wales.

→ W of Newcastle Emlyn on A484 (near SA38 9JL), with a large pay car park by bridge. A footpath leads upstream and it's a good place to launch a canoe. There's also access to riverside footpath and space to pull off a mile downstream on A484 from 52.0528, -4.5417. Museum open Easter–September, not Saturdays. (01239 710980).

2 mins, 52.0455, -4.5252 🅿️🄻🖼️

## 9 FFYNONE WOOD WATERFALLS

A surprisingly large waterfall for a tiny stream, flowing into a deep pool. There are rope swings galore, dens and tree climbing.

→ Turn S off B4332 just E of Newchapel, signed Cwm-ffynnone. After 1¼ miles find a large car park on R past SA37 0HQ. Follow track ½ mile up past lake and through woods.

15 mins, 52.0136, -4.5698

## 10 HENLLAN BRIDGE & WATERFALL, TEIFI

An exciting section of easily accessible gorge, deep pools and woodland upstream of the attractive arched stone bridge.

→ A484 E of Newcastle Emlyn, turn L over bridge for B4334/Henllan (signed Teifi railway, dir SA44 5TE). A footpath on R after bridge leads upstream 50m to pools after 50m. Or explore downstream to Pwll Glas, a big river bend and beach (continue on road 100m to find path on L via church).

2 mins, 52.0347, -4.3978

## 11 NEWCASTLE EMLYN, RIVER TEIFI

Easy access to this child-friendly ruin on a steep mound in a loop of the river near the town centre. There's loads of riverbank here, from which to swim or boat, and a weir too. Or just have fun rolling down the slopes.

→ Well-signed from the main high street (A475), past SA38 9AF.

2 mins, 52.0391, -4.4631

## 12 CILGERRAN, RIVER TEIFI

An impressive twin-towered Norman castle overlooks the deep, forested Teifi gorge. Swim down the river under the shadow of the castle, or take a canoe. Explore inside the ruins (free to NT members, and during winter) or outside on the public footpath.

→ Cilgerran is signed off the A478 S of Cardigan. The riverside car park is down dead end, signed from the village shop, past SA43 2SS. Downstream are steps. Walk back towards shop for Pumporth Road to the castle.

7 mins, 52.0671, -4.6341

## 13 LOWER TEIFI GORGE

Ferns and creepers hang from the cliffs over the dark, deep waters of the lower Teifi, home of otters and rich in birdlife. Enjoy an atmospheric swim from the little river beach; a mile upstream is Cilgerran (see listing).

→ From Teifi Marshes Reserve (see entry), walk to river and upstream on footpath ½ mile to beach. Experienced canoeists can canoe downstream, all the way to the sea.

15 mins, 52.0698, -4.6381

(16)

(14)

(15)

LOST RUINS

### 14 ST DOGMAELS ABBEY

St Dogmaels is a pretty village and worth a wander. At its centre are the ruins of the abbey founded in 1115 for Tironensian monks, a Benedictine order committed to labour and noted as skilled craftsmen. Good café and market (see listing).

→ Signposted from centre of St Dogmaels (W of Cardigan), down Mill or Church St dir SA43 3DX, with parking outside.
2 mins, 52.0805, -4.6807 🖼️✝️👫

### 15 LLECH Y DRYBEDD CROMLECH

Set on hillside meadows enjoying fine coastal views out to Mynydd Preseli, the fat capstone of this Neolithic tomb perches upon three uprights, with room under to sit and contemplate.

→ Start as for the Witch's Cauldron beach (see listing) but 1⅓ miles before Moylegrove, descending hill, find concrete farm track on R, with small footpath sign. Park and follow this up hillside, bearing L at fork after ½ mile, to stile into field on R after 200m.
15 mins, 52.0545, -4.7719 👫🖼️

### 16 CASTELL NANHYFER, NEVERN

The remains of a motte with simple tower ruins, atop grassy earthworks, surrounded by a bailey filled with trees. Now perfect for picnics and running wild, this was a great 12th century stone castle – one of the earliest in Wales.

→ Leave the B4582 at Nevern, Just E of Newport, dir SA42 0NF, across stone bridge, and up to find gate 120m after postcode on R, with signboard.
5 mins, 52.0260, -4.7972 🖼️👜🐾

### 17 BRONWYDD HOUSE RUIN

Built in the Gothic Revival style in 1850s, with great windows and turreted towers, this was gutted by a great fire after the Second World War and now lies abandoned and ivy-clad next to a farmyard.

→ From A475 E of Newcastle Emlyn turn N on B4334 at Aber-banc SA44 5NP (signed Rhydlewis). After 1½ miles turn L down dead-end road, dir SA44 5LY. Park and bear R around farm complex on bridleway, to find ruin on L after 200m.
5 mins, 52.0628, -4.4036 🖼️❓

## ANCIENT FORESTS

### 18 PENGELLI FOREST & CASTELL HENLLYS

This magical forest has one of the largest
expanses of oak woodland in western Wales.
Bluebells carpet the floor in late spring, and
later you can feast on its wild bilberries.
The fascinating Iron Age village of Castell
Henllys (entry fee) is a short distance away.

→ From Felindre Farchog (Velindre on some
maps) head E on A487 for ¼ mile, then take
small lane, dir SA41 3PX, up L for 1½ miles to
reserve gate on R and limited roadside parking.
Paths lead around the reserve. Castell Henllys is
signed from A487 1 mile E of turning to Pengelli.
5 mins. 52.0205, -4.7268 🍴🐾🚲🛶

### 19 NEVERN BLEEDING YEW & STONES

Pagans, Christians, and the botanically
curious come to experience the ever-flowing
red sap of the 'bleeding' yew – and to see
the finely carved 10th-century Celtic braided
crosses and the 5th-century Ogham stones
at the church of St Brynach, who was said to
commune with angels. In the nearby village
hall, a pop-up tea shop serves delicious
cakes and light lunches on Fridays in August.

→ Nevern is off the B4582 at SA42 0NF.
2 mins. 52.0253, -4.7952 🍴✝🏛

## WILDLIFE

### 20 LLANERCHAERON ESTATE NT

Enjoy the frozen-in-time charm of this
18th-century working farm estate. See
the historic Welsh breeds in the farmyard,
wander through wildflower meadows or
kitchen gardens with ancient fruit trees,
then walk along the river looking for otters
or hire a bike and follow one of the family
trails. Before you leave, buy seasonal organic
produce or meat from the farm in the shop
at the café.

→ SE of Aberaeron on A482 dir Ciliau Aeron,
turn signed National Trust Llanerchaeron 1
mile after SA48 8DQ, follow ¾ mile to car
park R before SA48 8DG and entrance, 01545
570200. Pur en lde Cycles 07806 905366
2 mins. 52.2191, -4.2262 🚲🍴🚗♿🐾👟

### 21 TEIFI MARSHES RESERVE

Water buffalo, sika deer, otters, barn owls,
salmon, bluebells; Teifi marshes is a wildlife
haven with award winning eco-visitor centre
and great local food at the café.

→ Entering Cilgerran from A478, Wildlife
Centre is signed L. Follow lane 1½ miles, past
SA43 2TB. 01239 621212.
5 mins. 52.0743, -4.6450 🚲🍴

### 22 CARDIGAN BAY DOLPHIN TRIPS

Book a dolphin boat trip with Cardigan Bay Marine Wildlife Trust and join the scientific researchers as they head out around the coast surveying the marine megafauna.

➔ Wildlife Centre, Patent Slip Building, Glanmor Terrace, New Quay, SA45 9PS, 01545 560032. 90 mins, 52.2139, -4.3580

## SLOW FOOD

### 23 LLWYNHELYG FARM SHOP

Good things come in small packages, and this friendly little farm shop has been selling home-grown vegetables, artisan Welsh cheeses, cakes and local delicacies for over 30 years.

➔ Sarnau, SA44 6QU, 01239 811079. 52.1257, -4.4823

### 24 BLAENCAMEL ORGANIC FARM

A small, organic family farm and farm shop selling seasonal fruit, vegetables, cut flowers and lots of lovely preserves. You are invited to share their love of the land, walking around the footpaths and woodland trails to see the springtime wild daffodils and bluebells that enrich their surrounding woodland. If you live nearby, veg boxes are available. Nearby is the Ty Glyn Davis Trust walled garden (Nant Camel, SA48 8DE), which often offers produce for a donation to the trust.

➔ Cilcennin, SA48 8DB, 01570 470529. 52.2183, -4.1881

### 25 NEW QUAY FISH SHOP

Fresh fish shack and fishing boat trips run by Winston Evans, one of the last fishermen of New Quay.

➔ South John Street, New Quay, SA45 9NP, 01545 561011. 52.2152, -4.3581

### 26 PENLON BREWERY

A beautiful farmhouse brewery producing vegan real ales. Open summer weekends for wood-fired pizzas and ale tastings in the granary shed, with sunset views overlooking Cardigan Bay.

➔ Panteg Farm, New Quay SA45 9TL, 01545 561492. Events on facebook or twitter. 52.2031, -4.3532

### 27 NEW QUAY HONEY FARM

It takes over 10 bees their entire lifetime to make one teaspoon of honey, and they are essential for pollinating our food crops.

Learn about bees and beekeeping and see how this precious edible treasure is made. Buy some honey or mead, or enjoy cakes and home-made ice cream at the tea shop.

➔ Cross Inn, Penrhiwgaled Lane, SA44 6NN, 01545 560822. 52.1822, -4.3435

### 28 THE PLWMP TART, PENBRYN

Enjoy cream teas, crab sandwiches, bowls of cawl, wood-fired pizzas and ice cream in this little café at Penbryn beach car park.

➔ Penbryn, SA44 6QL, 01239 758100. 52.1409, -4.4915

### 29 HAMMET HOUSE

This refreshingly contemporary country house hotel by the Teifi river serves two-AA-Rosette meals and tasting menus in stylish surroundings. Restaurant open to non-residents.

➔ Llechryd, SA43 2QA, 01239 682382. 52.0612, -4.6078

### 30 BARA MENYN BAKEHOUSE

Savour the best coffee, bread, breakfasts and lunches at this little artisan bakehouse and café in Cardigan town.

➔ 45 St Mary St, Cardigan, SA43 1HA, 01239 615310. 52.0823, -4.6606

### 31 PIZZATIPI & TAFARN SMWGLIN

Excellent wood-fired pizza tent, alehouse and café from the fantastic Fforest people (see listing). Overlooking the Teifi river.

➔ Cambrian Quay, Cardigan SA43 1EZ, 01239 612259. 52.0813, -4.6620

### 32 CAWS CENARTH

The oldest producer of Welsh Farmhouse Caerffili. Watch the cheesemakers and taste the different cheeses made on Glyneithinog farm – the Perl Wen brie is particularly good!

➔ Glyneithinog, Pontseli, Lancych, SA37 0LH, 01239 710432. Visit 11.30am–3pm Mon–Sat. 52.0150, -4.5266

### 33 CAWS TEIFI ORGANIC FARM TOURS

Love cheese? Take a tour and see how artisanal raw-milk cheese is made on this organic farm.

➔ Glynhynod Farm, Llandysul SA44 5JY, 01239 851528. Open 9am - 6pm Mon - Fri but best to call in advance. 52.0827, -4.3781

### 34 ST DOGMAELS MARKET & CAFÉ

Every Tuesday morning the small square outside St Dogmaels Abbey (see listing) is packed with producers, all from within a 30-mile radius, selling mouth-watering fare including freshly caught fish, from 9am–1pm. The café at the Coach House Visitor Centre next door is a real local hub and serves good home-made food daily.

→ Shingrig, St Dogmaels, SA43 3DX, 01239 615389.
52.0806, -4.6795 🍴

### 35 GLEBELANDS MARKET GARDEN

Stock up here on a fantastic range of home-grown organic salads and vegetables.

→ St.Dogmaels Rd, Cardigan, SA43 3BA, 07511 546701. Open 10am–5.30pm Thur-Sat, 11am–3pm Sun.
52.0810, -4.6700 🍴

## COSY PUBS

### 36 THE SHIP INN, LLANGRANNOG

Also called Tafarn-y-Llong, this is the pick of the pubs in this seaside village, serving up fresh mackerel salads, hearty fish and chips and good pints, best enjoyed in the sunshine on the patio.

→ Llangrannog, , SA44 6SL, 01239 654510.
52.1598, -4.4699 🍴

### 37 THE HARBOURMASTER, ABERAERON

Aberaeron is a pretty town filled with handsome, colourful houses. The Harbourmaster commands the best view over the little port, now bustling with pleasure boats. Come for locally caught lobster and fries, catch of the day or fried cockles. Nearby is The Hive, where you can buy ice cream sweetened with Welsh honey.

→ Pen Cei/Quay Parade, Aberaeron, SA46 0BT, 01545 570755.
52.2435, -4.2633 🍴

### 38 NAG'S HEAD INN, ABERCYCH

Really good food and ales are served on scrubbed wooden tables in this friendly country pub with rooms. We enjoyed excellent mackerel salad and burgers with fries out in the garden by the river.

→ Abercych, SA37 0HJ, 01239 841200.
52.0309, -4.5516 🍴

## RUSTIC HAVENS

### 39 FFOREST FARM, CILGERRAN

In a beautiful nature reserve on the River Teifi the family behind Fforest have created a magical get-away world with stylish cabins, domes, group tents, bell tents, crog lofts and a beautifully renovated Georgian farmhouse sleeping 14, decked out with cosy Welsh blankets. With a strong emphasis on local crafts and food, there is a whole calendar of events from winter feasts to week-long creative festivals.

→ Cwmplysgog, Cilgerran, SA43 2TB, 01239 623633.
52.0621, -4.6459 🔲🍴

### 40 THE DAIRY SHED, CILIAU AERON

Super-cute, cosy, rustic-minimalist retreat for two. Look out on the fields, snuggle up by the woodburner or sit out on the deck enjoying a feast of delights from nearby Blaencamel organic farm (see listing).

→ Ciliau Aeron, SA48 8BY, 01570 471436. airbnb.co.uk
52.2119, -4.1958 🔲

### 41 MORFA ISAF FARM GUEST HOUSE

With easy access to the amazing beach of Carreg-y-Tŷ (see listing) and along the coast path to Llangrannog, this little slice of heaven offers a quirky boathouse, self-catering barn and cottage, or B&B in the traditional farmhouse.

→ Morfa, Llangrannog, SA44 6RS, 01239 654699.
52.1490, -4.4823 🔲🔲

### 42 OVER THE RAINBOW B&B & RETREAT

Hippy-chic, vegetarian country-house B&B set in acres of quiet woodland. Lots of wonderful courses and retreats, including yoga and vegan cookery.

→ Plas Tyllwyd, Tanygroes, SA43 2JD, 01239 811155.
52.1055, -4.5042 🔲

### 43 NANTGWYNFAEN ORGANIC FARM

Sample the good life on this lovely organic farm and enjoy delicious produce from the farm shop or for your breakfast. Enjoy B&B in the farmhouse, rent the Glamavan or Ty Mamgu (grandma's house), play ping pong in the barn and meet the animals.

→ Penrhiwllan Road, Croeslan, SA44 4SR, 01239 851914.
52.0709, -4.3657 🍴🔲

### 44 PLAS-Y-BERLLAN & PEN LON LAS

Rustic-chic, renovated 19th-century workhouse, smothered in wisteria and enjoying views of the Teifi estuary. Perfect for a get together, Plas-Y-Berllan sleeps 14 – Pen Lon Las (attached) sleeps up to four.

→ Albro Castle, St.Dogmaels, SA43 3LH, 01239 614454.
52.0884, -4.6864 🖼

### 45 QUIET EARTH ECO RETREAT

Experience life in a Grand Designs award-winning straw-bale house in the woods near lovely St Dogmaels. Off-grid, a balcony with views, woodburners and utter serenity.

→ Cwmdegwel, St Dogmaels, Cardigan SA43 3JH. airbnb.co.uk
52.0780, -4.6814 🖼

### 46 TY GLAS & LITTLE BARN

Ridiculously idyllic stone cottage and a luxurious eco-barn, both sleeping two, set in 40 acres of meadows and wildlife.

→ Crymych, SA41 3XJ, 0844 5005101. underthethatch.co.uk
52.0403, -4.7659 🖼🏵

## WILDER CAMPING

### 47 NATURESBASE

Run a little wild at this bucolic, summer-only campsite set in woodland and meadows. There are fields set aside for games, wildflowers between mown pitches, and firepits already in place. Bring your our own tent, glamp in a furnished safari tent or cabin and enjoy pizza nights, bushcraft days and breakfasts in the barn.

→ Tyngwndwn Farm, Cilcennin, SA48 8RJ, 01570 471795.
52.2226, -4.1678 🔺🖼🍴🏵

### 48 ONE CAT FARM

Four little wooden cabins with turf roofs, set in three acres of wildlife-rich meadow, with firepits, a communal kitchen, dark skies and lots of space.

→ Bronfre Fach, Ciliau Aeron, SA48 7PT, 01570 470203.
52.2051, -4.2108 🖼🍴

### 49 FFOREST COAST, PENBRYN

A coastal sister site of Fforest Farm (see listing), Manorafan is a converted dairy farm. It offers not just its own domes and cabins, but the option to pitch your tent on a little site with a communal firepit, just 10 minutes from glorious Penbryn beach.

→ Manorafon, Penbryn, SA44 6QH, 01239 623633.
52.1404, -4.4856 🖼🔺

### 50 CWRT HEN, BEULAH

A quiet site in beautiful tree-lined surroundings set by a market garden. Buy fresh eggs, veg and fruit, or try some fishing on the lake. Campervans, tents and caravans all welcome. Greener Camping Club.

→ Beulah, SA38 9QS, 01239 811393.
52.0796, -4.5179 🔺

### 51 TOP OF THE WOODS, BONCATH

Camp in butterfly-filled wildflower meadows and enjoy starlit skies, cosy campfires and delicious feasts cooked in the Dutch barn. Fully furnished luxury tents, or bring your own.

→ Penrallt Farm, Capel Coleman, Boncath, SA37 0EP, 01239 842208.
52.0112, -4.5925 🍴🔺🍖🖼

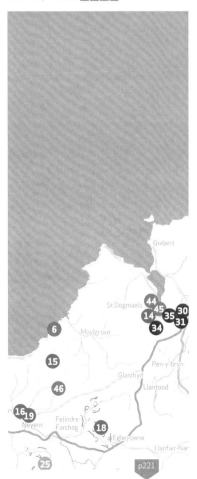

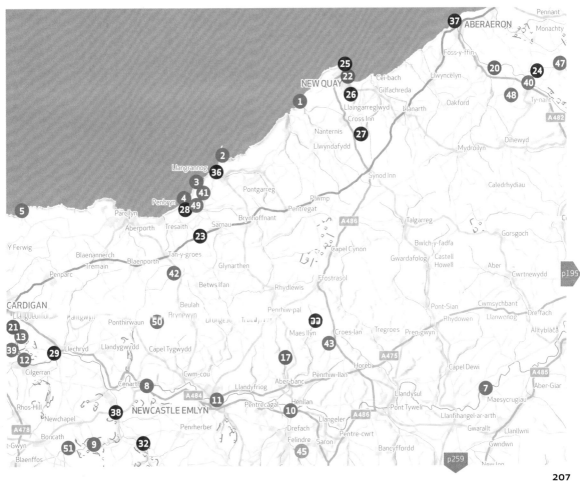

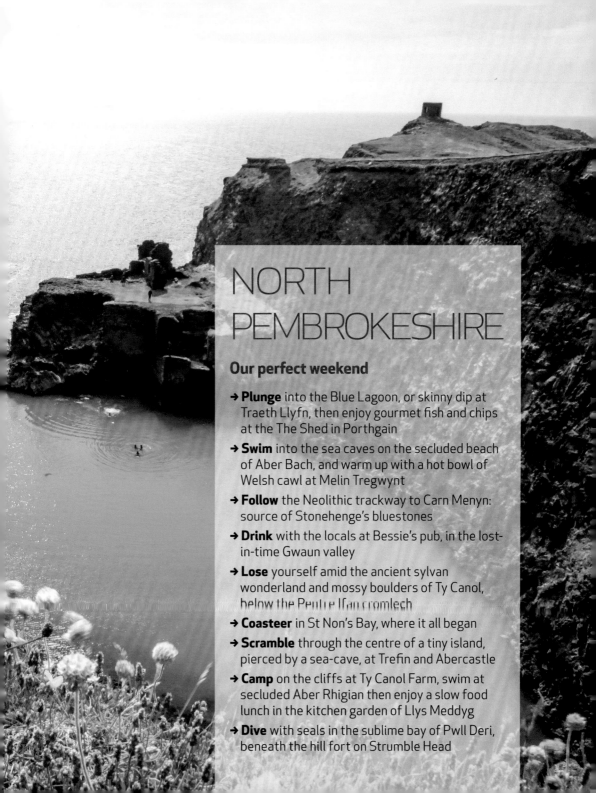

# NORTH PEMBROKESHIRE

### Our perfect weekend

- → **Plunge** into the Blue Lagoon, or skinny dip at Traeth Llyfn, then enjoy gourmet fish and chips at the The Shed in Porthgain
- → **Swim** into the sea caves on the secluded beach of Aber Bach, and warm up with a hot bowl of Welsh cawl at Melin Tregwynt
- → **Follow** the Neolithic trackway to Carn Menyn: source of Stonehenge's bluestones
- → **Drink** with the locals at Bessie's pub, in the lost-in-time Gwaun valley
- → **Lose** yourself amid the ancient sylvan wonderland and mossy boulders of Ty Canol, below the Pentre Ifan cromlech
- → **Coasteer** in St Non's Bay, where it all began
- → **Scramble** through the centre of a tiny island, pierced by a sea-cave, at Trefin and Abercastle
- → **Camp** on the cliffs at Ty Canol Farm, swim at secluded Aber Rhigian then enjoy a slow food lunch in the kitchen garden of Llys Meddyg
- → **Dive** with seals in the sublime bay of Pwll Deri, beneath the hill fort on Strumble Head

**From ancient woodlands to caves, coves and clifftop cromlechs that gaze out over sparkling seas, this is an area tangibly rich in nature, adventure and the mystical.**

Quite why the builders of Stonehenge chose Carn Menyn bluestones as their source remains a mystery, but walking the Preseli ridge, across the wild moorland of the Golden Road, past cairns and stone circles to the bluestone 'quarry' is a stirring experience and the Preseli mountains are far less visited than they deserve to be.

Indeed nearly all the sacred and ancient relics of the region occupy fabulous positions. Inland, Pentre Ifan is the portal to an enchanting woodland at Ty Canol, and on the coast Carreg Sampson overlooks the bay at Abercastle. Around Strumble Head, the lanes twist through a landscape of scattered Neolithic remains to remote Pwll Deri, where harbour porpoises, bottle-nosed dolphins and grey seals are common. Follow the rough path down through gorse to a rocky spur and you can dive into the deep, silky water and swim through dancing forests of kelp.

To the south west, miles of perfect coastline unfold. A difficult climb down via a rope and waterfall to remote and dramatic Pwllcrochan rewards you with low-tide sands and rock formations. Aber Bach, at the end of bumpy lanes and bluebell woods, reveals large sea caves with walls of pink and purple rock. And the tiny fishing village of Abercastle has an island with a cave right through its centre.

West of Porthgain, an adventure-packed coast peaks at Abereiddi's famous Blue Lagoon. This disused quarry has long since breached to the sea, and the old wheelhouse provides three platforms for leaping into the deep blue abyss below – a famous rite of passage for local swimmers and visitors alike.

Outside the tiny cathedral city of St Davids you can explore idyllic St Non's Bay. The chapel and holy well are where the princess-saint was said to have given birth to David; the well is still revered for its healing powers and the site remains a place of pilgrimage. Others head to the bay to try out 'coasteering', a term coined back in the 1990s by TYF Adventures and now almost a national sport. You can still head out on one of their courses, or with a wetsuit, some old trainers and a safe approach to adventure you can explore for yourself this incredible hidden coastline.

3

## SECRET BEACHES

### 1 ABER RHIGIAN & ABERFFORREST

Secluded cove with a pretty streamside walk through ancient forest. The stream forms a pool behind the beach and is perfect for paddling. West along the coast is Aberfforrest, with a waterfall in the woods behind.

→ 1 mile W of Newport on A487, park on wide verge on R by farm track turning for SA42 0SS. Follow track 200m, turn L down to house 300m, and take gate to woodland walk just before. Aberfforrest is ½ mile W on coast path (52.0193, -4.8786), or at end of track off A487 at SA42 0UG.

15 mins, 52.0195, -4.8688 🐚🏖️🏔️🚶

### 2 PWLL CROCHAN

A wonderfully dramatic and remote low-tide beach with a waterfall, sea stacks and sands. Difficult descent down the rocks via a rope.

→ 1 mile N along coast path from Aber Bach (see listing). Or ½ mile N on lane from Melin Tregwynt (see listing) and ¼ mile N of SA64 0LJ, find 2 gates on L with footpath sign, opp turn for a farm on R (tricky parking). Bear R then L around pool to descend at S end of beach.

15 mins, 51.9863, -5.0807 🐚📷

### 3 PWLLSTRODUR

The high cliffs between Abercastle and Aber Mawr look down on a spectacular string of islets, caves and inaccessible coves. This secluded shingle bay provides access for those wishing to coasteer or kayak. Swimming best at high tide.

→ Heading E out of Abercastle (SA62 5HJ) turn L down dead end after ½ mile. After another ½ mile find footpath on L between two field gates. Parking for one car on grass L just beyond. Or park back at junction.

8 mins, 51.9615, -5.1073 🐚📷🏖️🚶🅅

### 4 ABER DRAW, TREFIN & YNYS-FACH

Ruined Trefin mill sits forlornly above Aber Draw cove, two giant millstones worn by five centuries of use and two empty windows looking out on the sea. There's no sand, but good swimming at high tide, and caves and arches to explore for coasteering and kayaking. Westwards lies Ynys-fach island, connected to the cliff shore by a beach isthmus. On top is a grassy plateau, reached by a rope, and below a great sea cave pierces right through the rock – fascinating to explore if you can swim around to its entrance.

→ The cove is reached by footpath from layby parking just W/below Trefin SA62 5AX.

Continue up the hill W a little to find the coast footpath (signed Porthgain) just after SA62 5BA. Follow for ¾ miles W to reach Ynys-bach. It's a very steep scramble down over a fence.

2 mins, 51.9481, -5.1523 🐚📷🏖️🚶🅅

### 5 ABER BACH & SEA CAVES, ABERMAWR

This pretty shingle cove is backed by water meadows. Adjacent, via the coast path north you can climb down the boulder gulley to Porth Dwgan, a tiny secret low-tide cove which leads north to a huge sea cave, great for coasteering.

→ 4 miles SW of Fishguard A487, turn R signed Abermawr & Melin Tregwynt (see listing). Follow 1½ miles over crossroads, downhill and L before bridge (SA62 5UX) signed dead end. Pass footpath on R to Aber Bach (park at road end above shingle & sand Aber Mawr). Preseli Venture (01348 837709) run coasteering courses here. Sea cave is at 51.9761, -5.0845.

15 mins, 51.9739, -5.0824 🐚📷🏖️🚶

### 6 TRAETH LLYFN & PENCLEGYR

Traeth Llyfn is a superb west-facing, sandy beach, as wild and as beautiful as any in Wales. Walking there on the spongy, flowered coast path is equally delightful.

Nearby is Penclegyr, an exciting headland where you can swim through a chasm, and also a quarry and the ruins of an old tramway leading down to the huge brick loading hoppers in Porthgain.

→ Follow coast path ¾ mile N from Abereiddi Blue Lagoon (see listing) for steps down to Traeth Llyfn. Another ½ mile NE climb down on the far side of the second bay, Porth Dwfn, to swim around Penclegyr (51.9498, -5.1964) through the two chasms. The ruins are just beyond. You can also walk in W from Porthgain, SA62 5BL.

20 mins, 51.9435, -5.1992

### 7 PORTHMELGAN & COETAN ARTHUR
Sandy, secret cove just beyond popular Whitesands Bay, and below St Davids Head. Seek out Coetan Arthur cromlech (or quoit, for its flat capstone), a massive angled burial chamber.

→ Follow B4583 from St Davids to end, past SA62 6PS, for Whitesands beach car park. Follow coast path ¾ mile N, passing Porth Lleuog on way, to Porthmelgan. Continue on to headland for cromlech, about 200m NW of the cove (51.9045, -5.3081).

15 mins, 51.9033, -5.3044

### 8 CAER BWDY BAY & CAERFAI
The characteristic red and purple rocks of this coastline are most intense at Caer Bwdy, where the stone for St Davids magnificent cathedral was quarried. Sandy at low tide, this is a secluded alternative to popular Caerfai. The smooth yellow-and-purple 'barrel zawn' slab to the east is fun to dive off or climb along at high tide.

→ Follow A487 from St Davids E dir Solva. ¾ mile after Caerfair Bay turn off, turn R signed Trelerw dir SA62 6QP. NT grass parking on R after 130m. Follow lane 300m then track straight S at bend.

10 mins, 51.8728, -5.2456

### 9 PORTH Y RHAW FORT & LAKE
Beautiful woodland stream leads past a freshwater swimming lake to a low-tide cove with a waterfall and cave. There's a very deep rock pool along the rocks to left, into which you can leap into from above. Climb up to the eroded promontory fort above and look for the disintegrating shipwrecks in the next cove.

→ A mile W of Solva on A487, turn L into Nine Wells caravan site SA62 6UH, to find small NT parking on L. Follow woodland track down to cove, passing lake. Beach is accessed from other bank, cross stream at coast path.

10 mins, 51.8733, -5.2174

## 10 PORTHSELAU, WHITESANDS BAY

Beautiful little cove, great for rock pooling and sunset swims.

→ From St David's cathedral follow road 1¼ miles (signed St Justinian) and turn R for Pencarnan Farm Camping SA62 6PY, where you can park. Walk to bottom R of camping field to reach beach.

3 mins, 51.8866, -5.3049 🌊⛺

## 11 PORTHMYNAWYD, SOLVA

Remote shingle and sand low-tide cove, with a large sea arch and caves to left and a series of islets good for snorkelling to the right. Great coasteering in both directions.

→ A487, 2 miles SE from Solva, find R turn for SA62 6BA just after large layby. Walk past Pointz Castle farm buildings (now selling ice cream!) Take footpath signed on L, turn R and follow track descending to coppice / scrub, and then stream to beach.

15 mins, 51.8631, -5.1576 🐚⛴🚩🐾🍽

## BLUE LAGOONS & CAVES

## 12 PWLL DERI & PORTH MAENMELYN

Below the ancient promontory fort of Dinas Mawr, rocky ledges and a ladder lead to deep water and caves. You might well swim among seals here, but don't enter caves after August as it is pupping season. A short walk north at Porth Maenmelyn are the remains of an extraordinary flight of Victorian steps, hewn into the 60m sheer cliff, still just about navigable. Take care!

→ On A487 SW of Fishguard, ¾ mile beyond SA62 5XA, turn N dir SA64 0LR, 3½ miles to and through St Nicholas, to layby parking R before Pwll Deri YHA (see listing). Take coast path from hostel entrance downhill 500m. Bear off L on faint path to headland fort and after 400m, at bottom, bear L down gorse path for iron ladder to sea and caves. Continue on along coast path to Porth Maenmelyn to spot the old stairway.

15 mins, 52.0058, -5.0778 🌊🍽🚩🐾🐟

## 13 ABER CASTLE & CAREG SAMPSON

This tiny fishing cove has an island pierced by a long sea cave and connected at low tide by a rocky isthmus. A ruined grain store looks down from above, and the cove is good for kayak launching. On a hill above is Careg Sampson, a fine 5,000 year old cromlech with six uprights supporting the capstone.

→ From Mathry, 5 miles SW of Fishguard on A487, head to Abercastle and SA62 5HJ. Park by beach, island and ruin are R. Take coast

path L ⅓ mile to find Careg Sampson signed L (51.9583, -5.1330).
10 mins, 51.9618, -5.1291 🚶🏊🚲🏕🏊🚣

### 14 ROSEBUSH QUARRY, MYNYDD PRESELI

A deep blue lagoon, a grand old dressing shed and a fine arched tunnel into the hillside are the lasting relics of these 19th-century slate quarries. The lagoon was originally dug as a pit, allowed to flood and then used as a reservoir to drive the dressing sheds turbine. Good bilberry foraging.

→ Between Fishguard and Narbeth on B4313 turn into Rosebush village. Park and walk up the dead-end lane, beyond the cottages SA66 7QX, to find the dressing shed ruins L after 500m and path up to lake R.
10 mins, 51.9359, -4.7959 🏊🏊🚲🏊🏔

### 15 SEALYHAM WOODS, LAKE & RAVINE

Enter this enchanting ancient beech wood to find a mossy gorge, waterfalls and an old stone bridge over the Anghof river. There is a vast lake, from the slate-quarrying era, connecting to a fascinating man-made stream ravine (fun on an inner tube).

→ N from Haverfordwest on A40, just N of Wolf's Castle, turn R into cul-de-sac Quarry Lane (SA62 5ND, park here or layby off A40

just beyond). Follow footpath at end and bear R at junction down towards stream. 300m upstream, beyond activity camp, is the lake.
10 mins, 51.9080, -4.9675 🍴🏊🏕🏊🏊🚲

### 16 ABEREIDDI BLUE LAGOON

Spectacular and popular lagoon created when the old slate quarry was breached, connecting it – narrowly – to the sea. The winching tower ruins provide levels for jumping. Join in or just watch the daredevils from this wonderful stretch of coast path.

→ Abereiddy (SA62 6DT) is signed from the A487. Park at beach and follow coast path 300m N to lagoon. Do not jump from top tower at low tide. Bottom platform safe at all tides.
5 mins, 51.9379, -5.2087 🏊🏊🏊🏊

### 17 ST NON'S BAY CAVE & COASTEERING

This dramatic bay is the birthplace of St David – and coasteering. The spectacular sea cave/arch complex is great for an adventure swim; don your wetsuit and explore.

→ St Non's is signed L down a dead-end lane (Catherine St) leaving St Davids for Porthclais. Pass SA62 6BN and park at end. Walk R across field past chapel ruins, turning L onto coast path. Cave can be seen ahead, at E end of bay in headland. Either drop down via steep gulley

after 500m (far side) or continue on path beyond cave and then down on slabs beyond (51.8701, -5.2621) about halfway round to Caerfai Bay. W along coast path is Chanter's Seat, famous ledges for jumping (51.8690, -5.2725) and giant pyramid slabs in Porth y Ffynnon (difficult scramble down, or swim around from Porthclais).

15 mins, 51.8706, -5.2628 ⛏🍴🕱🅅🗻

## SACRED STONES & CIRCLES

### 18 GWAL Y FILIAST BURIAL CHAMBER

This remote cromlech, the 'den of the greyhound', is set in a clearing among beech trees above the course of the Taf.

→ From A478 at Glandy Cross take road SE to Llanglydwen. ½ mile beyond turn R dir SA34 0TU/Login. After 200m take driveway R (Pen-pontbren) then footpath along field edge down to woodland, ½ mile, to find on L.

10 mins, 51.8992, -4.6605 ⛏🗻

### 19 GARN TURNE ROCKS & CAIRN

The capstone of this collapsed burial chamber is thought to weigh 60 tonnes, making it much larger than Pentre Ifan (see Ty Canol woods entry). Although it has long since fallen, it is still fun to discover and survey the landscape

around. Look carefully and you can still make out some of the V-shaped stone forecourt.

→ A40 5½ miles S of Fishguard, turn L dir Sealyham. Follow 2 miles, past turn off for SA62 5DU, and the lane widens for a stretch. Park carefully here and find the tiny gap/gate in the hedge into the field. Slab is 100m to R.

2 mins, 51.9075, -4.9387 ⛏🍴

### 20 GORS FAWR STONE CIRCLE

One of the easiest and best stone circles in the Preselis, with 16 evenly spaced, low stones. A pair of outliers, one colloquially named the Dreaming Stone, may create an alignment for viewing the summer solstice sunrise or the Carn Menyn bluestone outcrop.

→ Lead to Mynachlog-ddu (W of A478), then take road SW 1 mile to find layby and kissing gate on R at SA66 7SE, leading to the circle 200m. Outliers are 130m NE.

3 mins, 51.9314, -4.7145 ⛏

## HILL FORTS & HILLTOPS

### 21 MYNYDD CARNINGLI, NEWPORT

Spend a night on Carningli and you'll either become a poet or go mad. The broad, heather-clad summit (337m) is scattered with Bronze Age remains and topped by the

Carn Briw cairn, while the craggy Carn (or Garn) Ingli hill fort (319m) contains obvious earthworks from the once-important settlement. Views of the coast and mountains are phenomenal; this is one of the most rewarding ascents of the Preselis.

→ From A487 W edge of Newport, take Ffordd Bedd Moirris, signed Cwm Gwaun. This eventually leads to Bessie's Pub (see listing) at SA65 9TP, but after 2 miles, near the top, is a cattle grid and parking on L. It's about 1⅓ miles to the hill fort. Quicker, but much steeper is following Church Street, then forking up off R after a mile for SA42 0QH. Parking can be found after ½ mile.

25 mins, 51.9980, -4.8326 🖼️🚗♿🌲✨

### 22 GARN FAWR, STRUMBLE HEAD

Sensational sea views and sunsets overlooking Strumble Head from this easy-to-access Iron Age hill fort. Fun scrambling for kids.

→ Climb up from behind Pwll Deri (see listing) or drive S then L, L and L again, signed Strumble Head, to find car park on other side, before SA64 0JJ. NB in fields S of St Nicholas, is Ffyst Samson, an unusual cromlech with a capstone poised on two uprights (51.9730, -5.0501, pull off near SA62 5UY).

10 mins, 52.0078, -5.0667 🚗🌊♿🖼️🔭

### 23 CARN MENYN & GOLDEN ROAD

Follow the Golden Road, a Neolithic trackway, along the Preseli ridge to the jagged tor of Carn Menyn, a long-assumed source of Stonehenge spotted dolerite bluestones. Climb to Foel Drygarn hill fort to find a trio of cairns, and discover Bedd Arthur, an eye-shaped stone ring said to be the grave of King Arthur. Just below here is Carn Goedog, another suggested source for Stonehenge. There's no actual quarry here – all the stones were carved out by the underbelly of a glacier.

→ The Golden Road bridleway starts from ½ mile NE of SA66 7SA (2 miles NE of Mynachlog-ddu). Detour R up Foeldrygarn first for the hill fort and cairns, then continue on 1¾ mile to Carn Menyn. Bedd Arthur circle remains are ¾ mile beyond (51.9598, -4.7205), and below this to R is Carn Goedog (51.9653, -4.7251).

50 mins, 51.9606, -4.7058 🚗🖼️

### 24 CWM GWAUN, GARN WOOD

Carved into a perfect V shape by the massive meltwater flows of the Preseli glaciers, this hidden valley is thick with beech and hazel,

25

ash and oak, watered by a bubbling stream with rapids and pools.

→ Opp Bridge End Inn SA65 9TB on B4313 (small layby just E above houses) cross river bridge to find the footpath upstream on the far side. Follow it a mile into the depths of the woods, continuing to Tre-ll⅓yn wood and returning on the N side via Court farm. There are also waterfalls 3 miles up valley (51.9673, -4.8550) beyond the fantastic Bessie's pub (see listing).

20 mins, 51.9792, -4.9186 🏠♨️📖

### 25 TY CANOL WOODS & PENTRE IFAN

This mystical ancient woodland has stood here for over 6,000 years; it is filled with twisted oaks, and foxglovos grow hon if huge mossy boulders. Nearby you'll find Pentre Ifan cromlech, dating from around the same time, one of the most impressive burial chambers in Pembrokeshire.

→ On A487 2 miles E of Newport, shortly before SA41 3XB, turn R signed Brynberian/ Burial Chamber, then R again after 1¾ miles, following same signs, to find parking layby after ½ mile for Pentre Ifan. After this, continue on ⅓ mile, beyond SA41 3TZ, to second bend to turn R through Tycanol farm gate over cattle grid and park on verge L. Go

up farm road and path immediately crosses fence into field R and heads NNW on ancient bridleway, into woods in ⅓ mile. You can loop W on track to Tycanol farmhouse to return. Bring a map!

15 mins, 52.0001, -4.7756 🏠♿🐕🍃

### 26 RAMSEY ISLAND RSPB RESERVE

Ramsey Island has dramatic cliffs topped by rich grass and maritime heathland that's smothered in bluebells, wildflowers and heather as the year progresses. Choughs, peregrines, guillemots and razorbills all flourish in this stunning habitat, together with large colonies of grey seals. Ogof Organ is our favourite sea cave cove, into which you can swim if no seal pups are present.

→ Open Easter to end of October; the only way to visit is by boat from St Justinian's lifeboat station, beyond SA62 6PY. Book with Thousand Island Expeditions (01437 721721). Sea cave is in NW corner, down ledge, at 51.8746, -5.3461; keep out of the tidal race if you swim in!

20 mins, 51.8646, -5.3335 🏊🚶🐕

25

26

## SLOW FOOD

### 27 CWTCH*, ST DAVIDS

Excellent creative food, sourced very locally in Britain's smallest city.

→ 22 High St, St Davids, SA62 6SD, 01437 720491.
51.8807, -5.2639

### 28 THE GOURMET PIG, FISHGUARD

Stock up your picnic basket at this lovely café and deli selling good coffee, Welsh ales, charcuterie and cheeses. They'll also advise where you can source fresh local crab.

→ 32 West St, Fishguard, SA65 9AD, 01348 874404.
51.9949, -4.9783

### 29 GWAUN VALLEY BREWERY

Sample and buy real Welsh ales at this remote, family-run microbrewery with small CCC campsite and holiday cottage. Open 10am–6pm Mar–Oct, 12pm–4pm Nov–Dec, by appointment Jan–Feb.

→ Kilkiffeth Farm, Pontfaen, SA65 9TP, 01348 881304.
51.9657, -4.8949

### 30 LAVENDER CAFÉ, SOLVA

Quirky licensed café in a converted chapel with gallery, selling delicious soups, tapas boards and lots of home-made cakes including gluten-free options.

→ The Old Chapel, 10 Main St, Solva, SA62 6UU, 01437 721907.
51.8755, -5.1880

### 31 THE SHED, PORTHGAIN

Our favourite fish and chips for miles are enjoyed sat outside The Shed in the sunshine: the freshest fish, delivered that day is cooked perfectly in light batter and served with Pembrokeshire hand-cut chips. The cosy bistro also serves great vegetarian curries and fish specials, including home-made fishcakes and dressed crab. Open daily Easter–October and school holidays in winter.

→ Llanrhian Rd, Porthgain, SA62 5BN, 01348 831518.
51.9482, -5.1816

### 32 THE OLD SAILORS, PWLLGWAELOD

Traditional red-and-white beachside pub set just back from Pwllgwaelod beach. Local seafood, bowls of cawl and fish and chips are served for lunch and dinner. Yes it's touristy, but just what you need after too long splashing in the sea!

→ Dinas Cross, SA42 0SE, 01348 811491.
52.0220, -4.9084

### 33 SOMETHING'S COOKING

If you're passing through Letterston stop and try one of Pembrokeshire's fish and chip masters. Try the local catch of the day fish or crab with chips to take away – it can be hard to get a table here!

→ 3 Haverfordwest Rd, Letterston, SA62 5SB, 01348 840621.
51.9277, -4.9903

### 34 THE BRASSERIE AT WOLFSCASTLE COUNTRY HOTEL

Runner up in the Observer food awards, the Brasserie offers a relaxed setting in which to sample Wolfscastle Hotel's 2-AA-Rosette food, using local produce. Delicious St Bride's Bay crab and first-class dry-aged filled steaks.

→ Wolf's Castle, Haverfordwest, SA62 5LZ, 01437 741225.
51.9003, -4.9708

### 35 MELIN TREGWYNT

See the tradition of Welsh weaving at this charming whitewashed working woollen mill and leave with a classic or modern blanket and a tummy full of delicious cawl from their little café. Free entry.

→ Castlemorris, SA62 5UX, 01348 891288.
51.9718, -5.0673

### 36 THE MILL, TREFIN

This café and gallery is the place for a proper Welsh breakfast, packed with cockles, laverbread, bacon and fresh eggs, eaten amid the art of local painters. Light lunches and afternoon teas too.

→ 37 Ffordd y Felin, Trefin, SA62 5AX, 01348 831650.
51.9486, -5.1484

### 37 GRUB KITCHEN, THE BUG FARM

Try some entomophagy – the practice of eating insects – at this innovative café serving delicious food made with edible insects. There's other great food too. The bug farm (entry fee) is well worth a visit.

→ Lower Harglodd Farm, St Davids, SA62 6BX, 07986 698169.
51.8894, -5.2357

### 38 LLYS MEDDYG, NEWPORT

A fantastic family-run restaurant with rooms in charming Newport. In the summer enjoy lunch in the kitchen garden, or savour the best Pembrokeshire seasonal food in the relaxed dining room or cosy cellar bar.

→ East St, Newport SA42 0SY, 01239 820008.
52.0169, -4.8300 🏠🍴

### 39 CRUG GLÂS COUNTRY HOUSE

A luxurious and relaxed country-house hotel and working farm, serving first-class locally sourced lunches and dinners. Restaurant open to non-residents.

→ Abereiddy Rd, SA62 6XX, 01348 831302.
51.9183, -5.1861 🍴🏠

## COSY PUBS

### 40 THE SLOOP, PORTHGAIN

Originally built for the slate workers who worked here, this characterful pub decorated with buoys and fishing nets is the place for a pint in the sun, overlooking the little houses and green of pretty Porthgain. Locally caught crab and fresh fish – or eat at The Shed bistro nearby (see listing).

→ Porthgain, SA62 5BN, 01348 831449.
51.9482, -5.1806 🍴🏠

### 41 BESSIE'S PUB, PORTHFAEN

In the wooded Cwm Gwaun (see listing) is Bessie's pub (technically the Dyffryn Arms), maybe our favourite pub in all of Wales. Local farmers and their dogs stand outside in the sunshine chatting in Welsh; go into the front room to buy your pint of draught Bass, served from a jug through the hatch. It's gloriously unchanged, very simple and utterly charming. No food.

→ Pontfaen, SA65 9TP, 01348 881305.
51.9697, -4.8747 🏠

### 42 TAFARN SINC, ROSEBUSH

Looking like a tin shed this cosy, quirky, remote village pub is filled with chatter, local music, steaming traditional Welsh food, local ales and a museum's worth of old photos and salvage from its mining and farming past. Recently saved from closure by community buyout – find updates on their facebook page. Take home some delicious artisan cheese from Pant Mawr Farmhouse opposite.

→ Rosebush, SA66 7QU, 01437 532214.
facebook.com/tafarnsinc/
51.9305, -4.8008 🍴🏠

## WILDER CAMPING

### 43 TIR BACH FARM CAMPSITE

With views of the Preseli mountains, this is a quiet campsite with a playground, clean facilities, fresh eggs and campfires. Ask for a secluded pitch in the hay meadow, or book a yurt or the boat for hassle-free glamping.

→ Llancefn, Clynderwen, SA66 7XT, 01437 532362.
51.8998, -4.7538 🏕️🔥🏠

### 44 HILLFORT TIPIS & CAMPING

Nestled against the mountain hills with views over Garn Fawr fort (see entry), the sea and Strumble Head, this is a wild place to camp and watch magical sunsets. Rent one of the four yurts or camp on one of their 11 tent pitches. Greener Camping Club.

→ Penparc, Pencaer, SA64 0JQ, 01348 891497.
52.0088, -5.0549 🏕️🔥🏠📷

### 45 TRELLYN WOODLAND CAMPING

Wonderful secluded eco-camping and glamping in a magical wooded valley near the sea. Yurts, geodesic domes, tipis and bushcraft courses are hosted by eco-camping pioneers Kevin and Claire. Greener Camping Club; book ahead!

→ Abercastle, SA62 5HJ, 01348 837762.
51.9570, -5.1249 🏠🏕️🔥

### 46 PWLL DERI YHA

Enjoy unbeatable sea views and spectacular sunsets from this great coastal youth hostel on the cliffs below Garn Fawr (see entry).

→ Castell Mawr, Trefasser, SA64 0LR, 0345 3719536.
52.0070, -5.0723 🏠

### 47 KITEWOOD CAMPING, TRE-GROES

Proper camping in nine spacious, private glades hidden in a traditionally worked woodland. Beautiful hand-built facilities include composting loos, hot showers, campfires and the sheepskin-strewn Dragon tipi. Greener Camping Club.

→ Tre-groes, Nr Fishguard, SA65 9QF, 07770 776402.
51.9802, -5.0013 🏕️🔥🏠

### 48 INTO THE STICKS, LETTERSTON

Birdsong, dark skies and five special off-grid tent-only pitches are set on a private nature reserve. It's a quiet place, abundant in wildlife. For a little more luxury rent their handmade Tiny Home with a woodburner,

solar electrics and super-king bed. Part of the Greener Camping Club.

→ Midland Ln, Letterston, SA62 5TF, 01348 840613.
51.9219, -5.0113 🔺🏕️↩️🔄🏃

### 49 BÔN CAMPING & YURT

Wild campfire camping in hay meadows. There's a simple compost loo and cold-water tap in the fields, but more loos, hot showers and washing up facilities in the communal shed. Yurt and vintage camper also available. Greener Camping Club.

→ Porterswell Farm, Roch, SA62 6JX, 01437 710744.
51.8557, -5.0951 🔺🔥🏕️

### 50 DUNES AT WHITESANDS

With easy access to lovely Whitesands Bay, this small campsite has ten secluded grass pitches, sheltered from the sea winds and each with their own loo and firepit. Greener Camping Club.

→ Craig-Y-Mor, Whitesands, SA62 6PT, 01437 720431.
51.8949, -5.2858 🔺🔥

### 51 CAERFAI FARM CAMPSITE

A rather large campsite, but the sea views and access to nearby Caerfai beach make it a great choice for families. Good facilities all run on 100% renewable energy. Yurts and cottages also available.

→ St Davids, SA62 6QT, 01437 720548.
51.8734, -5.2570 🔺🏕️↩️

### 52 PORTHCLAIS FARM CAMPSITE

A sprawling but uncrowded campsite on the fields overlooking the rocky coast Porthclais harbour – great for kayakers and crabbing.

→ St Davids, SA62 6RR, 01437 720616.
51.8710, -5.2784 🔺🏖️

### 53 TYCANOL FARM CAMPSITE

Simple campfire camping with sweeping sea views over Newport Bay, hot showers and

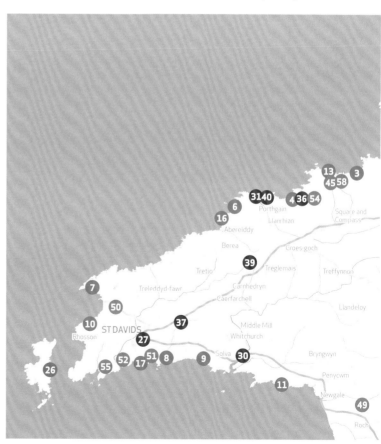

only a short walk to two beaches. You can also rent the rustic self-catering barn. Or for basic (and busy) camping right on the quay in Newport, try Morawelon.

→ Newport, SA42 0ST, 01239 820264. Or Morawelon Campsite: Parrog Rd, SA42 0RW, 01239 820 565.
52.0196, -4.8535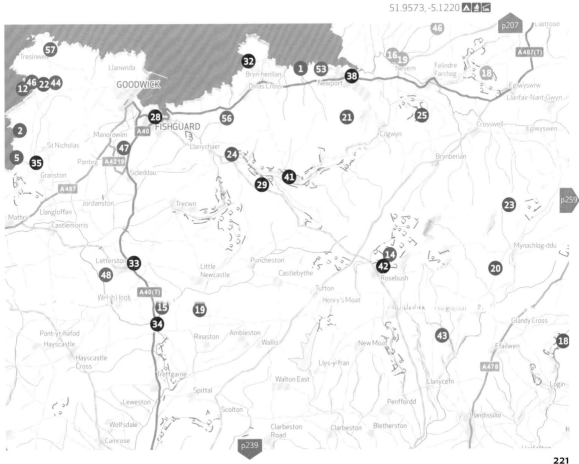

## RUSTIC HAVENS

### 54 OLD SCHOOL HOSTEL, TREFIN

A fun, super-friendly independent hostel. The rooms are small and basic but individually decorated with paintings, pictures and vintage finds. With B&B starting at £32 for a double, a clean kitchen to cook in and the lovely Mill café (see listing) and rocky coves all in walking distance it constantly gets great reviews.

→ Ffordd-yr-Afon, Trefin, SA62 5AU, 01348 831800.
51.9489, -5.1443

### 55 PORTHLLISKY FARM COTTAGES

Self-catering cottages on a secluded coastal farm. Perfectly located with access to Porthlysgi Bay – where you can launch your kayak, cast a fishing line and paddle round to Porthclais harbour.

→ Porthllisky Farm, Porthclais, SA62 6RR, 01437 720377.
51.8674, -5.2915

### 56 DYFFRYN FERNANT GARDEN BOTHY

At the foot of the Preselis, is a quiet place, abundant with wildlife and with a garden cultivated and tamed with such expertise that every corner is a delight. Set aside from the main house is a cosy garden bothy, Y Bwthyn Bach, that you can rent and enjoy the garden (open to visitors for an entry fee) at your leisure. Sleeps three.

→ Dinas, Fishguard, SA65 9SP, 01348 811282. Garden open 12–6pm April–Oct.
51.9956, -4.9234

### 57 BWTHYN TRESINWEN

In a quiet hamlet this traditional, authentically decorated cottage with a real fire and little garden makes for an idyllic holiday in an area where time feels suspended. It's a five-minute walk to the rocky cove (where we found a mother seal with her pup) or a short cycle to Strumble Head lighthouse and amazing sunsets.

→ Tresinwen, SA64 0JL, 0844 5005101. underthethatch.co.uk
52.0238, -5.0599

### 58 GARN ISAF, ABERCASTLE

Cosy, modern B&B with its own boat mooring, or self-catering in a cottage or converted barn, minutes from the coast path and a short walk from Abercastle. There is also Carn Gwely camping, the individual grassy pitches surrounded by wildflower covered hedges; caravans, campervans and tents welcome. Greener Camping Club.

→ Abercastle, SA62 5HJ, 01348 831838.
51.9573, -5.1220

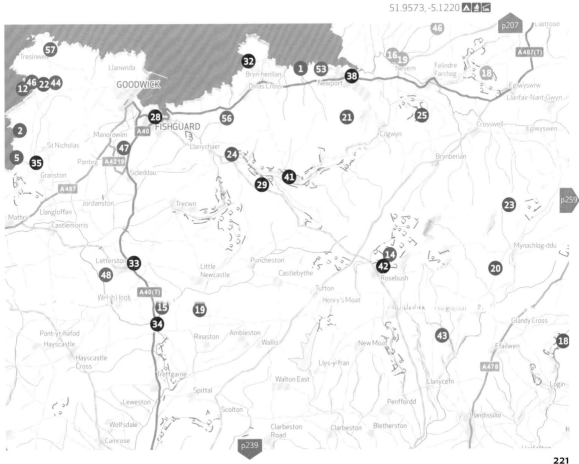

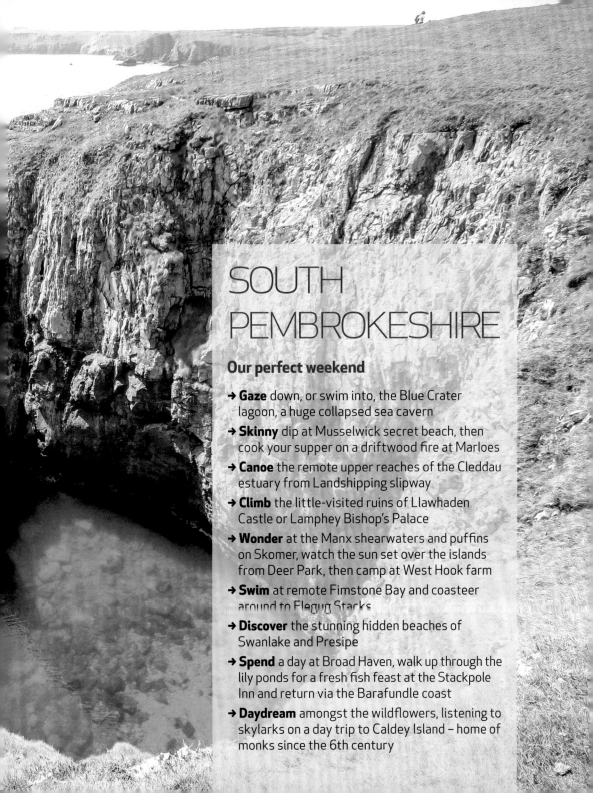

# SOUTH PEMBROKESHIRE

## Our perfect weekend

→ **Gaze** down, or swim into, the Blue Crater lagoon, a huge collapsed sea cavern

→ **Skinny** dip at Musselwick secret beach, then cook your supper on a driftwood fire at Marloes

→ **Canoe** the remote upper reaches of the Cleddau estuary from Landshipping slipway

→ **Climb** the little-visited ruins of Llawhaden Castle or Lamphey Bishop's Palace

→ **Wonder** at the Manx shearwaters and puffins on Skomer, watch the sun set over the islands from Deer Park, then camp at West Hook farm

→ **Swim** at remote Fimstone Bay and coasteer around to Flegug Stacks

→ **Discover** the stunning hidden beaches of Swanlake and Presipe

→ **Spend** a day at Broad Haven, walk up through the lily ponds for a fresh fish feast at the Stackpole Inn and return via the Barafundle coast

→ **Daydream** amongst the wildflowers, listening to skylarks on a day trip to Caldey Island – home of monks since the 6th century

As you venture into south Pembrokeshire, volcanic black basalts and rich red marls give way to golden limestone, the product of reefs, corals and plankton that once flourished in a shallow tropical sea. The sand it creates is silvery and soft, and wave-eroded clefts and cracks make a coastline abundant in caves and soaring arches, rich with bird- and sealife.

At the Druidstone you will find one of the classic family hotels of Wales – a blustery Victorian house standing proud and alone on a cliff above a spectacular beach, where horses gallop through the waves. Continue from here to the more forgotten and untouched parts of the coast around Marloes and Dale, where a Swallows-and-Amazons feel pervades, and life centres around the Dale sailing club and Westdale surf beach. Make driftwood campfires on delightful Marloes Sands and take a secret skinny dip at Musselwick.

Cheek-by-jowl with this idyllic coast are the vast oil refineries of Milford Haven, a gritty reminder of the modern world. Upstream on the Cleddau are the stately ruins of Carew Castle, and Cresswell Quay, and further up a timeless estuarine world of lost chapels and still waters. Here you can find – perhaps – the remains of a hospice used by pilgrims to St Davids.

Across the estuary is the Angle peninsula, once a critical location for Second World War defences. The old cliffside gun turrets and lookouts still remain and are an amazing place to spend a wild night, if you can reach them safely. From here the MOD occupies the coastline, but you can still walk the coast path to see picturesque limestone formations such as the Green Arch. One of our favourite sections for coastal wonders is Bosherston's Broad Haven beach. You can swim into a huge crater that fills up with each high tide, near a narrow chimney cave that climbers called Confucius Hole; they scale it without ropes, protected by the deep water below. Next to this is Box Bay, with amazing caves and sand but only accessible via a scramble and a swim, or a kayak from Broad Haven. The other side of Stackpole Head, tree-fringed Barafundle Bay opens out, recently named one of the best beaches in the world, ornamented by a trio of gothic arches.

Close to this coast but in a world of their own are the islands of Skomer and Skokholm to the west, and monastic Caldey to the south-east. All are havens for wildlife and a slower pace of life, and the ferry ride offers chances to see dolphins and porpoises.

4

## HIDDEN BEACHES

### 1 WESTDALE BAY, DALE

The best beach for surfing and sunsets, with an Iron Age promontory fort at one end. Easy access but difficult parking along the lane. Beware of rip currents.

→ At end of B4327 in Dale, park and walk along Castle Way or Blue Anchor Way to single-track road from Castle Way, opp church (W of SA62 3RN) – or limited parking and turning space up at the road end. Continue W on footpath to join the coast path. Walk down to beach or head S to the rocky promontory and fort.

30 mins, 51.7083, -5.1873

### 2 MUSSELWICK SANDS, MARLOES

North-west facing, low-tide sandy beach hidden beneath cliffs, within walking distance of Marloes.

→ Almost at the end of the B4327 to Dale, turn R through Marloes and 250m after final house, past SA62 3BE, find the footpath on R with rough layby opp.

5 mins, 51.735, -5.2093

### 3 MARLOES SANDS & GATEHOLM ISLAND

A favourite beach, enjoying a vast sweep of low-tide sands. Make your way to the far western end, beyond Raggle Rocks, and climb up Gateholm Island to an amazing high, grassy plateau and remains of an ancient settlement, accessible only at low tide.

→ Head to Marloes, as for Musselwick Sands (see entry) but turn L before church, past SA62 3BH, to find large car park at end. Walk back 100m to track/bridleway and follow to beach. Continue W at low tide along beach to Gateholm. Return on coast path.

5 mins, 51.7237, -5.2138

### 4 WATWICK BAY, DALE

White sand cove set below a secret wooded valley, popular with sailors who anchor their boats in the little bay and swim to shore.

→ Follow the B4327 to Dale and follow seafront, L past Griffin Inn and park on verge L after ¾ mile, beyond SA62 3RD. Take gate and footpath R across field down to Castlebeach Bay and then onto Watwick. Or for Watwick only, follow signs dir St Ann's Head and park by SA62 3RP. Follow footpath R 80m down drive to Maryborough Farm.

20 mins, 51.6924, -5.1597

### 5 LINDSWAY BAY, ST ISHMAEL'S

These secluded low-tide sands with views over Milford Haven and Thorn Island are kept peaceful by the dramatic climb down, which ensures they get very few visitors.

→ St Ishmael's is signed from B4327. Park by recreation ground just E of SA62 3TB. Follow asphalt footpath ½ mile to coast path then turn L to find steep steps down after 200m.

15 mins, 51.7165, -5.1240

### 6 FLIMSTON BAY & GREEN BRIDGE

Admire the fantastic Green Bridge of Wales rock arch and seabird-smothered Elegug Stacks (elegug is Welsh for guillemot), then descend to this secret golden beach. Accessible via a steep scramble down a gully – there's usually a rope in place – and the adventurous could swim back around towards the Cauldron, Stacks and Green Bridge for once more in this totally sensational scenery. Bullslaughter Bay is further east along the coast path, with caves and arches.

→ On B4319 2 miles W of Bosherton turnoff, ⅓ mile after Merrion Cross (SA71 5EB), turn L for Stack Rocks viewing platform and parking. Bear L on coast path ¼ mile to descend to Flimston Bay in gully at NW corner. Continue ¾ mile to E corner of Bullslaughter for easier path down gully (51.6099, -4.9739). MOD range usually open at weekend, (info 01646 662367).

10 mins, 51.6126, -4.9902

### 7 BROAD HAVEN & BOSHERSTON LAKES

This is a beautiful and exciting beach, backed by dunes and serene lily ponds and (whisper it), just as good as Barafundle. You'll find a little island, Star Rock, which kids jump from at high tide, while the bigger Church Rock sits offshore beckoning the stronger swimmer or kayaker. To the west are two secret coves not named on maps, Trevallan and Little Horn, connected to each other by a sea cave and accessible from the coast path (or by swimming around). The path to the first is below the dell/bottom camping field and the other is from the MOD range hut nearby. From here continue onto New Quay.

→ From B4319 follow signs to Bosherston, then signed on L after St Govan's Inn SA71 5DZ. Toilets, shop and café van near the NT car park.

5 mins, 51.6079, -4.9204 🏖🍴🐾🚻

### 8 BOX BAY & BLUE CRATER

The limestone cliffs of Saddle Point headland are riddled with sea caves. One of the most impressive is a cavern that has collapsed into a huge blue crater that fills with water at high tide, accessible from the adventurous from about mid-tide and below. You can swim on a little further for more blowholes, including a chimney known to climbers as Confucius Hole, and eventually into Box Bay (also called Saddle Bay, not named on maps), a steep-backed Robinson Crusoe beach with more sea caves.

→ As for Broad Haven (see entry), but cross E onto Saddle Point, then ¼ mile to tip to find big crater (51.6084, -4.9149). Scramble down to water and swim in through a small cave from mid- to low tide. Smaller caves/blowholes 25–50m E. Continue 150m on until beach comes into a view. Take path down onto rock promontory (51.6094, -4.9137), scramble down and swim into the beach. There is a sheerer rock scramble at 51.6101, -4.9142, but a rope is advisable.

20 mins, 51.6111, -4.9145 🍴↖◁▽

### 9 BARAFUNDLE BAY & ARCHES

Backed by dunes and ancient woodland, this beach has won many awards for its beauty. On the far right corner is Griffith Lorts Hole, with three interconnected rock arches, perfect for snorkelling through at high tide. On the left is Lorts Cave, which leads through to a secret cove at low tide.

→ Signed from B4319 just E of SA71 5DL; park at Stackpole Quay car park SA71 5LS (the quay here is popular for jumping at higher

11

tide) and follow coast path ¾ mile. Or from Broad Haven (see entry), just over a mile.
20 mins, 51.6181, -4.9031 🌊⛱🏊

### 10 PRESIPE, MANORBIER

Low-tide secret beach with crimson rock stacks and deep tidal pools and lagoons in the sand.

→ As for Church Doors (see listing) but find footpath over stile R by first army camp gate, before L turn (some roadside parking). Follow path W around perimeter and across a field to steps at W end of beach. Or a slightly longer but lovely coast path walk E from Manorbier Bay passes King's Quoit.
15 mins, 51.6377, -4.7896 🌊

### 11 SKRINKLE HAVEN & LYDSTEP CAVERNS

Dramatic Church Doors cove has an arch and, at mid- to low tide, a secret cave tunnel through the cliff to spectacular Skrinkle Haven with its own impressive caverns. You can also swim round to Skrinkle, but it's further than it seems, and the stairs to Skrinkle itself are closed due to instability. At nearby Lydstep Caverns there are even more impressive sea caverns and huge arches. Walk in at very low tide, or swim at high tide.

→ On B4585 ½ mile E from Manorbier turn R to army camp (signed Skrinkle Haven/youth hostel, SA70 7TT). Turn L at army gate and park beyond youth hostel at large concrete picnic parking area. 100m SW find metal staircase to Church Doors. Or head ½ mile E on coast path to follow valley down to Lydstep Caverns (51.6451 -4.7660, foot access at low tide only).
5 mins, 51.6423, -4.7747 🐚⛱🏊

### 12 SWANLAKE BAY, MANORBIER

Very secluded, part-naturist beach, with steps and some sand at all tides. Backed by handsome red sandstone cliffs.

→ From B4585 in Manorbier follow road to beach and castle and continue ¼ mile up hill to find footpath on L and some parking on R, after SA70 8QR. Follow ¾ mile, past East Moor Farm, then dropping down to beach.
20 mins, 51.6466, -4.8262 🌊

## RIVERS & ESTUARIES

### 13 LANDSHIPPING QUAY

Explore the remains of the great quay, pier and harbour wall areas, plus the remote foreshore beach beyond. This is the site of Garden Pit coal mine and Pembrokeshire's

10

12

worst mining disaster. In 1844, workings beneath the river collapsed under the high tide and flooded, killing 40 miners – men, women, and children.

→ Landshipping is signed from A4075 at Cross Hands. Follow to parking with mining memorial ¼ mile S of SA67 8BE. Follow S edge of bay along old quay to remains of old pier and beach. Also, ¼ mile N of SA67 8BE, on the corner, follow the road down to the slipway for canoe launching by the derelict mansion (51.7691, -4.8831).

5 mins, 51.7602, -4.8892 🏊🎣🚶

### 14 GARRON PILL, LAWRENNY

Quiet Daugleddau estuary is surrounded by deep ancient woodland; this stretch around Benton Castle is narrow and secluded. Best swimming is at high tide (watch out for currents), or let the flow take you down to Lawrenny Quay or up to Landshipping Quay (see listing).

→ Lawrenny is signed from A4075. ½ mile N, at SA68 0PU, find rough footpath along S side of Garron Pill. Park and follow ½ mile along wooded shore to reach main channel and grassy, rocky shore area for swimming.

10 mins, 51.7321, -4.8833 🏊🚶

### 15 CAREW CASTLE MILLPOND

Take a swim in the tidal millpond under one of the most magnificent castle ruins in south Wales, an Elizabethan pile with many grand, mullioned windows. Slighted in the Civil War, it fell into dereliction after.

→ Off the A4075, at SA70 8SN; millpond parking is on the N side. Walk down the path W along the shore a little way to a beach. High tide only. The Carew Inn has a wood-panelled bar and hearty pub dishes (SA70 8SL, 01646 651267).

2 mins, 51.7002, -4.8317 🍴🏊

## WILD RUINS

### 16 EAST BLOCKHOUSE BATTERY, ANGLE

There's plenty of history to discover around the strategic entrance to Milford Haven. Remains of Henry VIII's blockhouses, built in 1539, can be seen on the cliff edge. The main construction, from 1905, sits slightly behind. These five gun turrets were also used in the Second World War, accompanied by new gun lookouts placed in the cliffs below. It's still just possible to reach them, and the adventurous can even camp out overnight.

→ Follow B4320 to Angle and West Angle Bay car park, shortly before SA71 5BE. Take

coast path SW ¾ mile. Down to R find first gun lookout with stairway leading down gated gully to lower lookout on rock (51.6837, -5.1200). Another 200m leads around to the main artillery complex of underground bunkers and gunhouses. The final lookout is 250m S on promontory along coast path, a tricky descent but a good place to bivvy.
20 mins, 51.6820, -5.1218 ▣🔆▽

## 17 WISTON CASTLE

Little known, but easily reached, this petite 13th-century stone castle sits atop a pretty mound in a big meadow. It was built by the wonderfully named Lord Marcher Wizo Flandrenis.

→ Signed on R, 2½ miles W of Canaston roundabout A40. Then signed on L after 2 miles. Park at telephone box SA62 4PN, castle is opp.
2 mins, 51.8268, -4.8711 ▣🔆

## 18 LLAWHADEN CASTLE & CLEDDAU

A very fine ruined 14th-century castle complex, free to enter and with much to explore, including a five-storied gatehouse, which you can climb. Great fun for kids. In the valley are pools on the Eastern Cleddau.

→ Llawhaden is signed N from A40/A4075 roundabout at Canaston. Castle at road end

beyond SA67 8HL. Below to the E (a mile by road to SA67 8DH, or shorter on the footpath) an old stone bridge crosses a river pool R. There is another pool, better for paddling, 2 miles upstream at Gelli Bridge (SA66 7HR).
1 min, 51.8223, -4.7976 ▣▣🔆

## 19 LAMPHEY BISHOP'S PALACE

A gateway in the great walls leads into the exquisite ruins of this garden palace retreat built by Henry de Gower, bishop of St Davids in the 13th century. There were over 20 rooms to entertain the bishops, a vast undercroft to store wine, fishponds, orchards, fruit and herb gardens. Great fun for kids. Free entry, open 10am–4pm.

→ Signed off A4139 E of Pembroke, SA71 5NT
2 mins, 51.6717, -4.8669 ▣🔆

## 20 SCOVESTON FORT, NEYLAND

This massive hexagonal fort was built in the 1860s as part of the Palmerston fortifications against feared French invasion. A whopping 250m across, with a moat and kitted out for 128 men, its now completely overgrown and overlooked amid the fields, the entrance sealed.

→ On B4325, 1½ miles NW of Neyland, turn R at bend signed Little Honeyborough (dir SA73

21

21

22

1QU) and find gate immediately on L. Fort is the area of woodland beyond. Apparently the well-preserved interior is accessible by determined urban explorers. Private but viewable from road.

2 mins, 51.7194, -4.9773 🖾❓🖼

## SACRED & ANCIENT

### 21 ST GOVAN'S CHAPEL & NEW QUAY

Climb down the steps to this tiny, dark hermit's cell, built into a cleft in the high cliffs with stupendous views out over the sea. You can scramble down the rocks below and coasteer to Huntsman's Leap in calm weather. Or bear due east from the car park ½ mile to New Quay beach, a long, snaky, sandy inlet also known locally as Tank Beach.

→ Start for Broad Haven beach (see listing) but follow signs straight on at Bosherston, past SA71 5DP, to road-end car park. Chapel is straight ahead.

5 mins, 51.5986, -4.9365 ✝🌊🐚

### 22 BOULSTON CHURCH & MANOR

On the banks of the Cleddau estuary lie the ruins of 15th-century Boulston Manor and church. Now derelict, trees and ivy grow through the floors and drape the walls. Look out for the openings to the cellar below the medieval hall, and the many inscribed stones still legible in the church.

→ From A40/A4076 roundabout in Haverfordwest, follow minor road signed Uzmaston S for 2 miles, to ⅓ mile before SA62 4AQ. Before Boulston Manor a drive / public byway leads L into Puntingbud Farm. Park respectfully and take bridleway on farm's far R, leading S down old drive to the manor on shore, ½ mile. Church is 200m SW, upstream.

10 mins, 51.7722, -4.9304 ✝🖾🖼

### 23 SISTERS' HOUSE & MINWEAR WOODS

A collection of ruined buildings on the shores of the Cleddau estuary, possibly a hospice for pilgrims to St Davids, linked to the ruined church on the bank opp (Slebech, see food listing). But maybe a 16th-century manor, with the words 'systerne house' on an early map, meaning a cistern for a pool. Take a look and make your own guess.

→ Signed Black Pool Mill/Minwear off A4075 just S of A40. Turn R after 2½ miles and park by the church at Minwear Farm, SA67 8BJ. Go through farmyard and follow footpath ⅓ mile NW to shore. Lovely loop back via Long Wood/ Minwear Wood to E.

15 mins, 51.7862, -4.8537 ✝🖾🐿

## WILDLIFE

### 24 ST BRIDES HAVEN

At low tide this little fisherman's cove reveals a sandy beach but the real draw is the sea life. The rocky outcrops are rich with anemones, making this a great spot for rock pooling. The braver can snorkel in the surrounding kelp forests. West along the coast is Huntsman's Leap inlet.

➔ St Brides is signed off B4327. A short walk from the St Brides and car park, just above the cove at SA62 3AJ.

2 mins, 51.7536, -5.1862 🏊🏖

### 25 SKOMER ISLAND

Skomer Island and smaller Skokholm are home to the world's largest colonies of breeding Manx shearwaters, but also teem with puffins, razorbills, gannets and fulmars, and in the sea you can often see seals, dolphins and the extraordinary sunfish. Spring heralds bluebells and moulting seals, in summer puffins and Manx shearwaters return to their island burrows, and wildflowers are visible from the mainland, and in autumn you can see seal pups. The island is open from April–September, closed Mondays. Book a day trip or stay the night in one of the cottages or the hostel. You'll need to bring your own food and be able to climb the steep steps from the ferry.

➔ Boats depart from Martin's Haven – follow B4327 and lanes through Marloes past SA62 3BJ. Buy tickets (no advance booking) from Lockley Lodge Visitors Centre (car park).

10 mins, 51.7364, -5.2968 🐦🍴🏖

### 26 CALDEY ISLAND

Caldey Island is a special place, rich in Viking, and Bronze, Iron and even Stone Age history, and a place of monasticism on and off since the 6th century AD. Today it is home to some 40 residents and a Cistercian order. Wildlife is bountiful; in summer skylarks fill the air, choughs and fulmars gather on the cliffs, wildflowers decorate the grass and golden sand beaches are backed by turquoise waters. The island is open to day visitors from Easter to October.

➔ Ferries run Easter–October (not Sundays), from Tenby harbour SA70 7BN, 01834 844453.

20 mins, 51.6397, -4.6939 🐦🏖🍴🏊

### 27 MINWEAR STARLING MURMURATIONS

Come at dusk in winter to experience the wondrous swirling shapes made by thousands – or tens of thousands – of birds joining

28

31

32

together before they roost for the night in the reedbeds of the Eastern Cleddau. Arrive an hour before dusk on a mild, clear and still night from November to January.

→ Start as for Sisters' House ruins (see listing) but ¼ mile W of SA67 8AA find layby and park. Walk NW down hill a short distance to viewpoint. Paths continue in both directions along the river.

5 mins, 51.7891, -4.8227

### 28 DEER PARK, MARTIN'S HAVEN

This most westerly point was once an Iron Age coastal fortress, and the views out over the water to Skomer are stunning. Take a circular walk around the cliffs and see choughs and porpoises at Wooltack Point and grey seals pupping from August to December in the inaccessible coves. Excellent sunsets.

→ Follow B4327 and lanes through Marloes and past SA62 3BJ to park at Lockley Lodge Visitor Centre, and walk W. Wooltack Point is at the NW corner.

10 mins, 51.7353, -5.2483

### 29 WILLIAMSTON PARK

The salt-marsh mudflats at the confluence of the Carew and Cresswell rivers are rich feeding grounds that attract curlew and oystercatchers. This is a quiet place, decorated with bee orchids and rare butterflies in late spring and summer.

→ Follow lanes from A4075 crossroads SA68 0SX to West Williamston, S of SA68 0TL, then walk W, following footpath signs along lane and then across fields towards Carew shore. Path then continues N.

15 mins, 51.7161, -4.8545

## SLOW FOOD

### 30 CAFÉ MÔR

From this little mobile beach café come great things – it's worth travelling here just to eat their fresh, seasonal seafood, always served with a smile and colourful salad. Breakfast rolls come with laverbread patties, and lobster rolls with Welsh Sea Black Butter (spiced laverbread in organic butter), but there is so much more including great veg options, sweet treats and coffee. Always perfect after a slightly-too-long swim in Freshwater's wild seas.

→ Freshwater West car park, B4319, SA71 5AH, 01646 278101.

51.6547, -5.0576

### 31 QUAYSIDE, LAWRENNY

If you find yourself in this forgotten world around Cresswell Quay and Lawrenny, make haste to this tea room and enjoy a Pembrokeshire Smokey (locally caught and oak-smoked mackerel), fresh crab sandwiches, cakes and salads, either inside or on the terrace overlooking the Cleddau. Open 11am–5pm Tues–Sun and bank holidays Easter–Sept.

➔ Lawrenny Yacht Station, Lawrenny, SA68 0PR, 01646 651574.
51.7191, -4.8814 🍴

### 32 THE BOTHY TEA ROOM AT COLBY

What a find! This lovely National Trust tea room in the old estate workers' houses serves up colourful, flavoursome platters of locally sourced delights. Enjoy a delicious cheese platter with home-made bread and chutney (so good we had to take some home). Cakes, soups and a specials board have made this a destination in its own right, but there's also a lovely NT woodland garden and walled garden to discover. Open 10am–4.30pm.

➔ NT Colby Woodland Garden, Stepaside, SA67 8PP, 01834 814163.
51.7409, -4.6701 🍴

### 33 SLEBECH PARK & RUINED CHURCH

In a beautiful location on the banks of the Cleddau estuary, this grand estate hotel has a fine restaurant serving award-winning Welsh produce, including herbs and vegetables from their own kitchen garden. The romantic remains of an 11th-century church sit on the shore, and the estate teems with wildlife.

➔ Slebech Park Estate, SA62 4AX, 01437 752000.
51.7900, -4.8546 🍴🍷🖥🏕✝

### 34 ULTRACOMIDA & NARBERTH CASTLE

Plan a stop in Narberth to stock up on the wonderful cheeses, delicious Spanish deli items and wine, and have lunch – either eat in on the long tables or pack it up to take to the nearby ruins of Narbeth Castle (at Castle Terrace, just above SA67 7BD).

➔ 7 High St, Narberth, SA67 7AR, 01834 861491.
51.7994, -4.7439 🍴

### 35 COAST, SAUNDERSFOOT

With its bright, airy interior and large windows overlooking the bay, this imposing restaurant is a good local choice for a beachside lunch or supper of fresh seafood.

→ Coppet Hall Beach, Saundersfoot,
SA69 9AJ, 01834 810800.
51.7169, -4.6951 🍴

### 36 BUBBLETON FARM SHOP & KITCHEN
Fifth-generation farm selling locally grown and
reared produce. Artisan crafts and tea room.
→ Bubbleton, Penally, SA70 7RY,
07814 035005.
51.6579, -4.7508 🍴

### 37 YE OLDE WORLDE CAFÉ
If the cutesy spelling puts you off, think of
it as Bosh Tea Rooms, which has become its
alternative name. Either way, this is a pretty
place for a cup of proper loose-leaf tea and
slice of home-made cake. Check out the local
crafts in the old school house down the road.
→ Bosherston, SA71 5DN, 01646 661216.
51.6144, -4.9389 🍴

### 38 BOATHOUSE TEA ROOM, STACKPOLE
The National Trust manages the large
Stackpole Estate, and it's worth exploring
the wonderful bluebell woods and lily ponds
in addition to the stunning beaches. Down
at the old quay you'll find the little tea room
serving ice creams and light lunches to
those heading to Barafundle Bay (see entry).
Nearby the old farm complex now houses
a range of holiday cottages, some of which
enjoy sea views.
→ Stackpole Quary, SA71 5DQ, 01646 672672.
51.6233, -4.9286 🍴

### 39 STACKPOLE WALLED GARDENS
Discover the old walled kitchen gardens, still
abundant thanks to the gardening skills of
local adults with learning disabilities. Run as
a social enterprise where you can pick your
own soft fruit, buy seasonal veg and eat in
the tea room.
→ Stackpole, SA71 5DJ, 01646 661442.
51.6273, -4.9301 🍴

### 40 THE GROVE, NARBERTH
A luxurious country house hotel with
three-AA-rosette fine dining, using organic
produce from their kitchen garden and the
best Pembrokeshire produce. Restaurant
open to non-residents.
→ Molleston, Narberth, SA67 8BX,
01834 860915.
51.7827, -4.7650 🍴

### 41 SWAN INN, LITTLE HAVEN
From a pint of prawns with your pint of real
ale or a fresh fish supper with wine – all
can be enjoyed at this beachside pub with
upstairs dining room.
→ Point Rd, Little Haven, Haverfordwest,
SA62 3UL, 01437 781880.
51.7738, -5.1085 🍴

### 42 THE STACKPOLE INN
When the rain threatens a day on the beach,
take a wet walk through Bosherston's lily
ponds up to Stackpole's celebrated pub.
Everything that a pub should be – leave
muddy boots in the porch and sit down
in the fire-warmed pub to a delicious fish
meal. Crabs are served simply with buttered
bread, catch-of-the-day specials come with
laverbread butter, all enjoyed with good
wines and beer. Rooms available.
→ Jasons Corner, Stackpole, SA71 5DF, 01646
672324.
51.6310, -4.9142 🍴

### 43 THE GRIFFIN INN, DALE
Even in high season The Griffin is filled
with a mix of locals and visitors coming for
the acclaimed fresh fish, landed that day
from the local waters. Or maybe they're just
having a pint and watching the boaters and
windsurfers coming in off the jetty. Enjoy a
fish-and-chip lunch on the terrace and prepare
for more crabbing and cold-water antics.
→ Dale, SA62 3RB, 01646 636227.
51.7073, -5.1689 🍴

### 44 THE OLD POINT HOUSE, ANGLE
This is a superb location for a sundowner
pint, overlooking Angle Bay. Food is by-the-
sea pub grub, but whether you're sitting
outside in the sunshine or cosy and squashed
the fireside snug you can't beat the location
or history. Look out for the 14th-century
tower house on the way.
→ Angle, SA71 5AS, 01646 641205.
51.6865, -5.0777 🍴

### 45 CRESSELLY ARMS, KILGETTY
Historic pub, beautifully situated near
the water's edge in a wooded reach of the
Cleddau estuary. Beer is served from the
barrel by jug, and there's a roaring fire in
winter. No kids and no dogs.
→ Cresswell Quay, Kilgetty, SA68 0TE,
01646 651210.
51.7250, -4.8246 🍴

## WILDER CAMPING

### 46 WALTON WEST CAMPSITE

Only a mile from sandy beaches, this is a lovely open site with large pitches mown out of the meadow – or rent the little cabin. Greener Camping Club.

→ Lower Foxhill, Little Haven, SA62 3UA, 07980 622673/706001.
51.7732, -5.0923 🏕️🛖

### 47 MILL HAVEN PLACE, TALBENNY

This old Pembrokeshire farm has three Mongolian yurts, three whitewashed holiday cottages and camping space for six lucky tents, campervans or caravans, just one mile from the coast. Greener Camping Club.

→ Middle Broadmoor Farm, Talbenny, SA62 3XD, 01437 781145.
51.7647, -5.1478 🏕️♨️🛖

### 48 WEST HOOK FARM CAMPING

A lovely and simple clifftop campsite, enjoying vast sea views gilded with colourful sunsets. Walk out to the Deer Park and see the wild horses grazing against the backdrop of Skomer Island – or the other way you're just minutes from the golden beaches of Marloes Sands (see entries for all).

→ Marloes, SA62 3BJ, 01646 636424.
51.7353, -5.2387 🏕️

### 49 POINT FARM CAMPSITE & TAWNY

Just a short walk from Dale, this tiny and sheltered family campsite is the perfect base for exploring the amazing beaches of Marloes Sands and Westdale Bay or the vibrant rock pools of Watwick Bay (see listings). Pitch up on one of the grassy terraces or rent Tawny, the shepherd's hut. Excellent facilities.

→ Dale, SA62 3RD, 01646 636842.
51.7039, -5.1638 🏕️♨️🛖🚶

### 50 SKRINKLE BAY CAMPSITE

Wonderfully sited above Skrinkle Haven and Church Doors coves, this quiet and very basic site provides cold showers, portaloos and campfires alongside incredible sea views. Can get windy!

→ Campsite is on R just before YHA Manorbier, SA70 7TT, 01834 871005.
51.6475, -4.7695 ♨️

### 51 TREFALEN FARM CAMPING

A fantastic campsite to while away a happy summer, set just back from lovely Broad Haven beach (see listing). You can walk up the past the lily ponds to the Stackpole Inn (see listing) or take a kayak round to one of the secret beaches. Facilities are basic, with no hot water. Booking essential, minimum two nights.

→ Bosherston, SA71 5DZ, 01646 661643.
51.6071, -4.9273 🏕️♨️

### 52 NT GUPTON FARM

This wild and windy campsite and simply furnished farmhouse are the only accommodation close to the surfers' paradise of Freshwater West. To the south-east and north-east, vast dune systems and Castlemartin Corse are a twitcher's heaven and rich in wildflowers and fungi.

→ Castlemartin, SA71 5HW, 01646 661640.
51.6500, -5.0456 🛖🏕️🚽🏕️

### 53 STACKPOLE UNDER THE STARS

Bordering the lovely Stackpole NT estate this is a small, intimate site, with handmade yurts, bell tents, luxury pod and five meadow tent or caravan pitches, all with compost loos, fire pits and luxury hot showers. Greener Camping Club.

→ North Lodge, Cheriton, SA71 5BX, 01646 683167.
51.6403, -4.9299 🏕️♨️

## RUSTIC HAVENS

### 54 PENALLY ABBEY

Hidden away in the village of Penally with views out to the sea (and not a caravan park in sight) is this beautifully decorated, family-run country hotel with a fine Pembrokeshire-produce focused restaurant. There is always a fire burning and the restaurant is open to non-residents.

→ Penally, nr Tenby, SA70 7PY, 01834 843033.
51.6607, -4.7233 🛖

### 55 DRUIDSTONE HOTEL & BEACH

The Druidstone stands on the cliff looking straight out to sea, and below is a long sandy wild beach which curves to a point. A family favourite for a winter weekend beachside escape, as well as summer holidays. Open fires, large family bedrooms (even the dog is allowed), incredibly friendly staff and avant garde artsy decor – or five self-catering choices including the eco-cottage Roundhouse with stunning sea views. The cosy downstairs pub and upstairs restaurant are both open to non-residents.

→ Welsh Rd, Druidston, SA62 3NE, 01437 781221.
51.8095, -5.1021 🛖🍴ℹ️🚶

### 56 CLIFF COTTAGE

St Brides is a sheltered little cove with sand and rock pools at low-tide. Overlooking it all, the old fisherman's cottage makes for the perfect family retreat. Sleeps up to seven.

→ Windmill Park, St Brides, SA62 3AJ, 01646 636242.
51.7547, -5.1855 🏖 🚶

### 57 ALLENBROOK, DALE

Hospitality, hearty breakfasts and comfortable beds make this country house B&B the perfect overnight stop for coast walkers. Families can rent the two clifftop homes a short walk from the village centre.

→ Dale, SA62 3RN, 01646 636254.
51.7098, -5.1691 🏖

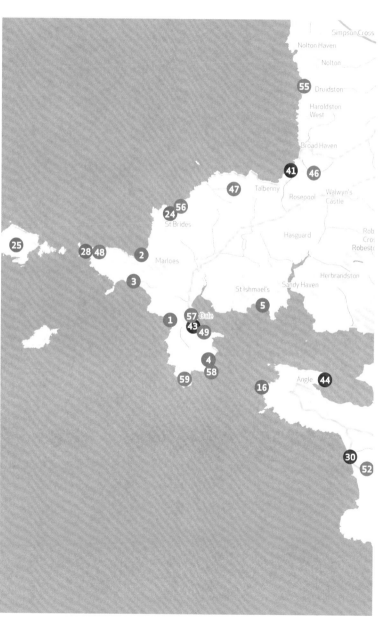

## 58 WEST BLOCKHOUSE, DALE

Renovated by the Landmark Trust, this 19th-century fort on the cliff edge still guards the entrance to Milford Haven. You can rent the garrison, sit by the fire and watch the sea life from the roof. Sleeps eight.

➜ Dale, SA62 3RT, 01628 825925.
51.6884, -5.1580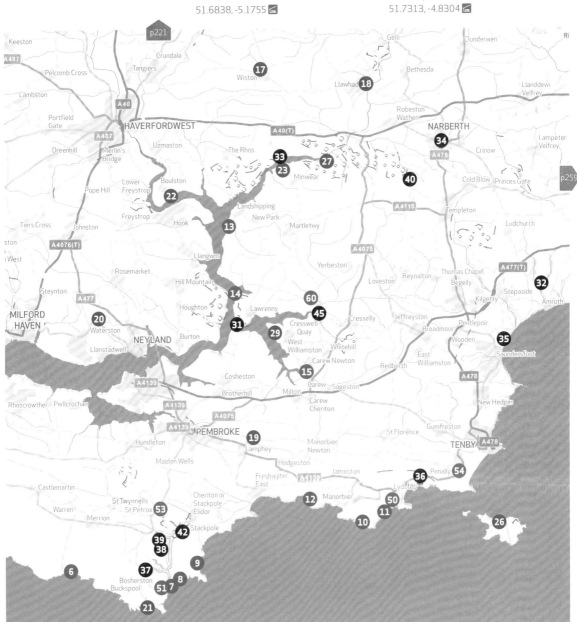

## 59 THE OFFICER'S HOUSE

St Ann's head is a wild promontory at the entrance to Milford Haven and the ideal location for a lighthouse. The Officer's House was built by the Admiralty in 1908 for the captain of the Coastguard station, and today is resurrected as a remote B&B.

➜ St Ann's Head, Dale, SA62 3RT, 01646 636407.
51.6838, -5.1755

## 60 KINGFISHER HOUSEBOAT

Start the morning with a refreshing dip straight from the deck of your floating wooden houseboat and spend the day relaxing and listening to birdsong. Shepherd's hut also available. Greener Camping club.

➜ Dragonfly Camping, New Pencoed, Lawrenny, SA68 0PL, 07967 291348.
51.7313, -4.8304

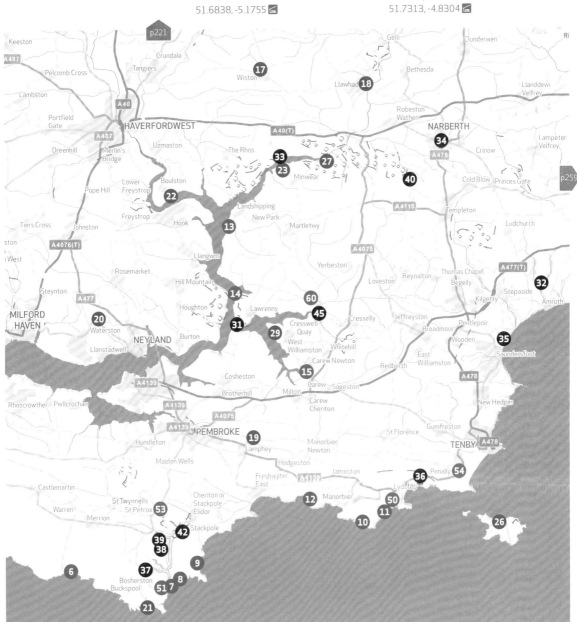

# GOWER

## Our perfect weekend

→ **Swim** through the rock arch, paddle in the stream and explore the ruined castle at the Gower's most spectacular beach, Threecliff Bay

→ **Venture** across the causeway onto the Worm's Head and listen for the sea below through the blowhole at its nose

→ **Plunge** into Britain largest rock pool, at Bluepool Bay, then search for shipwreck booty and find the chapel ruins on Burry Holmes island

→ **Run** wild around the secret sandy coves of Mewslade and Fall Bay

→ **Wriggle** inside the eerie Culver Hole, a fortified cave in the sea cliffs, with four storeys inside

→ **Sleep** in Paviland cave with the spirit of the mysterious man who was buried here 33,000 years ago

→ **Take** a windswept walk across the vast sand dunes of Whiteford Burrows, stopping for home-made cake at the @ Cwm Ivy café

→ **Eat** delicious salt-marsh lamb, reared below the impressive ruins of Weobley Castle

→ **Watch** the sun go down from the ruins or cairns on Rhossili Downs

**The Gower peninsula has long been a magnet for holidaymakers drawn to its endless sandy beaches backed by rolling dunes, dramatic limestone cliffs pocked with caves and culverts, and ancient remains still standing proud and commanding the very best views.**

Head down a remote little valley, just above the ocean foreshore, and you can clamber into large, dry Paviland cave, one of the oldest ceremonial burial sites in all of western Europe. In 1823 the 'Red Lady of Paviland' was found here, named because of the ochre-stained bones. We now know the bones belonged to a man who died 33,000 years ago. Interred with sea shell jewellery, his burial was ceremonial, and the site was possibly a shamanic one, visited by many people. Today the waves come crashing in below the entrance at high tide, marooning you here if you are not careful, but in those times, the cave looked out on a vast plain, where bison and mammoth roamed, and the Bristol Channel was just a shallow meandering river.

There are more such ancient caves to be found on Gower, many formed long before the last ice age, when the sea levels were much higher. At Port Eynon you'll find Culver Hole or 'pigeon cave', a possible smuggler's retreat with walls, windows, floors and staircases. On the north coast is another Culver Hole, next to the Three Chimneys cave arches, where gold moidores and doubloons from an 18th-century shipwreck have been found in the past – try your luck.

For wonders of the natural kind head to Bluepool Bay, named after its great rock pool, one of the largest in Britain. I still remember my first visit, in the late afternoon sun, the cliffs tinted bronze and a glinting sea pulling at the sand as the tide began to ebb. It is a perfect tub, scoured out of the rocks by waves that tumbled giant cobbles in its depths.

From here you can explore Burry Holms, a tidal island with the ruins of a medieval hermit's chapel and a fabulous view down the miles of Rhossili sand. Midway along the beach is the Old Rectory, built by the vicar in a desolate spot equidistant between his two parish churches. You can rent it by the week – it is popular, despite its haunted reputation. The crowning glory, however, must be Worm's Head, a giant serpent-shaped tidal promontory; its name is derived from 'wurm', the Norse word for dragon or serpent. This is also a moving place to bivvy – as Dylan Thomas once did by accident – if it starts to rain, as there is a cave at the far end of the peninsula. Autumn and winter only though, please, for the sake of the nesting birds.

1

## WILD BEACHES

### 1 BLUEPOOL CORNER & CULVER HOLE

One of the best rock pools in Wales, this is a deep tub into which you can leap from the rock ledges. It sits in the corner of a superb beach with the Three Chimneys rock arches and caves at the far end, said to contain gold coins from a Spanish shipwreck. Further on, the adventurous can scramble to the narrow slit-like entrance of Culver Hole (not the famous walled cave, see entry), opening into a large chamber that has yielded prehistoric finds.

→ In Llangennith take lane from mini-roundabout dir Broughton/SA3 1JP and park L after ¾ mile at entrance to Broughton Farm Caravan Park. Walk through the park, bearing L onto coast path. After ¾ mile Bluepool Corner bay is below with pool at the E end. Tricky scramble down. Culver Hole is 200m beyond W end at 51.6124, -4.3050, low tide only.
20 mins, 51.6141, -4.2986

### 2 MEWSLADE & FALL BAY

A pretty valley walk leads down past caves to this low-tide bay. Climb up and over via the promontory fort to Fall Bay and explore inside the Giant's Cave, popular with climbers. Both beaches connect at low tide.

→ In Pitton a mile before Rhossili on B4247, turn L opp SA3 1PH for Mewslade car park and take footpath on R to Mewslade. Or walk to Fall Bay (51.5627, -4.2922) from the W (see Worm's Head entry), or via the footpath from Rhossili Bunkhouse (51.5670, -4.2792).
10 mins, 51.5604, -4.2823

### 3 OXWICH BAY NNR, PENMAEN

Long, curving golden sand beach backed by dunes, marshes and woods. In spring swathes of cowslips decorate the burrows, bluebells follow in the woods and then it's time for the orchids. Birdwatchers should head for the reedbeds and follow the boardwalk. There is a big beach car park in Oxwich, or follow our lesser-known route through Nicholaston woods and along the stream to reach the remote central portion of the beach or head to Tor Bay (see entry).

→ Signed off A4118 by ruined lodge gates/postbox then 1¼ miles to SA3 1LS for main beach pay car park. Alternatively, 300m from main road, find small gravel pull-in on L (parking for one) at 51.5720, -4.1621 and path down through woods. Or camp at clifftop Nicholaston Farm, SA3 2HL (01792 371209) and access over Nicholaston Burrows.
20 mins, 51.5691, -4.1446

### 4 TOR BAY & CAVE, PENMAEN

Descend via steep dunes to the beautiful sheltered sands between Great Tor and Little Tor, at the far east end of Oxwich Bay (see listing). En-route explore a burial cairn and hill fort, enjoying views over Threecliff Bay (with path down). The adventurous could even try to reach Leather's Hole cave in the end of Great Tor, high on its east side.

→ Park near top of the hill in Penmaen by bus stop/post box at SA3 2HJ (or in overflow parking up lane with cattle grid opp 80m E). Take bridleway SE down through fields to headland. Bear L for Threecliff Bay, the cairn and the hill fort, or R for Tor Bay and the far end of the headland, Great Tor, where you can find Leather's Hole (51.5689, -4.1224).
15 mins, 51.5688, -4.1254

### 5 POBBLES BEACH, THREECLIFF BAY

A wide sand beach is revealed at low tide below the famous three peaks. There are tidal pools and a sea arch. As the tide advances retreat via Pennard Pill river and stepping stones.

→ From NT car park at the far end of Southgate (SA3 2DH) follow coast path W a mile, dropping down via a little dune valley to the sand in front of the arch. At high tide, drop

down/retreat on the rear side of the arch, up the Pill nearer the stepping stones.
20 mins, 51.5687, -4.1082 🏊🚶

### 6 PWLLDU BAY

Magical approach by stream and woodland to a remote shingle bay. At mid- to low tide a sand bay (Bantam Bay) also appears on the south-west side of Pwlldu, accessible over the sand. It's also a lovely walk a mile east for Brandy Cove, returning in a loop via Pyle.

➔ From Pennard church on B4436, take dead end to Widgate. At bottom of hill, 200m before SA3 2AB, park by wooden gates L on bend. Follow the footpath (muddy in winter) down to and along stream through woods. At the house bear R to find cave and swing.
20 mins, 51.5639, -4.0565 🏊🚶

### ISLANDS

### 7 WORM'S HEAD

Looking like a dragon's head rising from the ocean, this stunning, rocky, mile-long tidal island is only accessible for about 2½ hours either side of low tide. The Devil's Bridge is an impressive rock arch to the Outer Head where you will find a cave-arch shelter, and may see the blowhole erupt below from the bottom of the cliff. On the very tip of the head, a steep and tricky scramble leads down to a secret cave near water level. No access to Outer Head March–August, to protect nesting birds. Great rock pooling on the causeway, and dolphins can often be seen offshore.

➔ Set out at least 2 hours before low tide; the causeway has very dangerous currents when in flood. From NT Rhossilli car park, SA3 1PR, follow coast path SW to the NCI Lookout Station (double check tide times here) and down across the rocky causeway.
30 mins, 51.5649, -4.3317 🚶🚴👟📹⛺🏖

### 8 BURRY HOLMS, RHOSSILI BAY

At the far end of beautiful Rhossili Bay this tidal island connects to the mainland by a tiny isthmus of sand. It carries the remains of a ruined chapel to St Cenydd, abandoned to the sea as a baby and raised by seagulls and angels on Worm's Head (see listing), a cairn at the western tip.

➔ Park as for Bluepool Corner bay (see listing) ½ mile and walk directly across the dunes.
30 mins, 51.6103, -4.3095 🚶📷✝♿

## CAVES

### 9 CULVER HOLE, PORT EYNON

This wild and spooky walled cave sits in a tall cliff recess, and is thought to have been used as a smugglers' store, or for keeping pigeons. Vast rocky foreshore at low tide. Also find a large low-tide cave below Port Eynon point.

→ Park at the beach car park in Port Eynon, following road R past SA3 1NN. Take coast path S past campsite, YHA and salthouse ruins. Narrow path continues through bush, onto headland via old quarry. 50m NW of triangulation point a rough path descends directly to the recess. Port Eynon point cave is at 51.5372, -4.2102.

20 mins, 51.5389, -4.2142 🏊🚫⛰🔦

### 10 MINCHIN HOLE CAVE, FOX HOLE

Minchin hole is a prehistoric cave in a cliff, reached over rocks from a low-tide cove. First excavated in 1851, it has yielded rhinoceros and elephant bones, and over 750 pieces of pottery, combs, bone spoons, bronze brooches and Roman coins. Bacon Hole is further along the coast with the remains of a gate at the rear put in when red bands beyond it were thought to be ancient paintings. Do not disturb hibernating bats in winter.

→ Park as for Pobble beach (see listing). Take on path S to Fox Hole cove at low tide, then traverse E around the rocky beach 400m to reach the 20m tall slit entrance to Minchin Hole. Bacon Hole nearby has a much wider entrance; follow East Cliff road E take track SE from opp No 29 to cliff and steep narrow path down at 51.5619, -4.0782.

15 mins, 51.5622, -4.0857 🏊🚫🔦

### 11 PARC LE BREOS & CATHOLE CAVE

In a wooded clearing lies a long-chambered Neolithic tomb, of a type built in Wales and the South West around 3500 BC; also called Parc Cwm and Giant's Grave. The bones of at least 40 people were found here; bodies may have lain in nearby Cathole Cave before the bones were moved here. Also find a ruined limekiln.

→ Signed Coed y Parc from A4118 just W of Parkmill (SA3 2EH). Parking on L after ½ mile at road end. The cave is at 51.5900, -4.1124.

2 mins, 51.5884, -4.1129 🐕🚶🚫↩

### 12 PAVILAND CAVE

In 1823 the red-stained bones of 'The Red Lady of Paviland' were discovered here. Actually a male, he lived around 33,000 years ago in the Palaeolithic era, when the

14

14

15

**sea was miles away and the cliffs overlooked vast plains, making this the oldest known ceremonial burial in western Europe.**

→ Heading to Rhossili on the B4247 find footpath S signed Foxhole Slade house at Pilton Green (NT sign), 200m W of SA3 1PE; parking opp on common land. Cross fields and at the coast keep L of the drystone wall, down into the gulley then climb up to the R. Low tide only. Or walk SE on coast path from Mewslade Bay (see listing).

20 mins, 51.5501, -4.2553

## HILLTOPS & RUINS

### 13 MOUNT HERMON CHAPEL

**This now-derelict chapel is the perfect place to view the great Loughor estuary. Built in 1807, its white walls were an important landmark for ships navigating the treacherous sand banks. Above and across the lane is the Pen-y-gaer hill fort.**

→ Following B4295 along the estuary, turn dir SA4 3RR at Crofty and find chapel R after 300m, car park opp.

1 min, 51.6380, -4.1212

### 14 PENNARD CASTLE, THREECLIFF BAY

**With sublime views down Pennard Pill to Threecliff Bay, this 13th-century Norman castle still sports a huge gatehouse and towers, and is perfect for sunsets. It is part-buried in sand, apparently because the Norman baron upset the beach-dwelling 'tylwyth teg' (fairy folk). From here a steep sand path leads down to the valley and onto the beach.**

→ There is a pay car park on the A4118 at Parkmill (by turning SA3 2EH) outside the shop or in the field opp in summer. Take path by field over stream and bear L steeply up through the woods to the cabins, bear R around edge of the golf course. You can return via the low route, along the stream the entire way. Or drop down to the Pill, around the arch to Pobbles beach (see listing) and up to Southgate or back across the golf course.

20 mins, 51.5765, -4.1023

### 15 RHOSSILI DOWN RADAR & TOMB

**Walk these heather-clad downs for incredible sea views, and for the remains of the Second World War radar station and two Bronze Age burial chambers at Sweyne's Howes. There's not a lot left of either, but the grand vistas make it worthwhile.**

→ From St Mary's Church car park in Rhossili, opp SA3 1PN, follow track/lane N, signed for the downs, up to ridge line. Pass the Beacon trig point (193m) and continue on ¾ mile to find the burial cairns to the R and large concrete bases of the old radar station below L. Drop down to Hillend Burrows dunes, by the caravan park, and return along the beach.
30 mins, 51.5860, -4.2844 ⬛🏊🖼🚶

### 16 ARTHUR'S STONE, CEFN BRYN

**Cefyn Bryn is a long red sandstone ridge jutting out of the limestone and known as 'the backbone of Gower'. At its highest point is Arthur's stone, or Maen Ceti, a Neolithic burial chamber from 2500 BC. It has a huge capstone, now broken in two, and even bigger views.**

→ A mile E of Reynoldston (signed Llanrhidian, dir SA3 1EB) find car park on L at the brow of the hill. Walk ½ mile N to the stones. Broad Pool, 1½ miles NE along the road, is well known for its birdlife.
10 mins, 51.5935, -4.1793 🏊⬛🌳

### 17 CILIFOR TOP HILL FORT

**This is the largest hill fort on the Gower peninsula, dating back to at least two millennia, and very possibly occupied into the Roman period; likely medieval**

ringworks can also be seen to the south east. Spectacular panoramas reach out across the Gower, Llanelli and the Brecon Beacons.

→ From B4271 just E of Llanrhidan, take L fork dir SA3 1EX/Welsh Moor and pull over tight R opp set back gate L after 350m. Walk on 150m to stile by next gate L. Hill fort is N.
10 mins, 51.6097, -4.15796 ⬛

### WILDLIFE

### 18 WHITEFORD BURROWS NNR

**Gower's wildest beach, with forested sand dunes stretching for miles. At the far tip of the peninsula are the very finest white sands, perfect for sitting around driftwood fires. Across a bank of low-tide cockle and oyster shells, the haunting remains of the iron lighthouse stand defiant. You can reach it, but watch the tides.**

→ Take lanes through Llanmadoc dir Cwm Ivy SA3 1DJ, to car park 80m after dead-end sign, in field R. Walk on, past @ Cwm Ivy (see listing) to dunes and beach. Fine views from the tor L, which can be climbed, or turn R and head along the burrows or beach for over 2 miles to the lighthouse. Loop back via the woodland path along the back of the burrows, past birdhides.
20 mins, 51.6342, -4.2487 ⬛⛰🖼⬛⬛⬛

### 19 LLANRHIDIAN MARSH & CASTLE

Stride out on the causeway into the salt marsh, across a maze of rivulets and pools towards the tidal estuary and see wintering wildfowl and waders. Once this area was busy with cockle pickers loading their harvest onto donkeys, but now the flats are used to graze award-winning salt-marsh lamb. Buy some at the Weobley Castle shop (see listing), and explore the handsome shell, one of the few Welsh fortified manor houses still standing (entry fee).

→ Weobley castle is signed at fork W of Llanrhidian; follow ¾ mile for second R, past SA3 1HB turn. Head down the track to the marshes. The farm shop is in the farmyard by the castle (01792 390012).
20 mins, 51.6193, -4.2031 🐦🍴🖼

## SLOW FOOD

### 20 @ CWM IVY CAFÉ & CRAFTS

Delicious home-made cakes, coffees, proper pots of tea, organic ice creams and light lunches, all served in the wooden cabin café and on the sunny terrace, both enjoying the big views out over the estuary.

→ Cwm Ivy, Llanmadoc, SA3 1DJ, 07873 746207.
51.6205, -4.2564 🍴

### 21 GOWER SALT MARSH LAMB

This little farm shop specialises in highly acclaimed salt-marsh lamb. It has a stunning location looking out over the salt marshes where the lamb is raised, by the medieval remains of Weobley Castle (pay for entrance at the shop). Also a basic CCC campsite.

→ Weobley Castle Farm, Llanrhidian, SA3 1HB, 01792 390012.
51.6126, -4.1993 ⛺🍴

### 22 BEACH HOUSE RESTAURANT, OXWICH

Large windows overlooking the bay and simple nautical décor provide the perfect backdrop to colourful plates of award-winning Gower fare. We had high expectations of our candlelit dinner, and they didn't let us down.

→ Oxwich Beach, SA3 1LS, 01792 390965.
51.5570, -4.1611 🍴

### 23 THE BAY BISTRO, RHOSSILI

A welcome sight after a windy walk, this lovely beach café serves fresh seasonal and local breakfasts, vegetarian meals, crab sandwiches and wagyu beef burgers.

→ Rhossili, SA3 1PL, 01792 390519.
51.5695, -4.2883 🍴

### 24 LITTLE VALLEY BAKERY

Good bread can make a meal, and at this little artisan bakery you'll find sourdoughs, rye loaves and laverbread focaccia, sausage rolls and enormous cinnamon buns. Open 8.30am until they are sold out (usually 3–5pm) Thurs–Sat.

→ Old Hay Barn, Gower Heritage Centre, SA3 2EH, 01792 371346.
51.5833, -4.1033 🍴

## COSY PUBS

### 25 THE SHIP INN, PORT EYNON

Newly renovated with old wood and nautical finds; enjoy Gower ales, sustainably caught fish and Welsh meats and cheeses.

→ Port Eynon, SA3 1NN, 1792 390204.
51.5456, -4.2109 🍴

### 26 THE PLOUGH & HARROW, MURTON

A glance at the kids' menu alone suggests you're in for a treat. Pork belly with roasted apple, mussels Breton style, hake en papillote, all served up with faultless service in this food-focused village pub.

→ 88 Oldway, Murton, SA3 3DJ, 01792 234459.
51.5830, -4.0438 🍴🐾

### 27 BRITANNIA INN, LLANMADOC

This cosy, wooden-beamed pub has a smart and simple restaurant and terrace views to the Loughor Estuary. Sample cockles with laverbread, Gower salt-marsh lamb or bowls of traditional cawl with home-made bread.

→ Llanmadoc, SA3 1DB, 01792 386624.
51.6161, -4.2458 🍴🛏

### 28 THE KING ARTHUR HOTEL

A large pub offering real ales, a cosy bar with roaring fires inside and tables on the village green outside. Rooms available.

→ Reynoldston, SA3 1AD, 01792 390775.
51.5876, -4.1923 🛏🐾

### 29 KINGS HEAD, LLANGENNITH

With lots of local ales on tap, including their own Gower Brewery craft ales, this is the place for a sundowner after a day on Rhosili beach. Pool table, hearty local-produce meals served all day.

→ Llangennith, SA3 1HX, 01792 386212.
51.6002, -4.2696 🍴

## WILDER CAMPING

### 30 THREE CLIFFS BAY HOLIDAY PARK

A large and windy site, but a stunning location overlooking the magnificent Threeliff Bay (see Pobbles Beach entry). Sea-view pitches do get booked up, and if you have a tent you can't book ahead. Couples and families only.

➜ North Hill Farm, North Hill Lane, Penmaen, SA3 2HB, 01792 371218.
51.5775, -4.1158 ◬

### 31 EASTERN SLADE BARN & CAMP SITE

Between Horton and Oxwich is the oldest campsite in the Gower. It's a basic site on a working farm, enjoying an easy walk down to wild Slade Bay. The spanking new bunkhouse (converted from the old farmhouse) sleeps up to 15 and offers great value for group adventurers.

➜ Eastern Slade Farm, SA3 1NA, Oxwich, 01792 391374.
51.5529, -4.1834 ◬ 🏠 B

### 32 HILLEND CAMPING PARK

Basic, exposed campsite just behind the dunes, enjoying unrivalled access to Rhosilli beach – but you are next to the massive caravan park.

➜ Llangennith, SA3 1JD, 01792 386204.
51.5954, -4.2903 ◬

### 33 YHA PORT EYNON

On a spring tide the waves crash at the door of this beachside YHA, formerly the lifeboat station. Great views and a fantastic beach. Just behind is Carreglwyd, a massive family camping site hosting caravans and tents in the fields overlooking the beach.

➜ Old Lifeboat House, Port Eynon, SA3 1NN, 0345 3719135.
51.5414, -4.2098 🍴🏠🚶

## RUSTIC HAVENS

### 34 HILLSIDE FARM, LLANGENNITH

Love camping on the Gower peninsula but don't want to be at a large caravan site? Hillside is only five minutes from Rhosilli and boasts gorgeous views and luxurious, fully equipped Feather Down Farm safari tents on a working family farm.

➜ Llangennith, SA3 1JR, 01420 80804.
featherdown.co.uk
51.5965, -4.2563 🏠🚿🚶

### 35 QUABS LOG CABIN AT PARC LE BREOS

The perfect wooden cabin, sheltered by ancient oak woodland in the grounds of

Parc-Le-Breos House B&B. Renovated using reclaimed materials, it has a large veranda and a lovely outdoor fireplace.

➜ Parkmill, SA3 2HA, 01792 371636.
51.5846, -4.1245 🏠

### 36 THE OLD RECTORY, RHOSSILI

You'll have to book many months – maybe a year – in advance but this secluded NT property stands completely by itself in an enviable position overlooking Rhossili Bay. Sleeping seven, it's perfect for a special beachside celebration.

➜ Rhossili, SA3 1PP, 0344 8002070.
nationaltrust.org.uk
51.5788, -4.2869 🏠

36

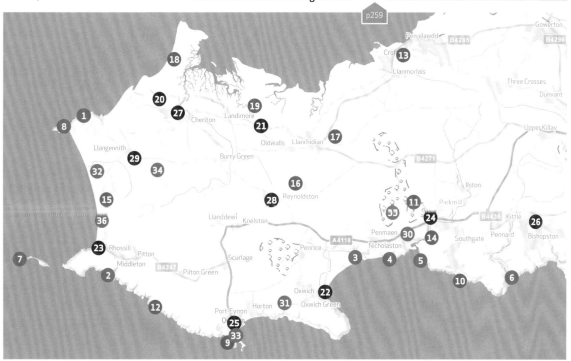

# CARMARTHEN & WEST BRECONS

## Our perfect weekend

→ **Explore** Carreg Cennen, one of the most dramatic castle locations in Wales

→ **Gallop** through the surf on horseback at Marros or look for the curious pyramid tank defences on Morfa Bychan beach

→ **Camp** for the night on Pendine Sands, one of the longest and wildest beaches in south Wales, and try your hand at night fishing

→ **Climb** the 12th-century ruins of Lansteffan Castle and walk on Scott's Bay

→ **Wild** camp at the high, magical lake of Llyn y Fawr, and in the morning find the Cerrig Duon stones and plunge into the waterfall

→ **Wander** the ruins of Talley Abbey, then enjoy a riverside lunch and dip at the Black Lion

→ **Capture** Dryslwyn Castle on its dramatic knoll and then swim in the beautiful Towy river

→ **Climb** the ancient oaks and the high tower of Dinefwr Castle, then feast at the Gin Haus

→ **Seek** out ancient cairns and caves on the wild heart of the Black Mountain at Garreg Las

**From the soaring limestone karst plateaus, down through the castles of the lush Towy valley, to the vast beach sands of the coast, this is a region often bypassed by travellers, but rich in beauty and antiquity.**

The Black Mountain, at the far westerly end of the Brecon Beacons National Park (not to be confused with the Black Mountains to the east) is a mysterious area of sinkholes and escarpments, ancient stones and caves. There are no jagged peaks here, but two ethereal tarns hide under the summit. Llyn y Fan Fach is the legendary home of the Lady of the Lake, the mother of the most famous healers of Wales. She was said to rise from the lake shimmering on the first Sunday of August, and in Victorian times entire families would climb up the mountain in the summer sun in the hope that she would appear. Today it's a good place to wild camp. Llyn y Fan Fach faces north-west and is best for sunset, Llyn y Fan Fawr faces north-east and is best for swimming. A wall of bare scree rises up on the south of both, and many miles of central Wales' most remote interior drops away in undulating vistas to the north. Venture into the waters on some summer evenings and great sheets of mist roll down the escarpment to surround you in the water. At moments like this, you feel anything could appear.

From here the land drops for 20 miles towards the Towy valley, providing perfect sunsets. There are hill forts at Carn Goch, and the great brooding hulk of Carreg Cennen Castle sits on a massive outcrop of sheer rock. In the south-eastern corner of the inner ward, a steep set of steps leads down to a passageway and eventually a pitch-black cavern with natural pool.

More castles await on the river Towy near Llandeilo. Dinefwr is now in the hands of the National Trust and offers ancient parkland, a bunkhouse and a brilliant ruin with a four-storey-high lookout to climb – not for the giddy. Dryslwyn is even easier, right on the banks of the river and decorated with pastoral wild-swimming spots; particularly good are the meanders where the river forms gravel beaches with deeper holes. Llandeilo itself is worth lingering in, with some fine artisan food suppliers, including a superb deli café that specialises in charcuterie and 240 varieties of gin.

The river emerges on the coast in a sprawling estuary, meeting the Taf and Gwendraeth near Llansteffan – with yet another fabulous castle – and Laugharne, famous as the home of Dylan Thomas. The beaches here are vast and remote, and the wild shores replete with wading birds and solitude.

## LAKES

### 1 LLYN Y FAN FACH & FAWR

These two high, wild lakes lie in the shadow of the Black Mountain's steep escarpments and offer fantastic views, amazing sunsets and good wild camping. Above are several summits for a high-level circular walk, returning via the lakes. Fach (the small one) is the legendary home of a fairy woman, mother of the famous Physicians of Myddfai, who married a local farmer but returned to the lake after he struck her three times. It's also a drinking water supply, so dip at Fawr (the big one) instead.

→ For Llyn y Fan Fach, leave A4069 between Brynamman and Llangadog, following signs for Llyn y Fan and YHA hostel at Twynllanan, and then head on to Llandeusant SA19 9UL. Continue past church 1 mile to Blaenau Farm (see Farmyard Campsite listing) and on up to road end, then by foot on up track (Beacons Way). Llyn y Fan Fawr another 2 miles trek E around the mountainside. To visit for Fawr first, drive on up ¾ mile from Cerrig Duon stone circle (see listing) to gravel parking L and follow path up W.

30 mins, 51.8833, -3.7386 🏊🏖️🛶📷🧗

### 2 USK RESERVOIR

Set in forested mountain scenery, and mostly encircled by a track and lane. The north road has south west-facing beaches, great for picnicking and paddling. No swimming.

→ On A40 Trecastle turn by antiques shops and follow 4 miles to pull off L, beyond LD3 8YF.

2 mins, 51.9502, -3.7097 🛶🏖️❓

## BEACHES

### 3 PEMBREY BURROWS

This vast wild wilderness of sand, dunes and forest nature reserve extends almost 10 miles, up the coast to Cefn Sidan sands and MOD area, and down to the Loughor estuary. Explore on foot along the beach, or by bike via the forest tracks (coastal route 4). A good place to bivvy.

→ Follow Country Park signs from A484 Burry Port. After ¾ mile turn L, signed cycle route 4, just before the main country park sign (400m before SA16 0EJ). This avoids the more commercial area. The lane continues 1½ miles to arrive at final parking area in dunes. Strong estuary currents, swimming is safest at high tide.

5 mins, 51.6717, -4.3017 🐚🏖️🐾🚴🏞️

### 4 SCOTT'S BAY, LLANSTEFFAN

Wild sandy estuarine beach backed by red sandstone cliffs, with a little holy well behind. Only at high tide or on a rising tide.

→ Turn off B4312 in Llansteffan dir beach/ SA33 5LW and park in beach car park at road end. Walk along the sands ⅓ mile to the steps up the cliff (or head up the slipway road at high tide). Turn L at top of steps, then ½ mile. Or just follow sands at low tide. Continue on to Wharley Point at low tide. For a loop, head back via St Anthony's well path and Castle Hill to Llansteffan Castle ruins (see listing).

20 mins, 51.7628, -4.3973 🏖️🧗

### 5 LAUGHARNE SANDS, GINST POINT

Three estuaries meet here at a massive expanse of shimmering shell sand. Very remote MOD location where you probably won't see a soul.

→ All MOD range, but open daily 4pm–8am. Turn off A4066 (signed Corran Resort/Nine Acres) and follow S past campsite and SA33 4RS through MOD gates and L for 2¼ miles to lookout towers (no one in these at night) and carpark on L. Popular with night fishermen. Take care of strong, confusing tides, and only swim on a rising or high tide. The marsh can flood on spring tides, so don't get cut off.

5 mins, 51.7435, -4.4232 🏖️⚠️🧭🏞️🛶

## 6 TELPYN & MARROS SANDS

Escape the crowds at Telpyn, at the far end of Amroth beach, with caves and flat rock platforms for sunbathing. For a truly wild beach continue on the coast path around Telpyn Point a mile (or via the sand past caves at low tide) and drop down onto Marros Sands. Look for the outline remains of the schooner, wrecked in the sands in 1886. The ruins of Marros Mill are another mile on, or climb up to Top Castle hill fort for sensational views and a good area for bivvying.

→ 1¼ miles E of Amroth find red MOD sign and footpath, with parking layby, ¼ mile before SA67 8NR. Hannah's Plain seasonal camping is ahead on L. The wreck is at 51.7367, -4.6104. Or access Marros beach via the footpath behind Marros church, past SA33 4PN.
10 mins, 51.7345, -4.6327 ⛺🔆🐾

## 7 MORFA BYCHAN & PENDINE

A white pebble beach with sand at low tide, used for 1943 Normandy landings preparation. High up on one side is a hill fort, on the other is a collection of chambered cairns. Walk around on the sand at low tide from Pendine, where via Gilman Point there is an interesting three-chambered cave thought to contain ancient bones and rock art. The riding centre above arranges horse rides along the sands.

→ Rough byway tracks leads down behind the postbox opp and just S of SA33 4PQ, ½ mile N of Pendine on B4314. Also from 150m W of The Green Bridge pub SA33 4PL, which is sometimes driveable, and you can park at the back of the cove. There is also the steep coast path from Pendine, taking in the sea (51.7411, -4.5621) and hill or t. Marros Riding Centre is at SA33 4PN, 01994 453777.
20 mins, 51.7375, -4.5774 🏕🖼🐾🏇

## 8 MILLENNIUM COASTAL CYCLE PATH

This superb super-flat, surfaced coastal cycle path leads out to some beautiful wild beach and estuary terrain. Our favourite is the section out to the sand flats and wetlands of Machynys, south of Llanelli. There is also a lovely northern section via Pembrey Burrows and forest.

→ National Cycle Network route 4. Start at the Discovery Centre, Llanelli, SA15 2LG and head S for Machynys and return via Bynea train station (about 5 miles). Or head N for Pembrey and return via Kidwelly station (about 12 miles).
30 mins, 51.6554, -4.1479 🚴🚲

## 9 DYLAN THOMAS & RIVER TAF

Walk along the broad path beneath Laugharne Castle and swim at high tide from Dylan Thomas' boathouse, or on a rising tide let the current carry you up the estuary. At Black Scar on the opposite bank is the old ruined bellhouse that was used to call the ferryman across. The adventurous could try swimming up to St Michael's ruin (see listing) with the flow and returning with the ebb.

→ Park in the main car park at the bottom of Laugharne village (below SA33 4SS). Follow the broad path around the base of the castle and along the foreshore upstream to reach the boathouse. The tidal currents in this estuary can be dangerous.
10 mins, 51.7718, -4.4570 🏊▽🚶

## 10 PWLLYMERCHED, RIVER AMMAN

A traditional swimming hole in a high mountain stream. It's small, but remote and wild, so you will probably have it all to yourself.

→ Turn off A4068 E of Rhosaman, dir SA9 2WN, and park at the cattle grid after 250m. Bear L onto dirt track ⅓ mile NW across the moor for the stone sheepfolds, then on again to where the river bends.
15 mins, 51.8197, -3.8237 🏊⛰

## 11 CWM CLYDACH, LOWER CLYDACH

Paddle below the ancient stone packhorse bridge in this secret wooded valley. Create a loop via Carn Llechart stones (see entry), part of the Cwm Clydach Walk.

→ From B4603 in Clydach head NW through Craig-cefn-parc and then turn R to Pont Llechart/SA6 5TL; 300m beyond postcode, find footpath on L signed Mynydd Carnllechart (park R by bridge just beyond – nice little pool below here too). Continue 1 mile N. Main pools ⅓ mile upstream at 51.7401, -3.9097.
20 mins, 51.7361, -3.9062 🏊🚶

## 12 AFON SAWDDE

Easy spot for a picnic, paddle and plunge, in meadows with a small weir by the road.

→ Just S of Llangadog on A4069, turn R (dir Bethlehem, SA19 9BU) to parking either side before bridge. Better weir to the L 180m.
3 mins, 51.9310, -3.8826 🏊🚲

## 13 HENRHYD FALLS

The tallest waterfall in southern Wales, with a drop of 27m and a small plunge pool below – you can also walk behind. Sessile oak cling to the cliff walls. Follow the footpath downstream along the Nant Llech another mile for a smaller waterfall with a larger pool, and the ruins of Melin Llech mill by a footbridge.

→ Signed from the A4221 via Coelbren. Continue through the village beyond SA10 9PG then turn L to NT car park. Walk down to the stream (two gates) and turn L upstream.
15 mins, 51.7942, -3.6641 ▨▧▨▨▨

### 14 ABERGORLECH, AFON COTHI

The footpath opposite the forest car park leads upstream to a wooded gorge, fun for an adventure dip. Or follow the five-mile forest loop to Brechfa arboretum, planted in the 1950s. There is also a river pool in the village behind the church hall, opposite the Black Lion pub (see listing).

→ Abergorlech is on B4310, at SA32 7SJ, 9 miles N of Llandeilo. The forest car park is 100m E of village.
1 min, 51.9818, -4.0568 ▨▨▨▨▨▨

## SACRED & ANCIENT

### 15 CARN LLECHART STONE CIRCLE

This ring of slab stones with a burial cist at its centre lies on a remote moor. Many standing stones nearby.

→ A mile NW from Pontardawe A474, turn L after Travellers Well, past SA8 4RR. Take hairpin L (dead end) and park by gates when road turn L (51.7376, -3.8804). Continue straight on track onto moor to find circle 200m NW. Standing stones start ⅓ mile S on slope above Cwm-bryn.
15 mins, 51.7399, -3.8880 ▨▨▨

### 16 CERRIG DUON STONE CIRCLE

A Bronze Age stone circle and a standing stone (Maen Mawr) just by a mountain lane above a waterfall plunge pool. It's a beautiful and easy location, leading up to the Llyn y Fan lakes (see listing).

→ Turn L off A4067 a mile N of the Dan-yr-Ogof showcaves on unsigned road dir SA9 1GT. Continue 2¼ miles and park on L by stream (also layby ¼ mile back). Cross stream to find stones NW 200m.
3 mins, 51.8722, -3.6701 ✝▨

### 17 NANT TARW CIRCLES

Two stone circles (much of the western one barely breaking the surface) in close proximity to each other, just east of the headwaters of the River Usk.

→ Start as for Llyn y Fan Fach tarn (see listing) but at Twynllanan continue to Glasfynydd forestry car park, 2 miles E of and beyond SA19 9YP. Walk S a mile, along the young Usk stream, bearing L up Nant Tarw tributary.
20 mins, 51.9184, -3.7180 ✝

### 18 SAITH MAEN STONES

High on the slopes of Cribarth (ridge of the bear) stands an unusual and unexplained row of seven standing stones. Underneath is a swallow hole in which you can hear the water gurgling, and a large shakehole just north.

→ Park at Craig-y-nos country park car park SA9 1GL on A4067 (near Dan-yr-Ogof showcaves). A lane opp leads up to a farm, and from there the footpath heads straight up the mountainside to the L of the house.
25 mins, 51.8249, -3.6948 ▨▨

### 19 TRECASTELL CIRCLES

This pair of Bronze Age circles sits in moorland close to the Y Pigwn Roman marching camps and the Roman road that once transported gold from Dolaucothi gold mines. Vast views, wild camping.

→ In Trecastle (A40) take the lane W by the antique stores (past LD3 8UL). Turn R (unsigned) after ½ mile. At the road end park at the gate or continue on the byway another mile (says unsuitable for motors, but a decent stone track) then bear off R ¼ mile to the circles. Camps are NW, find boundaries crossing at 51.9652, -3.7087.
30 mins, 51.9658, -3.6997 ▨▨▨

## HILLTOPS & HILL FORTS

### 20 Y GAER FAWR & FACH, CARN GOCH

With bilberries, heather and views of endless hills, these two Iron Age hill forts on the far west edge of the National Park occupy a fine position above the valley and are an easy climb. The larger fort, on the summit, has a long cairn within it.

→ SW of Llagadog on lanes to Bethlehem, then signed/S dir SA19 6YW; ½ mile past postcode turn L into the small parking area and board.
10 mins, 51.9014, -3.9088 ▨▨▨

### 21 CARNAU'R GARREG LAS

If you need an excuse to strike into the real wild heart of the Black Mountain wilderness then seek out these two summit cairns on Carreg Las (635m). On the slopes below, half-worked millstones date from the Napoleonic War period when millstone supplies from France became scarcer. Then climb Carreg yr Ogof (585m, 'hill of the caves') for fine views from the trig point and a small cave.

→ Most direct approach is from end of the public lane at Gellygron (51.8986, -3.7777). Start as for Llan y Fan Fach tarn (see listing) but at Llandeusant take lane S down side of graveyard.
100 mins, 51.8674, -3.7769 ▨▨▨

25

→ Just N of SA32 8JQ, about 7 miles W of Llandeilo. You can swim from the far bottom end of the car park (push through the balsam, following the fishermen's paths) or head downstream a little through the fields for more bank. Eventually you come to a huge gravelly meander with beaches and deep pools (no official right of way, so be discreet).
10 mins, 51.8624, -4.1013

## 24 TALLEY ABBEY & LAKE

This lakeside abbey was founded in 1185 by the Premonstratensian 'White Canons' order and fell into ruin after the Dissolution. The stones were used to build the adjacent white church and many of the village houses, but one lofty corner with arches remains. The footpath through the churchyard leads down to one of the biggest ash trees in Britain and you can also hop over the church wall to explore the lakes – once fish ponds for the monks.

→ Parking in front, at SA19 7AX. 6 miles N of Llandeilo on B4302. Be discreet if you dip (W shore). Ash tree at 51.9777, -3.9888.
2 mins, 51.9766, -3.9920

## 25 LLANSTEFFAN CASTLE

This large 12th-century hilltop ruin has brilliant views out over the Towy estuary and sands. You won't have it to yourself, but it's worth the hike. Best as part of a loop with Scott's Bay (see listing).

→ As for Scott's Bay, but R at the top of steps, along woodland track and then steeply up to L once castle appears.
20 mins, 51.7657, -4.3905

## 26 ST MICHAEL'S CHURCH, TREFENTY

This imposing 11th-century bell tower, now overgrown with ivy, sits in a large lost graveyard on the edge of the tidal river. Look for the 12th-century 'pilgrims graves' – this may have been an important church for

24

## WILD RUINS

### 22 CARREG CENNEN CASTLE

The 'castle on the rock' sits on a remote limestone cliff above the Cennen, its low hulk both forbidding and magnificent. Within the walls, steep steps descend to a vaulted tunnel leading to a cave with a pool below the castle, where Roman coins and ancient remains have been found – bring a torch. There is a time capsule barn museum with doves opposite the café, unchanged for hundreds of years.

→ Parking and café are at SA19 6UA, just E of Trapp. There is an entrance fee to the castle. Our favourite approach, especially at dusk after everyone else has gone home, is from the SE. 200m before the main car park a steep R turn leads a mile down to the road end and a fenced parking area. Follow the woodland path ½ mile, then switch back L up to the castle ½ mile.
20 mins, 51.8545, -3.9354

22

### 23 DRYSLWYN CASTLE & RIVER TOWY

Captured by Edward I in 1287, the dramatic ruin stands on an isolated knoll on the banks of the Towy valley. There is good river swimming here too – from the car park and further downstream.

23

pilgrims travelling to St Davids. Less than a mile away across the marshes is another ruined church, St Teilo's. Wander down to the river and swim if you wish; at high tide the water is warmed as it rises over the sands downstream.

→ Signed Llan-y-bri off A40 E of St Clear's. After 2 miles take R down dead-end road, then park on lane just before the white gates of Trefenty Farm (SA33 4NG). Continue on foot, turning L through farmyard, then SE down across field. St Teilo's is further along the Llan-y-bri lane, at 51.7903, -4.4528.

15 mins, 51.7928, -4.4627 🖼🏊🏞

## WOODS & WILDLIFE

### 27 DINEFWR CASTLE & WOODS

A romantic ruin situated on a crag above the Towy valley, set in medieval parkland. There are hundreds of venerable trees, many over 400 years old, and spring brings bluebells galore. In autumn look out for fungi, woodpeckers and fallow deer. It is also home to the ancient breed of cattle the White Park Cattle – the oldest herd of its kind in the UK.

→ NT members can park by the house and enter the parkland for free (SA19 6RT). Otherwise you are free to park and walk in (about a mile) from the dead-end lane by Llandeilo Bridge (S of SA19 6BN). This is a beautiful route, much quieter, and passes the little estate chapel and woods, and then direct to the castle, bearing SW.

30 mins, 51.8769, -4.0185 🖼🏰🚶

### 28 CARMEL TURLOUGH & CILYRCHEN LAKE

At Carmel NNR find Britain's only turlough – a seasonal lake on limestone filled only by spring water from below. It also has the disused Pant-y-llyn Quarry and the Cave of the Twelve Knights. Human skeletons were found here in 1813, reportedly with enormous skulls. Nearby Cilyrchen's great azure quarry pool is slowly returning to nature.

→ Signed Pentregwenlais off the A483, N of Llandybie. After ¾ miles turn R and, 100m beyond SA18 3JR, find kissing gate entrance to turlough on L, and path leading into quarry area. Cave off path to R after 100m (near 51.8319, -4.0252 but tricky to find). Cilyrchen quarry lake, usually fenced, is across the road to E, at 51.8296, -4.0147, but best accessed from 100m beyond / E of SA18 3JQ (find kissing gate on L by telegraph pole, then N into the woods 5 mins).

5 mins, 51.8309, -4.0241 ❓📹

### 29 OGOF FFYNNON DDU NNR & QUARRY

Dan-yr-Ogof showcaves are great fun and recommended, but if you want to escape the crowds, seek out the interesting old silica quarry and brick factory across the valley at Penwyllt, with ruins and an old railway. Ogof Ffynnon Ddu, the deepest cave network in the UK, lies below. A path and old tramway route leads up the mountainside, passing the top cave entrance, and eventually onto the summit of Carreg Cadno and the nature reserve. This wonderfully wild, broad and empty summit is pocked with sinkholes, scattered with glacial erratics and has sensational views. Perfect for a wild camp – you might hear the churring of a nightjar.

→ Head S from Dan-yr-Ogof showcaves 1¼ miles, A4067, turn L signed Penwyllt and continue up to working quarry. Bear R down dirt tracks (past gravel area and fenced quarry with cave entrances) for SA9 1GQ, the caving club cottages. Beyond cottages are remains of quarry tramway and bridge, limekiln and other buildings. A branch of tramway leads up the hillside to the top gated cave entrance (51.8297, -3.6506).

5 mins, 51.8277, -3.6593 🏕🖼🏔🏞⛰

### 30 NOMNOM, LLANBOIDY

NOMNOM Chocolate is perhaps the best in Wales, and their home in The Abandoned Chocolate Factory is a strange and wonder-filled world with super friendly people and chocolate hugs all around. Big plans are afoot to bring a chocolate utopia back to Llanboidy whilst collaborating with artists in their Maker's Village, but for now the farm is open to the curious, with a shop selling their handmade chocolates and other Welsh produce. Ring ahead so they can put the kettle on.

→ The Abandoned Chocolate Factory, Llanboidy, SA34 0EX, 01994 448761.
51.9000, -4.5978

### 31 THE FERRYMAN DELICATESSEN

A lovely family-run café and deli selling Welsh craft beers, charcuterie and cheeses. Enjoy a delicious Welsh breakfast of cockles, laverbread and black pudding or a chorizo, avocado and potato plate, accompanied by great coffees. Also stocks crafts: we left with a lovely vase from a local potter.

→ King St, Laugharne, SA33 4RY, 01994 427398.
51.7714, -4.4624

### 32 YR HEN DAFARN, LLANSTEFFAN

People rave about this little homely restaurant, with food prepared and served by the warm owners. Seafood platters, fresh fish and perfectly cooked lamb suppers are all talked about long after. Booking essential.

→ High Street, Llansteffan, SA33 5JY, 01267 241656.
51.7725, -4.3907

### 33 MYDDFAI FARMERS' MARKET & CAFÉ

Need to borrow a laptop, want free wifi? Maybe a bowl of cawl, a coffee or cake? Then come to this buzzing eco-community centre, craft shop and café and learn about the powerful herbalists that worked in this area. Workshops throughout the year, and a farmer's market every last Wednesday of the month 9am–1pm.

→ Myddfai, SA20 0JD, 01550 720449.
51.9558, -3.7887

### 34 WRIGHT'S FOOD EMPORIUM

Excellent lunch platters, suppers, breakfasts and cakes, with coffee and wine served in informal surroundings. Now with rooms and a cottage so you can properly indulge.

→ Llanarthne, SA32 8JU, 01558 668929.
51.8616, -4.1315

### 35 THE GIN HAUS DELI, LLANDEILO

Llandeilo narrow lanes are filled with independent shops, and NT Dinefwr estate is nearby (see listing). Come here for sourdough toast, fresh craband pizza. The coffee is good and the organic wines and gins even better.

→ 1 Market St, Llandeilo, SA19 6AH, 01558 823030
51.8827, -3.9936

### 36 CWMCERRIG FARM SHOP, GORSLAS

Home-reared Texel lamb and Hereford beef, veg, fruit and pies. Also a café.

→ Cwmcerrig Farm, Gorslas, SA14 7HU, 01269 844405.
51.8063, -4.0844

### 37 BLACK LION, ABERGORLECH

A traditional little pub with good food and seating by the Afon Cothi (see listing).

→ Abergorlech, SA32 7SN, 01558 685271.
51.9830, -4.0616

### 38 WHITE HART INN, LLANDDAROG

Rich in brewing history, this 600-year old thatched pub still brews is own ale, lager and cider. Eat hearty pub grub, cooked in the open kitchen, whilst relaxing on carved wooden settles warmed by the real fire. Closed Wed.

→ Bryn Hyfryd, Llanddarog, SA32 8NT, 01267 275395.
51.8277, -4.1742

### 39 THE FOREST ARMS, BRECHFA

Perfectly located for those riding the Brechfa Mountain Bike trails, this friendly dining pub with rooms serves good pub grub.

→ Brechfa, SA32 7RA, 01267 202288.
51.9509, -4.1490

### 40 THE SALUTATION INN, PONTARGOTHI

Renovated traditional pub with a fresh locally sourced menu, cooked by the landlady and head chef Lavinia.

→ Nr Nantgaredig, SA32 7NG, 01267 290824.
51.8744, -4.1693

### 41 Y POLYN, CAPEL DEWI

Excellent pub food where the suppliers' attention to detail – in Himalayan rock salt, dry-aged Welsh steaks, coracle-caught home-cured salmon and local harvested seasonal vegetables – are able to really shine.

→ Capel Dewi, SA32 7LH, 01267 290000.
51.8555, -4.1872

## WILDER CAMPING

### 42 THE FARMYARD CAMPSITE

Simple farm camping on a remote working farm. Set up in the rich wildflower meadows and watch the kites soaring above.

→ Blaenau Farm, Llanddeusant, SA19 9UN, 01550 740277.
51.9016, -3.7537 🏕

### 43 CAMPING AT YNYSFAEN, TRECASTLE

Quiet dark-sky campsite taking tents and a very few small classic-VW-style campers. You'll find otters and owls, but no wifi or phone signal. Bell tent and shepherd's hut available.

→ Cwmwysg, Trecastle, LD3 8YF, 01874 636436.
51.9411, -3.6693 🏕🔥🥾

### 44 COASTAL WOOD CAMPING

Camp in wildflower meadows and enjoy starlit campfires and woodland walks. Only seven pitches to choose from, each with a canvas shelter and picnic bench. Cottages also available. Greener Camping Club.

→ Clungwyn Farm, Marros, SA33 4PW, 01994 453214.
51.7510, -4.6151 🏕🔥🥾

## RUSTIC HAVENS

### 45 GYPSY CWTCH

Stay in a beautiful restored gypsy wagon and wake up to woodland views and bird song. Set on an organic smallholding where you can buy seasonal produce, and there's an eco-cabin for you next door with kitchen, loo and shower. Sleeps two, plus space for a small child.

→ Yr Hendy, Penybanc Farm, Drefach-Felindre, SA44 5XE, 01559 370211.
52.0134, -4.3869 🥾🍴

### 46 BRYN EGLUR

The perfect rural Welsh cottage, rescued from ruin. Its white washed walls, wooden settles and cosy fires are the epitomy of rustic chic and with no wifi, its the perfect place for curling up with a good book. Sleeps four, dogs allowed.

→ Pen-y-bont, nr Trelech, SA33 6QR, 0844 5005101. underthethatch.co.uk
51.9108, -4.4814 🥾

### 47 THE LOG HOUSE STUDIO

A charming hand-built Swedish-style log cabin on stilts with a veranda overlooking the fields and swallows nesting in the eaves.

Inside is a woodburner, two double beds (one being high up on an unguarded mezzanine), and the owner's paintings and easels. Outside is a hot shower and loo.

→ Cwm Farm, Capel Isaac, SA19 7UE, 01172 047830. canopyandstars.co.uk
51.9124, -4.0665 🥾

### 48 WHITLANDUNDER STARRY SKIES

A thoughtfully converted haybarn sleeping four, or two off-grid wooden cabins each for two, set within their own wildflower meadows and enjoying lovely views.

→ Llwynbwch, Llanwrda, SA19 8LP, 01550 777499.
51.9645, -3.9162 🔥🥾❄

### 49 DINEFWR BUNKHOUSE NT

The National Trust estate of Dinefwr offers not only wildlife, woodlands, and a ruined castle (see listing), but also a luxurious bunkhouse with woodburners and cosy sofas, sleeping up to 16 in dormitories that once housed the estate servants.

→ Dinefwr Estate, Llandeilo, SA19 6RT, 0344 3351296.
51.8830, -4.0150 🥾🔥Ⓑ

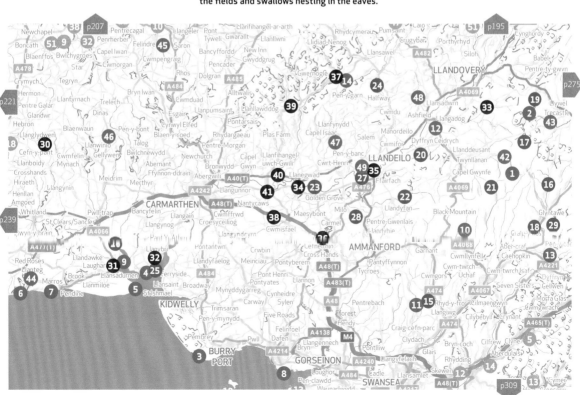

# BRECON BEACONS

### Our perfect weekend

→ **Descend** from Pen y Fan to discover the magical waterfalls and woodland of the Nant Sere valley

→ **Climb** behind waterfalls and find secret cascades along the Mellte and Nedd rivers

→ **Delve** inside the echoing natural cavern of Eglwys Faen, the 'stone church'

→ **Cycle** the old railway to find the ruins of Clydach lime and ironworks, exploring Ogof Clogwyn deep in the gorge below

→ **Watch** Maen Llia's shadow drink from the river on a midsummer eve, then wild camp with wondrous views on the flanks of Fan Nedd

→ **Picnic** by the river Usk in Llangynidr or try shooting the rapids on a rubber ring

→ **Canyon** up the Sychryd gorges, cross a huge waterfall pool, and enter a tunnel into the most important silica mine in the world at Ddinas

→ **Wild** camp and skinny dip at Llyn Cwm Llwch

→ **Plunge** in the wonderful waterfall of Blaen y glyn then climb up to the old Wellington bomber on Waun Rydd

**Coed y Rhaiadr, literally the 'waterfall woods', are the sublime handiwork of the Mellte and Nedd rivers meeting contorted seams of limestone, sandstone and gritstone, and you'll not find a more impressive network of forest lidos and falling water anywhere in Britain. There are canyons to swim through, waterfalls you can climb behind and emerald-azure pools nestled in great moss- and fern-bound amphitheatres.**

In the higher reaches whole sections of river flow underground through great river caves, in one part leaving a dry river canyon that last felt water flowing an ice age ago. The waters re-emerge through further mysterious caves, such as White Lady cave in the Nedd valley. In the lower reaches, river flows were harnessed to grind gunpowder and mine silica at Craig y Ddinas.

At the head of these valleys, the peaks of the Brecon Beacons rise in great crests of old red sandstone, then plunge away in sheer escarpments sculpted by glaciers. You can find impressive ancient remains, including one of the best-preserved sections of Roman road in Wales and two great Bronze Age standing stones, hiding en route to the less-visited peak of Fan Nedd, perfect for wild camping.

To the east, the river Usk cuts a more gentle scene, passing charming village inns and ancient yews, and criss-crossing the Monmouthshire and Brecon Canal. There are idyllic river swimming pools all the way. Our favourite is at Llangynidr, where the river runs rocky with rapids and pools under the narrow medieval bridge. The red sandstone bedrock is polished as smooth and gentle to the touch as soapstone and struck through with dazzling cream and red quartz bands.

In the hills south of the Usk, the stone is rich in iron that fuelled the industrial revolution. Blaenavon town grew around an ironworks that opened in 1789, the first purpose-built multi-furnace ironworks in Wales, and Clydach soon followed. A mile-long tunnel was driven through the hillside to the Pwll du limestone quarry, and the tramway continued around the Blorenge to the canal at Llanfoist. When the railway came in 1860, via a series of viaducts up the Clydach gorge, this route was abandoned in favour of the train. Today both routes are abandoned and provide a fascinating way to explore these industrial remains.

## THE WATERFALL WOODS

### 1 YSTRADFELLTE FALLS, AFON MELLTE

A dramatic and very popular gorge with many waterfalls, best in hot weather! Often more dramatic than the others listed, but with smaller pools. Work your way down past the Clun-gwyns (many little pools on this stretch) to our favourite: y Pannwr (more secret and with a bigger pool). Then on to yr Eira (on the Hepste) – a big pool, and you can walk behind the falls.

➜ Entering Pontneddfechan from B4242, follow road up L at the Dinas Inn. After 2½ miles, before SA11 5US, find car park R by cattle grid. Follow footpath down ⅓ mile, past Clyngwyn bunkhouse (see listing) to footbridge. Cross and explore downstream on river L path. Y Pannwr is at 51.7813, -3.5631, on the lower green path. Yr Eira/Eira is another ⅓ mile on from here.

20 mins, 51.7838, -3.5625 🏊🚶💧🅿🚻🚶

### 2 GUNPOWDER WORKS, AFON MELLTE

A large, deep pool beneath a ruined weir, good for jumps and next to the old gunpowder works. Explore upstream through sylvan glens to find the upper weir and pools, then discover the upper waterfall with deep canyon pools.

➜ Entering Pontneddfechan from B4242, bear R past the Dinas Inn and go straight on at village hall past SA11 5NB. Park at road end and walk another ⅓ mile to footbridge with weir, pools and ruins. Continue another ⅓ mile for the upper weir, and ⅓ mile again for the waterfall, keeping to river R (near side).

15 mins, 51.7639, -3.5671 🏊🚶👥🅿🚻🚶

### 3 DDINAS SILICA MINE & SYCHRYD FALLS

Once the most important silica mine in the world. One path leads into the lower Sychryd gorge falls, under the great folds of Bwa Maen. Confident scramblers could climb this following the route of the old tramway, along a precipitous track along the canyon wall, with remains of rusting old mine trucks in the river below. If this wet short-cut doesn't appeal, a climb up and over the sheer Craig y Ddinas (a hill fort said to be inhabited by fairies), leads to the upper gorge. The Sychryd waterfall and large plunge pool thunder below a bridge which leads to the long silica mine tunnel. Popular for gorge scrambling.

➜ Entering Pontneddfechan from B4242, bear R past the Dinas Inn. Parking is signed R just before the village hall, SA11 5NU. Follow old tramway path around back of rocks to lower gorge. Or bear L on a steep path up and over Craig y Ddinas, for the upper gorge and bridge (51.7598, -3.5711).

20 mins, 51.7577, -3.5689 🏊🚶🚴🚶🚻🚶

### 4 SCWD DDWLI & HORSESHOE FALLS

The graceful arc and large pool of Ddwli on the Nedd Fechan is probably the quickest waterfall swim to reach. Further on, Horseshoe Falls is also great fun and has a big, deep jump.

➜ Entering Pontneddfechan from B4242, follow road up L at the Dinas Inn 1¾ miles, then L dir SA11 5UR, to find Pont Melin-fach bridge and car park on L after ¾ mile. Walk downstream ¼ mile for Upper Ddwli. It's another lovely ¾ mile on to Horseshoe Falls (51.7720, -3.5949) or 1¼ to Lady Falls (see listing).

5 mins, 51.7771, -3.5876 🚶🚶🚻🅿🚶

### 5 LADY FALLS & EINION GAM

A graceful column of water in a wooded amphitheatre falls 10m into the large, deep plunge pool of Sgwd Gwladus; you can climb behind and dive back in. Upstream find imposing Einion Gam, 21m high and rarely visited. It requires some criss-crossing of the stream, but you are rewarded with a huge plunge pool, best in the morning sun.

→ Entering Pontneddfechan from B4242, find woodland 'waterfall woods' through metal gate behind Angel Inn L (SA11 5NR, 01639 722013, parking opp). About half way is a little canyon stretch for jumping and swimming (51.7639, -3.5978). Eventually arrive at a large junction pool below footbridges. Cross first bridge and bear L up the Afon Pyrddin to Lady Falls, ¼ mile. (Bear R to continue to Horseshoe and then Ddwli falls, see listing). To continue to Einion Gam, bear up R above falls, and follow river for ½ mile. Also accessible from the N, at Bronwydd, end of road by SA11 5UR.
30 mins, 51.7714, -3.6011 🏊🚶🅿️♈️🅅🧍🚻

## WATERFALLS

### 6 PWLL-Y-WRACH WATERFALL

By name and local legend this was the 'witches pool', where suspected witches were tried by immersion. Today it is a peaceful, wooded glen, vibrant with woodland flowers in springtime.

→ In Tallgarth turn up Bell St by the Bridge End Inn. Continue ¾ mile (past turning to LD3 0DU) to reserve signboard, gate and some parking R. Head upstream ¾ mile. Falls are W facing so best in the afternoon.
15 mins, 51.9862, -3.2109 🚶🅿️❇️

### 7 NANT SERE WATERFALLS & WOODS

A string of enchanting, moss-covered shallow waterfalls in magical woodland, under a heather-covered hillside in a secret valley. Amazing mossy hummocks can be found in the woods below.

→ Spectacular approach by bushwhacking down from Cribyn or Pen y Fan ridge to S as part of a loop. Or from B4601 W approach into Brecon from A40 turn by church dir LD3 8LL to end of road (Cwmcynwyn Farm pay parking L), continue on bridleway 300m then follow wall all the way along to stream ½ mile (small waterfall) and continue up ½ mile. Probably nicest walk is from Cwm Gwdi car park at 51.9127, -3.4203 (over cattle grid ½ mile E of LD3 8LE, good overnight parking spot), then around bottom of Allt Ddu, 2 miles.
35 mins, 51.8936, -3.4195 🚶🅿️

### 8 PONT-SARN BLUE POOL & CHURCH

The Taf Fechan churns through a narrow, deep chasm under the old bridge to reach what's known locally as the Blue Pool – more black than blue. You can find further pools downstream in ancient woodland, or upstream under the viaduct. Upstream are the lost remains of Vaynor Church.

→ From A465 roundabout in Merthyr Tydfil,

9

head for Abagavenny then immediately L dir CF48 2TW; 250m beyond find car park on L or park down nearer bridge on L. Cross bridge and follow footpath on L down to base of falls. Back on the road, continue to T junction and turn R past pub. After ¾ mile turn R signed Vaynor Church. Park by new church but continue on grass track to find old church lost in the woods 200m (51.7832, -3.3812).
3 mins, 51.7780, -3.3854 🏊🏞️🪧

### 9 BLAEN-Y-GLYN FALLS, CAERFANELL

Find your perfect pool on this popular mountain stream. The deepest are downstream of the footbridge, some with grassy banks. Above the bridge there are rock slides and paddling leading up to the tallest falls. Beyond and above is a quieter stretch with orchid meadows, shallow pools and ancient oaks, continuing for half a mile.

→ From Pontsticill follow the reservoir road, signed Talybont-on-Usk. About 1¼ miles after CF48 2UT top car park is off L, but it's easier to continue down to bottom parking area, another ¾ mile, just before bridge. Follow the river path up from the bridge (far side). Scout as you go, then choose your pool to swim in on the way back.
20 mins, 51.8485, -3.3650 🏊🏞️🥾

### 10 UPPER CWM BRIDGE, LLANBEDR

Old stone packhorse bridge over the bracing Grwyne Fechan stream. Pool below, and beach with small waterfall pools just upstream.

→ In Llanbedr (NP8 1SR) follow the dead-end lane past church, becoming a footpath down to the river.
5 mins, 51.8767, -3.1028 🪧🏊🐾

10

## RIVER USK

### 11 USK PROMENADE, BRECON

Pleasant stretch of deep water above the weir, with pedalos to rent, easy swimming and grass banks for picnics.

→ Follow Cradoc Rd towards cemetery and bear L signed for promenade, past LD3 9LL to large carpark on L.
2 mins, 51.9505, -3.4034 🏊🚣🐕🏕️

### 12 CRICKHOWELL, RIVER USK

A large, deep pool beneath the arched stone bridge. Paddling, picnics and shallow pools upstream along riverside path.

→ Access from steps below green, opp Bridge End Inn (NP8 1AR, 01873 810338, parking by old chapel). Avoid if fishermen are present.
2 mins, 51.8561, -3.1405 🏊🏞️🍺❓🚶

12

### 13 LLANGYNIDR, RIVER USK

Beautiful river section. Just upstream of the old bridge are deeper pools, shallower rapid sections and plenty of flat rocks for picnics. Downstream by a wooded crag is a large pool below a waterfall good for a jump, but this can be shady in the afternoon. There are more excellent and secluded pools downstream ¼ mile. The whole of the Usk has private fishing rights, so do not swim if fishermen present.

→ Signed off A40 7½ miles SE of Brecon. Cross the bridge, turn R and park by post office café/shop. A path behind leads down to riverbanks. Downstream of bridge on same bank a path leads to the waterfall ½ mile (51.875, -3.2230). A mile further downstream is Dyfnant riverbank (51.8707, -3.2038), but also popular with fishermen. Just E of NP8 1PX cross the roadside canal bridge (good point for canal canoe access too) then turn L.
5 mins, 51.8749, -3.2349 🏊🏻‍♂️🚶‍♂️❓🅿️🏞️

## LAKES

### 14 LLANGORS LAKE

The largest natural lake in South Wales, with a reconstructed 10th-century crannog lake house. Fringed with reeds, it offers an important roost and stopover for migrant

birds and habitat for otters. Hire a canoe, sailing dinghy, rowing boat or pedalo. On the more remote shores, behind the church, you can have a quick dip among the water lilies if you are discreet.

→ On A40 2 miles E from Brecon, L signed Pennorth/Talyllyn. Then L after LD3 7PJ signed Llangasty to a small car park beyond the church. A path leads NW around the shore to the main visitor centre, passing a bird hide and a few places to access the shore.
5 mins, 51.9276, -3.2623 🏊🏻‍♂️🚶‍♂️🚗🏞️

### 15 LLYN CWM LLWCH & CORN DU

High in the beautiful Cwm Llwch valley, a remote tarn with a gently shelving shore and superb view. A good approach to the summit ridge of Corn Du and Pen y Fan.

→ From B4601 W approach into Brecon from A40, turn first R into Ffrwdgrech Rd and follow straight for about 3 miles, past LD3 8LD, to road-end Nant Cwm Llwch car park beyond gate. Continue 2 miles up the valley to the lake.
30 mins, 51.8878, -3.4516 🏊🏻‍♂️🥾📷

### 16 BLAENAVON CHIMNEY & LAKE

The fantastic ironworks site in town is worth exploring but so too is the wilder industrial landscape of these hills. A short walk leads

up past lunar slag heaps to the smart, square stack of Hill Pits, the chimney for steam-powered extraction of coal and iron ore. Continue on to the secret lake for a dip.

→ Parking L off B4248/Garn Rd NW from Blaenavon, 270m before NP4 9SE. Walk on from parking to find track opp postbox, by the bus stop. Follow this up ⅓ mile bearing L behind slag hillocks, to find chimney. Bear L on the level tramway ⅓ mile to the lake/reservoir (51.7889, -3.1093), nice camping spot. Descend on path below via Garn-yr-erw, or climb higher to old coal and ironworks lake at 51.7961, -3.1120. Blaenavon Ironworks are open 10am–4pm Thu–Sat (NP4 9RQ, 01495 792615, free entry).

10 mins, 51.7858, -3.1045 🏕🏊📷✚

## 17 KEEPER'S POND & PWLL DU

There are superb views from this high-level 'pond' (Pen-fford-goch), and it's perfect for a summer swim. Built in 1817, it once powered the Garn Ddyrys iron forge below, and you can still see the remains of old furnaces and huge, weirdly shaped slag. Hill's Tramroad passes below. It linked the ironworks at Blaenavon via the Pwll Du limestone quarry, a place of rock walls and wilderness, to the canal at Llanfoist below the Blorenge. It

included the longest horse-drawn tramway tunnel in Britain and the route is now known as the Iron Mountain Trail.

→ On B4246 a mile N from Blaenavon, find pond and car park opp turn off for NP4 9SS. From N side of pond, cross back over B4246 onto footpath down valley to the old tramway (500m). Signed L is Pwl Ddu quarry (the old tramway precariously follows the top edge of the quarry, but the main path enters from below, 10 mins) or R for Garn Ddyrys forge (51.7992, -3.0784, 10 mins) which then leads around the Blorenge to Llanfoist. The entrance to the old tunnel is below the road by the Pwll Du Adventure centre at 51.8103, -3.0541.

2 mins, 51.7910, -3.0817 🏊📷🚗

## 18 TALYBONT RESERVOIR

Sheltered by trees and with grassy banks, this gently shelving lake warms up nicely in summer. There's bird hide from which to spot pochard, tufted duck, mallard and teal.

→ As for Blaen y Glyn falls (see listing), but continue NE 3 miles from the bridge. Find a gate in fence R, and bird hide (just under a mile SW from the dam wall). If you dip, make sure no one is using the hide and be discreet. Bigger parking and picnic area ⅓ mile on.

2 mins, 51.8641, -3.3097 🏊❓🚗

## CAVES & CAVERNS

### 19 PORTH YR OGOF RIVER CAVE

Explore inside the huge chambers of this famous cave, which swallows the Mellte whole and spits it out ¼ mile downstream. Easy access.

→ Pass Ystradfellte falls (see listing), then turn R after a mile (CF44 9JF) to the find car park and small visitor centre on L (Cwm Porth). The river and cave are below on path.
2 mins, 51.800, -3.5558

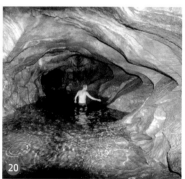

### 20 WHITE LADY CAVE & PWLL-Y-RHYD

A fascinating area of easy gorges and caves in the very upper reaches of the Nedd valley. Much of this is now dry, the river having found underground routes, but downstream the remains of waterfalls can be found, with a huge (usually dry) sinkhole abyss, and a ravine beyond that has not seen water since the last ice age. Behind the old waterfall is a stunning cave passage, like an entry into a secret underworld.

→ Pass Ystradfellte falls (see listing), then ¾ mile after turn L, signed Nedd Valley. Near road end, ⅓ mile before CF44 9JG, find parking and track L down to bridge over and woodland meadows. (Bridge Cave is just R,

in wooded depression, a wide low entrance starting with a 20m crawl before opening up into 300m of impressive high passageways). Follow dry riverbed L 200m downstream (this section floods in spate) to a large hole, with cave and pool in bottom (Pwll-y-rhyd). Continue 'downstream' over a stile and into a dry, wooded rock gorge. After 200m find dry waterfall with White Lady cave beneath. You can bypass the entrance pool to the R to explore the inner passages (about 50m). Take care before or during heavy rains.
10 mins, 51.8111, -3.5809

### 21 EGLWYS FAEN & CRAIG Y CILAU

The 'stone church' is a towering, broad cavern, filled with mist and strange echoes. It's an excellent and easy introduction to the wonders of the underworld and a truly majestic location under the steep cliffs of Craig y Cilau with views out over the Black Mountains. This NNR is famous for its limestone-loving plants, but especially the many whitebeams. The walk in traverses many remains of the 18th-century limestone quarry: conical heaps, old tramways, great scars and riffs in the cliffs. After you could climb Mynydd Llangatwg to Pwll Gwy-rhoc lake for a really wild return loop.

→ Follow Hillside Rd N out of Llangattock, becoming lanes. Turn R ⅓ mile after bridge and wiggle up to the very top. 150m past NP8 1LG the old tramway is R with dead end sign and no parking. (Continue ⅓ mile L for car park signed R - great views for wild campers - and follow path back through old quarries above). After ¾ mile arrive at a little waterfall cleft as path bends R. 50m beyond a clear path climbs up L to the main entrance. High above, the lake is at 51.8305, -3.1854.

25 mins, 51.8333, -3.1725 🏊🏞️💧🧗🥾🚶

## 22 CHARTIST'S CAVE OR OGOF FAWR

Tradition says this large cavern, hidden on Mynydd Llangynidr, was used by Tredegar Chartists to stockpile pikes for use in the pro democracy attack on Newport in 1839. Human bones were also found here.

→ From A465 roundabout in Tredegar take Trefil road to 1¼ miles past NP22 4ET, where a switchback turns R up to the old Trefil quarry (boulders and some layby). A rough track leads up onto the broad peak E/NE. Entrance under a low S-facing crag, a passage at back R leads 30m towards a lower chamber. Bring a map.

30 mins, 51.8289, -3.2672 🏊🏞️🌲🧗🚶

## 23 OGOF CLOGWYN & CWM CLYDACH NNR

Descend into the deep, dark, hidden world of Cwm Clydach and the Devils' Bridge and you'll forget that the dual carriageway sits just above. Cwm Pwca is upstream, translated as Puck's Valley and enthusiastically claimed as the inspiration for A Midsummer Night's Dream. Above the stream, in the cliff face, is Ogof Clogwyn, from which a small waterfall flows. Its oval passageways were dissolved outwards by water (phreatic shelving) rather than just eroded downwards, creating intriguing layered formations, some of the best in Wales.

→ From Clydach village hall follow quarry road 1½ miles (also Cycle Route 46) and turn R at postbox. Bear L, past NP7 0NN, to arrive after 200m at parking L in broadly wooded double tunnel exit. Continue on foot 100m and turn R after building, down footpath, through woods, around cliff, to cave entrance above stream gorge. The entrance is 1.5m up on a shelf and is wet and low! Devil's Bridge and waterfall is 400m downstream: from parking follow cycle path E (not road) then footpath down L after 200m. Below it are very deep, dark slot canyon pools, accessible from much further downstream.

10 mins, 51.8046, -3.1429 🏊🏞️💧

### WILD RUINS

#### 24 CWAR YR YSTRAD QUARRY, TREFIL

It's a post-apocalyptic, moonscape world up here, with huge views, quarried ravines and plenty of remains of limestone processing, including giant hoppers and crushers. Easy place to wild camp.

→ Leave A465 at the Tredegar roundabout, signed Trefil. Continue straight, over 5 miles, past NP22 4ET, to road end on the mountain plateau at the quarry zone. All open access.
5 mins, 51.8239, -3.3262 🖼🏔🏕

#### 25 CASTELL BLAENLLYNFI & TRETOWER

Built around 1215, ruinous by 1340, and hidden in woodland, there are only a few remaining parts of the castle curtain wall and main tower to be seen. It's an atmospheric place with easy access from the lane, and a small signboard welcomes you in. Nearby Tretower Court and Castle (entry fee) are better preserved.

→ N of Bwlch, turn off B4560 signed Pennorth, dir LD3 7PZ, and find wooden gate on L after 100m (you could park tight in front of gate if you aren't long). In Tretower, at NP8 1RJ, castle is visible from the main road, but costs £6.50.
2 mins, 51.8981, -3.2442 🖼

#### 26 CLYDACH VIADUCT, RUINS & GORGE

Passing high above the spectacular Clydach gorge, the old Heads of the Valleys railway is now Cycle Route 46. Find the old viaduct and station. Far below are waterfall pools. Upstream are the ruins of a limeworks with staircase, and then a dry ravine. Further along the route are railway tunnels to explore.

→ From Clydach village hall, follow Quarry Rd ¾ mile to parking area on L just before NP7 0AQ. Head back E along railway cycle track, past the old quarry and railway double tunnel on R, past old station house on road (NP7 0RB much closer, but poor parking) to viaduct. Upstream 100m on the far (R) bank are the limeworks ruins and dry gorge. Downstream, deep below, are waterfall pools.
15 mins, 51.8079, -3.1152 🖼🚶🌊🐟🚲🏛

#### 27 CLYDACH IRONWORKS & STREAM

Two towering masonry furnaces, connected by tunnels and passageways, lie overgrown and forgotten by the side of a pretty stream. Built the 1790s, the workings were in production for over 70 years, and employed over 1,350 people. Once the beating heart of the industrial revolution in this important valley, it's now an eerie, unvisited place. Nice plunge pools below the iron bridge.

→ On the S side of the new A465, W of Gilwern. From Quarry Rd in Clydach village NP7 0NL, turn L down Station Rd, L again after 200m down dead-end lane signed Clydach Old Iron Works. Cross the stream and turn L to find the iron bridge on L, into site.
3 mins, 51.8124, -3.1196 🚗

### 28 WELLINGTON BOMBER, WAUN RYDD

A Wellington bomber R1465 crashed here, killing its five Canadian crew, on 6th July 1942. A cairn memorial has been built, and surprisingly large pieces of the wing and fuselage remain scattered around.

→ As for Blaen y glyn falls (see listing), but park in top car park and follow woodland track NE for 2 miles.
80 mins, 51.8700, -3.3653 ⛰🚶📷

## SACRED & ANCIENT

### 29 MAEN LLIA & FAN NEDD

Colossal, roughly hexagonal Bronze Age monolith in splendid wild moorland. Legend says that the 4m stone wanders down to the river Mellte on midsummer eve to drink – probably this means its long shadow. A little way along the road, a grassy track leads to Llech Llia, one of the few places wild camping is officially allowed. Continue on up to the summit of Fan Nedd (663m), a rarely visited peak but an easy climb with superb views and a great cairn.

→ Continue 2 miles on road from forestry parking for Sarn Helen (see listing) to find tree, gravel verge, stile and stone to R. For Fan Nedd summit (51.8573, -3.5780) walk N 200m to find path L.
2 mins, 51.8608, -3.5636 🚴📷✨⛺

### 30 SARN HELEN & MAEN MADOC

One of the best-preserved stretches of Roman road in Wales, with its original cobbles still visible. Maen Madoc is a Bronze Age standing stone, inscribed in Latin commemorating a Roman, Dervacus, son of Justus, who lies here.

→ Follow the road N dir Sennybridge from Ystradfellte (CF44 9JE) 2¼ miles, past forestry parking signed R, to parking at switchback turn L. The trail leads SW uphill, past the site of a Roman camp, through forest, to the stone L and best-preserved section of the road.
20 mins, 51.8301, -3.5712 ✝

31

29

31

### 31 LLANELLY YEWS & TY UCHAF BIRCHES
A rare, almost complete circle of 13 yews surrounds St Elli's church. Tree lovers might also seek out the secret twisted birches at Ty Uchaf on the hillside above.

→ Church is at fork S of Church Farm, NP7 0HG. The birches can be reached on the footpath heading W up the hill opp Church Farm, ¾ mile to 51.8310, -3.1306 (quicker from top road near bunkhouse turn off).
2 mins, 51.8269, -3.1153 📍♦

### 32 PENCELLI YEWS & CANAL
Hidden up a lane is the church of St Meugan, encircled by 12 giant and ancient yews, older than the current church. This is also a lovely and easy spot to the join the languid waters of the Monmouthshire and Brecon Canal, if you have a canoe.

→ Heading N on the B4558 into Pencelli, take L signed Taff Trail, dir LD3 7DQ. After 100m turn L signed for church, or on R find parking for the canal.
2 mins, 51.9118, -3.3291 🛶📍

## SLOW FOOD

### 33 INT. WELSH RAREBIT CENTRE
A charming bright, vintage café serving delicious seasonal rarebit specials, moussakas, soups, salads and excellent coffee. Take home a loaf of sourdough or croissants from the onsite artisan bakers. Open Wed-Sun 10am-5pm.

→ High St, Defynnog, LD3 8SL, 01874 636843. 51.9377, -3.5631, 🍴

### 34 THE FELIN FACH GRIFFIN
Sister pub to the Gurnard's Head in Cornwall, with the same relaxed, arty ambience. Excellent local produce is combined with fruit and veg from the organic kitchen garden to make consistently good meals – perfect for a long lunch or candlelit dinner. Rooms available, but it is right on the busy A470.

→ Felinfach, LD3 0UB, 01874 620111. 51.9898, -3.3243 🍴🛏

### 35 TALGARTH MILL & THE BAKERS' TABLE
A restored watermill and café selling local produce and of course bread made with Talgarth stoneground flour. Excellent cake and coffee, and bread-making courses. Closed Mondays. Entry fee to mill.

38

→ The Mill House, The Square, Talgarth, LD3 0BW, 01874 711352.
51.9957, -3.2324 🍴

### 36 BEACONS FARM SHOP, BWLCH

Watch the deer and enjoy a gourmet venison burger. Deli, seasonal home-grown vegetables and crafts.

→ Middlewood Farm, Bwlch, LD3 7HQ, 01874 730929.
51.8969, -3.2535 🍴

### 37 GLIFFAES COUNTRY HOUSE HOTEL

Enjoy a slow-food summer lunch on the terrace overlooking the river Usk. Spend the weekend at the hotel and you can learn to fly fish.

→ Gliffaes Rd, Crickhowell NP8 1RH, 01874 730371.
51.8716, -3.2062 🍴

## COSY PUBS

### 38 THE LAMB & FOX INN, PWLL DU

On your way back from a a swim at Kepper's Pond or a vista-filled walk around the Pwll du quarry (see listing), stop for a pint and some friendly local banter at the highest pub in Wales. If the evening air is cooling, the

fires will be burning and laughter emanating from every small table. Music nights and food (usually) served. Nearby Pwll Du bunkhouse is good for groups (01495 791 577).

→ Pwll Du, Blaenavon, NP4 9SS, 07790 682832.
51.7970, -3.0936 📷🚶🅱

### 39 THE WHITE SWAN INN, LLANFRYNACH

We've enjoyed some good food here at the White Swan. Closed for much-needed refurbishment at the time of writing, fingers are crossed for when it reopens. Across the road the churchyard boasts an avenue of ancient yews, and there's a nice short walk along the Menasgin stream passing the grand old oak.

→ Llanfrynach, LD3 7BZ, 01874 665277. For oak head E following signs for Centref, to signed bridleway on L along the stream. Oak is R in field at 51.9226, -3.3541.
51.9226, -3.3453 🍴

### 40 THE STAR INN, TALYBONT-ON-USK

With a pleasant garden overlooking the Usk, this multi-CAMRA-award-winning pub is the place to sample the local breweries latest ales and enjoy a game of scrabble or pie and chips by the fire. Across the road you'll find

38

39

Talybont Farm Campsite (01874 676674) and The White Hart just down the road offers bunkhouse accommodation (01874 676227).
→ Talybont-on-Usk, LD3 7YX, 01874 676635. 51.8949, -3.2889 ⛺🚶🅱

### 41 NEW INN & BEACONS BACKPACKERS
A bustling pub and bunkhouse packed with walkers and bikers filling up on big plates of pub grub and exchanging muddy-boot stories about the day's adventures.
→ Bwlch LD3 7RQ, 01874 730215. 51.8902, -3.2380 🅻

### 42 THE DRAGON'S HEAD INN
Cosy stone country pub smothered in memorabilia and serving Welsh home-cooking, with a small campsite at the back.
→ Llangenny, NP8 1HD, 01873 810350. 51.8550, -3.1049 🚶⛺

## BUNKHOUSES & HOSTELS

### 43 CLYNGWYN BUNKHOUSE
Great location for exploring waterfalls (The Four Waterfalls Walk, and see Ystradfellte listing), this large bunkhouse sleeps 19 and with its glorious views, a BBQ, and fields to play in, it's a great choice for large groups.
→ Ystradfellte Rd, Pontneddfechan, SA11 5US, 01639 722930. 51.7846, -3.5653 🅻🐾🅱

### 44 DAN-Y-GYRN NT BUNKHOUSE
This National Trust bunkhouse sleeping 15 lacks charm, but is warm, modern and at the foot of Pen-y-fan – perfect for a group hike.
→ Dan-y-Gyrn, Blaenglyn, Libanus, LD3 8NF, 01874 625515. 51.8936, -3.4873 🅻🅱

### 45 YHA BRECON BEACONS DANYWENALLT
Converted farmhouse still retaining some of its original character. Situated on the edge of woodland near the Talybont reservoir dam, with waterfall trails and mountain walks nearby. Camping available in the orchard.
→ Talybont-on-Usk, LD3 7YS, 0345 3719548. 51.8767, -3.2977 🅻⛺

### 46 WERN WATKIN BUNKHOUSE
A rather luxurious private bunkhouse and combined YHA hostel at the base of Mynydd Llangatwg, enjoying views over the Sugarloaf and down the Usk valley. Sleeping 30 in seven en-suite rooms, step outside and you are straight into ancient woodland with an easy walk to Llangattock caves.

→ Hillside, Llangattock, NP8 1LG, 01873 812307. 51.8311, -3.1410 🅻🚶🅱

## WILDER CAMPING

### 47 ABERBRAN FAWR CAMPSITE
A Camping & Caravan Club site on a long flat, grass field bordering the tree-lined river Usk. Up the road is Matthew's fruit farm – pick your own soft fruits and enjoy cream teas.
→ Aberbran, LD3 9NG, 01847 623301. 51.9514, -3.4744

## RUSTIC HAVENS

### 48 WANDEROO, PENTRE NABOTH

Wanderoo is a cosy hideaway for two looking out over Pen-y-fan. With total privacy you can stargaze from the hot tub, and snuggle up in the cosy converted horsebox. Friends can join you and camp.

→ Pentre Naboth, Libanus, LD3 8NR, 07717 813322.
51.9178, -3.5273

### 49 PENPONT CAMPING & COURTYARD

In the grounds of a glorious country house deep in the Usk valley you can camp in the old rose garden or the orchard, or rent the Courtyard wing – perfect for a large party. The onsite organic farm shop sells local meats and produce from their gardens (open 10.30am–6pm, Wed–Sat, June–Dec).

→ Penpont, LD3 8EU, 01874 636202.
51.9480, -3.4982

### 50 TY DONKEY

The perfect hideaway for a family with young children, this rustic handcrafted cabin has little cabin beds for the kids, and a big bed in the eaves looking out at the stars for the adults, and nearby the donkeys watch over. Quiet valley position.

→ Llanbedr, NP8 1SY, 01237 459888.
51.8966, -3.1056

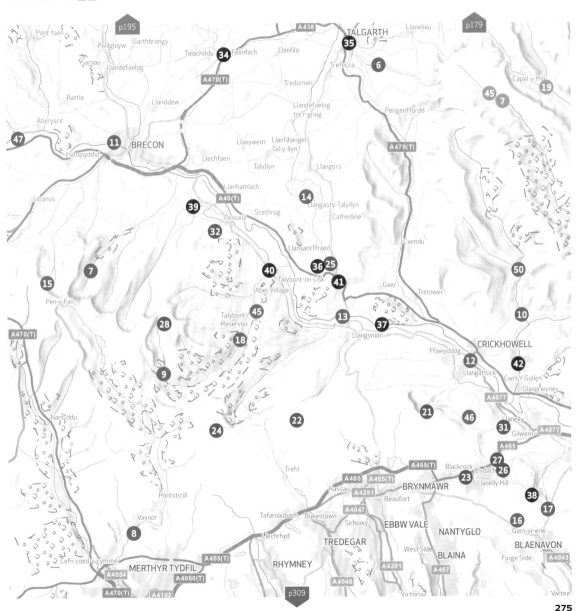

# WYE & BLACK MOUNTAINS

## Our perfect weekend

→ **Follow** the Wye downstream from the riverside church at Holme Lacey, past Fownhope and Capler Camp hill fort, to the famous Arts and Crafts church at Brockhampton

→ **Camp** by the river at Maes-y-Beran in the Vale of Ewyas, march over Offa's Dyke to Longtown Castle, and return for a drink in the cellar bar of the Llanthony Hotel at the ruined priory

→ **Bothy** and swim at remote Grwyne Fawr Reservoir, then find the hidden church of St Issui

→ **Scale** the battlement at perfect Grosmont Castle, visit the local producers' market in the church and stay at the pretty riverside campsite

→ **Swim** and explore at Skenrith Castle, enjoying fantastic food at The Bell

→ **Live** the good life in the Golden Valley with a few bottles of perry from Gwatkin's Farm, a visit to the county market at Vowchurch and tea in the stables at Abbey Dore Court Gardens

→ **Sleep** in ancient Lord's Woods, sheltered within King Arthur's Cave

**Arcadian valleys dominate the lush borderlands of England and Wales. Watered by clear streams, they are adorned with ancient churches, lost castles and ruined abbeys, and some of the finest food produce in Wales – slow travel at its best.**

At the heart of the Black Mountains is the Vale of Eywas, once a Welsh kingdom in its own right, but later home for the Augustinian monks of Llanthony Priory. It is a profoundly peaceful and sheltered spot, nestled deep within a steep-sided, verdant glaciated valley. A few miles further up the valley is the tiny and utterly charming chapel of Capel-y-ffin from where the road rises to gain spectacular views from Hay Bluff and Lord Hereford's Knob. Lower down in the valley is the endearingly wonky church of Cwmyoy, built on unstable glacial moraine from the last ice age. Beyond to the south, Sugar Loaf and Ysgyryd Fawr rise up above Abergavenny, as iconic and satisfying little mountains as you could hope for.

One of our favourite places in summer is the aptly named Golden Valley of the Dore, blessed with the river Monnow and its tributaries – here is the good life in all its manifestations. There are many lovely places to stay, from luxury tree tents to gypsy caravans and yurts in meadows. Good food and old ways are in abundance, from a home-made tea in Abbey Dore to local-produce, gastro-pub fare at The Bell at Skenfrith and Kilpeck, and where you can see some of the finest 12th-century masonry in Britain. A trio of isolated Norman Castles remind us of the turbulent past of the region: Grosmonth, Skenfrith and White Castle, built as a strategic triangle of Norman defences, are all set well off the beaten track and free to enter.

Wide and meandering, it feels as if the Wye forms the real, pre-Norman boundary with England. Lucky to be one of the several rivers in England where an Act of Parliament enshrines the right to navigate and to swim, it is deservedly loved. A remote and bucolic stretch reaches for several miles from the little church at Holme Lacy to well beyond Capler Camp hill fort and Brockhampton's famous church, perfect for a safari with your own canoe. The waters, relatively untouched by towns and their pollution, are deep and clear and offer instantaneous absolution from the stresses of our modern world with one single dip. Come and go slow.

## RIVERS & POOLS

### 1 HOLME LACY, RIVER WYE

Remote pastoral plain giving easy access to the river and a beach. St Cuthbert's church stands alone by the river to the south in a bucolic graveyard. Downstream, access the river from the old railway bridge at Ballingham.

→ Entering Holme Lacy from Hereford bear R (signed Holme Lacy House). After ½ mile turn L signed Church Rd. After ½ mile kissing gate on L by bend (parking for one) before church at HR2 6LX. Or pass Church Rd and continue another 1½ miles for the bridge and track on L to river (51.9925, -2.6347). Also see Capler Camp hill fort listing for river access.

2 mins, 52.0121, -2.6767

### 2 BACKNEY COMMON, RIVER WYE

This piece of ancient common land juts out onto a tight meander of the river Wye. Good shingle and sand beach, shelving to a large pool at the far end.

→ From A449 Ross take A49 Hereford road then first R, signed Backney. After 2 miles, bear R to Foy and find car park on R after 250m (just before HR9 6QX). Track to meadows is adjacent. Continue ⅓ mile upstream to beach.

10 mins, 51.939, -2.6009

### 3 SELLACK COMMON & HOARWITHY

Beautiful open meadows by a small church. An elegant white suspension footbridge crosses the river by a shingle beach.

→ As for Backney but L for Sellack Church instead of Foy, then R at sign after a mile. Or park at 51.9461, -2.6556 (bus route) & follow river path a mile downstream. Also footpath and swimming downstream from Hoarwithy bridge, right bank, leading to beaches and simple riverside campsite (Tressacks) and pub (New Harp Inn).

5 mins, 51.9483, -2.6323

### 4 KERNE BRIDGE, RIVER WYE

On the site of the vanished railway bridge, steps lead down into the water for canoe launching or swimming. A short way upstream through the meadow is an old stone landing stage, perfect for a secluded swim.

→ On B4234 from N into Kerne Bridge, 300m after the Inn on the Wye and 100m past turn to HR9 5QT, find carpark on R.

2 mins, 51.8662, -2.6089

### 5 SYMONDS YAT EAST & BIBLINS

Both sides of the river here are heaving in summer, with nightmare parking, but the eastern side is still enjoyable. You can swim or canoe from the steps and relax outside the Saracens Head in the afternoon sun. There is a small riverside campsite, if need be, and you are not too far from Biblins, where there is a suspension footbridge and youth camp, deep in the forest. Walk, swim or canoe downstream to here and enjoy the Wye rapids.

→ S from Goodrich on B4229, signed on R after ½ mile, dir HR9 6JL for 2 miles. Camping and canoe hire, 01600 891376; pub 01600 890435. Walk downstream on the riverbank footpath to explore the river – it's about a mile to the suspension footbridge. On the W side, there is a good beach behind the Paddocks Hotel.

2 mins, 51.0401, -2.6303

### 6 TREGATE BRIDGE, RIVER MONNOW

A quiet, wooded stretch of the Monnow flowing down to an old weir and bridge. Other deep pools, islands and beaches can be found up and downstream.

→ Take turning next to Bell Inn/bridge at Skenfrith (see listing). Continue 2½ miles S dir NP25 5QG, then turn L to bridge (signed). Follow footpaths on far side.

5 mins, 51.8516, -2.7607

## 7 GRWYNE FAWR RESERVOIR

It's a long walk up into the upper reaches of this remote valley, but efforts are rewarded with a fine Victorian dam and lake, and a bothy (see listing). In high water the far end has ledges good for jumping.

→ From A465 Llanvihangel Crucorney (signed Llanthony), turn L after 1¼ mile signed Partrishow/Forest Coal Pit. Continue straight for 7½ miles (1¾ miles N of/past NP7 7LY) to Myndd Du forestry car park near road end. Walk on to gate and bear R up trackway, arriving at top of dam.

45 mins, 51.9709, -3.1189 🏊🏕🛏

### WILD RUINS

## 8 SKENFRITH CASTLE & RIVER MONNOW

This is a super 13th-century castle ruin, with lots of space on the grassy slopes for children to play, right alongside the River Monnow with an island, deep section and great rope swing. There's a delightful seasonal shop and café opposite.

→ Skenfrith is on B4521, 7 miles N of Monmouth (via B4347). Castle signed dir NP7 8UG, with parking.

2 mins, 51.8793, -2.7908 🏰🏊🎣🍴🚲

## 9 GROSMONT CASTLE

Perfectly quaint in every way, Grosmont just might be the perfect ruined castle. Boasting a moat and bridge, and a pretty winding section of River Monnow below, not to mention a pub, a campsite and a village farmers' and craft market at St Nicholas' church on the second Saturday of the month.

→ Park on main road near pub/shop, N of NP7 8LW. Short path to castle is opp shop; the Angel Inn is further up (01981 240646). ½ mile SE on B4347, find layby on bend L (51.9129, -2.8564) with gap in hedge leading to river.

2 mins, 51.9155, -2.8657 🏰🍴🚲

## 10 LLANTHONY PRIORY, VALE OF EWYAS

Graceful 12th-century Augustinian priory ruins, in an equally perfect valley – the poet Walter Savage Landor owned them, and Turner painted them. Follow the footpath to the back of the priory to Offa's Dyke ridge, or down through the farm on the lane opposite to find a river beach by the footbridge. Bar and restaurant at the Priory Hotel (see listing).

→ From A465 Llanvihangel Crucorney (signed Llanthony). After 6 miles find ruins on R just before NP7 7NN.

2 mins, 51.9446, -3.0361 🏰🍴🏔

## 11 WHITE CASTLE

With a fine moat, bridge and towers to climb, this is the best preserved of the Three Castles. Built with Grosmont and Skenfrith to defend transport links, they were largely redundant within 150 years, but remained bound together in the same lordship for almost seven centuries. Tucked away down little lanes.

→ E of Abergavenny 5¾ miles on B4521, signed on R 1 mile, past NP7 8UD and R up dead end. Free entry, open 10am–3.30pm.
2 mins, 51.8458, -2.9019

## 12 CRASWALL PRIORY

All that survives of this priory, founded around 1225, are the stumps of the once grand gothic pillars, and a few walls and doors. It's a beautiful location – private, but open to the public by kind permission of the farm owners.

→ 6½ miles N of Longtown (see listing), turn R down straight drive, past HR2 0PX, for Abbey Farm. Priory on R, large barn on L.
2 mins, 52.0330, -3.0616

## 13 LONGTOWN CASTLE & CLODOCK

A delightful small ruin under Offa's Dyke, built around 1200. Its imposing tower with

five-metre high walls stands on a high motte, and looks out over a bailey ringed by stone walls and a gatehouse. Much of the grounds are laid to meadow. A mile downstream at Clodock, adjacent to church, are a series of shallow pools and deep section above weir.

→ Longtown signed N from A465 at Pandy, 4½ miles; castle signed in the centre of the village, HR2 0LE. Turn in and park outside. Clodock is at HR2 0NZ, follow up from bridge.
2 mins, 51.9569, -2.9897

## 14 KILPECK RUINS & CHURCH

Ruined Kilpeck Castle still enjoys fine views from its motte; wall sections with chimney remnants survive above the hummocks of the long-vanished medieval village, mostly to the east. Sitting among them is perhaps the finest small Norman church in the UK, and certainly the best-preserved example of the 'Herefordshire School' – blended Saxon, Celtic, and Romanesque motifs, showing influences from as far as Santiago de Compostella, all beautifully carved.

→ Church signed off the A465 SW of Hereford, dir HR2 9DN, and after ¾ mile R at crossroads. The castle is behind the church.
2 mins, 51.9700, -2.8105

## SACRED & ANCIENT

### 15 KING ARTHUR'S CAVE & LITTLE DOWARD

Set within the ancient forest of Lord's Wood is a strange double-entranced cave in the limestone cliff. Its multiple chambers are rich with legends, but we do know that people lived or used these caves as far back as the Old Stone Age or Upper Paleolithic, 50,000–10,000 years ago. Flint tools and woolly mammoth bones have been found, along with lion and rhinoceros remains. Above is the hill fort of Little Doward with earthworks and a large, recently opened clearing on its plateau (51.8416, -2.6715).

→ From Whitchurch/Symonds Yat A40 junction, follow the signs all the way to Doward Park Camp Site (Crockers Ash/Doward road, turn L after a mile, pass turning to HR9 6DT). Find a woodland layby on R, with track leading down into woods, about 120m before the campsite. Follow this ¼ mile to the caves. The hill fort is ½ mile to NW.

5 mins, 51.8370, -2.6608 🏕️📷🔦❇️

### 16 ST ISSUI, PARTRISHOW

This remote mountain valley church contains an exquisite carved tracery rood screen and loft separating the altar area from the main church. In the late Middle Ages nearly every church had one but they fell from favour in the Reformation, so this one is rare for both its beauty and its survival. Dedicated to St Issui, a hermit who lived here in the 6th century; his holy well is still here.

→ From A465 Llanvihangel Crucorney (signed Llanthony), turn L after 1¼ mile signed Partrishow/Forest Coal Pit. After 1¾ miles take second L, signed. Church is on R 100m beyond/N of NP7 7LP. The well is on the L.
1 min, 51.8958, -3.0493 ⛪

### 17 CWMYOY CHURCH & GAER HILL FORT

The tiny mountain church of St Martin tilts with a rakish charm and the short, buttressed church tower is said to lean more than Pisa's campanile tower. Y Graig, a little rocky knoll above the church, is great fun to climb, but the finest views are from the Gaer hill fort on the opposite side of the valley.

→ From A465 Llanvihangel Crucorney (signed Llanthony), turn R after 2¾ mile, signed Cwmyoy. Bear L up steep lane to church on L (before NP7 7NT). Tricky parking. Footpath bears up R to knoll from lane above church. (Previous L, steep dead end lane opp Queen's Head, leads up to the Gaer, 51.8917, -3.0274).
2 mins, 51.9043, -3.0202 ⛪📷

### 18 HAY BLUFF & STONE CIRCLE

Not much is left of this stone circle – just a single stone is standing, next to the car park – but the location and the views are magnificent. For the ultimate panorama climb Hay Bluff (677m) over the road. The landscape here was used in the opening sequence of 'American Werewolf in London', so take care if you are camping.

→ Continue N from Llanthony Priory ruins and St Mary's church (see listings) to just N of turning to HR3 5RJ; find parking L and stone beside. Lord Hereford's Knob is 680m (52.0083, -3.1307) but is 80m less climb, from parking up at Gospel Pass.

1 min, 52.0293, -3.1101 🅿️🖼️➕

### 19 ST MARY'S, CAPEL-Y-FFIN & YEWS

This tiny white chapel is as cute as an owl, with its big wide windows looking out onto the hills. It is surrounded by a semicircle of seven ancient yews, and in the graveyard are two gravestones with elegant script carved by the artist Eric Gill, who lived here in the 1920s.

→ 3½ mile N beyond Llanthony (see Priory ruins listing) on R, just before the turning to NP7 7NP.

1 min, 51.9772, -3.0863 ✝️🏞️

### 20 DORE ABBEY, ABBEY DORE

In the quiet setting of the Golden Valley, this parish church was created from the remnants of the ancient Cistercian Monastery. Inside additional salvaged parts are laid out to be seen, and show the exquisite skills of the master masons.

→ Abbey Dore village N of A465 on B4347, just before HR2 0AA. Open 9am–5pm.

2 mins, 51.9686, -2.8933 🅿️🖼️✝️

## HILLTOPS & HILL FORTS

### 21 CAPLER, WYE & BROCKHAMPTON

The roadside viewpoint enjoys fine views out over the river Wye. From here it's a short walk up to the open plateau and earthworks of Capler Camp hill fort, a good place to bivvy. Paths also lead down the steep, wooded banks to the river Wye, and a little swim. Then visit Brockhampton's All Saints' Church, one of the most important and beautiful Arts & Crafts buildings of the early 20th century.

→ Signed Capler S from B4224 at Fownhope. After a mile find footpath on R down to river to follow bank in either direction, a good canoe put in. Another ½ mile, at top of hill, find Capler Lodge parking, viewpoint and picnic

table, ⅓ mile before turn to HR1 4SE. Hill fort track is on L into woods N, just before lodge. Church is a short drive/walk further on, first L to HR1 4SD.

15 mins, 51.9883, -2.5973 🖼️🏊🏕️⛪🚂♿🅿️♻️

### 22 YSGYRYD FAWR/SKIRRID

The Skirrid has long been regarded as a holy mountain – legend has it that it rose up at the time of the crucifixion. A small chapel was built on the summit, of which only the doorposts really remain. Below is a rock table left by a landslip, known as the Devil's Table and reputedly used for card games between the devil and the local giant.

→ A465 Abergavenny bypass, turn off for B4521 signed Skenfrith. Head 2 miles E to find carpark on L, 250m before NP7 8AP. Climb the ridge (Devil's Table is below L 100m before trig) and return along the W base, through woods.

50 mins, 51.8591, -2.9727 🖼️🅿️

### 23 CRIB Y GARTH/CAT'S BACK, BLACK HILL

This narrow, steep-sided ridge and peak (640m) has fabulous views over Herefordshire and out to the Malvern Hills. Return loop down the Olchon Valley with stream.

→ ⅓ mile N of Longtown (see castle ruins listing) turn L signed Llanveynoe/Black Hill.

Continue straight 2¾ miles and turn R just before HR2 0NL, for car park 350m.

50 mins, 52.0070, -3.0579 🖼️

## TREES & FORESTS

### 24 LLANVIHANGEL COURT CHESTNUTS

Llanvihangel Court is a beautiful Tudor estate with peacocks wandering its high walls, and you can rent it for your wedding or grand gathering. To the south-west of the house a long avenue of sweet chestnut trees planted in the 1660s march out along the hill. They can just be seen off the footpath by the farm buildings. From here The Beacons Way continues across the fields towards Pen-y-parc, giving glimpses of the giant gnarled beasts and offering stunning views of the Skirrid.

→ From Llanvihangel Crucorney (with historic Skirrid Mountain Inn), take the footpath, opp church (100m NE of NP7 8DQ), E crossing the A465 carefully. Continue up the dead-end road past the Court on L to the farm buildings on R, from where the avenue can be viewed. Just after find footpath SE across fields, to get a little closer.

3 mins, 51.8769, -2.9780 🅿️

### 25 ST MARY'S VALE & SUGAR LOAF

This secret valley is thick with sessile oaks, their twisted shapes coated in rare lichens and vivid green mosses. A beautiful ancient place and a lesser-known approach to the Sugar Loaf.

→ A40, W suburbs of Abergavenny, head up Chapel Rd and continue a mile. Turn L, pass turn for NP7 7HU, skirting L around hillside, to find car park on L at end. Straight on for ½ mile to enter the woods proper.

10 mins, 51.8439, -3.0474 🚶

### 26 NUPEND WOODS & CHERRY HILL

The ancient oak and ash woodland of Nupend sits astride the steep limestone ridge of Wenlock. Dotted with old yews and large, gnarled coppice stools, it is a beautiful place throughout the year. In May, bluebells flood the slopes, and in winter fieldfares flock to feast on the yew berries. Loop back via Cherry Hill with its hill fort ramparts, also rich in ancient oaks and spring flowers.

→ From Fownhope take Woolhope Rd (signed Woolhope) for ½ mile, past HR1 4PD. On L find flat concrete bridge over stream, park respectfully here if room and cross bridge to follow path NW into woods. After ½ mile return via paths S over the top of Cherry Hill, to return near Fownhope village.

15 mins, 52.0136, -2.6119 🚶

### 27 LEA WOOD & PAGET'S WOOD

Strewn with bluebells and ramsons in April and May, this sessile oak woodland is one of the best ancient stands in the area and is protected and accessible thanks to the Herefordshire Wildlife Trust.

→ E of Fownhope at junction of Common Hill Lane & Hawkers Lane, just E of HR1 4PZ, find footpath on R sign (limited parking can be found further up Hawkers Lane). Follow path SE into woods.

10 mins, 52.0076, -2.5909 🚶

## SLOW FOOD

### 28 THE STABLES TEA ROOM, ABBEY DORE

Open to the public for over 40 years, Abbey Dore Court Gardens is the life's work of Charis Ward and family. Take an inspirational walk around the eight acres of charming garden then enjoy a lovely lunch in the old stables: homemade pâtés, soup, warm bread and cakes, all using as much organic and locally sourced produce as possible. Open Apr–Sept, Thurs–Sun. Entry fee to gardens.

→ Abbey Dore, HR2 0AD, 01981 241126. 51.9733, -2.8929 🍴🚶

### 29 LLANTHONY PRIORY HOTEL CELLAR BAR

Right next to the stunning ruins of Llanthony Priory is the Priory Hotel, and in the cellars is a cosy vaulted bar and restaurant with open log fire. Enjoy Welsh ploughman's lunch, local ham, egg and chips, casseroles and nut roasts.

→ Llanthony, NP7 7NN, 01873 890487. 51.9446, -3.0369 🍴

### 30 KILPECK INN

A green-minded pub with rooms, whose well-sourced menu is as local as can be. Sunday lunches are delicious, and you'll find a good selection of local game and vegetarian meals.

→ Kilpeck, HR2 9DN, 01981 570464. 51.9692, -2.8074 🍴🛏

### 31 ROWLESTONE COURT

More than just award-winning ice cream in the café, this family farm also serves up glorious views and acres of lovingly tended wildflower meadows. Open 11am–4pm Wed–Fri, 11am–5pm weekends and bank holidays, mid-Apr–Sept. Also a family-friendly campsite.

→ Rowlestone, HR2 0DW, 01981 240322. 51.9392, -2.9099 🍴⛺

28

37

42

47

48

### 32 VOWCHURCH COUNTRY MARKET

Village farmers market selling local artisan breads, cheeses, eggs, meats and veg as well as local crafts. Teas, cakes and bacon butties. Last Saturday of every month, 10am–1pm.

→ Memorial Hall, Vowchurch, HR2 0RB, 01981 550 022.
52.0234, -2.9314 ⚏

### 33 GWATKIN CIDER & FARM SHOP

Perry is an underrated alcoholic drink, and this is one of the few areas where it is still grown and made. Visit Gwatkin's cider and perry farm and stock up your cellar.

→ Moorhampton Park Farm, Abbey Dore HR2 0AL, 01981 551906.
52.0016, -2.9084 ⚏

### 34 THE WALNUT TREE

A rural inn run by chef Shaun Hill, offering Michelin-starred relaxed fine dining using fresh herbs and seasonal vegetables from the garden. Rooms available.

→ Llanddewi Skirrid, NP7 8AW, 01873 852797.
51.8433, -2.9640 ⚏

## COSY PUBS

### 35 BRIDGE INN, MICHAELCHURCH ESCLEY

Hops hang from the ceiling, local cider is on tap, lovely riverside seating, rooms and a camping field. (This was our dearly departed connoisseur brother Mungo's favourite place for a Sunday rib-of-beef-on-the-bone).

→ Michaelchurch Escley, HR2 0JW, 01981 510646.
52.0011, -2.9947 ⚏

### 36 THE CROWN AT PANTYGELLI

Nestled between Sugar Loaf and Ysgyryd Fawr, this is a friendly, real ale gastropub serving up fancy plates of locally sourced fare against a mountain backdrop.

→ Old Hereford Road, Pantygelli, NP7 7HR, 01873 853314.
51.8555, -3.0150 ⚏

### 37 THE BELL AT SKENFRITH

With views of the ruined castle and the pretty river Monnow, this dining pub with rooms really takes its food seriously. Lists of their suppliers proudly line the walls, and you can wander around their organic gardens to guess what might be on today's menu.

→ Skenfrith, NP7 8UH, 01600 750235.
51.8777, -2.7892 ⚏

### 38 THE MILL RACE, WALFORD

Locally sourced to within a 30-mile radius, this village gastropub offers everything from locally hunted game to meats, fruits and fungi reared and foraged on their very own farm. Closed Mondays.

→ Walford, HR9 5QS, 01989 562891.
51.8772, -2.6014 ⚏

## CAMP WILD

### 39 MAES-Y-BERAN & RIVER HONDDU

A very minimal, meadow campsite marked by a white stone at the turning – arrange directions in advance – among the ancient trees and water meadows next to the Honddu. Perfect for climbing Offa's Dyke. Many small beaches and pools. There is a deeper section in the river, deep enough for the annual New Years' day jump, a mile upstream below Bugle Bridge.

→ Meadow is at Llanthony, NP7 7NL, 01873 890621. It does not belong to the farm, so please do not disturb them.
51.9321, -3.0262 ⚏

### 40 LOWER TRESENNY FARM CAMPING

A large field along the banks of the River Monnow, just below lovely Grosmont Castle. Very basic.

→ Grosmont, NP7 8LN, 01981 242026.
51.9142, -2.8590 ⚏

### 41 CHAPEL HOUSE FARM, CRASWALL

Idyllic, remote campsite site spread out over 10 acres of wild flower meadows and bordered by ancient bluebell woods. Smart, rustic facilities, and for even more luxury, beautifully furnished bell tents look out over the Black Mountains. Greener Camping Club.

→ Craswall, HR2 0PN, 01981 510590.
52.0196, -3.0510 ⚏

### 42 HIGH MEADOW YURTS

Two secluded yurts on a working family farm sit surrounded by buttercups and butterflies looking out over the verdant Escley valley and mountains behind.

→ Glebe Farm, Michaelchurch Escley, HR2 0PR, 01981 510333.
51.9926, -2.9982 ⚏

### 43 YHA WYE VALLEY

Spacious YHA hostel and riverside campsite on the banks of the Wye. Canoe-landing and restaurant/bar.

→ Nr Goodrich, HR9 6JJ, 0345 3719666.
51.8566, -2.5946 ⚏

## 44 TIPI ADVENTURE, PENCRAIG

Eleven luxury furnished tipis on the banks of the River Wye. Each sits within an unrivalled bit of parkland on the meander of the lovely Wye. Gravel beaches lead down to the water – perfect for a dip or canoe.

→ Ashe Farm, Pencraig, HR9 6HP, 07966 061480.
51.8887, -2.6313

## 45 GRWYNE FAWR BOTHY

At the north-western tip of this remote mountain reservoir you'll find the tiny Mountain Bothies Association bothy, with room for three people. Bring your own fuel, and a tent in case it's full.

→ As for Grwyne Fawr Reservoir (see listing). Continue on path along the northern edge to reach the bothy.
51.9743, -3.1286

## RUSTIC HAVENS

## 46 WARMTH & WONDER, CLODOCK

A simple and cosy converted barn for five enjoying far-reaching views and with a special hideaway for star gazing. You can run wild in the adjoining hills and woodland, and at night listen out for the wildlife – including the elusive polecat.

→ Garn Farm, Clodock, HR2 0PE, 01873 860885.
51.9343, -2.9741

## 47 TY-COCH FARMHOUSE

The perfect Black Mountains rustic farmhouse, south-facing, with mountain views, seclusion, ancient woodlands and trout fishing on your own bit of riverbank. Sleeps seven.

→ N of Forest Coal Pit, NP7 7LU, 01873 890190. blackmountainsholidaycottages.co.uk
51.8951, -3.0383

## 48 MIMI'S TREE YURT & PHOENIX TREE

Two stunning hand crafted tented abodes. Mimi's is a tactile yurt with a copper bath and wooden mess cabin. The Phoenix Tree is an eclectic tree-top tent, built for star gazing and daydreaming.

→ Walterstone, HR2 0DT, 01873 890190. beneath-the-stars.co.uk
51.9168, -2.9457

## 49 WOOD SHACK

Stylish handmade ash cabin in the woods with a veranda, hammocks for daydreaming and a woodburner for cosy evenings in. Sleeps two.

→ Bettws, Nr Abergavenny NP7 7LH, 01873 776238. holidaycottages.co.uk
51.8680, -3.0203

## 50 LLANTHONY COURT & CAMPSITE

At the magnificent Llanthony Priory ruins (see listing) stay in the medieval 'farmhouse', originally the prior's lodging, or the smart, rustic bunkbarn – or camp in the fields (basic facilities only, no showers).

→ Llanthony, NP7 7NN, 01873 890359.
51.9438, -3.0369

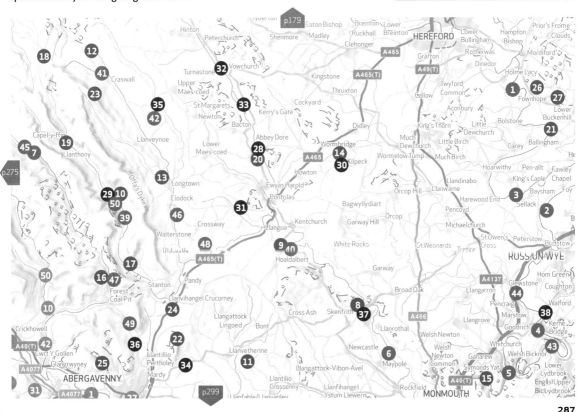

# LOWER WYE & USK

## Our perfect weekend

→ **Canoe** downstream through pastoral meadows of the Usk valley to enjoy fine food in the riverside gardens of The Newbridge on Usk

→ **Explore** the woodlands to find the mysterious abandoned remains of Llangybi and Troggy Castles, once great Norman strongholds, now consumed by forest

→ **Swim** the Usk from islands and beaches at The Bryn or Llanvihangel-Gobion

→ **Picnic** by the Punchbowl lake and climb the curvy beech trees on the Blorenge

→ **Follow** paths through the high cliffs of the Wye gorge, to find grottoes, tunnels, ruins and an eagle's nest lookout at Wyndcliff

→ **Warm** yourself by a campfire at Beeches Farm campsite after drinking in views from Offa's Dyke and the Devil's Pulpit

→ **Descend** deep into the wilderness at the heart of the Wye gorge, treading little-known footpaths at Livox and Tintern Quarries or Lancaut

**Bounded by the rivers Usk and Wye, running parallel on their final stretch to the sea, southern Monmouthshire is a graceful landscape of deep gorges and ancient forest, with exquisite ruins and sacred sites that have long entranced artists and travellers.**

The Wye valley gorge was a major draw for 18th-century Romantic school artists in search of the picturesque, and then for the gentry tourists who followed them. Tintern Abbey's exquisite ruins were a primary attraction, but the whole valley was admired for its classical beauty. In places such as at Piercefield Park and Wyndcliff, further adornments included man-made ruins, grottoes, a giant's cave and an eagle's nest lookout, which impressed both Wordsworth and Coleridge.

The Wye was also a working river, with large sea-going 'trows' sailing right up to the old quay at Brockweir, and swapping their goods for iron and timber from the Forest of Dean. More modern industrial remains can also be seen at the quarries cut from the grand cliffs at Tintern and Livox.

There are fine walks to be had along the east ridge here, through superb ancient woods along the path of Offa's Dyke at the Devils' Pulpit. This is one of the finest areas in Britain for native trees, and as well as heron, otters and kingfishers, you may see peregrine falcons and the red kite.

To the west, towards the Usk, are a number of intriguing sacred sites, including Trellech's Virtuous Well, the extraordinary yew at Bettws Newydd and the wonderfully remote 8th-century Church of the Holy Cross in Kilgwrrwg. Penterry church sits on the site of a now-lost village and can only be reached through a meadow. On a hot summer day a colourful meadow is a thing of fecund beauty, dense with wildflowers dancing below the blue sky; lie back and you can daydream to the soundtrack of humming insects. Boasting some of the best-preserved meadows in Britain, nature reserves such as New Grove Meadows, Pentwyn Farm and Springdale Farm are heart-lifting places to encounter.

The Usk has no dramatic gorge but often flows away from any main roads, retaining its sense of the secret and feel of the wild. Beaches and rapids are common, and its waters and pools are mountain-clear, making them popular with fishermen, canoeists and wild swimmers alike. Canoeing is allowed anywhere downstream of Crickhowell all year, and a high-summer foray along its verdant waters, with a picnic of artisan cheese, bread and ale stowed away, will not be forgotten.

## RIVERS & LAKES

### 1 LLANWENARTH, RIVER USK

Walk across the field from the church to this long pebble beach with an island to explore. There are also deeper spots downstream.

→ Heading W out of Abergavenny bear first L after hospital past NP7 7EL. Continue to church ¾ mile to find parking R, footpath on L.
5 mins, 51.8248, -3.0581 🏊🏃🐕

### 2 ST CADOC'S AT THE BRYN, RIVER USK

A path leads down to the river near the church (look out for the ancient yew growing in the graveyard wall). There are beaches and a pool downstream. Upstream, beyond the railway bridge, are more pools and an island.

→ B4598 at Penpergwm SE of Abergavenny, signed The Bryn (dead end) over A40. Follow round to village end and St Cadoc's past NP7 9AP and park on junction grass verge. A footpath leads down lane L through the gate into field and down to river.
5 mins, 51.7794, -2.9718 🏊👁✝🐕

### 3 LLYWN CORNER & CLYTHA, RIVER USK

In remote pasture, on a tight bend of the river, find a large gravel-and-sand beach, shelving to a very deep pool. Continue along the river for another mile and back by the lane for a lovely circuit and more dips.

→ On B4598, S of Llanvihangel Gobion and NP7 9AY find footpath on L on far side of bridge (parking 50m further along road on R by gate). Walk downstream to Llwyn Corner. You can also reach the far (non beach) side of this meander very quickly from Clytha road, at the footpath gate SE of NP7 9BA at 51.7792, -2.9299. The NT Clytha car park at 51.7719, -2.9273 gives access downstream. Also explore ½ mile upstream of bridge via path (same bank) for secret, very secluded beaches at 51.7755, -2.9563, good for bivvying.
20 mins, 51.7790, -2.9308 🏊⛺🏃

### 4 NEWBRIDGE ON USK SWIM & CANOE

A footpath leads a shingle beach with a deep section above the bridge, and a good pub. For miles upstream find many hidden meanders; the best way to explore this section is by canoe.

→ From M4 J24 follow signs for A48 then after ¾ mile Cat's Ash, and follow the minor road along river. For pub and bridge take unsigned L for NP15 1LY after 3 miles; a footpath from E side of bridge leads to shingle beach just downstream, or a rough path almost opp leads to the deeper section upstream of the bridge. Or continue on to explore points where the river comes close to the road: 51.6543, -2.8850 is good for a quick deep swim. Canoe put-ins include 51.6632, -2.8852 for 1½ miles to Newbridge or 51.6858, -2.8846 for 3½ miles. None have formal access rights, so respect fishermen and be discreet.
2 mins, 51.6481, -2.8896 🏊🛶❤🍴

### 5 BROCKWEIR & BIGSWEIR, RIVER WYE

The quay at Brockweir, the last tidal section of the river, was once the limit for the larger sea-going 'trows' from Bristol. Iron and timber from the Forest of Dean were loaded on, while imports from Bristol were transferred onto smaller boats and pulled upstream by bow hauliers. Now the grassy banks make an easy place for a summer picnic and dip, or a good place to launch a canoe.

→ Turn R off the A466, 1 mile N from Tintern, for NP16 7NG. The quayside is on L after the bridge; some parking L a little further straight on. The path continues upstream for miles, although the main road is always on opp bank. There's also swimming from the bank paths, both up and downstream, at Bigsweir bridge, three miles up the A466, NP25 4TS.
2 mins, 51.7080, -2.6694 🏊🛶

### 6 PUNCHBOWL LAKE & BEECHES

This forested cwm was carved by glaciers and now shelters an islanded lake. There are big views and a large tree to climb by the embankment. The walk down is via an old trackway lined with twisty veteran beeches.

→ From the transmitter station car park on top of the Blorenge (½ mile E from Keeper's pond and B4246), continue on E downhill 1 mile to find a bridleway on L by stone wall and cattle grid (parking for one car, more parking back up the hill in layby), about ½ mile SW of NP7 9LE. Path links to the Iron Mountain Trail.

10 mins, 51.7988, -3.0424

### 7 LIVOX QUARRY BLUE LAKE

Deep, clear azure blue waters are edged with flat ledges and white quartz beaches. This huge spring-fed lake lies in a vast, abandoned quarry amphitheatre guarded by circling buzzards. It is visited by locals, and a public footpath leads right to its edge, but the lake is private.

→ Footpath is from NP16 6HF on A466 (by bus stop, opp Livox Cottages), but most discreet approach joins this below Livox Farm from woods under Wyndcliff Eagle's Nest hilltop (see listing). Bring a map!

20 mins, 51.6744, -2.6625

### 8 CAS TROGGY CASTLE

This truly lost ruin was built by the Earl of Norfolk as a hunting lodge in 1306. There was a rectangular court; today two octagonal towers, fireplaces and an impressive window still remain, entwined with incredible twisted tree roots.

→ At Pen y cae-mawr on lanes from Usk SE to Wentwood, turn off at chapel for NP15 1ND, about 200m. Find footpaths opp (park beyond, away from house), take L into field and head down to clump of trees. The ruins are within, about 50m up to R of path (S side of clump) – actually easier from far side. Rather overgrown.

5 mins, 51.6527, -2.8474

### 9 LLANGYBI CASTLE

Atmospheric hidden ruins deep in the woods. This large 13th-century castle complex, with tumbling remains and beautiful masonry, was built by the powerful de Clare family. The outer bailey is now tended as a woodland garden. On private land, but the footpath runs very close.

→ Woodland approach (lovely walk, easy parking, most discreet) starts from footpath on R, 400m N from NP15 1NY and heads

9

across field, woods, another field and a forest track – but bring map. Castle is up on L, off footpath, so be respectful. To approach from W, Llangybi road, a footpath begins at the private drive at NP15 1NJ, through farm.
20 mins, 51.6716, -2.9210 [icons]

### 10 ST JAMES'S CHURCH, LANCAUT

Deep in the base of the Wye gorge, on a remote oxbow, the 12th-century church of St James is all that remains of the medieval village of Lancaut. It sits on the banks of the tidal river, dramatic white cliffs rising up all around; continue downstream to explore the woodland reserve.

→ On B4228 ⅓ mile N from Woodcroft turn hard L dir NP16 7JB (Woodcroft, Lancaut Lane). After ⅓ mile park by houses and find footpath on L. Head straight across field to bottom L corner behind trees.
5 mins, 51.6652, -2.6708 [icons]

### 11 ST MARY'S CHURCH & TINTERN

Spooky ivy-wrapped church ruins, destroyed by fire in 1977 and enjoying views of spectacular (but often busy) Tintern Abbey.

→ From Tintern Abbey car park (NP16 6TE, take time to walk along the river and view the ruins here) cross main road, ascend lane with

postbox, then take the footpath opp to find church above.
10 mins, 51.6965, -2.6809 [icons]

### 12 TINTERN QUARRY & OLD RAILWAY

Descend into the overgrown lost world of this monstrously large limestone quarry, often used by climbers, although unstable. The path continues down to the abandoned Wye Valley Railway and reaches the wild, remote banks of the tidal Wye; follow the railway upstream through the woodland to Tintern.

→ On B4228 at Tiddenham Chase, turn into an unsigned lane at NP16 7JW. There is parking to R of green gate. Public footpaths or access land lead down along N edge of quarry to the old railway with a tunnel beneath it to the river. The ancient forests of Shorn Cliff and Worgan's Wood to N can be reached via the wooden gate on R by parking.
15 mins, 51.6795, -2.6581 [icons]

### 13 HOLY CROSS CHURCH, KILGWRRWG

Alone in a field, this is one of the oldest Christian sites in Monmouthshire, founded in 722AD or earlier (the rounded churchyard suggests a Celtic site), though the church

10

11

is 13th century. In the early 1800s it was described as a dilapidated sheepfold, but it has since been much restored.

→ S of Devauden ⅓ mile on B4293, turn R signed Kilgwrrwg. Turn R at crossroads/postbox, continue past turn to NP16 6PD on byway to Kilgwrrwg House, to find footpath behind house leading 300m N through field to the church.

10 mins, 51.6822, -2.7793 ✝ ⚐ ⛰

### 14 PENTERRY CHURCH & LOST VILLAGE

Reached through a pretty meadow, St Mary's Church is an exceptionally peaceful place with views out over the Wye valley. The earthworks of a medieval village are visible in the adjoining field, and the church (much reconstructed) dates to 955AD.

→ N of St Arvans village, off A466, turn R signed Penterry, and 500m beyond NP16 6HH find metal field gate and small layby on R.

3 mins, 51.6854, -2.6962 ✝ ▣ ⌦

### 15 HAROLD'S STONES & VIRTUOUS WELL

Three Neolithic standing stones sit in a row, all at odd angles, and give the village of Trellech its name, 'town of stone'. The nearby well, also called St Anne's, is well-loved and adorned. Fairies are said to drink its

water from the abundant harebells here on midsummer's morning, and girls would drop pebbles in, counting each bubble that rose as a month until they might marry.

→ Head S out of Trellech village, at B4293 bend (NP25 4PE) turn L and L again (signed Llandogo) to find well signed on L after 250m with green gate, parking R just beyond. Continue S on B4293 to find stone on L 160m from bend.

2 mins, 51.7428, -2.7265 ⚐ ✝

### 16 CAERLEON AMPHITHEATRE

Wander around this impressive remain, built to serve the Roman legionary fortress of Isca in the 1st century. It could hold 6,000 spectators and may be the origin of the 'round table' in Arthurian legend; Geoffrey of Monmouth placed Arthur's capital here in his tales. Suburban location.

→ Entering Caerleon from J24/25 of M4, small Roman helmet sign L opp the church 300 N of the Hanbury Arms. Beyond NP18 1AY, park by the football club. Free, open 10am–4pm.

2 mins, 51.6080, -2.9567 ⚐ ⌂

### 17 VENTA SILURUM, CAERWENT

The ruins of the grand Roman town are scattered all over this tiny village: the forum and basilica, perimeter walls, shops, houses

19

and temples can all be clearly seen, and date from 1,600 years ago.

➜ Large CADW car park E of NP26 5AU. Wander the village at will. The impressive walls are S of the church.

2 mins, 51.6121, -2.7696 ✝

## HILLTOPS & CAVES

### 18 WYNDCLIFF EAGLE'S NEST

In the 18th century a series of picturesque and romantic walks were built around Piercefield Park. Climb the 365 steps up to the cliff, and follow passageways to the amazing Eagle's Nest viewpoint over the Wye gorge, or explore the Giant's Cave tunnel. Eventually, find the ruins of Piercefield Park itself, with many crumbling outbuildings and a grotto.

➜ A466, about 2 miles N from Chepstow Racecourse roundabout, find Tintern/Lower Wyndcliff forestry carpark on R, 250m before NP16 6HD. Cross road for 365 steps, then R at bench for Eagle's Nest. E facing cliffs so best in morning. From carpark, the Wye Valley Walk heads W then S ¾ mile to the Giant's Cave (51.6633, -2.6887) and another ½ mile S to the ruined house (51.6580, -2.6834).

15 mins, 51.6737, -2.6837 🚗📷🚶🐾

### 19 LLANMELIN WOOD HILL FORT

This Iron Age hill fort is well off the beaten path. Built around 150BC, most likely by the Silures, a fierce, mountain-dwelling tribe who resisted the Romans fiercely.

➜ SW of Shirenewton off B4235, follow lanes dir NP16 6LN but at 1⅓ miles, find parking for two in small woodland layby on L, opp entrance to Coombe Farm.

5 mins, 51.6295, -2.7799 🚗🐕🐾

17

### 20 DEVIL'S PULPIT & OFFA'S DYKE

The embankments of Offa's Dyke are at their most beautiful here, amid ancient woodland with sunset views down to Tintern and the river far below. The pulpit is a limestone rock jutting out from the cliffs, from which the devil tried to tempt the monks below to follow him.

➜ Quickest route is from the footpath from track 250m N of NP16 7JR (Miss Graces Ln, Tiddenham Chase). Best approach includes a section of the Offa's Dyke, either S from Tintern (NP16 6TE; over the river footbridge and up into woodland to the ridge) or N from beautiful Worgan's Wood (from B4228 at NP16 7JW). An exciting circular route taking in the length of the ridge might return to Tintern via the old riverside railway below Tintern Quarry (see listing).

15 mins, 51.6926, -2.6630 🐾🚗🐕

18

## 21 COED Y BWNYDD HILL FORT

This is one of the finest Monmouthshire Iron Age hill forts and its multiple ramparts are uniquely well-preserved. A walk up its wooded slopes is particularly stunning in spring, when tapestries of primroses, then bluebells and orchids, colour the forest floor and open glades.

→ On B4598 3 miles N from Usk take R before bridge to Bettws Newydd (see listing) and on to L up lane at NP15 1JS. After 500m find NT sign and path on L. Tricky parking – narrow layby.
10 mins, 51.7566, -2.9205 🏰🌳👣🚻

### WILDLIFE & WOODS

### 22 BETTWS NEWYDD YEW

Three glorious yews, but one over 1,000 years old is pitted and twisted and you can see right through it. Even better, within is a darker, younger trunk – this is not a different tree, but new growth from an aerial root of the old. An amazing survivor.

→ Find village as for Coed y Bwynydd bluebells (see listing) and head S; 30m past NP15 1JN and entrance to golf club, find footpath and lane up to church (no parking at end so find a place on the main road).
5 mins, 51.7478, -2.9254 ✝️🌳

### 23 BEACON HILL NIGHTJARS & SKYLARKS

Beacon Hill is a quiet place, not long ago covered by forestry plantation. Now a reserve, the heathland is recovering thanks to the Welsh mountain ponies grazing it. But what makes this heather-covered hinterland special is its birdsong. You can hear skylarks and cuckoos here, and the elusive nightjar – come at dusk on a warm evening in late May and June to hear the spine-tingling churr.

→ From the Virtuous Well in Trellech (see listing) continue SW and turn L to Beacon View forestry car park NP25 4PR (51.7441,
-2.7103); the path heads uphill and continues in a circular route.
10 mins, 51.7436, -2.7020 🚶📷🌳

### MAGICAL MEADOWS

### 24 SPRINGDALE FARM MEADOWS

A traditional farm, now wildlife reserve, enjoying glorious views out over the Brecon Beacons and Usk Valley. Come in spring to see unrivalled displays of woodland flowers in Coed-Cwnwr, including violets, wood anemones and bluebells. In summer the flower-rich meadows are the highlight, dense with knapweeds and common spotted orchids below clouds of butterflies.

→ From B4235 at Llangwn head W to NP15 1NF Coed-Cwnwr, and turn L to parking and reserve entrance opp red sandstone almshouses on Llanllowell Lane. Please stick to paths and beware of any grazing cattle.
5 mins, 51.6880, -2.8539 🌳🌸

### 25 NEW GROVE MEADOWS, TRELLECH

Four fields by the road form a small but utterly delightful nature reserve, especially splendid in May and June, when masses of orchids carpet the already colourful hay meadows. This is one of the best examples

25

of wildflower-rich traditional hay meadow in Britain and the perfect place for a summer daydream. Meadows are cut in August but are rich in fungal blooms throughout autumn.

→ B4293, 1¼ mile N of Trellech (see Harold's Stones listing), and ½ mile N of NP25 4PH, find 'Wet Meadow' sign L. Park off track and take stile into field R. Follow corner stiles into N fields for best displays.

5 mins, 51.7592, -2.7241 ❂

### 26 PENTWYN FARM HAY MEADOWS

Enjoy a wildflower walk around this old farm nature reserve on the Trellech Ridge. Unchanged for centuries the meadows are decorated with cowslips and early purple orchids in spring, and greater butterfly orchids and knapweeds in summer. The hay is cut at the end of summer. Nearby Prisk Wood, bordering the Wye, has bluebells in spring.

→ Park by modern barn next to The Inn at Penallt (NP25 4SA, see listing). Follow path through orchard or continue on green lane N to medieval barn with disabled parking.

5 mins, 51.7810, -2.6925 ❂ ➡

**SLOW FOOD**

### 27 THE KITCHEN AT THE CHAPEL

The café to stop at if you're passing through Abergavenny – wholesome breakfasts with home-made bread and great coffee, and organic lunches with biodynamic wine, together with evening events, exhibitions and (around the corner at the linked Art Shop) art supplies.

→ Market Street & 8 Cross St, Abergavenny NP7 5EH, 01873 852690.

51.8228, -3.0172 🍴

### 28 THE HARDWICK, ABERGAVENNY

Ignore the blocky exterior and inside you'll find a friendly gastropub serving mouth-watering plates using the finest ingredients from producers and growers in the area.

→ Old Raglan Road, Abergavenny, NP7 9AA, 01873 854220.

51.7974, -2.9952 🍴

### 29 BROCKWEIR VILLAGE SHOP & CAFÉ

This model village shop with licensed café/ art gallery has been serving up hot meals, cakes and organic coffee along with lovely views for nearly 15 years. Stop off if you are walking Offa's Dyke or call in and pick up

26

some local cheeses, Hobbs House bread or wild boar sausages. Post office and wifi.

→ Mill Hill, Brockweir, NP16 7NW, 01291 689995. Open daily.

51.7124, -2.6590 🍴

### 30 THE NEWBRIDGE ON USK

Overlooking the Usk, this is a great restaurant to enjoy views of the river and its fly-fishers. Sit outside and enjoy perfectly pink roast Usk beef and fish and chips in the sunshine.

→ Tredunnock, NP15 1LY, 01633 451000.

51.6484, -2.8908 🏠🍴🛏

### 31 THE WHITEBROOK

Fresh, foraged and local foods are prepared and served with care and unfussy artistry at this rather unassuming Michelin-starred restaurant with rooms. If the weather is fine, enjoy a more relaxed lunch outside on the terrace. If you visit in March be sure to see the wild daffodils that illuminate neighbouring St Margaret's wood.

→ Whitebrook, NP25 4TX, 01600 860254. Footpath into wood is 150m W on same side. 51.7596, -2.6867 🍴🛏

## COSY PUBS

### 32 CLYTHA ARMS

Making the most of the vast array of first-class local produce available in the area, vegans, carnivores and real ale enthusiasts are all catered for wonderfully in this rustic and rural inn.

→ Clytha, NP7 9BW, 01873 840206. 51.7744, -2.9162 🍴🛏

### 33 KINGSTONE BREWERY

Micro-brewery and glamping in furnished tents and a shepherd's hut.

→ Tintern, NP16 7NX, 01291 680111. 51.7051, -2.6734 🍺🛏

### 34 RAGLAN ARMS, NR TINTERN

Excellent Hereford steaks, Welsh cheeses and head chef James Miller's pies can all be enjoyed at this award-winning village gastropub with garden and cosy bar area.

→ Llandenny, Usk, NP15 1DL, 01291 690800. 51.7306, -2.8498 🛏🍴

### 35 THE BLACK BEAR INN

Order a pint of Butty Bach take a seat by the fire or in the garden. Good home-cooked local game, pies and soups and a jolly landlady.

→ Bettws Newydd, NP15 1JN, 01873 880701. 51.7504, -2.9277 🛏🍴

### 36 THE INN AT PENALLT

After a walk around the summer hay meadows of nearby Pentwyn Farm Reserve (see listing) relax in the garden and soak up the sun with a pint of local ale. Inside, local rare-breed meats and seasonal vegetables are served against a backdrop of local art.

→ Penallt, NP25 4SE, 01600 772765. 51.7791, -2.6939 🛏🍴🍺

## CAMPING & HOSTELS

### 37 PENHEIN GLAMPING

Luxury 'alachigh' Persian-style tents make for cosy and spacious glamping, each one fitting up to a family of six. These have skylights for stargazing and sit on a family farm enjoying big views out over the Severn valley.

→ Penhein Farm, Llanvair-Discoed, NP16 6RB, 01633 400581. 51.6353, -2.7964 🍺🏕

### 38 BEECHES FARM CAMPING

Wake up to a magical, mist-filled Wye Valley and enjoy sunset evenings from your grassy plateau on the Tidenham Chase. Classic family camping on an eco-minded farm.

→ Miss Grace's Lane, Tidenham Chase, NP16 7JR, 07791 540016. 51.7019, -2.6555 🏕🔥🐄

### 39 MIDDLE NINFA FARM

Six-bed bunkhouse in a converted barn, and lovely tent-only secluded camping, with incredible views over the Vale of Usk and the Skirrid, and wonderful vegetables, fruit, salads and eggs fresh from the farm. Solar-powered showers, compost loos and coracle and willow workshops.

→ Middle Ninfa, Llanellan, NP7 9LE, 01873 854662. 51.7986, -3.0377 🏕🍺🅱

### 40 THE SECRET GARDEN YURT

Set on a cheese-making farm, with views out over the rolling hills, a woodburner and a firepit, and kitchen and bathroom cabins built with timber from the farm woodlands. A perfect getaway for two – although you can add your own tent for two more.

→ Lower Gockett Farm, Lydart, NP25 4RL, 01600 860984. canopyandstars.co.uk 51.7739, -2.7301 🍺

### 41 YHA ST BRIAVELS CASTLE

The impressive 13th-century castle is a former hunting lodge of King John and, unlike many of the YHA hostels, retains much of its unique character. If you're here on a Saturday, stop off at the local produce market in the Assembly Rooms on East Street 10am–12.30pm.

→ Church St, St Briavels, GL15 6RG, 0845 3719042. 51.7380, -2.6407 🍺

## RUSTIC HAVENS

### 42 ALLT-Y-BELA B&B

The perfect medieval farmhouse, renovated in keeping with its history, surrounded by rolling, secluded countryside and boasting stunning gardens by Chelsea gold-winning owner Arne Maynard.

→ Llangwm, NP15 1EZ, 07892 403103.
sawdays.co.uk
51.7000, -2.8552

### 43 PENPERGWM LODGE B&B

This chintzy B&B has old-world charm to spare, but it's the garden that is the real draw. Beyond the summer swimming pool are fairytale brick follies smothered in roses, offering great viewing platforms from which to survey the garden. The loggia garden room is the perfect place for a glass of wine as the sun goes down.

→ Penpergwm, NP7 9AS, 01873 840208.
51.7886, -2.9652

43

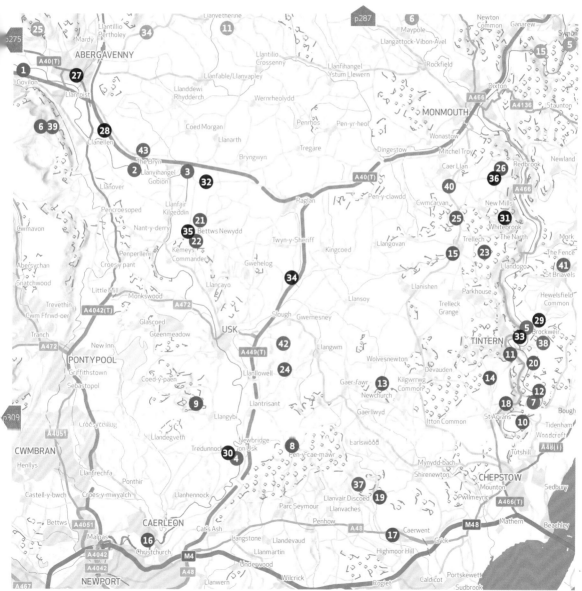

# GLAMORGAN & THE VALLEYS

## Our perfect weekend

→ **Seek** out the rare fen orchid among the dunes and pools of Kenfig

→ **Plunge** into one of the Rhondda Valley waterfalls – fach or fawr, take your pick

→ **Walk** between ruined castles and explore beaches and streams at Ogmore and Merthyr Mawr

→ **Skinny** dip beneath blue lias cliffs at Traeth Mawr, and warm up by the inglenook of the Plough and Harrow, built from a ruined abbey

→ **Stand** under the largest and heaviest gravestone, which shielded the bones of a village for centuries at Tinkinswood

→ **Find** the overgrown ironworks and climb the wooded gorge to the huge amphitheatre waterfall at Melin Court

→ **Climb** Twmbarlwm hill fort, a great Norman motte within high Iron Age ramparts, for wild horses and views over the Bristol Channel

→ **Feast** on vale of Glamorgan fare at the food-focused, open-kitchened Hare & Hounds in Aberthin

**Although this southern stretch is highly populated for Wales, you'll still find miles of superb coastline, blessed with remote beaches, cliffs and dunes, while inland are waterfalls, dramatic mountain passes and, of course, the valleys. The whole area has a wealth of intriguing historical sites, from otherworldly industrial ruins to ancient and sacred remains lost in time, and worth detouring off the M4.**

The coastline is majestic south of Bridgend, where the cliffs are composed of layers of blue lias, and flat limestone pavements stretch into the sea. Monknash makes a perfect base from which to explore – follow the stream with ruined mill to the vast beach of Traeth Mawr, and return to the atmospheric Plough and Harrow Inn, built from the ruins of the adjacent monastery. It specialises in real ales and ciders, and with a fire roaring in the inglenook, this is the ideal spot to warm up after a day of swimming and beachcombing.

At Merthyr Mawr and Kenfig, just up the coast and only a minute off the motorway, you'll find some of the largest and most important dune systems in Europe. It's easy to lose yourself and the rest of the world here, and a fine place to bivvy for the night if you want to sleep under the stars to the sound of crashing waves. Both dunes have castles partly buried by the sand, though the best is Candleston Castle. From here it's a short walk across the river and stepping stones to Ogmore Castle, and there's a riding centre if you want to ride out onto the beach. More medieval remains can be uncovered at Twyn Tudur mound, Twmbarlwm hill fort and the lost ruins of Castell Morgraig.

For ancient relics, the 6,000-year old Tinkinswood tomb has the heaviest chambered cairn in Britain and possibly Europe, and needed over 200 people to heave its heavy stone into place. Nearby is St Lythans cromlech with holes that let the spirits pass through. For more recent remains, seek out the alien-mothership form of the Hafodyrynys coal washery, the last remnant of the mine, or Cwm Coke, where a footpath leads past derelict chimneys and conveyor belts in the sky – for all their industrial looks, now an important home to wildlife including over 50 species of bee. For truly wild places discover the Coed y Bwl woods, with drifts of snowdrops and rare Tenby daffodils, or Gelli-gaer moor, where wild horses roam and you can stand under vast skies in the footprint of one of the earliest churches in Britain.

## WILD BEACHES

### 1 KENFIG DUNES & BEACH

A world away from the chimneys of nearby Port Talbot is one of Europe's largest and most important active dunes systems, backing a long sandy beach and harbouring several freshwater pools. A haven for fungi and orchids – it's the only place in Britain where you can see the rare fen orchid. Head for the beach or seek out the topmost remains of the 13th-century castle, almost entirely buried in sand and ivy.

→ M4, J37 head S on A4229, then B4283 North Cornelly (back under motorway), then signed L at crossroads after a mile, car park after another mile opp CF33 4PT. Footpath for castle (51.5302, -3.7297) is on R, 100m before the Prince of Wales pub, then ¾ mile N.

15 mins, 51.5153, -3.7287 🏰🚶🌊⊞

### 2 MERTHYR MAWR DUNES & CASTLES

The substantial remains of 12th-century Candleston Castle tower stand on the edge of extensive dunes that lead to a wild beach. There is also a small pool for paddling with kids, and a stream leading up to Ogmore Castle (see listing).

→ Follows signs for Merthry Mawr (CF32

0LS) from A48 Bridgend bypass. Continue past church to the dune car park at end and find castle in the trees on R. It's over a mile to the beach through the dunes. You can walk to Ogmore Castle from the village too; turn L before the church to find parking and a footbridge at the end, leading ½ mile along the river to the castle. For easier access to just the beach, head to Ogmore-by-Sea, car park off R 300m before CF32 0PD.

2 mins, 51.4829, -3.6267 🏰🚶🌊🚣🏊🚶

### 3 DUNRAVEN BAY & CASTLE

Beautiful, quiet sandy bay with easy access and parking. Above on the headland of Trwyn y Witch are the remains of Dunraven Castle, including an ice tower, stone arches and walled gardens, and an older hill fort.

→ 2 miles S of Ogmore-by-Sea, via Southerndown, past CF32 0RP to car park at end. The ruins are on headland ⅓ mile on, and gardens can be entered via the ruined archway.

2 mins, 51.4465, -3.6054 🏰🚶🌊

### 4 TRAETH MAWR & NASH POINT

A woodland stream cascades past a ruined mill onto remote tidal sands and rock pools beneath layered blue lias cliffs, and fossils can be found. Flat rock ledges with drifts of cobbles provide places for sunbathing, and the beach becomes naturist the further north-west you go. A mile sout-east down the coast path is the dramatic pinnacled headland of Nash Point with intriguing rock formations. Good campsite nearby.

→ From B4265 1½ mile s from St Brides Major turn R signed Broughton, then in Monknash turn into the lane past the Plough and Harrow (CF71 7QQ see listing). Park near the end of lane by farm at corner (Heritage Coast Campsite, see listing). Continue on lane, bear L over stile and follow woodland path down ¾ mile to beach. Bear R (N) ½ mile to find best sands and, if enough low-tide time, continue another ½ mile on for Whitmore Stairs back up the cliffs.

15 mins, 51.1105, -3.5767 🚶🚗⊞🏊⛺

## RIVERS & WATERFALLS

### 5 MELIN COURT WATERFALL

Waterfall cascading 24m into a great rock amphitheatre. The path is through ancient oak woodland, abundant in many fern species and spring wildflowers, and passes the remains of an 18th-century iron blast furnace. Above the main fall are several more pools and some deep plunge pools.

→ Car park at SA11 4AP off B4434 at Melincourt. The lazy can park at the cemetery on Waterfall Rd. Footpath opp follows S bank of the stream, with ironworks on opp bank after 300m. Footpath on lane above the falls climbs on the straight mine track for ¾ mile to meet stream again and several new waterfalls with pools starting at 51.6969, -3.6908.
15 mins, 51.7008, -3.6996 🚶♿🚗

### 6 RHONDDA FACH WATERFALL

On splendid open moorland, a cycle route and track follows the mountain stream to a waterfall plunge pool. This links up with Castell Nos reservoir, set under a medieval motte.

→ A 1¼ mile N of Maerdy/CF43 4BE on A4233, find car park on L. Follow the cycle route SW then NW for 1¾ mile, perhaps returning S ½ mile to Castell Nos if you fancy a second dip.
40 mins, 51.7007, -3.5080 🚶🏊🚴

### 7 RHONDDA FAWR WATERFALLS

Two high waterfalls plunge and tumble over verdant cliffs to collect in this large dammed pool; other smaller falls are found nearby.

→ N from Treherbert on A4061, 2½ miles beyond turn to CF42 5PH, Hendre'r Mynydd car park is on R. Cross road and down the slope SW.
5 mins, 51.7034, -3.5663 🏊🚶

## MODERN RUINS

### 8 LAVERNOCK BATTERY

Intriguing network of ruined Second World War lookouts, gun turrets and a house, set on the cliffs above beautiful Lavernock Point and St Mary's Well Bay. This was also the site of the first ever wireless transmission across water in 1897.

→ Signed Lavernock Point/Marconi Inn from the B4267 just S of Penarth. 100m past CF64 5UL, before the Marconi Inn holiday village, find gate and footpath on R with some parking. Cross field ⅓ mile. Cosmeston County Park medieval village is also close (CF64 5UY).
5 mins, 51.4042, -3.1796 🚗♿

### 9 CWM COKE, TYNANT

A footpath leads alongside this giant former coke works, with towers, chimneys and conveyor belts in the sky. Closed in 2002, some of the buildings will be conserved, but much of the site will eventually be redeveloped for housing.

→ Head for Windsor Gardens (CF38 2PS) in Tynant, just off B4595 E of Beddau. Park and walk in; the footpath continues into woodland and old quarries.
5 mins, 51.5662, -3.3488 🚗❓

12

## 10 COAL WASHERY, HAFODYRYNYS

A bit like something from an old sci-fi movie, this is the last remnant of the Hafodyrynys coal mine, which until 1966 took up this entire valley with railway tracks, wagons and concrete pit buildings, all long since pulled down and landscaped away. The washery processed coal from other mines for a while, and is now listed.

→ From Hafordyrynys Inn (NP11 5BE) head E 1 mile on A472 and turn L down unsigned lane. Washery is a little further on by field gate on R with layby.
2 mins, 51.6849, -3.0952 ▣

## 11 ST LUKE'S, ABERCARN

One of the most striking churches in Britain, built in the 1920s in a dramatic and forbidding simplified Gothic style. It began to suffer subsidence in the 1950s and the pitched roof was replaced with flat concrete, but by 1980 it was abandoned. Now it's a vast austere empty shell with two crypts.

→ Turn L at St Luke's Surgery, Abercarn by telephone box into Twyn Rd (NP11 5GU). Continue up hill 200m to gates on R. Park in layby just before on L.
2 mins, 51.6491, -3.1341 ▣ ? V

## WILD RUINS

## 12 NEATH ABBEY RUINS

These grand ruins offer a quiet retreat by the canal, tucked away among the industrial sprawl of Neath. It was once the largest and most powerful abbey in Wales.

→ Signed off the A4230, 1 mile NW of Neath town centre. Take Monastery Rd towards SA10 7DW and park on road opp gates. Free, 10am-4pm, or view from canal towpath.
2 mins, 51.6610, -3.8261 ▣

## 13 NANT-Y-BAR RUIN & GROTTOES

The preserved ruins of an old farmhouse and stone grottoes, set within the Afan Forest Park, encircled by hills, returning in a loop on the Afan Valley cycle route.

→ From A4107/Station Rd in Cymer follow signs to Abercregan (L after bridge) and past SA13 3LH on Hopkins Terrace, becoming a dirt road. Beyond hairpin are grottoes, mostly now gated, but 50m before hairpin take footpath down to footbridge to connect with St Illtyd's Way, heading up W slopes and then 2 miles on contour W to ruin – bring a map, many paths. Bike hire from Afan Valley Bike Shed (01639 851406) at the Visitor Centre, SA13 3HG.
45 mins, 51.6537, -3.6903 ▣ ▣ ▣

9

11

### 14 THE IVY TOWER, GNOLL PARK

A shell of a two-storey castellated tower from 1795 draped in ivy. Great views, and 100m further up lane is a wooded reservoir. The country park below has formal cascades, more ruins and an ice house.

→ Take Fairyland Rd R off B4434 on Neath to Tonna road. Find a car park just W of SA11 3QE. Continue along road on foot and at L turn (lane/bridleway to Dan-y-lan Farm) find gate with path up across field up to woods. Continue up NE 300m, above the woods.
10 mins, 51.6700, -3.7709 🖼️📷❓🔁

### 15 CASTELL MORGRAIG

The ruined tower and keep of a mystery 13th-century castle. It straddled the border between Welsh Senghennydd and English Glamorgan, but nobody knows for sure which side built it, and it was never finished.

→ Head S from Caerphilly on A469/ Thornhill Rd for the Travellers Rest, past CF83 1LY. The castle is on the ridge line, in the woods, 100m behind the car park.
5 mins, 51.5518, -3.2139 🖼️❓

### 16 CEFN CRIBWR, BEDFORD PARK

The Cefn Cribwr ironworks, built in 1780, are reached on a cycle route along the old railway line. The entire area is renowned for its meadow flowers.

→ Signed N from B4281 in Cefn Cribwr on dead-end Bedford Rd, beyond CF32 0BW. 200m W of car park, just off the cycle path.
5 mins, 51.5383, -3.6580 🖼️❂🏃

### 17 RUPERRA CASTLE

Fabulous ivy-clad mock-castle mansion built in 1626, and where King Charles I once stayed. It was rebuilt in 1785 after a fire, but another in 1941 led to its final dereliction. Now a romantic ruin, it has been saved from redevelopment by its colonies of greater horseshoe bats.

→ Situated on private land but easily visible from footpaths to N and W. From the Hollybush Inn, Draethen (NP10 8GB), take Rymney Valley Way footpath across field and into woods. Castle is behind the coach houses.
15 mins, 51.5703, -3.1272 🖼️❓❂🔁

### 18 OGMORE CASTLE, RIVER & RIDES

In a pretty location by the River Ewenny, children can play on the stepping stones, paddle in the river, run around on the lawns, and roll down the grassy moat. Tea rooms and pub adjacent, and there's a riding school for a hack down to the Methyn Mawr beach.

20

→ Reached as for Methyn Mawr beach (see listing). Ogmore Farm Riding Centre CF32 0PQ (01656 880856).
2 mins, 51.4805, -3.6121 🐴🧺🏊

## SACRED & ANCIENT

### 19 CAPEL GWLADYS, GELLIGAER COMMON
The foundations of a 5th-century Celtic chapel, with a memorial stone cross marker, stand proud on the top of Gelli-gaer Common where wild horses roam.
→ Signed Dowlais from B4254 at Gelligaer; 450m after CF82 8FZ, turn R. After 400m, see memorial on hill to L and park at bend.
5 mins, 51.6856, -3.2671 🖼️✝️

### 20 CAPEL MAIR, MARGAM
Founded in 1147, Margam abbey is a splendid ruin with a 12-sided chapter house. Now set in a popular country park, climb up through the beautiful ancient woodland to escape the crowds and to find a 15th-century ruined chapel on the hilltop looking out to sea; it was built for parishioners not allowed to worship at the abbey below. There's also a café and museum, which houses early Christian crosses, next to the abbey.
→ At J38 on M5 take the Pyle A48 exit and turn immediately L (dir Margam Stones museum, Weds–Sun, entry fee) but after 350m take L fork (dir SA13 2TB) and park 280m further on, by the start of lake. A footpath runs up into woods opp NW, leading up to chapel, 200m.
5 mins, 51.5648, -3.7307 ✝️🖼️💧🖼️

### 21 TINKINSWOOD CHAMBERED CAIRN
This 6,000-year-old tomb has the largest, heaviest capstone in Britain, and possibly Europe, weighing about 40 tonnes. Some 200 people would have been needed to position it, and this site was used for millenia; the bones of at least 40 people and Neolithic and Bronze Age pottery were found within. Set among fields and fun to go inside. Stones to the south may be a fallen Bronze Age tomb.
→ Head S from A48 in St Nicholas dir CF5 6TA, to find parking and sign on R after ½ mile.
5 mins, 51.4515, -3.3078 🚲🌿

### 22 ST LYTHANS BURIAL CHAMBER
Another intriguing burial chamber to creep inside. This one has a curious pierced hole in one stone, an unusual feature but found occasionally across Europe and thought to permit the ancestors free passage in and out. NT Dyffryn is less than a mile down the lane.

18

21

→ As for Tinkinswood cairn (see listing), but continue along lane, then L at end (dir CF5 6BQ) to find the sign 200m on R.
2 mins, 51.4425, -3.2950 🎽

## HILLTOPS & HILL FORTS

### 23 GRAIG-FAWR, RHONDDA

The steep curving cliffs of this dramatic ridge (550m) were scooped out by a glacier. Below is Cwm Parc, and views over the Rhondda valleys.

→ Follow A4107 for 5 miles E from Cymer (see Nant-y-Bar ruin listing), past SA13 3YW, park at the very brow of the hill, by a gated dirt track (51.6448, -3.5609) and follow the footpath opp.
10 mins, 51.6550, -3.5589 🖼️

### 24 TWYN TUDUR MOTTE

This great mound on a hill has far-reaching views. Said to be the resting place of giants, but more likely a Norman motte. Next door is a white-towered church, surrounded by ancient yews, and a basic pub (cash only).

→ From A472 dual carriageway (Blackwood exit), head S for 2 miles signed Mynyddsilwyn, to shortly beyond NP12 2BG.
2 mins, 51.63739, -3.1670 🎽🖼️🍺🚻

### 25 TWMBARLWM HILL FORT

A great medieval motte and Iron Age ramparts give this hill a distinctive profile. Wild horses and views out over the Bristol Channel reward those who make the hike to 419m.

→ In Risca, head for leisure centre and school and behind them Mountain Rd (NP11 6JD). Follow this NW 1½ miles, past the reservoir, to the car park L where road and track fork.
20 mins, 51.6271, -3.0964 🖼️

## MEADOWS & WILDLIFE

### 26 COED Y BWL WILD DAFFODILS

Locals call it the Daffodil Wood and in early spring the dainty and rare Tenby daffodil, a local variant of the native Lenten lily, brightens the woodland floor. Later, bluebells carpet the northern slopes; also look out for treecreepers scuttling up the trunks. The River Alun clapper bridge is a pretty place to picnic.

→ On B4265, S from St Brides Major, turn L at The Farmers Arms, pass the trekking centre, straight over at crossroads and continue on L fork. Find entrance on L with layby at clapper bridge. Further parking further after railway bridge (CF32 0TL).
2 mins, 51.4648, -3.5708 🍎🎽

### 27 PARC SLIP NATURE RESERVE

Surrounded by hundreds of acres of flower-rich meadows, wetland and woodland, this is a great place for kids, with a café and full calendar of interesting events. Traffic-free cycle paths, footpaths and disabled access paths lead around this wonderful example of a re-wilded open-cast mine.

→ The Nature Centre, Fountain Rd, Aberkenfig, CF32 0EH, 01656 724100. On National Cycle route 4.
10 mins, 51.5454, -3.6145 🚻🦌🌿🐕🚶

## SLOW FOOD

### 28 COBBLES KITCHEN & DELI

Super coffee in a converted barn with creative vegan/veggie options, and all meat locally sourced for selected farms. Afternoon tea served in vintage china, or a Gentlemen's Tea with pork pies, pickles and a bottle of real ale. Monthly supper clubs.

→ Ty Maen Farm Buildings, Ogmore-by-Sea, CF32 0QP, 01656 646361.
51.4821, -3.5945 🍴

### 29 RESTAURANT TOMMY HEANEY

The decor is fresh and contemporary. Organic, local and Welsh ingredients are served by very friendly staff. Rooms available, and summertime afternoon teas in the garden.

→ The Great House, 8 High St, Laleston, CF32 0HP, 01656 657644.
51.5058, -3.6226 🍴🛏️

### 30 ELEPHANT & BUN

Stock up on Alex Gooch sourdough, artisan cheeses, Portuguese tarts, vegetarian pies and basketfuls of mouth-watering treats.

→ 31 High St, Cowbridge, CF71 7AE, 01446 773545.
51.4620, -3.4480 🍴

### 31 HENDREWENNOL PYO

Relive your childhood and pick blueberries, strawberries and raspberries to your heart's content. Hay bales for climbing and good ice cream. Entry fee.

→ Bonvilston, CF5 6TS, 01446 781670. Follow yellow signs. May–September.
51.4705, -3.3820 🍴🐕

## COSY PUBS

### 32 PLOUGH & HARROW, MONKNASH

Built into the side of a ruined monastery, whitewashed and cosy with an inglenook. Open fires, wooden beams and an amazing array of local ciders and ales as well as good pub grub. Just the job after a wild beach walk.

→ Off Heol Las, Monknash, CF71 7QQ, 01656 890209.
51.4240, -3.5550 🍺

### 33 HARE & HOUNDS, ABERTHIN
The perfect village pub with a cosy locals' bar and a scrubbed wood and whitewashed dining area. Serves up veg and herbs from their very own kitchen garden up the road, local Vale of Glamorgan meats and cheeses, foraged finds and home-baked sourdough.

→ Aberthin, CF71 7LG, 01446 774892.
51.4674, -3.4293 🍴🍺🛏

### 34 THE RED LION AT PENDOYLAN
It's a rare country pub where vegetarians enjoy a tempting and varied choice from the menu, but the unassuming Red Lion won us over with their fresh food, using seasonal produce cooked simply and served

with a big smile. If only the decor was more characterful, we'd have loved it even more.

→ Pendoylan, CF71 7UJ, 01446 760690.
51.4809, -3.3552 🍴

### 35 BLUE ANCHOR INN, ABERTHAW
Award-winning, thatched, stone and wood-beamed pub with open inglenook fires and real ales, serving Brecon lamb, roast local beef and a very good vegetable soup.

→ East Aberthaw, CF62 3DD, 01446 750329.
51.3909, -3.3884 🍴🍺

## SLEEP WILD

### 36 NASH POINT LIGHTHOUSE COTTAGES
Ariel and Stella are two 19th-century lighthouse cottages enjoying wild panoramic views of the moody Glamorgan heritage coast.

→ Marcross, Lantwit Major, CF61 1ZH, 01386 897282. ruralretreats.co.uk
51.4009, -3.5523 🏠

### 37 HERITAGE COAST CAMPSITE
With the Plough & Harrow (see listing) up the road and Traeth Mawr (see listing) down the road, this is a great campsite from which to enjoy sunset views, campfires, and coffee, beer and ice cream from the camp kitchen.

→ Off Heol Las, Monknash, CF71 7QQ, 01656 890399.
51.4227, -3.5588 ⚓▲

### 38 HIDE, ST DONATS
Cosy-up in super-chic, hand-crafted 'cabans', hidden away in a seven acre arboretum, over-looking the coast. The 'Bugail Hut' is sheltered under a tulip tree. Or 'Walden Lodge' is inspired by the American transcendental movement and Thoreau's classic book. All come with a wood burner and Welsh blankets.

→ Tresilian Wood, Dimlands Road, CF61 1ZB, 01446 794362. hide.wales
51.4034, -3.5212 🏠

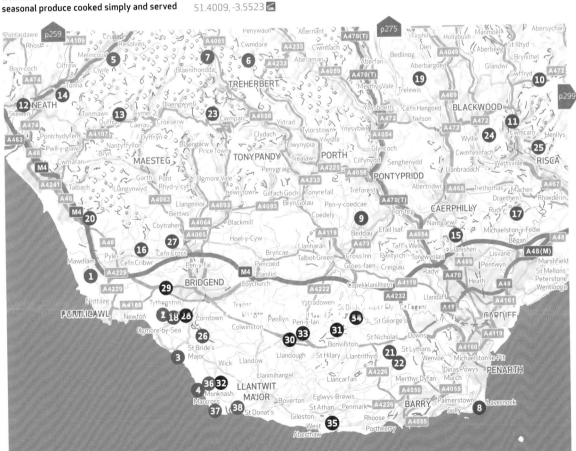

# Ordnance Survey National Grid References

**1 Anglesey & Menai**
1  SH 389 628
2  SH 335 682
3  SH 271 750
4  SH 291 917
5  SH 366 655
6  SH 300 750
7  SH 242 796
8  SH 295 877
9  SH 402 946
10 SH 489 886
11 SH 206 823
12 SH 335 931
13 SH 545 659
14 SH 418 633
15 SH 262 754
16 SH 630 807
17 SH 328 707
18 SH 507 701
19 SH 497 861
20 SH 455 606
21 SH 597 764
22 SH 388 950
23 SH 588 815
24 SH 616 793
25 SH 443 904
26 SH 482 924
27 SH 512 862
28 SH 496 870
29 SH 456 878
30 SH 518 828
31 SH 461 684
32 SH 301 891
33 SH 340 852
34 SH 325 725
35 SH 430 650
36 SH 453 666
37 SH 490 676
38 SH 557 720
39 SH 581 720
40 SH 506 628
41 SH 271 755
42 SH 270 756
43 SH 319 864
44 SH 529 810
45 SH 302 890
46 SH 513 855
47 SH 477 863
48 SH 297 877
49 SH 275 748
50 SH 479 934
51 SH 559 725

**2 Llyn Peninsula**
1  SH 365 472
2  SH 273 410
3  SH 230 375
4  SH 203 343
5  SH 185 325
6  SH 168 317
7  SH 165 298
8  SH 207 264
9  SH 281 264
10 SH 311 247
11 SH 146 266
12 SH 185 255
13 SH 139 251
14 SH 373 446
15 SH 364 461
16 SH 345 445
17 SH 326 427
18 SH 274 368
19 SH 427 412

20 SH 430 488
21 SH 236 281
22 SH 117 215
23 SH 329 314
24 SH 242 345
25 SH 281 405
26 SH 172 264
27 SH 172 264
28 SH 349 447
29 SH 319 261
30 SH 354 352
31 SH 318 264
32 SH 275 415
33 SH 149 259
34 SH 324 419
35 SH 232 374
36 SH 214 362
37 SH 307 251
38 SH 239 285
39 SH 398 486
40 SH 417 504
41 SH 377 433

**3 Conwy & Llandudno**
1  SH 763 604
2  SH 724 653
3  SH 764 596
4  SH 774 661
5  SH 756 683
6  SH 668 700
7  SH 678 649
8  SH 817 826
9  SH 778 838
10 SH 780 829
11 SH 759 618
12 SH 775 653
13 SH 780 601
14 SH 765 621
15 SH 751 833
16 SH 833 802
17 SH 770 831
18 SH 722 746
19 SH 740 717
20 SH 841 811
21 SH 759 778
22 SH 688 715
23 SH 662 636
24 SH 875 674
25 SH 755 843
26 SH 797 773
27 SH 780 775
28 SH 796 722
29 SH 797 617
30 SH 809 597
31 SH 750 608
32 SH 784 820
33 SH 798 616
34 SH 856 789
35 SH 817 803
36 SH 781 632
37 SH 776 740
38 SH 863 764
39 SH 705 664
40 SH 774 729
41 SH 752 612
42 SH 756 844

**4 Snowdon & Llanberis**
1  SH 511 509
2  SH 595 543
3  SH 618 557
4  SH 573 610

5  SH 643 521
6  SH 634 596
7  SH 623 516
8  SH 634 530
9  SH 626 654
10 SH 518 561
11 SH 564 519
12 SH 556 597
13 SH 566 609
14 SH 581 540
15 SH 500 533
16 SH 586 597
17 SH 589 602
18 SH 595 605
19 SH 600 603
20 SH 599 521
21 SH 613 524
22 SH 555 577
23 SH 557 537
24 SH 551 526
25 SH 666 598
26 SH 660 586
27 SH 646 589
28 SH 619 537
29 SH 676 537
30 SH 646 598
31 SH 584 618
32 SH 626 505
33 SH 560 627
34 SH 578 600
35 SH 660 557
36 SH 685 600
37 SH 627 511
38 SH 649 524

**5 Glaslyn & Cwm Pennant**
1  SH 620 437
2  SH 532 476
3  SH 479 395
4  SH 595 461
5  SH 652 412
6  SH 633 471
7  SH 560 369
8  SH 570 378
9  SH 585 367
10 SH 478 371
11 SH 523 374
12 SH 616 388
13 SH 616 422
14 SH 525 477
15 SH 549 433
16 SH 571 452
17 SH 646 446
18 SH 656 455
19 SH 548 499
20 SH 517 443
21 SH 549 389
22 SH 605 483
23 SH 606 492
24 SH 567 388
25 SH 505 381
26 SH 632 446
27 SH 568 387
28 SH 589 481
29 SH 564 374
30 SH 561 401
31 SH 633 465
32 SH 523 444
33 SH 516 454
34 SH 522 434
35 SH 633 483
36 SH 636 451
37 SH 594 460

**6 Blaenau to Betwys-y-Coed**
1  SH 798 543
2  SH 806 528
3  SH 798 573
4  SH 735 570
5  SH 779 569
6  SH 707 409
7  SH 659 469
8  SH 753 423
9  SH 665 461
10 SH 680 461
11 SH 678 454
12 SH 711 461
13 SH 733 469
14 SH 739 461
15 SH 729 562
16 SH 721 523
17 SH 815 543
18 SH 716 454
19 SH 728 429
20 SH 708 545
21 SH 693 439
22 SH 770 524
23 SH 792 566
24 SH 745 418
25 SH 799 556
26 SH 724 578
27 SH 678 412
28 SH 800 580
29 SH 815 535
30 SH 832 487
31 SH 854 511
32 SH 768 559
33 SH 804 499

**7 Central Snowdonia**
1  SH 601 370
2  SH 597 358
3  SH 568 315
4  SH 568 282
5  SH 634 313
6  SH 666 388
7  SH 628 261
8  SH 735 274
9  SH 717 193
10 SH 645 344
11 SH 653 294
12 SH 734 327
13 SH 711 200
14 SH 579 288
15 SH 613 160
16 SH 645 365
17 SH 647 352
18 SH 613 205
19 SH 603 228
20 SH 634 235
21 SH 631 188
22 SH 626 270
23 SH 626 162
24 SH 632 376
25 SH 610 324
26 SH 738 210
27 SH 668 383
28 SH 568 329
29 SH 618 288
30 SH 723 244
31 SH 705 386
32 SH 742 385
33 SH 738 225
34 SH 614 156
35 SH 581 310
36 SH 581 312

37 SH 709 193
38 SH 557 267
39 SH 714 297
40 SH 645 314
41 SH 608 267
42 SH 690 357
43 SH 737 238
44 SH 601 319
45 SH 622 165
46 SH 596 358
47 SH 634 319
48 SH 743 260

**8 Southern Snowdonia**
1  SH 707 137
2  SH 621 121
3  SH 658 143
4  SH 834 061
5  SH 710 094
6  SH 776 100
7  SH 681 066
8  SH 647 144
9  SH 704 149
10 SH 559 037
11 SH 592 026
12 SN 614 958
13 SN 626 962
14 SH 696 185
15 SH 571 071
16 SH 667 085
17 SH 722 055
18 SH 852 139
19 SH 746 092
20 SH 769 103
21 SH 644 068
22 SH 663 150
23 SH 728 178
24 SH 729 116
25 SH 728 177
26 SH 586 008
27 SH 750 008
28 SH 746 008
29 SH 677 069
30 SH 587 008
31 SH 754 079
32 SN 612 959
33 SH 858 140
34 SH 766 166
35 SH 759 059
36 SH 745 007
37 SH 720 990
38 SH 819 043
39 SH 694 184
40 SH 859 148
41 SH 654 157
42 SH 651 148
43 SH 684 159
44 SH 798 084
45 SH 566 058
46 SN 663 972
47 SN 816 987
48 SH 624 133
49 SH 649 078
50 SH 854 048
51 SH 704 159
52 SH 653 093
53 SH 847 053
54 SH 808 027
55 SH 678 159
56 SH 851 183
57 SN 813 991

**9 Denbigh & Flintshire**
1  SJ 026 776
2  SJ 415 621
3  SJ 418 601
4  SJ 298 598
5  SJ 037 510
6  SH 983 574
7  SJ 057 792
8  SJ 297 494
9  SH 928 774
10 SJ 246 733
11 SJ 315 655
12 SJ 288 675
13 SJ 256 519
14 SJ 052 651
15 SJ 015 710
16 SJ 086 800
17 SJ 184 762
18 SJ 079 633
19 SJ 029 710
20 SJ 145 661
21 SJ 197 588
22 SJ 133 782
23 SJ 004 621
24 SJ 125 552
25 SJ 059 559
26 SJ 124 848
27 SJ 204 668
28 SJ 112 604
29 SJ 367 572
30 SJ 324 652
31 SJ 255 578
32 SJ 121 634
33 SJ 107 651
34 SH 974 757
35 SJ 209 703
36 SJ 345 533
37 SJ 151 715
38 SH 952 590
39 SJ 190 562
40 SJ 331 616
41 SJ 031 709
42 SJ 102 803

**10 Bala & River Dee**
1  SJ 113 433
2  SJ 365 419
3  SJ 195 433
4  SJ 176 443
5  SJ 268 420
6  SJ 021 374
7  SH 891 401
8  SH 982 406
9  SJ 453 392
10 SH 901 321
11 SJ 435 329
12 SJ 186 380
13 SJ 108 424
14 SJ 222 430
15 SH 847 306
16 SJ 222 449
17 SH 826 369
18 SJ 157 328
19 SJ 264 376
20 SJ 424 328
21 SJ 061 424
22 SJ 056 371
23 SJ 280 363
24 SJ 053 436
25 SJ 031 372
26 SH 925 358
27 SJ 349 448

**11 Berwyn & Vyrnwy**
1  SJ 073 294
2  SJ 067 126
3  SH 944 231
4  SJ 351 173
5  SJ 393 154
6  SJ 032 154
7  SJ 143 113
8  SJ 156 129
9  SJ 332 165
10 SJ 268 212
11 SJ 205 258
12 SJ 384 193
13 SJ 055 266
14 SH 999 215
15 SJ 034 097
16 SJ 024 265
17 SJ 209 281
18 SJ 222 129
19 SJ 295 144
20 SJ 172 247
21 SJ 066 318
22 SJ 286 247
23 SJ 242 307
24 SJ 142 194
25 SJ 444 135
26 SJ 219 105
27 SJ 189 203
28 SJ 313 250
29 SJ 220 283
30 SJ 270 218
31 SJ 310 177
32 SJ 109 088
33 SJ 175 203
34 SJ 173 287
35 SJ 322 244

**12 Shropshire Hills**
1  SO 436 946
2  SJ 186 008
3  SO 019 974
4  SO 023 880
5  SO 208 983
6  SO 330 731
7  SO 374 730
8  SO 453 749
9  SO 481 766
10 SO 403 738
11 SO 366 779
12 SO 221 967
13 SO 151 950
14 SO 090 754
15 SO 298 809
16 SJ 374 022
17 SO 476 954
18 SO 383 831
19 SO 327 837
20 SO 368 991

21 SO 460 850
22 SO 440 942
23 SO 357 967
24 SO 382 016
25 SO 449 939
26 SO 466 936
27 SO 351 936
28 SO 358 713
29 SJ 200 000
30 SO 258 895
31 SO 304 983
32 SO 055 710
33 SO 453 937
34 SO 108 915
35 SO 309 827
36 SO 034 913
37 SO 193 989
38 SO 356 979
39 SO 389 833
40 SO 315 727
41 SO 483 770
42 SO 222 964
43 SO 507 744
44 SO 393 964
45 SO 405 738
46 SO 403 738
47 SO 454 792
48 SJ 286 024
49 SO 222 964
50 SO 324 889
51 SO 322 884
52 SO 300 808
53 SO 364 928
54 SO 440 919
55 SO 324 897
56 SO 384 733
57 SJ 454 021
58 SO 353 959
59 SO 218 849
60 SO 457 898
61 SO 348 849
62 SO 289 994
63 SO 115 754

**13 Radnor & Upper Wye**
1  SO 029 523
2  SO 090 437
3  SO 123 402
4  SO 336 446
5  SO 221 425
6  SO 226 425
7  SO 278 653
8  SO 429 635
9  SO 465 613
10 SO 458 656
11 SO 529 508
12 SO 390 584
13 SO 359 603
14 SO 090 630
15 SO 101 481
16 SO 483 702
17 SO 083 468
18 SO 408 692
19 SO 256 682
20 SO 318 431
21 SO 123 520
22 SO 155 444
23 SO 078 471
24 SO 086 560
25 SO 443 668
26 SO 084 612
27 SO 545 601
28 SO 532 410

SO 276 647
SO 271 649
SO 326 645
SO 395 564
SO 313 644
SO 314 640
SO 059 611
SO 419 586
SO 490 620
SO 119 400
SO 229 424
SO 402 515
SO 180 392
SO 390 581
SO 329 597
SO 414 690
SO 425 654
SO 310 496
SO 250 591
SO 376 425
SO 310 656
SO 062 460
SO 209 491
SO 275 425
SO 222 427
SO 198 409
SO 100 533
SO 240 566
SO 403 689
SO 296 653
SO 284 566
SO 251 592
SO 107 415
SO 224 422
SO 255 480
SO 260 483
SO 298 432
SO 523 544

38 SN 583 817
39 SN 585 818
40 SN 878 467
41 SN 576 481
42 SN 738 722
43 SN 655 802
44 SN 655 892
45 SN 665 761
46 SN 680 596
47 SN 656 405
48 SN 862 940
49 SN 784 437
50 SN 967 677
51 SN 753 400
52 SN 689 811
53 SN 938 985
54 SN 948 956
55 SN 927 916
56 SN 947 715
57 SN 766 444
58 SN 775 425
59 SN 750 534
60 SN 806 561
61 SN 977 584
62 SN 583 614
63 SN 586 536
64 SN 823 753
65 SN 964 856
66 SN 773 790
67 SN 611 924
68 SN 900 704
69 SN 836 792
70 SN 805 611

**15 Cardigan & Teifi**
1 SN 362 582
2 SN 315 551
3 SN 300 534
4 SN 292 524
5 SN 193 519
6 SN 101 450

**14 Aberystwyth & Cambrians**
1 SN 891 888
2 SN 739 930
3 SN 743 874
4 SN 713 831
5 SN 791 673
6 SN 897 683
7 SN 809 514
8 SN 859 499
9 SN 844 824
10 SN 951 715
11 SN 842 547
12 SN 966 656
13 SN 970 675
14 SN 781 466
15 SN 729 780
16 SN 767 729
17 SN 730 719
18 SN 884 627
19 SN 869 939
20 SN 707 939
21 SN 706 743
22 SN 746 657
23 SN 753 839
24 SN 748 790
25 SO 016 554
26 SN 608 940
27 SN 605 925
28 SN 682 961
29 SN 964 717
30 SN 979 677
31 SN 685 626
32 SN 716 784
33 SN 610 785
34 SN 955 844
35 SN 682 958
36 SN 660 923
37 SN 580 811

7 SN 474 413
8 SN 269 415
9 SN 237 381
10 SN 356 400
11 SN 311 407
12 SN 195 431
13 SN 192 445
14 SN 164 458
15 SN 100 431
16 SN 081 400
17 SN 353 432
18 SN 129 392
19 SN 083 400
20 SN 480 602
21 SN 188 450
22 SN 389 599
23 SN 301 503
24 SN 506 600
25 SN 389 600
26 SN 392 507
27 SN 350 503
28 SN 296 521
29 SN 213 435
30 SN 177 460
31 SN 176 458
32 SN 267 381
33 SN 371 453
34 SN 164 458
35 SN 171 458
36 SN 311 541
37 SN 455 630
38 SN 250 400
39 SN 187 437
40 SN 500 593
41 SN 302 529
42 SN 285 482
43 SN 379 440

44 SN 160 467
45 SN 163 455
46 SN 103 416
47 SN 520 604
48 SN 490 586
49 SN 300 520
50 SN 275 453
51 SN 221 379

**16 North Pembrokeshire**
1 SN 032 395
2 SM 885 364
3 SM 866 337
4 SM 834 324
5 SM 883 350
6 SM 802 320
7 SM 727 279
8 SM 766 243
9 SM 786 243
10 SM 726 260
11 SM 826 229
12 SM 888 386
13 SM 851 338
14 SN 078 300
15 SM 959 274
16 SM 795 314
17 SM 754 241
18 SN 170 256
19 SM 979 273
20 SN 134 293
21 SN 056 370
22 SM 896 336
23 SN 141 325
24 SM 996 352
25 SN 095 371
26 SM 705 237
27 SM 754 252
28 SM 956 371
29 SN 012 336
30 SM 806 244
31 SN 814 325
32 SN 005 399
33 SM 944 296
34 SM 957 265
35 SM 894 348
36 SM 837 324
37 SM 774 261
38 SN 059 391
39 SM 809 292
40 SM 815 325
41 SN 026 340
42 SN 075 294
43 SN 106 259
44 SN 904 388
45 SN 853 333
46 SM 892 387
47 SM 939 355
48 SM 930 291
49 SM 869 219
50 SM 710 269
51 SM 760 244
52 SN 744 242
53 SN 043 395
54 SM 840 324
55 SM 734 238
56 SM 993 370
57 SM 901 405
58 SM 855 333

**17 South Pembrokeshire**
1 SM 798 058
2 SM 784 089
3 SM 781 076
4 SM 817 040
5 SM 842 065
6 SR 930 946

7 SR 978 939
8 SR 982 942
9 SS 991 968
10 SS 070 968
11 SS 081 973
12 SS 045 979
13 SN 007 107
14 SN 009 007
15 SN 044 039
16 SM 842 027
17 SN 022 181
18 SO 072 174
19 SN 018 008
20 SM 944 064
21 SR 967 929
22 SM 979 122
23 SN 032 135
24 SM 801 109
25 SM 724 093
26 SS 136 968
27 SN 054 138
28 SM 758 090
29 SM 029 057
30 SR 885 995
31 SN 010 061
32 SN 157 080
33 SN 032 140
34 SN 108 147
35 SN 139 054
36 SS 098 990
37 SR 966 947
38 SR 973 956
39 SR 972 961
40 SN 093 129
41 SM 856 129
42 SR 984 964
43 SM 811 057
44 SM 873 031
45 SN 050 066
46 SM 867 128
47 SM 828 120
48 SM 764 090
49 SM 814 053
50 SS 084 979
51 SR 973 938
52 SR 894 989
53 SR 973 975
54 SS 117 992
55 SM 862 168
56 SM 802 110
57 SM 811 059
58 SM 818 035
59 SM 805 031
60 SN 046 074

**18 Gower**
1 SS 409 930
2 SS 418 870
3 SS 514 877
4 SS 527 876
5 SS 539 876
6 SS 575 870
7 SS 384 876
8 SS 401 926
9 SS 465 845
10 SS 555 868
11 SS 537 898
12 SS 437 858
13 SS 533 953
14 SS 544 884
15 SS 418 899
16 SS 491 905
17 SS 506 923
18 SS 444 952
19 SS 475 934
20 SS 438 937
21 SS 478 927
22 SS 502 864

23 SS 415 881
24 SS 543 892
25 SS 467 852
26 SS 584 891
27 SS 446 931
28 SS 482 899
29 SS 429 914
30 SS 534 886
31 SS 487 860
32 SS 414 909
33 SS 468 848
34 SS 438 910
35 SS 529 894
36 SS 416 891

**19 Carmarthen & West Brecons**
1 SN 804 219
2 SN 825 293
3 SS 409 995
4 SN 346 098
5 SN 328 077
6 SN 183 072
7 SN 221 074
8 SS 515 973
9 SN 305 109
10 SN 743 150
11 SN 684 058
12 SN 706 275
13 SN 853 119
14 SN 588 334
15 SN 697 062
16 SN 851 206
17 SN 819 258
18 SN 832 153
19 SN 833 310
20 SN 687 242
21 SN 777 202
22 SN 668 190
23 SN 554 202
24 SN 632 327
25 SN 351 101
26 SN 302 133
27 SN 611 217
28 SN 606 166
29 SN 857 156
30 SN 213 255
31 SN 301 109
32 SN 351 109
33 SN 771 301
34 SN 533 202
35 SN 628 223
36 SN 563 140
37 SN 585 336
38 SN 502 165
39 SN 524 302
40 SN 507 217
41 SN 494 196
42 SN 794 240
43 SN 853 282
44 SN 195 090
45 SN 362 376
46 SN 294 265
47 SN 579 257
48 SN 684 312
49 SN 614 224

**20 Brecon Beacons**
1 SN 923 106
2 SN 919 084
3 SN 918 077
4 SN 905 099
5 SN 896 092
6 SO 169 326
7 SO 024 226
8 SO 045 097
9 SO 060 175
10 SO 241 203

11 SO 036 289
12 SO 215 181
13 SO 150 203
14 SO 132 262
15 SO 001 220
16 SO 239 102
17 SO 254 108
18 SO 099 192
19 SN 928 124
20 SN 911 136
21 SO 193 156
22 SO 127 152
23 SO 212 123
24 SO 086 147
25 SO 144 229
26 SO 232 127
27 SO 229 132
28 SO 060 199
29 SN 924 191
30 SN 918 157
31 SO 232 148
32 SO 086 245
33 SN 926 277
34 SO 091 332
35 SO 154 337
36 SO 138 227
37 SO 170 199
38 SO 246 114
39 SO 075 257
40 SO 114 226
41 SO 148 220
42 SO 239 179
43 SN 921 107
44 SN 977 227
45 SO 107 205
46 SO 214 153
47 SN 987 291
48 SN 950 254
49 SN 971 287
50 SO 240 225

**21 Wye & Black Mountains**
1 SO 563 350
2 SO 587 268
3 SO 566 279
4 SO 581 188
5 SO 561 159
6 SO 477 172
7 SO 232 308
8 SO 456 203
9 SO 405 244
10 SO 288 278
11 SO 379 167
12 SO 272 377
13 SO 320 291
14 SO 444 304
15 SO 545 155
16 SO 278 224
17 SO 299 233
18 SO 239 373
19 SO 254 315
20 SO 387 303
21 SO 590 323
22 SO 331 182
23 SO 274 348
24 SO 327 202
25 SO 279 166
26 SO 581 351
27 SO 595 345
28 SO 387 309
29 SO 288 278
30 SO 446 303
31 SO 375 271
32 SO 361 365
33 SO 377 340
34 SO 336 165
35 SO 318 340

36 SO 301 179
37 SO 457 201
38 SO 586 200
39 SO 295 264
40 SO 410 243
41 SO 279 362
42 SO 315 331
43 SO 591 177
44 SO 566 213
45 SO 225 312
46 SO 331 266
47 SO 286 223
48 SO 350 246
49 SO 298 193
50 SO 288 277

**22 Lower Wye & Usk**
1 SO 271 145
2 SO 330 094
3 SO 358 093
4 ST 385 947
5 SO 538 012
6 SO 282 116
7 ST 542 975
8 ST 414 952
9 ST 364 973
10 ST 537 964
11 ST 530 999
12 ST 545 980
13 ST 462 984
14 ST 519 987
15 SO 499 051
16 ST 338 903
17 ST 468 906
18 ST 528 974
19 ST 461 925
20 ST 542 995
21 SO 365 068
22 SO 362 058
23 SO 516 052
24 ST 410 991
25 SO 501 069
26 SO 523 093
27 SO 299 142
28 SO 314 114
29 SO 545 017
30 ST 384 947
31 SO 527 069
32 SO 368 088
33 SO 535 009

34 SO 414 038
35 SO 360 061
36 SO 522 091
37 ST 449 932
38 SO 547 005
39 SO 285 116
40 SO 497 086
41 SS 558 045
42 SO 409 004
43 SO 335 104

**23 Glamorgan & The Valleys**
1 SS 801 810
2 SS 871 772
3 SS 885 731
4 SS 904 700
5 SN 826 015
6 SN 958 012
7 SN 918 016
8 ST 180 679
9 ST 066 861
10 ST 243 990
11 ST 216 950
12 SS 737 973
13 SS 831 963
14 SS 776 982
15 ST 159 843
16 SS 851 834
17 ST 219 863
18 SS 881 769
19 ST 125 992
20 SS 801 865
21 ST 092 733
22 ST 100 722
23 SS 922 962
24 ST 193 938
25 ST 242 926
26 SS 909 751
27 SS 881 841
28 SS 893 771
29 SS 874 797
30 SS 995 746
31 ST 041 755
32 SS 919 705
33 ST 008 752
34 ST 059 766
35 ST 034 666
36 SS 917 704
37 SS 921 680
38 SS 942 682

**Converting decimal degrees to minutes and seconds.** The whole number of degrees will remain the same (i.e. 50.1355° still starts with 50°). Then multiply the whole decimal by 60 (i.e. 0.1355 × 60 = 8.13). The whole first number becomes the minutes (8'). Take the remaining decimal digits and multiply by 60 again. (i.e. .13 × 60 = 7.8). The resulting number becomes the seconds (7.8").

## Wild Guide
## Wales & the Marches

**Words:**
Daniel Start
Tania Pascoe

**Photos:**
Daniel Start, Tania Pascoe
and those credited

**Editing:**
Candida Frith-Macdonald

**Proofreading:**
Jane MacNamee
Lucy Grewcock

**Design:**
Oliver Mann
Marcus Freeman

**Distribution:**
Central Books Ltd
50, Freshwater Road
Dagenham, RM8 1RX
02020 8525 8800
orders@centralbooks.com

**Published by:**
Wild Things Publishing Ltd.
Freshford, Bath, BA2 7WG

hello@
wildthingspublishing.com

the award-winning, best-selling adventure travel series, also available as iPhone and Android apps.

**Author acknowledgements:**
Dedicated to the memory of dear brother Mungo, who has returned home to the Black Mountains. Supreme thanks to editor extraordinaire, Candida Frith-Macdonald and proofer Jane MacNamee . Special thanks to those who travelled with us and supported our field research, particularly Rose and Toto Start, Marijka Pascoe, Petra Kjell, Julian Hodgson & family, Jack Thurston & Sarah Price & family, Jo & Will Webber & family, Ciaran & Leila Mundy & Mima Kearns, Yvette, Matt, Kaspar & Minna Alt-Reuss & Dorte, Isabella Peck, Vicki & Jules Peck & family, Maeve Hegarty & Hamish Kemp, Owen Davis, Richard Hammond & Rhiannon Batten & family, Kate Rew & boys, Emma & Jacob Heatley-Adams & family, Paul & Myla Rothwell, Jess, Paul Cobham & Leila Rodriguez & family, Lucy & Alex Stavri & family, Caroline & Paul Thomas & family, Harriet & Simon Pilkington & family, the Alcotts (Tom, Katie, Elodie, Reuben & Amelia), Tom & Julia Crompton & family, Liam Burgess, Carl Reynolds, Jen & Sim Benson, Chloe Kinsman, Dela Foster, Nick Cobbing, Sophie Evit, Flora & Rae Durgerian, Leander Thomas, Tom Parker, Emily Walmsley, Matthaeus Halder, Olivia Donnelly, Annie Vanbeck, Anna Pemberton, Luke Hudson, Oli & Tom Bullough (for additional photography), Iain Robinson, and to Richard Williams-Ellis, and Sheelegh and Angharad Stephens. Thank you to Geograph.org.uk contributors, especially and to those who provided photos so generously.

### Other books from Wild Things Publishing